MW01006530

Intellectual Life and the American South, 1810–1860

Michael O'Brien

FOREWORD BY DANIEL WALKER HOWE

The University of North Carolina Press   Chapel Hill

Intellectual Life and the American South, 1810–1860

AN ABRIDGED EDITION OF *Conjectures of Order*

© 2010 Michael O'Brien
All rights reserved
Manufactured in the United States of America

Designed by Courtney Leigh Baker and set in Whitman and Clarendon by
Keystone Typesetting, Inc. The paper in this book meets the guidelines for permanence
and durability of the Committee on Production Guidelines for Book Longevity of the
Council on Library Resources. The University of North Carolina Press has been a
member of the Green Press Initiative since 2003.

Library of Congress Cataloging-in-Publication Data
O'Brien, Michael, 1948 Apr. 13–
Intellectual life and the American South, 1810–1860 : an abridged edition of
Conjectures of order / Michael O'Brien ; foreword by Daniel Walker Howe. — [Abridged ed.]
p. cm.
Includes bibliographical references and index.
ISBN 978-0-8078-3400-8 (cloth : alk. paper)
1. Southern States—Intellectual life. 2. Intellectuals—Southern States—History—19th
century. 3. Southern States—Social conditions—19th century. 4. Southern States—
Relations—Europe. 5. Europe—Relations—Southern States. I. O'Brien, Michael, 1948 Apr.
13– Conjectures of order. II. Title.
F213.O27   2010
975'.03—dc22
2009046322

14 13 12 11 10   5 4 3 2 1

Contents

Foreword

Michael O'Brien's *Conjectures of Order*, his comprehensive intellectual history of the Old South, is a triumph of humane letters. The University of North Carolina Press originally published it in two large volumes. The present abridgment makes this distinguished work available to students and the general literate curious public.

In this edition, Michael O'Brien still displays the wide learning, acute intelligence, and refined sensibility that so impressed his fellow scholars. Professor O'Brien is a British academic (at Jesus College of Cambridge University) who has spent twenty-five years in the United States and obtained a secure familiarity with American history and habits, particularly those of the Southern states. Here he sets the finest thinkers of the antebellum South into a broad context. He writes with assurance, subtlety, and grace. Over and over again, he goes back to the original primary sources and reconceives his subjects with originality. A reader will find O'Brien's presentations fresh and imaginative.

Professor O'Brien shows us the Old South as an intellectually vibrant and modern society. He succeeds completely in redeeming the antebellum South from hostile accusations that it was a philistine cultural desert. He demonstrates that, on the contrary, its intellectual life was cosmopolitan and sensitive. And he accomplishes this feat without for a minute trying to defend the cavalier or proslavery legends. Instead he reveals a Southern culture that was lively, diverse, and in touch with the rest of the modern world.

O'Brien grounds his examination of Southern intellectual history in social reality, including an unshrinking recognition of the pervasive consequences of slavery. He is interested in the particular as much as the general, in the lived biographical experiences of individuals. The variety of characters and ideas in the book is truly remarkable. Thomas Jefferson and Edgar Allen Poe; expatriate radicals like Frederick Douglass and the Grimké sisters; brilliant, staunch conservatives like George Fitzhugh and Louisa McCord—all are treated with respect and insight. Thomas Dew, leading social scientist and historian, gets careful attention; so do the profound political reflections of John Taylor and John C. Calhoun; so do the autobiographical narratives of escaped slaves. O'Brien is as interested in the forms of Southern cultural life as he is in describing its intellectual content. Accordingly, he discusses conversation, correspondence, diaries, bookselling, libraries, and periodicals.

Michael O'Brien is leading a rebirth of American intellectual history after several decades in which few historians addressed the subject. His work bears on many aspects of American and Southern Studies, including literature, religion, politics, philosophy, society, gender, and race. He writes in a style complex and elegant yet lucid. It may take some getting used to, but readers will find it well worth the effort. O'Brien provides reflective Southerners of the present day—women as well as men, black as well as white—with an intellectual heritage they can look upon not only with sympathy but also with pride.

DANIEL WALKER HOWE
October 2009

Preface

In 2004 the University of North Carolina Press published *Conjectures of Order: Intellectual Life and the American South, 1810–1860*. It was in two volumes, divided into an introduction, six books, and an epilogue, and further subdivided into twenty-one chapters; there was a long bibliography of manuscript and printed sources; and in total, with the index, there were 1,382 pages. I was persuaded such voluminousness was necessary because of the breadth of the subject matter. Even critics agreed and gave evidence of having waded through everything, or almost everything. How readers coped is hard to say, though one presumes most browsed as their interests dictated. By Victorian standards, the book was laconically brief; by contemporary ones, inexcusably discursive. Even in 2004, it was gently suggested that a shorter version might be advisable. If the book was to have a wider readership, an abridgment was necessary.

To accomplish this task, I adopted a few elementary guidelines. First, it seemed undesirable to revisit the book's arguments and update them, partly because I have not kept up with recent Southern scholarship, and instead I ought to content myself with making the original text more succinct. Second, the structure would remain intact and its elements would, as it were, be miniaturized: books would be turned into chapters, chapters into sections, sections into paragraphs. Third, the scholarly apparatus would be drastically reduced, upon the reasoning that the retention of the old structure would make it easy for curious readers to refer to the original, if they wished to. So the bibliography has disappeared and the annotation now only cites direct quotations. Fourth, errors would be corrected and passages, if too long or too opaque, rewritten.

I cannot recommend the experience of abridging one's own work. An author is forced to reexamine prose with minute care and I, at least, ended up with the bleak conviction that I was once incapable of writing a competent sentence, fashioning an adequate footnote, or making a clear argument. On the other hand, there is an interest in observing how abridgment changes a book. In this instance, subplots had to be eliminated, swathes of evidence abandoned, quotations deleted or abridged, minor characters omitted, and biographical information lost. That is, thick description was thinned down, and the result is a different sort of intellectual history from the original, in which more than a handful of elite intellectuals and texts were explicated, great attention was paid to multiple cultural contexts, and anecdotal quirkiness was commonplace. This is a leaner book, more focused on the American South and fewer thinkers within it. For those who like canvases to look like Joshua Reynolds's *The Marlborough Family* and not Pieter Brueghel the Younger's *Fight between Carnival and Lent*, this will be an improvement.

Intellectual Life and the
American South, 1810–1860

Introduction · The Position and Course of the South

In 1829 Thomas Dew of Virginia felt it important to stress that "[t]his is a world of relations and dependencies, and consequent continual changes. The earth upon which we tread, remains not a moment in the same position in absolute space, but is in constant and endless movement. . . . Throughout all animated nature, we see still greater bustle, change and movement; we see event following event in quick succession; mind operating upon matter, and matter upon mind."[1] It was hard for an intellectual to live in the early nineteenth century and not have such opinions, for the culture of modernity conveyed this standpoint insistently. But such a message would not have been meaningful in places like Charleston and Williamsburg, unless the experience of the people who came to explain themselves as Southerners had not suggested mutability. For them, worlds moved, little settled into coherence, and contradictions were palpable. One way to comprehend these complexities is to observe that, in the early nineteenth century, Southerners were national, postcolonial, and imperial, all at once, and partly invented their culture in the tense encounters among these conditions.

That they were national is familiar. Southerners had helped to make the American Union, offered most of its early leadership, and furnished a disproportionate share of its governance even up to 1860. Thomas Jefferson, James Madison, Andrew Jackson, and John C. Calhoun were proprietary about the United States; it was their world, a thing whose meaning they felt capable of defining. Jefferson had explained that change was a moral duty, which ought to turn out for the best. More pessimistic men, like Madison, had suggested that, duty or not, change was a fate that humans could not evade. But certainly the experiences of change made a habit of mind. Having made a world, Southerners were aware that worlds could be made. Hence they liked to sit in judgment, not only on ordinary matters like who was in and who was out, but on the fundamentals of what made a society and how constitutions interacted with human nature. They retained a revolutionary frame of mind and, therefore, when they began to think that the United States was no longer a thing which they could control, many among them did not hesitate to destroy it and make another world.

Less familiar will be the proposition that Southerners were postcolonials, who had only recently repudiated a metropolitan authority and were anxious to possess and define their "place." But "postcolonial" is an omnibus term, which can obscure as much as it can illuminate, for empires take many forms, as do the regimes that succeed them. Like Australia, the South faced a small indigenous population which was pushed to the margins with considerable ease but which did not become extinct. But, like Brazil, the South imported slaves on a large scale, and, in time, they came to be a political force in their own right, though as a minority. However, as in South Africa, the settlers of the United States were disunited about what sort of society to make. Their differences (unlike those of the Boers and the English), though, arose less from ethnic and religious animosities carried from Europe than from social experiences and ambitions contrived in the colonial and early national years, which created different visions of how best to administer their newly conquered estate.

For the purposes of an intellectual history, what matters is that in the early nineteenth century Southerners' intellectual traditions continued to be formed mostly by the older cultures of Europe. Only a small proportion of their habits of mind can be said to have been produced indigenously. Indeed, it is surprising how little they were molded even by other Americans, who usually seem to have been viewed as competitors rather than as influences. To most Southerners, Madame de Staël mattered more than Ralph Waldo Emerson. Rather, Southerners had the habit of presuming that authority rested abroad; in ancient Rome, in modern Paris, in the libraries of Göttingen. They spent much time at home and abroad trying to comprehend these traditions; they imitated Demosthenes, read Livy, followed Calvin, painted like Reynolds, and admired Jean-Baptiste Say, while they traveled to Edinburgh, Paris, and Rome. They often saw the world through foreign eyes and did not always grant the premise that coming to see the world on native grounds marked an advance. These instincts bred a cosmopolitan imagination and mandated the outward gaze, but also delicately instilled the habit of doubt and a sense of provisionality. Always the metropolitan world elsewhere threatened to change the rules, to reinvent the paradigms, to transmute au courant knowledge into old-fashioned provinciality. A visitor could arrive, only to sneer at earnest young ladies playing Mozart and to say that Bellini was now the rage in Paris; the returned traveler could announce that Lamarck was an exploded theorist and someone called Darwin had a better idea. Southerners lived at the edge of the known world and, like figures in a Chekhov play, some in it wanted to touch the center. "If you go back to Paris," Yasha the servant says to Madame Ranevsky in *The Cherry Orchard*, "do me a favour and take me with you. I can't stay here. . . . You can see for yourself, this is an uncivilized country and no one has any morals. Besides it's boring."[2]

But Southerners were imperial, because their settler society was the heir of the conquerors, not of the conquered, nor of the people from Africa who had been stolen to make the settlement an economic success for the Europeans. Virginians and the rest had not rebelled against George III to repudiate the venture of European imperialism but to take the matter into their own hands. Movement was of this project's essence, what made it work. People came in their many thousands from beyond the South's limits, from Maine, Yorkshire, and Prussia, and by the pressure of their numbers and ambition assisted those born in the South to make an empire of liberty and slavery. The South was a moving target, a thing in process, never what it had been ten years before, never what it would be ten years later.

These three conditions of being national, postcolonial, and imperial mingled unstably. Postcolonialism inculcated doubt; it asserted only a thin margin for cultural invention, though the margin began to widen as the analytical presumptions of the Enlightenment began to yield to those of Romanticism, which legitimated the indigenous and licensed the will. Still, cultural anxiety was insistent. Were colleges good enough? Was it bad that novels were published in New York? Who reads a Southern book? Is someone, somewhere laughing at us, or sneering at us? Yet nationality and imperialism, to the contrary, sanctified a sense of mastery. Southerners were the children of the American Revolution, which all Americans (and some Europeans) agreed had commenced a *novus ordo seclorum*. Providence smiled on them, promised them not only the manifest destiny of a North American world but perhaps even that of a wider world. They felt themselves simultaneously to have the moral sanction of George Washington and God himself. While Europe punished itself with a generation of war, slaughtered people by their millions, and threw down and set up despotisms, the United States believed itself to have calmly and wisely ordered its affairs, expanded its domain, and acquired the habits of liberty. There might be little doubt here, only certainty and the expectation of a marble pedestal.

Yet there was doubt. To make a world while looking over one's shoulder at Niccolò Machiavelli and David Hume, at all those who smiled at the vanity of human wishes, was difficult. Even with a blithe spirit, it would have been hard. But the world did not offer easy reassurance. People in Massachusetts dissented, merchants in Liverpool pushed down the price of cotton, a slave in Virginia drove an axe through someone's skull, a politician could not get elected to the White House, there were disagreements about God. Dissent was habitual. Slavery itself was an education in uncertainty, a daily struggle of the will. An order was given, it was obeyed, or not. A smile might suffice to secure obedience, or a whip, or nothing would work. Here many Southerners faced an especial complexity, for they were ordering their world by compulsion. Making an empire, making a republic, making a democracy, making prosperity, all these would have been hard enough to hold together, but to drive the project forward while holding millions in bondage produced a cultural anxiety of stark proportions. Ambition and disillusionment became incessant companions in the Southern imagination. Indeed there were those who came to think that ambition could only work if predicated on disillusionment.

This book attempts to sketch the intellectuality that this confused world created. Its narrative runs from about 1810 to the eve of the Civil War, with a postscript on the Southern world after 1865. To use the terms favored by intellectual historians, this book describes the transition from a late Enlightenment, to a Romantic, then to an early realist sensibility, with the weight falling in the middle period. Broadly speaking, the organization of the book moves from society to thought, from the empirical to the abstract. The first half is partly social history, in which intellectuals are implicated in the broader patterns of society and it is presumed that their thoughts are explicable by what went on around them; this narrative offers contexts. The second half moves beyond the social and is, more strictly, an account of the Southern intellectual tradition and the men and women who made it. Not only idiosyncrasy matters here, as it must in any rigorous intellectual history, but also genre.

Chapter 1 is called "The Softened Echo of the World," a phrase Caroline Gilman coined to describe how Southerners interacted with those beyond their own culture.[3] The chapter describes how they located themselves, by a study of the Southern experience of the outside world. Mostly this involves seeing how people from the South responded when they were in Boston, London, or Buenos Aires, but it also involves seeing how strangers adapted when they came to live, permanently or not, in the South. Abroad was not only a place far away, but the house next door, if it was inhabited by an immigrant, as many Southern houses were. On the whole, this chapter confines itself to physical interactions: who went where, what they saw, what they concluded, whether they returned, what they said. The abstract act of cultural traveling, which occurred when someone in Tuscaloosa sat down with a text produced in Weimar or Boston preoccupies much in the rest of the book.

Chapter 2 takes its title, "All the Tribes, All the Productions of Nature," from a phrase of Stephen Elliott's, in which he tried to justify the modern passion for classification, both natural and social.[4] A major ideological shift of the early nineteenth century was how self came to be understood as implicated in social constructions. Romanticism did two things simultaneously: it told a person that he or she was alone and alienated, but it also claimed that the world was filled with cultural shapes, collectivities which contributed decisively to the sources of the self. Race, sex, ethnicity, class, place: all these freshly became salient categories. To the question "Who am I?" a Southerner by 1860 could make many answers, but increasingly the answer was produced in the alchemy of social identity. Yet not all categories were equally salient. Race, sex, and place became harder forms, more compulsory, more authoritarian in their demand for allegiance. Class and ethnicity, in a society so mobile, had a shape and pertinence more difficult to pin down. Still, in general, the South drifted away from the premise that mankind had a common nature toward the sense that society and, hence, self were segmented. Further, the troubling theory developed that bodies might matter as much as, if not more than, minds. Increasingly, it was believed that men and women, whites and blacks, Huguenots and Scotch-Irish, aristocrats and crackers, Virginians and Alabamians were not only cultural inventions but quasi-biological fates, not things that the human will had chosen. Few were sure of how this worked, but almost everyone was drawn into considering and accepting the proposition.

Chapter 3, "A Volley of Words" (a phrase from Elizabeth Ruffin), tries to describe how Southern society structured intellectual interactions, by a sequence of discussions that moves from the most informal of discourses (conversation), to the semiformal (letters, diaries), to the most formal (the printed word as it was read, then as it was written).[5] The rough movement is from the private to the public spheres, though these were unstable, interconnecting phenomena. Not all intelligence felt the need to express itself in a book or a periodical, and print may be understood as only a place where conversation went to achieve a form of permanence. Talking on the street or at a club, writing a letter to a friend or a relative, sitting alone with a diary to make sense of events, all these formed part of this culture's intellectual activity. These actions are hard to measure and narrate because they were often ephemeral, but they possessed a cultural logic. A club had rules, a letter had conventions, a conversation had habits of courtesy. Easier to understand is print culture. For good or ill, most of what was understood as the life of the mind did express itself in the printed word, which had a growing prestige. It mattered how this culture came by and produced printed words. Booksellers, libraries, publishers, and the business of authorship in the South had a distinctive shape, which formed much of what it was possible to know and to say.

The second half of the book is divided into what could be called the social and the metaphysical imaginations. Chapter 4, "The Shape of a History," is concerned, firstly, with historical writing: how the genre was justified and organized, how the South imagined its place in the trajectory of Western history and conceptualized its own local history, how it dealt with the genres of biography and autobiography. Then it considers what was then called "belles lettres": how the critical theories of the Enlightenment gave way to Romantic modes of understanding, how the idea of Southern literature fitfully developed, and how poetry and fiction were written in the South, in the forms (the Gothic, the romance, the frontier story, the historical novel) which became characteristic. Chapter 5, "Pride and Power," moves back to more worldly concerns: ideas of politics and the state, the venture of political economy, and the proslavery argument.[6] First, it examines political thought, in six phases: as it came from the Southern Enlightenment's most vigorous exponent and critic, John Taylor; as it was reassessed by Virginians in 1829–30, when a colder Burkeanism began to be expressed; as it was articulated by the South Carolinians of the 1820s, who ruthlessly exposed the contradictions of American constitutionalism and began to apply to it the social theories of cultural nationalism; as it was expounded by Andrew Jackson, the South's preeminent democrat and nationalist; as it was reassessed by the later Calhoun, who began to see that there was something between individualism and national culture, more local shapes which American history had produced; and, lastly, as it was redefined by Romantic theorists who came to think that one could have a self, only if first one had a society, and that society had come to be the South. Second, the chapter looks not only at how classical economics was understood and became a Southern orthodoxy but also at how it was criticized and flexibly applied. Last, it defines the shape of the developing proslavery argument, which moved from a fleeting moment of antislavery optimism at the turn of the nineteenth century, to a view in the 1820s and 1830s that slavery was a necessity that expressed men's social constraints, to a late antebellum position that tended sentimentally or playfully to express a hope that slavery might improve the human condition.

The content of Chapter 6, "Philosophy and Faith," is made clear by its title, which is taken from an article by George Frederick Holmes.[7] The first section is concerned with how Southerners responded to the analytical traditions of Scottish common sense philosophy and then experimented with other philosophical conjectures (mostly German, sometimes French). The second moves to ideas about the relationship between God and man. The transition here is mostly one of emphasis. There was little in metaphysics that was not engaged by religion, little in theology not troubled by metaphysics. Partly, this second section seeks to recover the importance of religious diversity in the South, by looking at the Jewish, Roman Catholic, and Episcopalian traditions, though only by a sampling. It ends with an analysis of Calvinist theology, at least as this theology was understood by its ablest Southern exponent, who knew that modernity and the ancient beliefs needed reconciling.

The epilogue's title, "Cool Brains," comes from a sentence of Mary Chesnut's when in 1861 she wrote in her diary of the mood and necessities of secession: "This southern Confederacy must be supported now by calm deliberation—& cool brains. We have risked all, & we must play our best for the stake is life or death."[8] This phrase captures one aspect of the Old South's youngest generation, who felt trapped but who were willing to hazard escape. They did not arrive at this stark conclusion without knowing that their predecessors had thought differently. Southern thought had undergone marked change over the preceding fifty years, as different options were considered, accepted, and rejected. Three moments are discernible. There was a late Enlightenment phase, which inclined to be individualist, skeptical of society, hopeful of human intelligence, and wary of human passion. Its figures included John Taylor, Isaac Harby, Thomas Cooper, Henry Clay, William Harper, and the young John C. Calhoun; their writings mostly ran from the 1810s to the early 1830s. The middle phase was Romantic and more interested in the pleasures of belonging, and hence was more sentimental and historicist, but jaggedly nervous about the possibility of failure. Its figures included Edgar Allan Poe, William Gilmore Simms, Hugh Blair Grigsby, Louisa McCord, Beverley Tucker, George Frederick Holmes, George Fitzhugh, and James Warley Miles; these flourished, roughly, from the mid-1830s to the early 1850s. Some thinkers were poised between these first two moments: among these one might count Thomas Dew and Hugh Legaré and even John Randolph and the later Calhoun. The last moment was bleaker; its cadres formed a sort of early realist generation who knew that life compelled choices and that all choices entailed loss. One might have God, or power, or belonging, but not everything, and not for everyone. This generation's figures included William Henry Trescot, James Johnston Pettigrew, Henry Hughes, Augusta Evans, and James Henley Thornwell. Their moment lasted from the late 1840s to the beginnings of the Civil War. Mary Chesnut had been one of them, and she it was who wrote their epitaph, in a work that after 1865 rendered a verdict on the intellectual and social ambitions of her culture, which had failed. With her, that world and this book ends, though not without an intimation that she glimpsed a further moment, the world that William Faulkner and Allen Tate would come to inhabit. It had been the illusion and the experience of antebellum Southerners to think that they could make their world, though they disagreed over what sort of world to make, and what sort of men and women existed to undertake the making. This creative vanity died on many battlefields, in many households that absorbed the reality of defeat, in the extinction of slavery, in the spread of poverty and constraint. But the old ambition was not surprised to be defeated, for it had often been unsure. It had tried to imagine and create order, but it knew that disorder existed, that society might be overwhelmed by disintegrations unless effort was unceasing. The will was strong in 1840, even 1860. Later was a different matter.

A few premises will begin to seem apparent. This is a book about those who were associated in the governing of the Southern world, but only obliquely a book about those whom, chiefly, they tried to govern. The imagination of the slave and free black communities in the South had different themes, origins, and ambitions. With good reason, Nat Turner, Frederick Douglass, and William Wells Brown had little or no cause to think themselves a part of Southern intellectual culture, which partly defined itself by their subjection. That some blacks, after the war which was their people's partial liberation, reconsidered this stance and that Brown, for one, later wrote a book called *My Southern Home* (1880) does not alter the plain, brutal exclusions of the world before 1861. White Southerners went to great lengths to silence their Africans, by denying them education and access to the printed word, and hence to writing, even in manuscript form. Almost all the African American intellectual tradition before 1861, written by those born in the South, was expatriate. It was the lessening and rescinding of that necessary tradition of exile which, in the late nineteenth and twentieth centuries, was to lead to the possibility of "Southern" and "black" becoming other than mutually exclusive identities, though even today the ambivalences remain unresolved. However, the discourse of the antebellum black community, in the South and abroad, since it was formed by contiguous experiences, offers opportunities for comparative understanding. African Americans lived their own lives, but they sometimes formed a chorus in the white South's House of Atreus, a chorus always watching, commenting, dissenting, knowing some parts of the same physical world, but experiencing it differently.

This case indicates how the defining of parameters for a Southern intellectual history is not simple. A few generations ago, it might have been easier. I would have defined the physical limits of the South, identified those writers who were born there, given a priority to those who were proslavery and secessionist, and set my narrative in motion, with frequent reminders to the reader that all, happily, would turn out badly. But now I have chosen and been compelled to live in times not more complex, but different. Historians used to accept more readily that making a national culture was a good thing, and one's chief duty was to judge the adequacy of the culture that was made; in the United States this was usually a moral judgment, in Europe often an aesthetic one. The Old South fared badly under this rubric, since it made an immoral culture which failed to gain a place in a world of nations, and succeeded only in contributing toward the making of a lesser thing, a regional culture, which occupied a politely subsidiary place in the greater project of American culture. Some historians still think this way. I do not, doubtless because I am not a Southerner, but also because recent intellectuals in the United States, Europe, and Africa have grown more agnostic about the merits of national cultures, which were once offered as things that God had made for human beings, eventually became secular religions, and now seem very available for skepticism. This book was mostly written in the twentieth century but was published in the twenty-first, in a world where the nation-state remains powerful but where the idea of culture has semidetached itself from the obligation of loyalty to such states. Women and men make cultures, but of many sorts, in many places, for many purposes; some of these are congruent, many not. Boundaries are invented and the nation-state is about enforcing these, insisting that this person belongs but that one does not, that he pays taxes and votes but she pays taxes and does not, that she may be illegal yet reside but he is illegal and must be sent away, that the world consists of "us" and "them." Historically, the democratic nation-state has tried to tell human beings that it defines them, while they define it; the circle is closed. Fortunately or not, we live in times when the circle begins to break down, where lives move in different patterns, sometimes interested or compelled by the circle of the nation-state, often not. (As they always have.) No doubt a culture like the South in the early nineteenth century is partly of interest because then the circle tried to close and we can study how what now may be being unmade was first made.

This is an abstract way of explaining a few practical decisions about whom to include and whom to exclude from this book. (Authors, alas, administer their own little worlds and stand at Ellis Island like petty policemen.) If one understands culture as a discourse, as people talking to one another with shared presumptions, if often in dissent, the criterion of nativity is of less interest, but it is not irrelevant. Strictly speaking, one might include Charles Sumner in this book, for in his own way, he was involved in the making of Southern culture. That seems more logical than sensible, however. Rather, I have gone with a mix of criteria. Firstly, I have taken an interest in those born in the South, which I take to be the slaveholding states which came to form the Confederacy, as well as those which did not. I go as far north as Baltimore, as far south as Florida, as far west as St. Louis and eastern Texas. However, the South distributed and encouraged its intellectuals very unevenly. So, in practice, the map is constructed differently. In the first tier are South Carolina and Virginia; of the two, the former had the most coherent and sophisticated of all the South's local intellectual societies, while Virginia was more diffuse but almost as complex. In the second tier, one might place Georgia, Alabama, Maryland, Mississippi, and Louisiana, all of which had significant thinkers, usually associated with urban centers. In the rear come Tennessee, Kentucky, Missouri, and Delaware, and behind the rear (being so new and little settled) are Arkansas, Florida, and Texas.

However, since I take an interest in how the South interacted with other cultures, I spend time following Southerners around the world; to live abroad does not seem to me to exclude someone from consideration, if he or she had an acknowledged connection to what was left behind. Henry James is properly considered a part of American literature, though he lived in Kent, just as James Baldwin forms part of black American culture, though he preferred Paris. Similarly, I consider the Charleston-born Sarah Grimké, though she came to live in the North and became an abolitionist, to have been a salient part of Southern culture, for she wished to influence the South and considered she had a right to do so, which had something to do with her social origins. But nativity is not everything. (If you were a slave, you were told your American origins were nothing, no matter how many generations they extended back.) The South exported people, but imported them, too, from Bermuda, or Prussia, or the Hudson River valley. Some of these stayed permanently and became Southerners, while others remained for a decade or longer before leaving. In general, I include most of the former, and some of the latter, if they sustained a presence in Southern intellectual culture and somehow influenced it.

These decisions create a motley crew, but not too much so. Mostly, these were people who shared a world of discourse, knew one another, sometimes were intermarried, and read one another's books. They formed an intelligentsia not so enclosed as that of England around 1900, for the South was a considerable part of a continent and such great distances diminished comity, but in the circumstances, it is more striking how much they shared than how little.

An intellectual history is not a democratic venture and hence has tended to be somewhat illegitimate in the modern discipline of history, which has made much of the moral importance of inclusiveness and equality. There are more complicated ways of expressing the rationale of intellectual history, but the cold truth is that its subject matter is clever people, who once expressed themselves in complicated patterns, which other clever people have taken seriously. Deciding who is clever and who is not was firstly a judgment made by contemporaries, but finally it is the historian's decision, based on experience and prejudice. Cleverness may be a personal quality, but it is authorized by society, which regulates who may acquire education, who has access to books, who is permitted to write, who is published, and who deserves criticism. Mute inglorious Miltons may form a subject matter for poetry, but not for intellectual histories, which are full of people less than mute, indeed often irritatingly garrulous. Nonetheless, an intellectual history is always the establishment of a canon, even if on a small scale. In general, I have tried to cast my net widely, occasionally as far as people whose claim to be thought intellectual might be regarded as tenuous. (Andrew Jackson and Henry Clay are dubious cases.) Some names have usually found their way, even into a tradition of American intellectual history which has thought the Old South to be mostly unworthy of attention: John Taylor, John C. Calhoun, Hugh Legaré, Thomas Dew, William Gilmore Simms, Edgar Allan Poe. Others have gained attention in a recent crop of valuable studies and editions: Beverley Tucker, Mary Chesnut, James Henley Thornwell, Edmund Ruffin, Louisa McCord, Henry Hughes. Others have been little or differently noticed: Hugh Blair Grigsby, James Johnston Pettigrew, Penina Moise, Mary Elizabeth Lee, Caroline Gilman.

A careful reader will discern that, in the wrangles among scholars, my positions, which stretch over various analytical traditions, are roughly the following. This is a book about the South, but also about intellectual culture, so it tries to bring together discourses not usually in conversation; what historians have said about the social structure of the Mississippi Delta is here relevant to the literature on the Scottish Enlightenment, or neo-Hegelianism, or the history of the book. My view is that a convincing intellectual history must, at once, reach into both biography and social history; texts are the necessary core, but where they come from, where they go to, ought to be a matter of interest.

So, briefly, let me say that, on the score of social history, I see the Old South as not premodern but deeply implicated in modernity, though an idiosyncratic version mostly based on slavery. However, I see the South as more than its slaveholding areas, as less than a coherent society, with significant tensions between the world the slaveholders made and the worlds the nonslaveholders made. (The notion that societies exist and are coherent is a premise which the nineteenth century itself especially sanctioned, and which is not self-evident.) As it happens, the South's intellectuals were caught in the middle of these tensions, for their lives mirrored a pattern of instability. Almost all experienced marked social and physical movement, and even those who did not looked out on a world where rootedness seemed an aberration. Without our grasping this instability, Southern thought is unintelligible. It used to be customary to conflate Southern intellectual life with the life of the plantation, understood as a fixed point. Thomas Jefferson has been the model. However much he moved away from Monticello, to Paris or Philadelphia, he has been understood to mirror and comprehend the moral economy of agrarian life, partly because that is how he preferred to represent himself, as one of God's chosen people. And certainly he embodied a social type, the man who was born to and lived upon land and slaves, inhabited a place for a lifetime, and wrote about its meaning. In the generations after Jefferson, the type recurred, as with Edmund Ruffin. Yet this was not the norm for Southern intellectuals: rather, they came from everywhere and nowhere; started poor, middling, and rich, and became middling, rich, or poor, as the world's luck and their talents dictated; they left plantations to become urban, or left cities to become planters, or oscillated between the two; they moved in place and status within the South and beyond its boundaries; they knew conflicting identities or, more rarely, felt themselves to be whole.

On balance, more intellectuals were urban than rural, a disproportion that ought not to be puzzling, especially as the South had one of the world's fastest rates of urbanization in the first half of the nineteenth century. Beyond that it helped to spark intellectual ambition and interest if a child had parents who dealt with words, needed books, and managed literacy. The lawyer with his Blackstone, the minister with volumes of sermons, the merchant with news from Liverpool, the physician with medical textbooks, the journalist, the bookbinder, the bookseller, all these made a child understand that print and ideas mattered. A plantation or farm could, of course, occasion intellectual curiosity. There were plantation libraries, from which a child could take books. Nonetheless, the intellectual who was born on, mostly lived on, and died on the plantation or farm without significant urban experience was not common. Very few, coming to the life of the mind, stayed in the countryside, though some, after or during urban experiences, took on plantations as an investment or a hobby. This helps to explain why there was little cultural warfare in the South between city and country, little between planter and merchant. Occasionally the stubbornly rural, like John Taylor, might speak against the city. But, for most people, the city and trade were respectable enough, not only because trade might invest in land, but because the planter was a commercial creature who knew about and needed trade.

In general, most came from the middling orders and stayed there, a few descended into poverty, and a few more ascended from it; a minority started and ended wealthy, at least before the impoverishments that the Civil War would bring. This is, of course, the common pattern for modern intelligentsias. The poor seldom have the means or occasion for intellectual enquiry, and the upper class tend to leave reflectiveness to those with less power, who need intellectual ingenuity to reason out their predicament and often want the attention that can go with publication. Equally usual is that the Southern intelligentsia was mostly composed of men, with only a few women; this was not a society that encouraged female intellectuality. Almost all had extensive experience of non-Southern society, either by origin, education, migration, or travel; perhaps a little over half had European experience. More than half ended up in states other than those in which they were born, but migration was complex and restless, with not a few returning to their native states after experiments westward. College education was very common, at least among the men. Very few lived upon their writings, but made a living in other ways: the ministry, journalism, the law, teaching, medicine, or officeholding were the most common pursuits. Slaveholding was habitual, though some did not have slaves and many owned only a few household servants; a minority were directly and extensively engaged in the political economy of slave plantations. Almost all were married with children, but they seem often to have been raised in households in which fathers or (more rarely) mothers had prematurely died. Of those unmarried, it is impossible to gauge how many were so because of sexual orientation, but it seems likely that a few were homosexual, intermittently or regularly. It is hard to know, because the antebellum South did not like to confess such matters, save in polite negations like "never married." And, of course, homosexuality is scarcely confined to the unmarried.

Though these were people whose intellectual lives tended often to be molded by local circumstances, the facts of migration and travel, the existence of gathering places (synods, court sessions, legislatures, spas, clubs), and the extent of kinship networks that extended through the South and beyond did much toward creating a wider discourse. Kinship, especially, should not be neglected as an encouragement to bringing minds into contact and (in the way of families) into conflict, nor should the existence of a cheap, efficient postal system. Such connections were uneven but fell into patterns, which tended to conform to the broader configurations of the South. Virginia was a world of its own (if divided between its east and west), but a world that had better connections with its western offspring, Kentucky, and the Chesapeake world than the world to its south. Maryland was poised between North and South, becoming more the former. Kentucky was part Virginian, part midwestern, and in its western parts connected to a river culture that extended northward to Pittsburgh and southward to New Orleans. South Carolina was linked closely to Philadelphia and New York up the coast, as well as to Georgia (with whom it had an old relationship) and to Alabama and Mississippi, to which many of its people migrated. Tennessee was linked to North Carolina, which itself faced two ways, south toward South Carolina and north toward Virginia. Mississippi faced partially toward Louisiana, which was a world of its own, linked mostly to Paris, and somewhat to the Caribbean. Arkansas was an offspring of Tennessee and the Mississippi River but, like Florida, was something of a remote orphan. Texas was semi-Mexican, but an empire to itself. Intellectual life followed all these social trade routes; books, periodicals, conversations tramped along plank roads, down rivers, on railroads, along with the herded slaves, the cotton bales, the itinerant preachers.

Nonetheless, these intellectuals tended to associate with the modernizing sector of society, a fact that explains their access and receptivity to advanced ideas. Hence the South's intelligentsia was in dialogue with its society, but it was not very representative, as most intelligentsias are not. What I describe in this book, the imaginative world created by Southern intellectuals, imperfectly mirrors the social world of the whole South, which was certainly more conservative than they were.

This untidiness was not absent from, or irrelevant to, the formal presumptions of Southern thought. If one considers not the contexts of social history, but those of intellectual history, the experience of studying the Old South does not weaken any sense that Romanticism marked a significant paradigm shift from the projects of the Enlightenment. It does, however, make one conscious (more than most intellectual historians allow) that paradigms persist, coexist, and come into conversation. The Enlightenment did not disappear in Southern culture in 1830 just because somebody was persuaded by reading August von Schlegel, any more than the evangelical culture of the Reformation ceased to be influential because somebody was reading Andrews Norton, or the Augustan imagination went away because William Wordsworth became more popular than Alexander Pope. Nonetheless, different times mandate different emphases, gather together the fragments of human experience into different patterns, and give them names, and intellectuals are peculiarly in the business of naming. (Those who have lived during the invention of postmodernism will be aware of how these things, puzzlingly, can happen.) So, because it is a philosophy of movement and change, Romanticism became and remains a formative influence on the modern imagination that offers a way to think about the fear of isolation and the pressure of society. But the perspectives of the Enlightenment have lingered, because they offer a glimpse of what the world might look like, if we could contrive to stabilize it, if we could but recover a sense of trust about all those other human beings, with knives in their hands.

Bringing together social history and intellectual history, however, affects another matter of boundaries, hence of narrative. Social history, on the whole, has been localistic. It has studied this county or that state, this social group or that gender. On the contrary, intellectual history, though not without microcosmic studies (the intellectual biography, the study of a local intellectual community), has been biased in favor of the free movement of ideas and hence of the permeability of frontiers. An American intellectual history cannot fail to be an intellectual history of other places, if Emerson read Carlyle, Carlyle read Goethe, Goethe read Hume, Hume read Epicurus, and Emerson, too, read Epicurus and Hume, who was reading Jonathan Edwards. Intellectuals, because they live in two places, their imaginations and places like Concord, live in more than two places. Their historians, likewise, must have a license to roam, if those imaginations are to be recaptured. Hence I have not hesitated to explicate, not only the texts Southern intellectuals wrote, but those they read. So the reader should not be surprised to come across passages where I pay attention to the works of, for example, Johann Friedrich Blumenbach of Göttingen or Hugh Blair of Edinburgh, since both had an influence on Southern thought.

This is another way of saying that a sort of globalization has been going on in intellectual life, and hence of intellectual history, for a long time. There are schools of thought which have debated the nature of these conversations *sans frontières*. The tradition of the history of ideas tended to write as though time and place mattered little, that the historian put Aristotle and William James in the same room to see how they coped with complicated questions put to them; this is an Enlightenment tradition, focused on what the Marxists like to call praxis or social action, not an intellectually fastidious thing. The venture of intellectual history, which is closer to Romantic historicism, has insisted that Aristotle belongs only in an ancient Greek room, William James only in a modern American room, and that, though James read Aristotle, Aristotle never read James, unless the Christian heaven or the Elysian Fields have good libraries. I am more sympathetic to the latter school, though I am conscious that anachronism is a very common human experience. Anachronism is an especial accomplishment of print culture, which allows so many words from so many times to survive together.

There is another cogent reason why a Southern history needs, partly, to be a history of people and places beyond the South, a reason which extends beyond the South's participation in the swirling patterns of physical and intellectual migrations. Once, it was usual to write the intellectual history of Europe as though it were only introspective. The colonies, the empires, the zones of influence of European cultures were understood as places where ideas made in Europe went to die or run to seed, but were not places whose existence was thought significantly to have influenced how Europeans thought at home. The development of postcolonial studies, especially the prominence of modern intellectual figures from what was once understood as the "periphery," has changed this. It is now clearer that the existence of empire has had a great bearing on how Europeans conceptualized their worlds. It follows that the resonance that Southerners found in European texts not only arose from the deference of ex-colonials but also stemmed from the fact that Southerners saw shapes in European ideas which existed because they, the Southerners, and others at the "margins" existed. Europe had faced the problem of ordering the multifarious knowledge which the project of empire had brought into its reckoning, while sustaining its political, economic, and cultural suzerainty. The pace quickened from the seventeenth, to the eighteenth, to the nineteenth centuries, as the knowledge piled up and as the agents of empire proliferated. The Enlightenment was a preliminary response, mostly a confident one. Romanticism was a more frantic response; the awareness of so many cultures, with so many values, with so many Gods, threatened the disintegration of intelligibility. Philosophers like Hegel found a way to finesse the problem, to describe the Bacchanalian whirl but to define patterns, albeit patterns full of movement; they were patterns they called history, society, culture. But it was no accident that the image, which seemed to Hegel to crystallize the problem of the modern self, was drawn from the experience of slavery.

So European conjectures of order appealed to Southerners, since the latter were among the custodians of empire. They were out in the field, felling the trees, managing nature, driving the slaves, building the institutions, filling their libraries with texts that tried to make sense of the whole business. Sometimes Southern texts went back and modified the metropolitan paradigms; this was the case, for example, with the ethnographic studies of Josiah Nott, which earned him election as an honorary fellow of the Anthropological Society of London and as a foreign associate of the Anthropological Society of Paris, and made him an influence upon Ernest Renan, the leading French Orientalist. Not infrequently, Southerners worked in imperial ventures into other continents: James Warley Miles and James Adger were both missionaries in the Near East; William B. Hodgson was a diplomat in North Africa, where he acquired an Orientalist's interest in Arabic languages; Southerners helped to found a colony on the western edge of Africa; Joel Poinsett and Louis Rémy Mignot followed in the footsteps of Alexander von Humboldt in South America. But, when considering the historic trajectory of the United States, Southerners were sharp judges of what worked in these European conjectures and what did not. Their margins were thinner, so they opted for a cautious version of Romanticism, one less receptive to disorder, more interested in hierarchy. For the disintegrative side of the Romantic vision often hinted at a subversion of the imperialist project, and Southerners resisted this, for they *were* the project. Nonetheless, many knew the darker side, and not a few were nervous. Edgar Allan Poe fashioned perhaps the sharpest, coldest images of disintegration of anyone in his century, and he contemplated what happened if you ventured, like Arthur Gordon Pym, to the edge of the world and "rushed into the embraces of the cataract, where a chasm threw itself open to receive us."[9]

1 · The Softened Echo of the World

There are many ways to understand the interchanges between the South and the northern United States, but four are instructive for an intellectual history: the Southern experience of Northern higher education, the responses of Southerners traveling as visitors beyond the Potomac, the character of Northern judgments about the adequacy of Southern culture, and the debate within the South about the comparative standing of its culture.

In education, there was an asymmetry. The student bodies of Southern colleges were far less cosmopolitan than their faculty. Of the students who attended the University of Virginia between 1826 and 1874, for example, just 1.7 percent came from nonslaveholding states, and this was a mirror image of the Northern situation. With the exception of Princeton, few Northern colleges were hospitable to hiring Southern teachers. However, on average, between 1820 and 1860, Southerners represented about 9 percent of Harvard students, 11 percent of Yale's, and 36 percent of Princeton's.

Those Southerners who graduated in the North before 1815 seem to have experienced little cultural tension, and difficulties during the next two decades turned mostly not on political, but on pedagogical issues. Earlier Southerners knew they were moving among strangers, whose odd ways needed definition, but not always strangers who threatened survival. With the onset of abolitionism, the mood changed. In 1847 William Elliott observed that, during his recent visits to the North, he had stayed away from his own college of Harvard, because he was aware of "a difference in the *tone*" which had grown "out of political and sectional estrangement." To his regret, his standing as a slaveholder now caused offense and seemed to place him in a position of "*moral inferiority*." What happened in the 1840s to a postgraduate like Elliott happened then to undergraduate Basil Manly Jr., who went to study at the Newton Theological Institution in Massachusetts. After talking to a faculty member about the refusal of Northern Baptists to permit slaveholders to serve on foreign missions, he had grown troubled to be enjoying the "conveniences, advantages, & privileges" of an institution sustained by "men who cast out as evil my name, & the names of all I love & hold dear," and decided to migrate to Princeton, where Southerners were more welcome.[1]

The impulse toward a growing separation was not only ideological but also institutional. The South in 1850 was richer in institutions of higher learning than in 1790, when effectively it had but one, the College of William and Mary. It was a pattern that fathers, born in the eighteenth century, went to English or to Northern colleges, but their sons to Southern. As the traveler John Melish observed even in 1815, "It was customary for a long period, for the more wealthy planters to send their sons to Europe for education; and even now they frequently send them to the northern states; but the practice is gradually declining, and the desire has become general to have respectable seminaries in the state."[2]

Many Southerners went north not for education but pleasure. They considered the fashionable walkers along Philadelphia's Chestnut Street and stayed at the Astor House in New York, from which they stepped out to be impressed (or not) by Broadway. There were bookshops, museums, and all the curious phenomena of modern life to visit: the new factories at Lowell, the great Fairmount Water Works in Philadelphia, the Shakers in New Lebanon. They went to churches, considered architecture, and judged preachers. They experienced landscape—Niagara, the Catskills, the Hudson River—and usually managed the required emotions of admiration or wonder. Above all, necessarily, they formed opinions on hotels, waiters, and menus.

Much was summed up by the word "manners," by which was meant both customs and courtesies. It was expected that the traveler would observe manners, perhaps even learn from them, and they were variously judged, often in reaction to settled stereotypes. In general, it was presumed that Northerners were avaricious, brusque, rapid, religious (and probably hypocritical), disciplined, diligent, self-improving, less courteous to women, less hospitable, uncharitable toward social inferiors, condescending toward outsiders, self-righteous, less adept at politics, and more prone to ideological enthusiasm. Those who found good words for the North did so by demonstrating the inaccuracy of such prejudices. Lucian Minor in 1833, for example, was willing to admit that he had met "some admirable female minds in New England," scant abolitionism, honesty, rational hospitality, and "a quiet, Sabbath-keeping, morals-preserving, good-doing, and heaven-serving religion." All this was self-consciously intended to diminish hostilities, upon the presumption that Southerners too little visited the North: "Our people ought to travel northward more often. It would be a good thing, if exploring parties were frequently sent hither, (as to a moral *terra incognita*,) to observe and report the particulars deserving of our imitation."[3] But there is little evidence that there was a deficiency of such expeditions. Each year Southerners swarmed forth, and each year the ruts of mistrust deepened.

Implicated in such debates was the matter of mind. Were the intellectual exertions of the North more advanced? Later, the verdict of Appomattox seemed to settle the matter. Before 1861, the issue was murkier, at least for Southerners. Most Northerners, even Northerners not abolitionists, however, had little doubt of Southern inferiority.

At first, the North tended to see the South as pastoral and gentlemanly, a sort of English country estate, which might make people ignorant by forcing them into a "paradise of indolence." In a Romantic age, this could be used by Northerners as a tool of self-criticism. In 1850, Emerson thought that the Southerner "has personality, has temperament, has manners, persuasion, address & terror," but "the cold Yankee has wealth, numbers, intellect, material power of all sorts, but not fire or firmness." Southern incompetence might occasion ambivalence, since it could be viewed either as a serious hindrance to national productivity or as merely a quaint nuisance. What sensible Northerner could feel challenged by what the *Albany Evening Journal* was later to assert of Southerners, that they were "dwarfs by the side of the giants of the North"? Did one need to fear what Henry David Thoreau called "a moral fungus"? Explanations for this inferiority differed. The rutted byways and dirty taverns might be blamed on slavery, but cultural etiolation might be understood as arising from a different descent; Northerners were energetic Anglo-Saxons, Southerners a mongrel people. Later, when it was clearer that an imperial South was less than supine, when the fungal dwarf bore the laurels of Mexico City on his brow, the images became darker. Then the North might be thought uncertain, the South purposeful. Theodore Parker put it starkly: "Southern Slavery is an institution which is in earnest. Northern Freedom is an institution that is not in earnest."[4] This was a class stereotype. If the South was aristocratic and the North democratic, the common man might be bewitched and herded by aristocrats who, if not intelligent, had ancestral habits of command and violence, even charm, and probably vice. The South came to embody what the North feared, that the great experiment of a moral, progressive republic might go awry. That is, the North saw the South as the continuation of Europe by other means; hence, to defeat her was to complete the project of the American Revolution. This was how Lincoln would come to explain matters over the dead of Gettysburg.

Francis L. Hawks of North Carolina, a historian and Episcopal minister in New York, felt the force of these condescensions in 1860. In his experience, Northerners "thought that the people of the South were a set of craven imbeciles" whose only purpose was to farm for the enrichment of Northerners, who in return "looked upon us as *inferiors*, morally, physically & intellectually." A Southerner had only to look into the writings of Theodore

Parker to find a sweeping indictment: "Whence come the men of superior education who occupy the pulpits, exercise the professions of law and medicine, or fill the chairs of the professors in the colleges of the Union? Almost all from the North, from the free States. . . . Whence come the distinguished authors of America? . . . All from the free States; north of Mason and Dixon's line!" Traveling little in the South, never attending its colleges, seldom publishing in or reading its periodicals, why should Northerners be able to arrive at an estimate? Some were aware of this problem and even regretted it. In 1861 the historian Hugh Blair Grigsby sent some of his publications to Cornelius Felton of Harvard, who in reply praised the Virginian's "eloquent and instructive pages" and mused on his ignorance of the Southern mind after the generation of Jefferson: "I could not help regretting that our country has not a common center where from time to time the men of letters, and leading professional gentlemen may meet, and become personally acquainted with each other. Your books have taught me how little I know of the literary works of Virginia, and how much there is in them which I and all our northern men ought to know."[5]

So Southerners observed the North more than they were observed and were very unsure about their standing. There was a school of opinion that believed the South was too dependent upon the North, both economically and intellectually. In the 1820s, Robert Young Hayne sought expansively to remedy this thralldom by proposing a periodical that might educate and stimulate the Southern elite, which, in turn, would give "tone to the sentiments and opinions of the people." Though they aimed at arousing and defining Southern intellectual energies as a counterpoise to Northern views, the founders of the *Southern Review* did not intend a closed world. Knowledge of "the improvements of the age" would be diffused in the South, intellect would arise from its slumber, write, and be read, but not only in the South. The place would come to define itself, but also would persuade others by a journal which might occasion "the diffusion of knowledge, the discussion of doctrines, and the investigation of truth," and so extend "the boundaries of human knowledge" and review "the opinions of the days as in their perpetual fluctuations they set on the characters and conduct of society."[6]

Intellectual life mattered because it molded public opinion, which controlled much of life. Knowledge was power, as Thomas Cooper passionately insisted in 1831, and it was worrying that in the "perpetual fluctuations" of modern society the South might lose ground. Any culture could fear that, even those which bestrode the world. Victorian Britain was riddled with doubt. So Basil Manly spoke of "the inferiority of our [educational] Institutions" and others looked at solid things like the *North American Review* in Boston and fretted when Southern periodicals tottered, as they regularly did.[7]

Not all the estimates, however, were self-abasing. Many considered the South as superior in the political arts and political thought. Conservative theologians thought little of Northerners who had strayed into liberalism, and, in general, Northern classical scholarship was deemed inferior. In the early 1830s, Edward W. Johnston, who had been librarian of South Carolina College, went north and found the experience discouraging. He had fallen into a respectable enough set, including William Cullen Bryant and James K. Paulding, but these, in comparison to the intellectuals of Columbia, seemed like lightweights. There was "nobody with Dr Cooper's Atlantean shoulders, fit to prop a whole world of volumes; nor none with Nott's nice fingers, that touch every thing, and know how to touch it so choicely and deftly; nor Lieber's sturdy German grasp, that wields so much, by dint of taking every thing by its handle; nor Preston's noble and elegant capacity that possesses itself, in a glance, of the better parts of all knowledge."[8] So, some were sure that the South was inferior, some that it was superior, some made distinctions within genres, others between institutions. Some were driven by a political vision; others were blithely indifferent to politics and cared only for God or verse forms.

In all this, it would be easy to exaggerate dissidence, even late in the antebellum years when tensions grew. Incomprehension was the norm, but a few set their boats against the current. Some relationships survived the strains, others even flourished. Nonetheless, amiability was impeded by the complexity of the American scene. To his friend Francis Lieber, then removed to New York, William Campbell Preston (the politician and college president) remarked in 1859 upon the evil of a "lack of a common center of thought" in the Union. "Washington is in no sense metropolitan, nor is New York except in respect to commerce," he observed. "The thought . . . of that great amorphous ag[g]regation of people and effort is hardly perceived here in Virginia."[9]

As the bitter history which created a civil war was to show, this fumbling ignorance could occasion hostility as often as indifference. Silence could be intimidating, when there was no center and no hope of any portion achieving intellectual dominance, but only fragments that postured, groped, and wondered.

THE SOUTH HAD ITS centrifugal forces, which touched its black population most powerfully: for Frederick Douglass, William Wells Brown, or Harriet Jacobs, this was a place to leave. But, for whites elsewhere, the South appeared prosperous, somewhere futures could be made. The presence of these "aliens" took many forms; visitors, settlers, sojourners—the temporary, the permanent, and the uncommitted.

Often noticed have been those who came briefly. These included friendly Northerners like James K. Paulding, ambivalent ones like Frederick Law Olmsted, hostile ones like Harriet Beecher Stowe. And then there were the foreign commentators, like Alexis de Tocqueville and Basil Hall. The early nineteenth century liked to travel, liked to write books about it, liked to have opinions about the alien. The South was on the circuit, though peripherally, being not so remote as to offer the shock of the new, nor so familiar as to provide the shock of recognition.

Foreign opinions rebounded back to the South, which took them with varying degrees of indignation, curiosity, and enthusiasm. Southerners, like other Americans, were notoriously sensitive about alien opinion. Table manners, the brutality of the roads, the brown slime of tobacco juice, the perils of democracy, such things were the standard topics of interest to foreigners perambulating in both Ohio and Alabama, and the standard occasion for local resentment. Slavery was an especial vexation. The institution, Southerners were persuaded, could only be understood by those who stayed more than a few months, certainly more than Mrs. Stowe's few days in northern Kentucky. A character in Susan Petigru King's novel *Lily* lays it down as a maxim that abolitionists should be obliged to stay for a year before they could earn their opinions.[10]

There was, especially, a steady supply of British writers who traveled through the South, though the trade routes were unhelpful. Invitations to American tours often came from Northern publishers, and the visitor's first contacts seldom encouraged a Southern venture. From New York in 1842, Charles Dickens wrote of his plans to go to Charleston, but upon advice he changed his mind: "The country, all the way from here, is nothing but a dismal swamp . . . [and] there is very little to see, after all." Slavery was a great barrier, especially for Dickens: "When we reach Baltimore, we are in the regions of slavery. . . . They whisper, here [in New York] . . . that in that place, and all through the South, there is a dull gloomy cloud on which the very word seems written."[11]

But visits by foreigners could bring into Southern culture a fund of knowledge, allusion, and gossip. The geologist Charles Lyell, for example, came often enough to become a familiar figure among Southern scientists. Thackeray became especially close during and after two lecturing tours in 1853 and 1856, when he was handed on from literary luminary to wealthy notable, from Baltimore via Charleston to New Orleans. In Richmond in 1853 he was a particular hit, his discourse later inducing fond memories of a "charming manner and musical voice," a geniality which altered previously critical opinion of the novelist's cynicism.[12] The fondness was reciprocal, enough to induce Thackeray to write *The Virginians* and not *The Bostonians*. The place was warm, the Médoc and bouillabaisse in New Orleans were excellent, there were agreeable and well-informed people. As a matter of principle, Thackeray leaned toward generosity, and, though a great admirer of Dickens, he had not approved of the *American Notes*, which he thought showed discourtesy and an ignorant temerity in hazarding a book on a culture which Dickens barely knew. Thackeray preferred to pocket his lecture fees, thank his audiences, and not add insult to benefit by dashing off a quick travel book. He was studiedly polite about what he saw, was only gently satirical, and tried to take no sides in American sectional disputes. But not to attack the South was, willy-nilly, to defend it. And, in truth, he saw little in slavery to trouble him. From Washington he wrote to his mother in 1852: "They are not my men & brethren, these strange people with retreating foreheads, with great obtruding lips & jaws: with capacities for thought, pleasure, endurance quite different to mine." In theory, he denied the morality of slavery, but not in extenso. Moreover, Thackeray felt that Southerners had a point when they indicated the inhumanities of English society: "God help us we are no better than our brethren."[13]

Then the South was full of migrants: some Northerners, some Europeans, some who came to stay, some who moved on. Among those who stayed, the case of Thomas Smyth, the theologian and Presbyterian minister, is instructive, because he tried to do what many migrants preferred, to effect a balance between his new place and his old one.

He started life as plain Thomas Smith, born in Belfast in 1808, and educated under the auspices of the Scottish Enlightenment. He came to America, partly to follow his emigrating parents, partly to escape disciplinary embarrassments at his college, partly to unburden himself of a failed romance. In the United States, he abruptly switched from Congregationalism to Presbyterianism, studied at Princeton, and was about to become a missionary in Florida, when he was invited to supply a pulpit in Charleston. There he found many Scotch-Irish who did not expect him to relinquish his former ties.

Smyth (as he became in 1837) turned into an assimilated Southerner and, what was extra, a proslavery Charlestonian, but he never abandoned his stake in North Britain, where he republished his works. As a theologian, he remained knitted into a transatlantic culture even while slavery complicated his relationship to it. In 1850, for example, he was nominated for an honorary degree at the University of Glasgow and the university's senate declined, believing it was unwise to meddle in the slavery question. This was but one of several incidents that indicated a gulf. In 1843, when the Free Church of Scotland had been founded, Smyth had taken up a very large collection in Charleston and sent it to Thomas Chalmers in Edinburgh. Thinking a Christian slaveholder to be no oxymoron, Chalmers was pleased, but others were not, including Frederick Douglass. In lectures in Belfast, Douglass had forcefully urged that there was, indeed, a contradiction and that morality required Christians to reject the fellowship of slaveholders. In Scotland, Douglass then urged that subventions from slaveholders be returned. "Send Back the Money," he demanded, in what became a popular chant. This lionizing did not please Thomas Smyth, back in Europe in 1846, only to learn of the celebrity of this "coloured man, formerly . . . a slave in Maryland." He heard many disparaging and damning things about Douglass. It seems likely that Smyth repeated some of these slanders. At least, Douglass threatened a libel suit against him and alleged that Smyth had called him "an Infidel" who "had been seen coming out a Brothel in Manchester."[14]

James Robertson, secretary of the Scottish Anti-Slavery Society, sent Smyth a letter full of harsh words about Smyth being a man stealer, "a *recreant Scotsman* and *an unfaithful minister of Jesus Christ*." Smyth was invited to debate the issue of slavery in public, but he declined. He was sent the draft of an apology, ready for his signature. Instead, prudently he wrote a letter to Douglass's solicitors, in which he denied ever having uttered the alleged libel.[15] Douglass, in turn, expressed himself satisfied with the explanation, and the matter was dropped. Technically, it was a tie. But, to Smyth, it was a humiliation. Charleston slaveholders were not accustomed to ties with those born into slavery. The incident showed that, when he confined himself to matters of Presbyterian theology, he could find many friends in his old home. Once the issue of slavery was raised, bitterness ensued, his expatriation was exposed, he became "a *recreant Scotsman*."

Smyth became a permanent Southerner, but there were many who were only sojourners. Among those who stayed longer, Francis Lieber, as an intellectual who lingered but never settled, offers the most illuminating instance. From 1835 to 1856 he served as professor of history and political economy at the South Carolina College. From the moment he arrived, he sent out a steady stream of unhappy letters to Northern friends that lamented his fate, stressed his isolation, and attributed his unhappiness to the culture around him. It was a lesson these friends were happy to see endorsed from within the Slave Power. As a Northern correspondent said to Lieber, the South was a place "where the sun ripens fruit, but not scholars, only here and there one, not indigenous to the soil."[16]

Why he came to the South was simple. South Carolina College paid him well. This was no small attraction for a man who had been born to modest circumstances in Berlin, had been exiled from Prussia for sedition, had fought in Greece, had removed to the United States and suffered a number of improvised and impecunious literary jobs, while unsuccessfully applying for a number of college positions. South Carolina College, by contrast, offered him a secure job at a very good salary. He went expecting a temporary expedient. Thereafter various jobs were cultivated by him in the North, but they all came to nothing and the temporary slipped into twenty years before he knew it.

Lieber spent those twenty years in confused suspension between Europe, the North, and the South. He spent the academic year in Columbia, but during most summers he went north, usually without his family. He often traveled back to Europe, though he came to regard himself as an American and was vexed when critics charged him with Germanic idiosyncrasies of style and thought. In 1851 Fanny Longfellow, the wife of the poet and an old friend, was to observe in a letter that foreigners found it hard to settle down in America, and Lieber fumed: "This is cutting. I, a foreigner—if I am not an American, what am I? German not—a sort of cosmopolitan dog, as the curs owned in Constantinople, owned by no one and owning nobody."[17]

Yet he did own somebody, several slaves. To friends in the North, he offered condemnation of the institution, but within his household he acted in ways indistinguishable from the Southerners around him. He kept condescending and sardonic note of his slaves' behavior, believed unhesitatingly in their sexual abandonment, checked a slave's teeth before buying, and grieved when a death deprived him of capital. He seems to have had little skepticism of local tales about racial characteristics, part of his hatred of slavery was that it condemned him to live among Africans, and he saw the issue of "negroism" as central. To be sure, he was disposed to believe that not all whites were superior to all blacks, partly because he wished to demonstrate that some whites were superior to other whites: above all, the cultured heartland of "some four or half a dozen white nations," especially France, Germany, and England, had of late pushed ahead.[18]

As a political economist and free trader, Lieber believed that slavery was an anachronism, doomed by the laws of progress and civilization. Yet he knew these were complicated issues and morality was not simple. For years he kept a notebook packed with clippings, random musings, and reports of conversations about slavery. Its pages show his instinct for contradictions. The slave was a chattel and a thing, yet he had rights and responsibilities. The master was theoretically sovereign, yet he often exercised a restricted power.

Slavery for blacks was supposed to elevate the white race, yet slave mechanics undercut their white counterparts and made them discontented. Slavery and commerce were honored, but the slave trader was a pariah.

Most fundamentally, he knew that many slaveholders had their own kind of honesty. Lieber was to break with his old friend Charles Sumner because the latter could not understand this, which Lieber knew to be true of others, because he thought it true of himself, the slaveholder. The senator would pointedly send down to Lieber in Columbia clippings from Boston newspapers about slave whippings and castrations, and Lieber grew irritated at the reproach to him, the morally complex man in a morally complex situation. Lieber felt himself to be a moderate, convinced that the problem of American society consisted in the threat to moderate men from Jacobin extremes in both sections, from Sumner and Calhoun.

But Lieber had to be discreet. In the classroom, though he lectured on history and political economy, he soft-pedaled slavery. In a farewell letter to the senior class of South Carolina College in 1849, which enunciated his basic principles of political economy, there was not a word about it. Few misunderstood his silence. As Lieber noted, "reticents are treated like accusers."[19] In truth, his unease was partly an example of a standing difficulty, the tension of criticizing a culture which employs you. Yet there was scarcely an opinion Francis Lieber held that did not unite him to a Southerner and divide him from a Northerner, or divide him from a Southerner and unite him to a Northerner.

The letters he wrote to Northern friends were, among other things, a means of advancement. He constantly lobbied and plotted for better jobs. Strategically, disparagement of his condition in the South was essential, as a way of validating his credentials for a job in a free state. More subtly, he thereby displaced responsibility from himself the slaveholder to the slaveholding society around him. He made himself a victim, a prisoner whom it would be virtuous to free. So these letters do not show Lieber the resident of Columbia in full measure, partly because when he left the South definitively in 1857, he destroyed thousands of his papers; doubtless a disproportionate number of Southern manuscripts found their way into the fire. And he did not need to correspond with people he met every day. But enough evidence has survived to show that, over time, he had developed extensive Southern connections and friendships, though also enemies. By 1856 Lieber had settled down in Columbia and accepted that his chances of a Northern position were slim. His children were grown and had become, somewhat against his will, ambivalently Southerners. He was fifty-seven and moving rapidly toward retirement. In publicly opposing separate secession, he had made enemies in the state, but also friends in a (for the moment) winning cause. He had reconciled himself to having lived less than youth had promised or wanted.

Late in 1855, Thornwell resigned the presidency of South Carolina College. Lieber's name was mentioned around the state to succeed in the post, and especially from the Unionists in the west. Factional support developed, with Petigru as Lieber's strongest backer on the board of trustees. In the balloting, Lieber came very close to success, but Thornwell balked him by the nomination of a lightweight but Presbyterian candidate in Charles McCay, the professor of mathematics newly arrived from an undistinguished career at the University of Georgia. The ploy had been intended merely to deadlock the election and make Lieber unacceptable, but McCay ended up elected. This was a matter of no little embarrassment, a nonentity filling the position once held by Thomas Cooper, Thornwell himself, and William Campbell Preston. Disgusted, insulted, Lieber resigned.

There were undoubtedly ideological matters in this departure. In the campaign against him, it had been mooted that Lieber was a foreigner, a weak Christian, an abolitionist, and a Unionist. Yet these had been accusations with which he had lived for twenty years, which had occasionally generated failed campaigns against him. There were other objections to him holding a position, like that of president, where sympathy with public opinion was of some legitimate moment. Lieber was well above the other canvassed candidates as a scholar, but he had grave disadvantages as an administrator, as a disciplinarian, and as someone who might be influential with the state legislature. The wonder is, not that Lieber lost the position, but that he came so close to winning it. Lieber left, then, because he had lost a faculty power struggle, because he, an old and distinguished man, had been insulted by his college preferring an inferior. His story at South Carolina College, then, is curiously modern: the tale of a man coming for a haven and a salary, staying for lack of an equally well paying option, enduring complicated ambivalence about the surrounding culture, leaving because of a feud and a slight.

There was a deeper ambivalence in Lieber's Southern career. He was a man in cultural flux, taking color from the cultures he encountered. The substructure of his ideology was European, bourgeois, and liberal. Early, the North gave him cool summers, admiring friends, agreeable conversation, publishers, and tantalizing prospects, but it is hard to document what ideas he received there. Curiously, it was the South, by tension, that gave Lieber his most characteristic doctrine, the notion of the tension between the ethics of change and the obligations of community. Above all, he came to insist that individuals should be free to move to make their contributions, that nativism was a moral blunder, and that emigration was a "great law . . . of civilisation," because by it individualism fertilized culture.[20]

Whatever the permanence or impermanence of all these various in-migrations, people such as Smyth and Lieber enlarged the stock of knowledge and analysis available to Southern culture. Many Southerners understood the value of such bridges; if they had not, far fewer aliens would have ended up as tutors and professors. Equally, many Southerners disliked such promiscuous connections. Their cultures were old enough to have achieved a workable distinction between the immigrant and the native, between them and us. Jefferson's acquisition of so many Europeans for the University of Virginia was widely distrusted, and, for some, the belief that Europe and the United States were culturally dissimilar created a sense that xenophobia was a moral duty. Basil Manly, soon after he had assumed the presidency of the University of Alabama, contemplated the appointment of a professor of modern languages who would likely be an outsider. "I have a great dread of these strolling Foreigners," he noted. Of course, if you were one of the strolling foreigners, the issue looked differently. In 1845, when there was criticism of strangers teaching at South Carolina College, Michael Tuomey, the geologist who had migrated from Ireland in 1830, observed tartly: "The world could not all have been born in S.C."[21]

MOST OF THE Southern cultural engagement with the world beyond the United States lay in Europe, the ancestral continent. Though Southerners did venture farther, to Africa, Asia, and Latin America, they did so in far fewer numbers. The European link was more complex, the categories of traveler more nuanced. After the Civil War, the historian William Henry Trescot was to express the opinion that "the American who has studied history in books, never understands until he has lived in Europe what history really is. He never comprehends where in the point of human progress he stands in America, until he looks back upon it from Europe. . . . He feels that the future, which to the genuine American looks so free, is, in fact, bound irrevocably to that humanity which has suffered and struggled and failed and achieved through so many centuries."[22] Not everyone felt this, and certainly not everyone would have agreed with Trescot that the European experience taught Americans that their lives were only variations on ancient ways. Most Southerners, in fact, concluded that they were living out a different drama.

There were those who went to Europe as young men, usually to complete an education begun in the United States. For some years after 1815, these went as Grand Tourists, but, by the 1830s, they often went formally as postgraduate students, usually to Germany if they were scholars of the law and the humanities, to Paris if doctors. Then there were those who toured in later life, usually with a family in tow, sometimes to teach their children French or Italian; the richer the family, the longer and more frequent the visits. After the coming of the steamship, the quality of these visits altered, because it was practical to visit for a few months in the summer. By the 1840s the world which Henry James was to chronicle later had been created and the Grand Tourist had become the tourist. Next were those who went on business: the South was part of the networks of international trade, which needed tending; and the region supplied about a third of the American diplomatic corps, at a time when it was not unusual to appoint men of letters to embassies and consulates. Occasionally Southerners came to Europe in search of health, to doctors in Paris or spas in Germany. More common were adult writers or artists in search of knowledge, conversation, or contacts. Frequent were returning immigrants who visited family or took children to be connected to cultural roots. Finally, there were the expatriates, who stayed in Europe for a decade or a lifetime, because they preferred it or despised their home.

The tradition of the American in Europe was older than the United States because it was continuous with the European travel traditions which stretched back beyond even John Milton in the cool woods of Vallambrosa, as far back as ancient Celts visiting Rome. For those on the western shore of the Atlantic, this tradition was disrupted by the American Revolution and the French revolutionary wars, but only by degrees. Thomas Jefferson in Paris was a new American in the Old World, but he was also a transplanted Welshman who had employment on the Continent. Networks of kinship and friendship did not stop at the American strand, but crossed and re-crossed the ocean in dizzying array. In such matters, nationality was only one consideration amongst many.

South Carolina indicates the kind of genealogical maze which engendered so many cultural and intellectual implications. Over several generations, from the late eighteenth century to the mid-nineteenth, the interconnected families of the Izards, Middletons, Pinckneys, Smiths, Kinlochs, and Manigaults produced men who were often educated abroad (at Cambridge, Oxford, the Inns of Court, Paris, Heidelberg), habitually accepted diplomatic missions (to Britain, Tuscany, Russia, Spain, and Portugal), were sometimes merchant adventurers (to the Far East and Latin America), and, as men and women, extensively intermarried with families beyond South Carolina and the South (the DeLanceys of New York, the Falconets of Naples, the Bentivoglios of Rome). There was scarcely a spot in the world that a member of the family did not visit, from Siberia to Chile, from Canton to Egypt. For a few, like John Izard Middleton, this led to permanent expatriation, but most served American governments, as signers of the Declaration of Independence, as governors, as senators, as wifely advisers to power. However, though these were unquestionably American families, indeed founders of the nation, the barrier they perceived between America and Europe was porous; it might require an effort of will to sustain it, and not all thought the effort worthwhile. The Jamesian image of British colonists become American patriots, dissevered from the courtly muses of Europe, then returning with shining morning faces as innocents abroad was irrelevant to their experience. They never lost their contact with Europe; it just gradually modulated. To visit Europe was to visit an aspect of home, a branch of the kinship network. Yet this was a cosmopolitan intimacy above the norm. Perhaps half the antebellum Southern intelligentsia never traveled to Europe in anything more than their reading and imagination, and the other half came to Europe with far less intimacy. One way to comprehend the discernment of those who did travel is to follow their routes.

If a Southerner traveled first to Britain, he or she first went north and took a ship from New York to Liverpool, fixed in the Southern mind as the place where cotton prices were decided and of peculiar interest as an introduction to modernity, impressive but dirty. There one decided whether to travel westward to Ireland or northward to Scotland, or to press on to London. Relatively few went to Ireland, which had yet to earn standing as a site for Romantic reveries, but Presbyterians sometimes went to Belfast and might go on to Dublin. Ireland came to be viewed in Southern discourse as the convergence of things characteristically mistrusted: British power, the enervations of Catholicism, the Malthusian perils of Europe, and the calamity of famine.

It was more usual to go to Scotland, ancestral home of so many Southerners, the kirk, common sense philosophy, and the wild charms of Ossianic and Romantic landscape. Unlike Ireland, Scotland was mostly a success story, a nation which had reasoned and felt its way toward prominence. Its climate might be grim, but that was not always seen as a disadvantage. William Campbell Preston thought in 1818 that such soddenness had left no option but intellectual pursuits and sociability. Early travelers might make as much of David Hume, William Robertson, and Adam Smith, and might dally as appreciatively in the elegant symmetries of Edinburgh's New Town as in the Highlands. Later visitors were more exclusive in their sympathies for "the romantic hills."[23] In truth, it was the combination that was appealing: philosophy and romance, head and heart.

If the traveler did not go north from Liverpool, he or she went south to London. (Almost no one went to Wales.) On the way to London, it was almost obligatory to stop in Chester, which raised the issue of antiquity and feudalism, for the city had Roman walls, a cathedral, and a stately home. Southward lay contradictions: industry in Birmingham, coal mines in the Black Country, Tudor cottages at Stratford, the immensity of London. Energy, squalor, vestiges, modernity, it was all confusing, often repulsive. Southerners who stayed home were more prone to Anglophilia: travelers seldom were, because encountering English hauteur was debilitating. Still, London was the center of a great empire, great despite the defeats of Yorktown and New Orleans. Modern Britain posed the question of the future of economic society. Abroad, she was supreme, with her fleet, her armies, her allies. At home, there was in London "the exchange of the whole world."[24] There was also wrenching poverty, which stared you in the face. For good or ill, England promised or threatened a future that might come to the South.

Nonetheless, few Southerners had reasons to dally in Britain. It had once been otherwise, but now there were no English colleges that a young man might wish to attend: Eton, Oxbridge, the Inns of Court were disused experiences. Since Washington Allston's departure from Bristol, England had been of little use to students of the fine arts, let alone music. The food was bad, the climate worse. Britain might be the future, but it had little interest in, few mechanisms for, instructing the alien about how to achieve or avoid that future, except its streets, its institutions, its externals. These were usually accomplished in short order, and the traveler hurried on to the Continent. But in climbing on to the Channel ferry, Southerners mingled in a great outward stream, for the English were reinventing travel with their enthusiasm and money.

It was customary to go to Paris, though a few made their way via Ostend to the Low Countries, usually if they were making their way down the Rhine toward Switzerland and Italy. Antwerp's Cathedral then held a fascination now vanished. But almost no Southerners spoke Dutch, let alone Frisian, which made things inaccessible. American culture had some conception of the Netherlands because of dim memories of William of Orange, after whom a Virginian college was half named, but almost none of Belgium, which tended to be regarded as an unsuccessful version of France. The Low Countries seemed little relevant, and even Southern Calvinists went elsewhere.

Making the more usual trip from Dover to Calais was to pass over a much-meditated cultural divide, was "like sunshine after darkness" as one approached Paris, the City of Light. Here one could study medicine, the fine arts, languages, dancing, the opera. Even walking the streets was thought to improve one's cultural standing. Preeminently, here was Europe's metropolis, where everything that rose converged. For Louisianans of French descent or birth, like Charles Gayarré the historian and Louis Moreau Gottschalk the composer, Paris was their metropolis. Religion was among the many reasons which brought Roman Catholic Southerners to France, but irreligion was part of the sensual thrill of French culture, perhaps especially for Protestants. John Young Bassett of Huntsville, who came to study medicine in 1836, had flattered himself a skeptic in Alabama. Upon arrival, he reflected that, in Alabama, religion seemed notable for "ignorance, bigotry, & deceit." But France was another world: *"God save me from a country without religion*; & from a government with it . . . & return me safe to a country with religion & a government without it—I am convinced that the evils of infidelity are worse, aye much worse, than any religion whatever."[25] This was a conventional judgment, common since at least the 1790s.

Paris had cruder temptations than irreligion, such as "the beautiful living proportions of the French girls' legs," but the city catered to more than bodies in search of sensuality.[26] In the eighteenth century, the Southern medical student had usually gone to Edinburgh to complete his education, after having studied in Philadelphia. Later, Paris began to outstrip Edinburgh by its clinical resources, and loyalty was increasingly transferred. In any given year in the 1830s, there were perhaps thirty to fifty American students in Paris, of whom just under half were Southerners. In fact the city, unlike any other European capital, attracted sufficient Americans and Southerners—abroad this distinction did not always matter—that they could huddle together as a community, partly in revulsion from Parisians, who were usually less popular than the amenities of their city.

Whatever else Paris meant, it meant revolution. This was a theme which occasioned ambivalence in Southerners, heirs to a revolution and sponsors of one to come, but persons who mostly accepted the standpoint of Edmund Burke on the meaning of 1789. But Paris furnished revolutions with convenient regularity for visiting students of society. In 1815 John Blair Hoge witnessed the flight of Napoleon from Waterloo, his abdication, and the return of Louis XVIII. The experience lowered his estimate of monarchs, those "very foolish or very wicked men" whose power rested only on force.[27] In 1848 Charles Izard Manigault saw the fall of the Orleanist monarchy and the July Days. This was serious theater, at the heart of modern history. Though Southerners felt some distance from these experiences, they were not confident and they considered anxiously what these fusillades might mean for their home.

Germany seemed less pertinent, at least at first. For many, it was little more than a pretty corridor down the Rhine toward Switzerland. For some, however, the response to prettiness became more complex. In 1829 the young Virginian Jesse Burton Harrison noted how the "romantic ruins of this river" next to a modern steamboat served to emphasize "the contrast between the reality of life & the spectral world of Rhine romance."[28] This lesson was historical, a corrective to a Southern education which had privileged the Mediterranean and classic. Harrison's came to be a habitual reaction, once Southern visitors had been trained to the thought.

Harrison was then on his way to study at a German university. In 1829, too, the elder Stephen Elliott was instructing Southern readers that German education was the world's "most varied, most extensive, most profound," offering a survey of its educational and cultural facilities, and recommending using them. The American position, he reasoned, was analogous to that of Germany. Decentralized and progressive American states, like those in Germany, might "by mutual and active competition, save each other from the negligence, the abuses, the lethargy which too often creep into or hover around old and privileged establishments."[29]

It was once customary, in narratives of the American mind, to stress the break in the pattern of the Grand Tour initiated by George Ticknor and George Bancroft, when they ventured to German universities in 1815 and soon thereafter. In truth, not only for New Englanders but also for Southerners this was more a modulation. Ticknor spent as much time on the Grand Tour as he did at Göttingen, and most early American students at German universities sampled the intellectual wares with casual incomprehension; they proclaimed the advances of German scholarship more than they understood them. Germany served as an addition to the old tradition, if one remembers that the Grand Tour could often be a serious intellectual and aesthetic endeavor.

As many as forty Southern students went to German universities before the Civil War. Most notable among the earliest were George Henry Calvert and Jesse Burton Harrison, who both went in the spirit of Ticknor, halfway between touring gentlemen and students. In addition, Calvert went as half a European. He had been born in Maryland to an unimpeachably Southern gentleman, but his mother was the daughter of a prosperous Brabant merchant who had fled the French Revolution in 1794 but returned in 1805. After expulsion from Harvard in 1823 for participation in a student rebellion, the younger Calvert sailed for Europe with no particular inspiration from Ticknor's German education but with a wish to extend his truncated education and a desire to visit his Flemish relatives.

Calvert decided to attend Göttingen partly because it was a university to which young English gentlemen of the era resorted. He joined more than fifteen hundred students in a city that housed the best endowed and most liberal German university, a preeminence contested only by Wilhelm von Humboldt's new university in Berlin. Göttingen had a distinguished faculty, among whom Calvert was free to roam. In his first semester, he listened to Arnold H. L. Heeren, the ancient and modern historian whose writings on Greece were later to be translated into English by George Bancroft. Less dry, more comic, and especially lucid were the lectures of Johann Friedrich Blumenbach, the naturalist, who was then over seventy but who had, half a century earlier, in his *De Generis Humani Varietate Nativa* (1775), been the first to venture a "scientific" study of human races. Forty years Blumenbach's junior was Karl Ottfried Müller, who was then beginning to revolutionize the study of ancient history by stressing the centrality of the Dorians and the local roots of Greek culture, its Romantic particularism, the nature of which could be located in mythology and the evidence for which could be lovingly traced by means of archaeology. From all these professors, Calvert got a steady dose of Göttingen's characteristic racialist social theory, ideas not puzzling to a Marylander.

Calvert never became a historian, except of himself, but he did later become a student and critic of Romantic thought. From Georg Friedrich Benecke, with whom Calvert studied German literature and language, he received the gift of a deep pleasure in Goethe and, in 1825, Calvert made his pilgrimage to Weimar, then the done thing. There Goethe was polite, asked about Calvert's travels and education, and quizzed him on the peculiar electoral process by which John Quincy Adams had recently been elevated to the presidency. After more time in Göttingen and a visit to Bonn, where he was granted interviews by Barthold Niebuhr and August von Schlegel, Calvert went on to Edinburgh, where he spent his time more idly, before joining his parents at Liverpool. But Germany had made the greatest impression on him. Back in Baltimore, he was to publish translations from the German (notably of Schiller's *Don Carlos* and the Goethe-Schiller correspondence) and to write on German literature for various American periodicals and, after the Civil War, a biography of Goethe, as well as memoirs which were modeled on Goethe's *Dichtung und Wahrheit*.

Jesse Burton Harrison, who set out for Göttingen in the same year that Elliott had urged the merits of Germany, was being au courant as well as imitative of Calvert, though the Virginian had few comparable ancestral motives for European travel. But he did have Thomas Jefferson as a mentor, who had cautiously endorsed a period of European education, and his cousin, Henry Clay, was anxious that Harrison report on economic and social conditions in central and eastern Europe. James Marsh, Harrison's teacher at Hampden-Sydney, was the chief American enthusiast of Coleridge, and Harrison's mentor at Harvard was George Ticknor. Beyond these influences were Harrison's own firm opinions that Virginia had too many semi-educated lawyers, too few "men of letters of the higher order; professional men, of high literary taste mingling with their professional feelings." So Harrison did what was becoming the usual things, propelled along by a network of friends and kin. In 1829 he visited Paris and proceeded to Göttingen, after calling on Schlegel in Bonn. He presented himself to Blumenbach, "a name dear to Englishmen and Americans for 50 years," and went on to Weimar to meet Goethe twice.[30] In May he proceeded to Leipzig, where he saw the Book Fair, and then made his way to Berlin, where he probably heard Hegel lecture. More certain is that Harrison met Wilhelm von Humboldt, the philologist and founder of the Friedrich-Wilhelm Universität. From Berlin, he went southward to Dresden (where he encountered James Fenimore Cooper), Munich, and Switzerland, and reached Venice by September; he spent October in Florence and the winter in Rome. After a brief visit to Naples, he returned to Paris in the spring. From there he made an excursion to England, to meet again George Long, once professor of ancient languages in Charlottesville, and Thomas Babington Macaulay, with whom Harrison had corresponded over antislavery matters. He returned to Virginia in the summer of 1831.

Harrison's German experience was less rigorous than Calvert's, the intellectual consequences less permanent. The former was more in the business of fashioning a public man informed by scholarship than of making a man of letters who might dabble in politics, which was Calvert's case. What Harrison shows, however, is that by 1830 it was becoming customary that such an ambition might demand an engagement with German culture, that pressures within the South might propel a young man into lodgings in Göttingen. More, he demonstrates that choosing Germany might involve a self-conscious rejection of English culture. The records of Southerners show how often England, seen from the Continent, seemed arrogant and contemptible, which only reinforced a Jeffersonian suspicion of the old enemy. Though Calvert was later to grow into an appreciation of English literature, of Wordsworth and Carlyle, in 1825 he mainly saw the English through German eyes. When Harrison came to consider the respective merits of English and German culture in an article for the *Southern Review*, he was to find little of merit in the former, corrupted into reaction by opposing the French Revolution and Napoleon, imperial in maritime policy, insensitive to ideality in the arts, persuaded of the merits of a Burkean prejudice, and merely commonsensical in philosophy.

The motives and procedures for studying in Germany began to shift later, certainly by the time that Thomas Caute Reynolds went to Berlin in 1839, then to Munich and Heidelberg. Hugh Legaré signaled the change in a letter of advice. Be brisker in your European studies than I was, he told Reynolds in 1841. "Nothing is more *perilous*, in America, than to be too long *learning*, and to get the name of bookish. Stay in Europe long enough to lay the groundwork of professional eminence, by pursuing the branches of knowledge most instrumental in advancing it." In 1825 Calvert had not bothered to acquire the "dry parchment" of a doctoral degree, nor did Harrison.[31] But Reynolds spent about three years at German universities and freely accumulated certificates of his studies, including a Heidelberg doctorate.

It was not that casual attendance at German universities disappeared as a phenomenon. Young men often wished to go to Europe, and a German university was as good an excuse as any to gull skeptical parents. But, by the time Basil Gildersleeve of Charleston went in 1850 for three years to study philology, there were those who went as nascent professional scholars. He had been born in 1831, the son of the struggling editor of religious periodicals. From the earliest age, the younger Gildersleeve had acquired languages: Latin, Greek, and French, and at Princeton in 1847 he had begun German, with a little Italian and Spanish on the side. He became interested in Carlyle, who led him to Goethe, who engendered what Gildersleeve later called a "Teutomania." Hence he went to Germany, not precisely to become a philologist, but to study *Altertumswissenschaft*, the science of antiquity, which was considered the foundation of humane knowledge. To this, he was then promised, philology was the key, an ideal whose "hopelessness" he was only later to realize without bitterness.[32]

In the winter semester of 1850–51, he studied in Berlin, mainly with August Boeckh, who was then lecturing on Demosthenes and Greek literature. Gildersleeve then proceeded to Göttingen, where he worked for two semesters; there he attended the lectures of Karl Friedrich Hermann on Greek and Roman literature, those of Friedrich Wilhelm Schneidewin on Latin and Greek syntax as well as Greek elegiac poetry, and those of Heinrich Ritter. For the winter semester of 1852–53, Gildersleeve went to Bonn, where he worked with several professors, but chiefly Friedrich Wilhelm Ritschl, the Latin philological professional par excellence. There was also the young Jakob Bernays, who lectured on Aristotle, Thucydides, and Cicero and who suggested the topic of Gildersleeve's dissertation on Porphyry. Some of these scholars were figures whose accomplishments Southern scholarship knew. As long ago as 1832, Legaré had analyzed Boeckh's *The Public Economy of Athens*, and George Frederick Holmes in 1844 had called Boeckh "the prince of writers" upon Pindar.[33] Gildersleeve, therefore, was perfecting rather than breaking with an aspect of the Southern tradition. Still, it was a long way from William Campbell Preston's reading in the Bibliothèque du Roi in Paris to Gildersleeve's dissertation, *De Porphyrii Studiis Capitum Homericis Trias.*

Beyond Germany was Switzerland, which was sacred ground for Presbyterians like Thornwell, because of Calvin's Geneva. But, for others less religious, Switzerland was two things, the modern European republic of greatest continuity and a further education in Romantic landscape. In 1822 John Taylor hoped that the United States might be "the Switzerland of the world," though by the late antebellum period, this theme of liberty was less urgent, because Southerners thought it had been safely accomplished at home.[34] But mountains remained impressive, even if Southerners were not given to indefatigable Alpine walking. To travel eastward from Switzerland was rare. Vienna was sometimes visited, but visits to Hungary and Poland were very unusual, Russia was remote, Scandinavia a silence. Most Southerners crossed the Alps and descended to Milan.

Italy was the most sacred of European destinations, central to understanding the dialectics of cultural identity. The English and Germans especially had invented the counterpoint between North and South from their Italian experiences, and these inventors (Winckelmann, Gibbon, Goethe, Byron) were familiar to Southerners. Crucial to the counterpoint was the theme of the cold rationality of the North contesting the imaginative freedom of the South, an idea which was to prove deeply influential in the other South across the Atlantic.

Southerners tended to like Italian scenery but less often the people who inhabited it, and they habitually despised both Italian government and religion. William Crawford thought Milan had been improved by the modern rule of the French, while Preston regretted that Napoleon had not continued his dominance of Italy, because the emperor had usefully weakened the clergy and suppressed the convents. Few had good words for the Roman Catholic Church. Despotism, cruelty, superstition, and parasitism were its characteristics. "It is astonishing," Crawford observed, "what numbers there are to be seen, parading the streets, of these holy loungers, these drones of society, that live on the labour of the industrious and are supported by ignorance and superstition."[35]

Armed only with such prejudice, few Southerners would have come. But their heads were full of antiquity and the Renaissance. Preston offered the formal reason for the former taste: "Americans from their republican sympathies are more interested in the history of Rome between the two Brutus' than any other people, and therefore we would visit the remains of that period with deeper feelings."[36] But this motive was overlaid with Romanticism. Crawford in 1833 punctuated his journal with long quotations from Byron's *Childe Harold*, and recommended that the ruins of antiquity be viewed by moonlight, the better to let imagination recreate the remote past.

The Southern engagement with Italy is perhaps best exemplified by the experience of Richard Henry Wilde, who was born in Dublin in 1789 but ended up by 1802 in Augusta, where he became a lawyer, politician, and poet. On and off he served in Congress, where he tacked between Nullifiers and Unionists in the early 1830s, but he drifted on to the states' rights ticket, and this led to his defeat in 1834. It was partly the tangled bitterness of politics that helped to drive Wilde away to Florence. He left as an expatriate, not only wishing to be somewhere else, but wanting to leave a dissatisfying home. Experience had indicated to him that he was unfitted for the life of a politician, and he was irked by the unreality of both public praise and vilification. Italy, by contrast, offered a people to whom he did not belong, to whom he owed nothing, to whom he was not accountable. Italy offered too the chance of "travel—study—science—literary occupation—the arts—the untroubled enjoyment of Nature."[37] As a poet, Wilde was more than primed for an Italian venture. The tradition of Byron, Keats, and Shelley was now well established, and for years Wilde's verse had conformed to their themes.

Wilde found in Florence an established if small American colony. Unlike most expatriates, however, Wilde did not confine himself to his own kind. It was through an invitation to the house of Count Mariano Alberti, where some newly discovered and controversial manuscripts of Tasso were read, that Wilde began literary researches which led him in 1842 to publish his *Conjectures and Researches Concerning the Love, Madness, and Imprisonment of Torquato Tasso*. It was a book that, consisting chiefly of excerpts from Tasso's writings, culled to demonstrate Tasso's sanity, shows great awareness of the historical problem of evidence. Unpublished was an anthology of Italian lyric poets, translated by Wilde himself, and an unfinished biography of Dante. In these ways, Wilde went further than most American visitors in the depth of his acquaintance with Italian culture. He did not content himself with picturesque descriptions in letters to American magazines nor even, as Madame de Staël had, with rapid judgments of Italian literature or society. He undertook serious research in Italian archives, and his Rankean energy carried him through some five hundred pages on Tasso and a thousand in draft on Dante before flagging.

Wilde wrote many verses in Italy. Most are lyrics, about women, death, loss, melancholy, parting. He continued to write his epic poem *Hesperia*, which was done in the manner of *Childe Harold*, with echoes of Wordsworth and Thomas Moore. It has four books, focusing on Florida, Virginia, Acadia, and Louisiana. Much is pastoral, reverie on nature, and the remembrance of places and people. There are modest passages of celebration of America's revolutionary history but still more assertion that America is the land of the future, a history-less land, inhospitable to poetry. A slice of the epic is a Romantic dissertation on the rise and fall of cultures, "the changing fortune of each various race," which was part of the grim lesson of Italy's past: "The soil we reap is of our ashes made, / Ruins on ruins rise, and tomb on tomb." Wilde tended toward the melancholy conclusion. Modern Italy was not free, but neither was America, for "all the earth are slaves! whom call we free?"[38]

As an expatriate, Wilde cared for home with enough ambivalence to embrace exile. Only financial necessity forced him to leave Florence in 1840, and he expected and wanted urgently to return. He was driven back on the law and politics with the utmost distaste, for he felt that America would kill his intellectual and literary endeavors. In New Orleans in 1846, a year before his death, he met Sir Charles Lyell, then visiting the Delta. Lyell presented him with a copy of Dante Gabriele Rossetti's *La Beatrice di Dante* and two other works on Dante, in one of which was reproduced the Bargello fresco which Wilde himself had uncovered. "This roused for a little while my 'passione Dantesca,' but it has all died away again," he wrote to the sculptor Hiram Powers, still in Florence. "Such things can't live in the atmosphere of Law and Commerce. It is like putting some innocent warm-blooded animal into carbonic gas."[39]

This sentiment, the usage of Italy as a refuge from an intrusively vulgar America, was to be echoed by Paul Hamilton Hayne in 1855: "I hear nothing about me now but politics, slavery, & anti-slavery ad nauseam. . . . Thank God! I shall have a prospect in time of living in Florence under a quiet despotism." Contempt for democracy often went with this prospect, as it did later for Henry James, who went to find solace in a purely aesthetic Italy. But this willingness to make light of the Founding Fathers and the beacon of commercial progress, to embrace the apolitical imagination, was rare among antebellum Southerners, for they seldom admitted a formal parallel between the South and Italy. Brantz Mayer of Baltimore was typical in remarking of a fortnight's visit in 1833 to Venice, that "curious city of palaces, prisons, shrines, art, despotism and degradation." There, he said, "amidst the solitude of her abandoned dwellings, against which the gondolas rested, unoccupied and motionless, our feelings came back with a rebound, from the grave of the old Republic to the active life and energy of our new one!"[40]

Italy was the heart of the European South. Spain, however, was off the beaten track. Henry Junius Nott noted in 1831 that Spain was "a country now almost as little traveled as Egypt or Mongolia."[41] It was true that a few from the Lower South traveled to Europe via Havana and Spain, instead of traveling around to New York and Liverpool. Nonetheless, even if little visited, Spain was thought about. Her importance as the founding imperial power of the New World gave her a large place in the Southern imagination. Spain had a significant place in the typology of Romanticism, and this tradition had been domesticated by Americans in works like Longfellow's *Outre-Mer* and Ticknor's *History of Spanish Literature*. Roncesvalles, the gardens of Córdoba, the Cid, Ferdinand and Isabella, Columbus and Cortes, all made for pretty reverie.

For the most part, however, Spain's image was dark, repressive, and gloomy. The United States had inherited from England a suspicion of the black ships of the Armada and the blacker robes of the Inquisition. To suspicion was added rancor, because half the South had once been Spain's possession and the South had an eye on yet more Spanish booty, in Cuba and elsewhere. The verdict of Southerners was stern. As De Bow wrote in 1850: "The victim of arbitrary and despotic power—the theater of court intrigues and revolutions—with a wealthy, dominant, but unscrupulous, hierarchy fattening upon the substance of the land, and repressing and crushing out the vital energies of the people by a system of intolerance the most perfect, and a total suppression of all light and knowledge . . . such is Spain."[42] With the exception of James Johnston Pettigrew, whose *Notes on Spain and the Spaniards* (1860) will be considered later, these were the common sentiments of progressive Southerners, who coupled Spain with Italy as evidence for the declension enforced upon countries by the intellectual enervations of Catholicism. But, while regret tinged accounts of Italy's decline, little but satisfaction can be found in most accounts of Spain's failure.

AT THE EASTERN END of the Mediterranean, more remote worlds began. Visits to Greece were infrequent, and more contemplated Attica than went there. As for Egypt, it became a somewhat more frequent resort, since Southerners had reasons to be interested, beyond the curiosities that the rage for Egyptology had created. Egypt featured largely in the debates over race, antiquity, and polygenesis, and it was developing cotton production, a matter which had long borne watching. The most significant Southerner in Egypt was Edwin DeLeon, the American consul-general from 1854 to 1861, who had grown up Jewish in Columbia, attended South Carolina College, had written for the *Southern Literary Messenger* and the *Southern Quarterly Review*, and became a Washington journalist of Democratic partisanship, which induced Franklin Pierce to send him to Egypt. There DeLeon played the exotic game of the Orientalist diplomat to the hilt. He rented an old palace in the Old Cairo Quarter, rode in the desert toward Suez upon Arab stallions, and lazed on luxurious divans. It was a perfect life for an amiable poseur, whose favorite poems included Shelley's "Prometheus Unbound," which spoke of the "flight of the eagle towards the sun, revelling in the blaze of light."[43] Such leisure was attendant upon a relative absence of duties, though there were American tourists, sailors, and merchants to tend, and the odd excitement.

However, missionaries were the most typical of Southerners in the Near East, where they went to reclaim holy lands from apostasy. Among these, notable was John Bailey Adger of Charleston, who spent twelve years in Smyrna between 1834 and 1846. He had been educated at the Princeton Theological Seminary, where he had talked to those who had been missionaries around the world. These conversations took him to Anatolia, where he was assigned the Armenians, thought to have a bastard version of Christianity in need of reform. Adger's duty was to enlighten them by the power of a press, upon which he came to set his modern American translation of the New Testament, of which in time three hundred thousand copies were to circulate. But Adger translated other works: the Psalms, the Presbyterian "Assembly's Shorter Catechism, and various religious tracts, relating to gospel doctrine, adapted to popular reading."[44]

Adger left in 1846, to return eventually to Charleston. Two years earlier, James Warley Miles of South Carolina had made his way to Istanbul, where he stayed until 1847. Miles did not go as an evangelical missionary, because the Episcopalians strove to work in concert with the traditional Christian hierarchies and even "sided with the Armenian ecclesiastics in the struggle against Protestant heretics in their communion."[45] In Istanbul, Miles labored among the Armenian Christians and, like Adger, offered them translations, though of Episcopalian texts like the Book of Common Prayer. Little of practical consequence flowed from this mission, which dissolved in ill-planning, impecuniousness, and dissension. But Miles himself was vastly educated by the experience of one of the world's great cosmopolitan cities, whose despotic amenities (colleges, libraries) he thought put the democratic South to shame. Such riches, and a sense of the abundance of the world's languages, was to make Miles into one of the South's most serious linguists, ill at ease back in the United States and pining for his Turkish coffee.

A similar legacy of languages was collected by William Brown Hodgson of Georgia, who was one of the first Southern Orientalists and served as a diplomat during the 1820s and 1830s in north Africa and Turkey, where he came to study Arabic, Persian, and Turkish. In 1842 he retired from the diplomatic service to settle down as a scholar in Savannah. Along the way, he sold valuable manuscripts to the British Museum, and in 1830 he was elected a foreign member of the Royal Asiatic Society in London and the Société de Géographie in Paris. In the United States, Paris, and London, he published brief, erudite pamphlets upon the cultural and linguistic history of northern Africa, as well as translating from Arabic the North African travel account of Ibn al-Din al-Aghwati. Further, he helped to translate into Berber the first twelve chapters of the Gospel according to Luke, which were published by the British and Foreign Bible Society in 1833.

Hodgson was among the few white Southerners to take a scholarly interest in Africa, though he was a student of the Mediterranean littoral, not the sub-Sahara. Once, when the slave trade had been active, Southerners had felt many reasons to discriminate among the peoples of Africa, but by the 1830s such practical discriminations had largely lapsed, though the occasional planter-érudit would grow curious about the ethnography of a slave. Such curiosity, however, was unusual, and it is striking that, in the learned treatises of the proslavery argument, though there are extended disquisitions on the slavery of ancient Greece and Rome, the patriarchy of ancient Judea, and the serfdom of the Middle Ages, from none of which Southern slavery immediately derived, there almost nothing written about African slavery, whose stepchild it was. With such an indifference, there was little reason for Southerners to visit Africa, unless you were a missionary like the Reverend John Leighton Wilson of South Carolina, who sailed for Liberia in 1834. Wilson was to produce what was perhaps the most elaborate account of Africa written by an antebellum white Southerner. *Western Africa: Its History, Condition, and Prospects* (1856) was no doubt structured by the characteristic hubris of the Christian missionary and the American racial theorist. Wilson was committed to Liberia because he felt the African had no future in the United States, though he was conscious that this was not exclusively the African's fault. Naturally, he had a low opinion of paganism and polygamy and regretted natives who did not wash regularly and who were unlikely to attain "the inventive powers of the white man." Still, he admired them for being "social, generous, and confiding" and thought they might come to be "examples of the purest and most elevated Christian virtues," and his tone was, for the most part, even.[46] Wilson was acutely aware that Africa was worth more than an easy generalization or a ready sneer and needed to be understood as a complicated mosaic of geography, cultures, religions, and languages. He knew the difference between the Mandingo and the Wolof, the Yoruba and the Pangwe. He noticed when one group was Islamic, another Christian, one was an autocracy, another an open society. He observed differences of physiognomy, who was light, who dark, who was tall, who short. He did not hesitate to prefer one group to another; the Ashantis came in for especial criticism, but he liked the Mpongwe for their intelligence, urbanity, and linguistic skill. In particular, Wilson had an interest in languages, and the concluding pages of the book are preoccupied with explaining the grammatical differences between Grebo, Mandingo, and Mpongwe.

In his sympathy for Africa, Wilson was unusual, but not for his Liberian interests. White Southerners had long been prominent in the leadership of the American Colonization Society. There was a period, in the 1820s, when it was fashionable and safe for a Southerner to help the Society's enterprise in West Africa. Liberia was, ironically, the most conspicuous outpost of Southern culture in the nineteenth century and the only colony, apart from the imperial territories of the United States, that the South helped successfully to found. Only 10 percent of Liberia's colonists came from the North, the rest were free blacks or ex-slaves from the South. In despised Africa, the South's names and customs and hierarchies were to be duplicated and modulated, including its habits of racial discrimination.

The colony strangely echoed the American experience of imperial expansion, colonial wars, and death at the hands of unwonted pathogens. Among the settlers there was nostalgia for the old country, talk of a New World conferred by God's beneficence, and a sense that colonization could only succeed if local labor was suborned. Yet this new country was also an old country, "this beautiful land of our forefathers," and oldness could be seen as providential: "This is the land of our fore fathers, the land from which the children went, back to the land they are Returning. Liberia is now spreading her rich perfume roun and about the big valleys of the World and introducing and calling out to her suns and Daughters to rise and come up out of the Valley of ignorence and Hethenism."[47]

Liberia was, fundamentally, a reproach to the South. As one of its first premises, the rules of the colony forbade slavery, a prohibition reiterated by the constitution of the independent republic to come. Though white American sponsors sent their manumitted slaves to rid themselves of a group whom they despised, felt charitable toward, or did not know how to assimilate, blacks themselves went to Liberia to rid themselves of humiliating constraints and signal their disillusionment with the hollow implications of a Virginian's Declaration of Independence. What they created in Liberia was, in part, a South and a United States, rid of the disadvantages peculiar to their previous conditions but possessed of what they remembered as beneficial; this was, after all, what the colonists of Virginia and Massachusetts, too, had wanted for themselves in the westward migrations of the seventeenth century. Certainly, few migrants to Liberia wanted to go home, and they were the South's most adamant expatriates.

To the east of Africa, the Southern engagement with Asia beyond the Levant was slight. The most exotic of American traders were the emissaries of New England and New York, though Baltimore did trade with China in the antebellum years. Brantz Mayer of that city was in Canton in 1821 and again in 1827–28, and later he was to write on the subject. Two of the American commissioners to China in the 1850s were Southerners, as was its minister plenipotentiary from 1859 to 1860. After the Civil War, Southerners were to be numerically important among American missionaries. Before 1861, however, they were far fewer, but at least one Southern missionary did not lack for impact.

In 1837 Issachar Jacox Roberts of Shelbyville, Tennessee, came to preach the Gospel in Canton, where he rented a small house, took to Chinese dress, and went around the local countryside with a convert to preach and distribute tracts. He studied the dialect of the Hakka, local migrants from northern China who had come to the area centuries before and were still a "guest people." One of them, called Hong Xiuquan, encountered Roberts in 1847. Hong was a frustrated young man and a mystic who in 1836 had been given on a Canton street a collection of Christian tracts. In 1843 he read them more closely and began to believe in a passionate syncretism of Confucianism and Protestant evangelicalism, which he started to preach. In his vision, God the Father had commissioned Hong in a dream to save mankind and maintain heaven and earth "in gracious harmony and convivial peace," and thus to succeed Hong's Elder Brother, Jesus Christ. Hong began to acquire converts, whom he formed into a "God-Worshiping Society."[48]

Early in 1847 Roberts's Chinese assistant wrote to Hong to urge that the latter visit Roberts's chapel. Hong came, studied a Chinese translation of the Bible, and asked to be baptized, though Roberts oddly refused. Hong left, gained more converts, acquired allies and an army, mounted a great rebellion against the Qing dynasty, came to control much of east central China, and until his death in 1864 unstably governed from Nanjing the Heavenly Kingdom of Great Peace, the Taiping Tienkuo. Hong harbored no resentment against the Tennessean, indeed wanted him as a moral guide. In 1854 he invited Roberts to visit Nanjing, but the latter was turned back by a Qing gunboat. In the succeeding years, Roberts did not fare well. His children and wife abandoned him, and he became bankrupt, his house and chapel being twice looted by mobs. A heavenly king for a friend came to seem a good idea, and Roberts finally reached Nanjing. There he was greeted with pomp, appointed "minister for foreign policy and of justice in all cases involving foreigners," and granted apartments in the palace. Roberts declined the offer of three wives, but he did accept Taiping court dress, "a blue satin fur gown, and yellow embroidered jacket over it, with red hood, and satin boots." Thereafter things went less well. Hong wished Roberts to preach Taiping Christianity, but Roberts wished to purify Hong's religion, and in time Roberts lost access to the king, who sat in his own apartments like Thomas Jefferson and wrote emendations and commentaries in the margins of his Bible, and (unlike Jefferson) came to think himself the voice of Melchizedek, the priest and king of Salem.[49] So Roberts fled in 1862 and took refuge on a British ship on the Yangzi. On that day, the Union army was moving south through Kentucky toward his native Tennessee and Shiloh. In China, too, there was civil war, more brutal than even Abraham Lincoln could imagine. The Taiping Rebellion had encouraged other dissidents, bloodshed spread, some six hundred walled cities were taken and lost, massacre was frequent. Certainly twenty million people died, perhaps as many as sixty million. No one is sure.

Southern influence on the rest of Asia was, happily, less significant. While secretary of the navy, John Pendleton Kennedy (the Maryland novelist) amplified the resources of the Matthew Perry expedition that reopened Japan to Western influence, and the editor of the expedition's first history was Francis Hawks. Nonetheless, the early contacts between American ships and Japan had little or nothing to do with the South, though the naval expedition of 1853–55 sent to reconnoiter the Bering Straits, the North Pacific Ocean, and the China Seas (and that spent time in and around Japan), was first commanded by Cadwalader Ringgold of Maryland and included, as its scientific officer, John M. Brooke of Virginia. As for India, there is little record of Southerners making physical contact with the subcontinent, although Southern intellectuals, though perhaps less than their New England counterparts, took some interest in Sanskrit and Hindu mythology.

On the other side of the Pacific and after the Civil War, about nine thousand disillusioned Confederates made their way to Mexico and Latin America to establish themselves among regimes that were either slaveholding or thought pliable. Nearly four thousand settled in Brazil, where their descendants still live. One might speculate that this migration grew from the perspectives of the antebellum South, which might have been expected to take an interest in other slaveholding regimes in the New World. Certainly the mid-twentieth-century South was to find the subject illuminating. But the Old South little shared this sense of relevance. It was its misfortune mostly to look toward Europe for its comparative cultural understandings, not to Brazil or

Cuba, with which it shared many experiences. Latin America, on the whole, seemed a countervision of what the South might have looked like, but for the grace of a Protestant God, and was a warning not a model. The southern continent did, however, acquire a languorous glamour, best captured in the work of the Charlestonian painter Louis Rémy Mignot, who traveled in 1857 to Ecuador. The outcome of this trip was a rich collection of sensuous painting: ominous volcanoes, intoxicating jungles, limpid lakes, solitary palms, and threatening moonlight and scenes in which humanity's contribution is superfluous and neat Spanish towns are dwarfed by the Andes.

The most visible of Southerners in Latin America, however, were the diplomats; forty-five of them served as heads of mission there during the early republic. Perhaps most important among these was Joel Poinsett, who went to be the American agent to Buenos Aires and Chile in 1810, was an envoy to Mexico City in 1822, then was the American ambassador to Mexico in 1825. In all three cases he threw himself into local politics, often disastrously. These experiences nonetheless made Poinsett one of the most knowledgeable of Southerners about Latin American affairs. His *Notes on Mexico, Made in the Autumn of 1822* (1824) is one of the earliest American studies of the new country and helped to form a minor literary tradition which was to reach a height during and after the Mexican War. Poinsett himself, as he freely acknowledged, was influenced by the pioneering work of Alexander von Humboldt, whose accomplishment lay in rediscovering the Americas which, in the long years of Spanish colonial rule, had slipped from view. Yet the German perspective and the American differed. Humboldt had stripped the people out of South America to leave only a landscape, but the South Carolinian did not.

Poinsett's *Notes* was driven by the comparative question of the Western Hemisphere. Could Mexico become another United States, if wisely directed? Poinsett thought it possible. When Waddy Thompson came as American minister and later published his *Recollections of Mexico* (1846), this conjecture had been weakened by twenty more years of contact and (in Texas) war with a Mexico often turbulent in its politics. Thompson was a cruder version of Poinsett, with the latter's subtlety modulated into prejudice, ironic hope into disdain. There was the same anti-Catholicism, but more dismissive. The same comparative question was asked but more decisively answered against Mexico, which was accused of throwing away the advantages of an early and splendid settlement, an excellent climate, a rich soil, and an abundant fund of resources, only to arrive at an unanswerably inferior position to Massachusetts, whose initial prospects and resources had been so less promising. Thompson was more interested in race than Poinsett, more attracted by it as an explanation, was closer to Rudyard Kipling than James Madison. While Poinsett took Britain to be a cultural and political enemy, Thompson saw her as a racial ally against the lesser, darker peoples. As a result, Thompson abandoned Poinsett's hope for Mexico as a democratic republic.

Neither Poinsett nor Thompson were scholars, but rather men of affairs who wrote at their leisure. Brantz Mayer of Baltimore was more assiduous. He had served between 1841 and 1843 as secretary of the U.S. legation in Mexico City, and in 1851 he published *Mexico, Aztec, Spanish, and Republican*, one of the more considerable accomplishments of Southern historicism, a self-conscious attempt to establish a longer perspective on Mexican culture, founded upon the best old and most useful recent authorities. The most striking features of Mayer's *Mexico* are completeness and patience. It was common enough to be interested in the period of the Conquest, whose romance had been so successfully narrated by Prescott. There were anti-quarian travel books about the pre-Columbian period, especially those by John Lloyd Stephens. There were contemporary works on modern Mexican society, like that by Thompson. But no American had tried to bring these matters together in a sustained, detailed historical narrative. And no one, in any language, had provided a connected history of colonial Mexico. The chronological balance of the first volume shows Mayer's interests: twelve chapters on the Conquest, two retrospective chapters on the Aztecs, sixteen chapters on the colonial period, seven on the Mexican revolution and its aftermath, ten on the war with the United States. His second volume was synchronic, an analysis of Mexico's geography, demography, economy, church, and constitution, to which was added a description, with their antiquities, of its various provinces, including those now annexed to the United States, California and New Mexico.

Mexico, Aztec, Spanish, and Republican has a rough force and an unconventional analytical intelligence. For Mayer, Mexico was the United States gone wrong or, rather, with insufficient preconditions for going right. He had the usual excoriation of Roman Catholicism's effect on Mexican culture and a pointed catalog of its huge ecclesiastical establishment, though as a Marylander, Mayer was differently scathing, by criticizing what the church had done in Mexico while not assuming Catholicism mandated such blunders. As for the indigenous population, Aztec civilization was deemed to have bequeathed a people with a culture of dependency and a reliance upon chance as the maker of fortune. In this view, Mayer was partially dissenting from Francisco Clavigero, the eighteenth-century Jesuit founder of Mexican history, who had been at pains to found Mexican identity upon what was shared between natives and Creoles, which grew out of the American environment. Clavigero attributed later degradations not to intrinsic incapacities, but to social conditions riveted upon natives by their conquerors. Mayer, too, sympathetically asserted that circumstances were adverse, that conquest had violently destroyed older institutions, but was unimpressed by Clavigero's claim for a shared Mexican identity. Rather, Mayer cataloged the myriad racial divisions in Mexican society, so as to demonstrate "the mongrel corruptions of the human race in Mexico." Race helped to explain why other cultures had advanced but Mexico had "remained comparatively fixed in the midst of a stagnant semi-civilization." Unlike the American colonies in 1776, Mexico had lacked a homogeneous people and had only the "discordant and heterogeneous materials of races, characters, politics and purposes."[50]

By the American annexation of Texas, Mexico stood on the borders of the South. The adjacent Caribbean produced more volatile emotions. At one time the South had been less south of the North, more north of the Caribbean. The plantations of the British Empire, based upon slavery and the staple crops of sugar and tobacco, had been a world that stretched from Trinidad to the Chesapeake. Within this world, there had been extensive movement, not least for the slaves who were often captured in Africa, sent to the West Indies, then transferred to the mainland. After American independence, this relationship changed. Albeit porous, trade barriers were created. Above all, the status of slavery changed. The French Revolution swept the institution away in the French West Indies, a measure briefly reversed by Napoleon. The British abolished it in 1833 and in Jamaica launched an experiment in apprenticeships that Southerners cynically monitored. In Cuba, however, slavery and even the slave trade lingered. But the emotional focus of Southern attitudes lay in Saint-Domingue, which had fallen to a slave revolt of ominous ferocity, a cataclysm which had sent to the mainland a flood of nervous and angry French refugees, often bringing their reluctant slaves. The possibility of butchery was a lesson the white South was eager to learn and seldom tired of reiterating, though for slaves Haiti was a flicker of hope. Gabriel Prosser, who led a slave rebellion in Virginia in 1800, had been partially educated in the possibility of success by Haitian slaves, carrying their "mischief" (as James Monroe put it) into the quarters.[51] When Denmark Vesey, who had been born on St. Thomas, planned his insurrection in 1822, it was to Haiti that he planned to escape, a place where he had once been a slave. But there was a more peaceable route to Port-au-Prince for free blacks, since Haiti served as a more local and cheaper Liberia for colonizationists. The Haitian government made concerted efforts to attract Americans, and they were encouraged by institutions like the North Carolina

Manumission Society. Several thousand migrated in the 1820s. The experience was mostly disillusioning, but not everyone on the mainland knew that. The idea of black liberty in the Western Hemisphere remained potently alive in the name of Haiti. In the 1850s William Wells Brown would celebrate the achievement of a black republic.

By contrast, for whites, migration was northward. George Tucker, for example, was born in Bermuda and, when twenty, came to the mainland United States for its wider opportunities. His autobiography, written in 1858, captures the way in which the United States and the South seemed in his childhood to brood, immense and metropolitan, over the scattered islands: "I had long felt that the little Island on which I was born was a sort of imprisonment which I was most impatient to break through, and in my solitary rambles on the sea shore, or in the narrow woods to be found there, I indulged my fancy on the various novelties I was to meet, the acquaintances I was to make, and the scenes I was to mingle in."[52]

In general, as the antebellum years proceeded, the Caribbean became more remote in the Southern literary imagination while retaining a political importance. A few thought that a wise policy for the future of Southern slavery might require a comparative analysis of slavery in the Caribbean, and, in such an analysis, Cuba would loom large. But for most, Cuba meant illness or geopolitics. The Spanish island became a place that a few, eccentrically, went for their health; Robert Wilson Gibbes published a *Cuba for Invalids* in 1860. Yet Poinsett's pause there on his return from Mexico in 1823 struck the more important note; his account is not preoccupied with Cuba itself, but passionate when discussing its strategic importance: "Cuba is not only the key of the Gulf of Mexico, but of all the maritime frontier south of Savannah, and some of our highest interests, political and commercial, are involved in its fate."[53] Above all, Cuba should be kept out of the hands of any great naval power. Hence there was a growing interest by later Southerners in the annexation of Cuba and the prospect of turning the Caribbean into a Southern lake. This interest sometimes turned to filibustering action, as when William Walker of Tennessee seized Nicaragua and became its president from 1856 to 1857. So, the Caribbean had to do with the cold necessities of power, real or imagined, it being so far from God and so close to the South.

From all of these travels (to Europe, Asia, Africa, and the Americas) Southerners took no clear lessons. The act of traveling acknowledged connection while refining difference, and individuals decided for themselves where the emphasis should lie. Still, in general, they learned to be competitive with the northern United States, as a matter of power and survival; this was a family quarrel, so it was alternately bitter and forgiving, and usually uncomprehending, because in a family everyone presumes knowledge of other family members but few try to acquire it. Oddly, Southerners' European experience led to better understandings or at least knowledge, because with Europe the conflict had ceased to be political once the matter of British, French, and Spanish power in North America had been settled. The issue of Europe became cultural, which for intellectuals was important enough but seldom urgent and so available for measured reflection. However, in Europe, Southerners were most torn between their identity as postcolonials, who wished the Atlantic to be wide, and their identity as migrant Europeans, who wished for comity with the old places. In Asia and Africa, matters were simpler because there European and Southern purposes ran together, however much there might have been subtle disagreements over how imperialism might be administered. In the Americas, on the other hand, what might have been a family relationship between societies which shared European origins, as well as the postcolonial experience and the brutal business of slaveholding, was almost never so. This lack of sympathy arose partly for religious reasons and mostly because Latin America was seen not as a partner but as an object of Southern imperialism, whether formal (as in Texas, Mexico, Nicaragua, or Cuba) or informal (almost everywhere else). If Southerners had known the Americas to their south as well as they had known Europe, they might have known themselves better. But the power of Europe, political and cultural, represented not only what Southerners had been but what they wished to emulate, even to transcend, so their minds (and their bodies) went more often to Paris than to Rio de Janeiro. There was a greater fascination in desire. But what sorts of beings existed in the South to express desire? As will be seen next, this, too, was not easy to decide.

2 · All the Tribes, All the Productions of Nature

Southerners thought about how mankind might be classified and where they stood in the order of nature. What was a race, a sex, a people, a class? Where did these things come from and how did they work? These were questions which had been inherited. For several centuries, the irruption of Europeans into the wider world had produced a torrent of problematic knowledge. Latterly, the projects of the Enlightenment tried to order this knowledge by inventing or reinventing intellectual disciplines which might cope. Ethnology, historicism, evolutionary theory, the study of mythology, and much of modern science itself flowed from this task of comprehension, which involved the subjection of particularity to a greater order. From Las Casas onward, figures like Locke, Linnaeus, Buffon, and Voltaire had struggled to keep pace, to reason out what early American societies, or Peruvian plants, or gazelles, or Confucianism said about God's order and man's nature.

In this endeavor, there was often little thought about implications. The New Hampshire moose presented by Jefferson to the Parisian savant and the Rosetta Stone plundered by Napoleon's armies, these might occasion understandings of unexpectedly dark significance. Objects arrived in disorder from the corners of the world, and men in periwigs tried to understand. They sat in Baroque libraries, they put artifacts in elegantly wrought cases, they drew patterns on manuscripts, but they seldom saw the world they sought to classify.

Races were part of the wider problem of the division of nature, which concerned even those who busied themselves with collecting flowers. Stephen Elliott of Charleston was by profession a doctor and banker but by avocation a botanist, whose *Sketch of the Botany of South-Carolina and Georgia* (1821–24) was the most considerable contribution made by a Southern botanist. In 1828 and 1829, Elliott wrote two essays on the philosophy of nature, which explained how some Southerners approached classification, not only of flora and fauna, but of "man in society." He had a sharp sense of the fecund connectedness of nature and the problem this posed for knowledge, because modern science had accelerated. Linnaeus once knew of ten thousand species of vegetable life, but now there were one hundred thousand and more.

Hence classification had become imperative, and it was natural history's purpose to group and arrange "on such principles, that the individuals of each group shall be connected by common qualities, by composition, by structure, by habit, and, as an almost necessary consequence, by their properties and uses."[1] So, as knowledge accumulated, the subdisciplines of inquiry multiplied.

Elliott distinguished between natural and artificial systems of classification, the former being the procedure of an earlier age, the latter of the modern. Once, naturalists had focused on individual objects, but this was now impossible; too much was known, too much to be known. With Linnaeus had begun the modern era of artificial classification, which looked only on "the peculiarities or discrepancies of external form." As Elliott saw it, this habit of thought was fundamental to natural history since about 1750, when the floodgates were opened and science became a great cooperative discipline, whose purpose was to "know all the tribes, all the productions of nature."[2]

Elliott dismissed the evolutionary theory of Jean-Baptiste Lamarck, because nature was not a chain but (as Buffon had explained) a web. Though knowledge was accumulating, the complexity of nature itself was static. For three thousand years, no mutations had been witnessed. Yet Elliott knew the fossil record; refusing evolution, he knew about change. Static forms did not mean constant ones: "When we examine the now existing forms, and compare them with the remains of the extinct races which are still so perfectly preserved, it becomes obvious that there have been successive creations." (By "races," Elliott meant all the groups of nature.) Early species had died, new ones had appeared, and a species, once created, might vary slightly. But permanence was more remarkable than chance variation, and Elliott refused the environment as an explanation for variation. Underneath all the movement was form, stillness. Only man had gained some exemption from the remorselessly "blind and uncontrollable instinct" which marked living creatures, by having "the awful responsibility of free-will" and reason, which made him a "wonderful anomaly in the system of life."[3] That being so, natural history had an obligation to investigate man himself.

Elliott nowhere mentioned the races of man. He scarcely needed to. Even in his silence on this score, his was a natural science for the South, progressive in knowledge, eager for understanding, convinced that reason would discover stability; knowing movement, wanting order. His was a mode of understanding which offered his blunter successors, who were less interested in plants and butterflies and more drawn to the shape of human bodies, an entry point. But Elliott's faith in the explanatory power of physical forms was consistent with a widespread stoic pessimism in the nineteenth century. His refusal of Lamarck, though driven by Elliott's theodicy, spoke to a reluctance to trust too much to man. After all, Lamarck offered the quintessence of free will as the key to the domain of nature. Elliott wanted the reassurance of free will, not its "awful responsibility."

Such pessimism was more marked in the Europe which had experienced the French Revolution, but even Southerners who inherited the American Revolution had known enough uncertainty and confronted enough necessity to be drawn to this darker view, characteristic of the age. This logic Alexis de Tocqueville tried in 1853 to explain to Gobineau:

> The last century had an exaggerated and a rather puerile confidence in the power that man exercises over himself and in that of peoples over their own destiny. That was an error of the time; a noble error . . . the failure of so many generous ideas . . . has now precipitated us in the opposite excess. . . . We believed ourselves capable of everything, today we believe ourselves capable of nothing, and we like to believe that from now on struggle and effort will be useless and that our blood, our muscles, and our nerves will always be stronger than our will and our virtue.[4]

So, to be preoccupied with bodies betrayed a want of confidence in minds. But what were the bodies, and where did they come from? Broadly speaking, the answers to these questions derived from two intellectual traditions converging upon Southern thought: the British tradition of ethnicity and the Continental scientific tradition of physical anthropology. The latter better addressed the philosophical problem, so it would be well to start there.

The modern conception of race began mostly with the biologists and botanists. Their driving question, at first, had been the problem of human nature. All the accumulating evidence was pointing to a dizzying variety of human cultures. Christianity, to which science was held responsible, said this diversity should not exist. Yet it did exist. Why? Most in the eighteenth century looked to the environment to explain how a single human race had diversified. But how this belief gave way to the axiom that diversity was encoded in bodies was not straightforward and might best be understood by looking at the case of Johann Friedrich Blumenbach, the man whom many intellectual Southerners came to see as the final authority on race.

In Blumenbach's Göttingen dissertation, *De Generis Humani Varietate Nativa Liber* (1775), physical appearance was regarded as only an epiphenomenon; what mattered was climate and custom, where men lived and what they did, in a world of plasticity and imperceptible gradation. In 1775 Blumenbach conferred no labels upon human racial variations, nor did he speak of hierarchy, because he defended the unity of the human race. That he changed his mind is a good instance of the proposition that method makes conclusion. Göttingen happened to possess a collection of skulls, and Blumenbach became interested in accumulating more. Most significantly, he acquired the skull of "a young Georgian female, made captive in the last Turkish war by the Russians."[5] Georgia is in the Caucasus. Thinking it pretty, wanting to use it as representative of the European variety, Blumenbach dubbed it Caucasian, but only eventually.

The *De Generis Humani Varietate Nativa Liber* went through several editions and, in each, method drove conclusion a little more. The second edition of 1781 broke from Linnaeus in raising the number of human varieties from four to five, and Blumenbach began to intermingle physical descriptions with moral discriminations. He observed, for example, that the Chinese were "distinguished for depravity and perfidious of spirit and manners." In the third edition of 1795 Blumenbach began to insist that nature did display "large gaps," a new opinion from a man who in 1775 had insisted of humanity that the world was seamless, that "all do run into one another." Now he observed that one could see how discontinuity worked by looking at the skulls, of which he was evidently proud, his collection being "unique in its kind." The first skull he named was that of "the middle, or Caucasian variety," of the unfortunate Georgian woman captive.[6]

Now, instead of beginning with climate, Blumenbach worked from bodily structure toward the mind, and he spoke more decisively about "racial varieties" and skin color. Now he had classes, ordered hierarchically from lightness to blackness; these were *"Caucasian, Mongolian, Ethiopian, American, and Malay."* His language was brisk: "I have allotted the first place to the Caucasian . . . which make me esteem it the primeval one."[7] From the Caucasian, there were two lines of divergence: one ran Caucasian-American-Mongolian, the other Caucasian-Malay-Ethiopian. The case was now being made that, in the beginning, all the world was Caucasian, and other races were degenerations from the original stock. Hence, Blumenbach had no conception of evolution. The history of the natural world did not move from the inferior primitive to the complicated modern, with certain races marooned at earlier stages of development, but began with God's creation of the beauteous Caucasian, from which others came to vary. In this manner, environmentalism mutated into something harder, unyielding, imposing.

Blumenbach was not alone in pondering species, human variety, unity, and environment and in inventing boxes into which human shapes might be fitted. The intellectual pace had quickened between his first and third editions. Others were contemporary or quickly joined in: in France, Georges Cuvier, François Péron, and Jean-Joseph Virey; in Britain, John Hunter, James Cowles Prichard, and Sir William Lawrence. The curious in Europe and the United States might, by the 1820s, have a substantial shelf of books on this subject. Among these, Blumenbach was a touchstone, the more so for being an anatomist who spoke with the authority of science.

Racial theory remained, for a long time, a matter for American naturalists and those who read them. Doctors were especially important, as they had been in Europe. Those who spent their lives prodding bodies, watching them, trying to understand what flesh meant, were vulnerable to the physiological explanation; their concepts used their experience. Such men in the South—the botanists, doctors, and anatomists—began to involve themselves in these controversies, and like Blumenbach they often gave the impression that only other men in disordered museums were listening. In the pages of the *Southern Review*, for example, between 1828 and 1832, science was a matter for concerted debate. Readers were kept informed about recent developments in medicine, botany, and geology, as well as the birth of a new science in phrenology. Virey, Cuvier, Gall, Spurzheim, Combe, Alibert, Broussais, these were names with theories which an attentive reader would notice. All had implications for concepts of race, because they touched on the age of the earth, the structure of the human body, the balances between reason and emotion, the relevance of Revelation. By the authority of science were races, as a construct of science, made to matter.

The idea of race had many attractions. The most obvious was its legitimation of conquest and subjection. Less obvious is that race gave intellectual authority to postcolonials. Once specimens had been sent to Linnaeus by Alexander Garden of Charleston, a cultural provincial on the edges of the world who thereby provided information to a European savant who decided what the world meant and placed the specimens in a *Systema Naturae*, about which Garden was not expected to have opinions. The world, by 1830, was different. It was not yet possible for Linnaeus to be a Charlestonian and receive parcels from Sweden. But Stephen Elliott was a citizen of the republic of science and, as a botanist, he held sway over South Carolina and Georgia; from him there was no appeal, until he should be displaced by another local. The botany and geology of the Northern Neck mattered no less than that of the Thames Valley or the Loire and might matter more, for science conferred glamour upon the remote, upon the frontiers of knowledge and space.

The attractiveness of racial theory for Americans was connected to this sense of comity and equality. However illogically for an environmentalist,

Blumenbach had extended the courtesy of including among the Caucasians those of the race who had emigrated to North America. This delivered Americans from the reproof of Buffon, which had vexed Jefferson. North American air, climate, miasmas, shortness, hairlessness, sexual feebleness—the threat of mutation implicit in Buffon's natural science—melted away. A Caucasian was a Caucasian in whichever Georgia he or she was found.

In the South this intellectual tradition of physical anthropology encountered a second, an English mode of thought. The word "race" itself came from Old Norse, where it had meant a rushing of water, a usage that survives in a phrase like "mill race." From this it came to mean a channel or course, and then the path of a life. By the late sixteenth century, it came to signify a collective name for those who shared a life, an ancestry, and a posterity. Usually, "race" was a way of translating the Latin word "gens" and this usage persisted until the nineteenth century, when a race might take many forms— the people of an American state, an ethnicity, a nation, or a kinship network.

There had been heady, if incoherent, debate in the seventeenth and eighteenth centuries about the genealogy of European races. William Camden (1551–1623), the historian, had wished to refute the old idea, touted by Geoffrey of Monmouth, that the British were the descendants of Brutus and the Trojans. Camden favored a Germanic origin, an Anglo-Saxon source, as one might understand the Germans from Tacitus's *Germania*. Later in the seventeenth century, Robert Molesworth preferred to derive the British from the Scandinavians, as another version of the Germanic. By 1703 the Celts had been imported into the debate, having been invented then by a Breton abbé, Paul-Yves Pezron, who ruled that the Welsh and Bretons were descendants of the ancient Keltoi. But there was confusion over whether Celts were a subdivision of the Germanic people or separate, whether they were more or less favorable to liberty than Anglo-Saxons. By the early nineteenth century, these matters had been swept up into the high Romantic argument. What did Ossian teach us of the Celts? Who were the Scythians? What did the Ostrogoths do in Italy? At stake was the shape of European culture. Had it begun in pieces and evolved toward coherence? Or had it begun with coherence and splintered into nations of rich particularity?

Southerners disagreed about this. Thomas Grimké, who knew more about these things than anyone else, inclined toward the theory that Europe had begun with the heterogeneous. There were, firstly, the "Northern nations" and "Celtic nations," and, secondly, the "Christian Latin" South, itself later influenced by the Arabs. These two groups had interacted to create modern European culture. With this Thomas Cooper disagreed and inclined to the Indo-European theory that there once had been a single race in "the high land of Asia," which had then radiated and diversified.[8] In either case, the European past was seen as being composed of these jostling races. Romantic literature crowded them into the Southern consciousness: Walter Scott's *Ivanhoe*, where Anglo-Saxons, Jews, and Normans competed; Robert Southey's poem *Roderick, The Last of the Goths*; the old Spanish ballads which spoke of the Moors, the Franks, and the Visigoths, which Hugh Legaré found so affecting; these and many more.

So the idea of race was commingled with this early modern discourse about nations and the origins of Europe. On the whole, the question of Africa had been peripheral. What changed things, eventually, was the shock of confrontation between the Old World and the New World, which compelled a reconsideration that, latterly, included Africa. The emergence of the idea of race-as-biology occurred because Europeans and their colonial descendants, from a sense of their superiority to those whom they had conquered, enslaved, and diminished, began to think it inapt to speak of the English, the Caribs, and the Hottentots in a language which implied equivalence. By the late nineteenth century, a separation grew almost absolute. Europe and North America had nations, Africa and Asia had tribes. All had races, but in a strict hierarchy.

There is little need to write an extended narrative about the emergence of racial theory in the South; the story has been often told. By the 1830s, the ethnic categories of Anglo-American thought had collided with the natural science of Blumenbach and his heirs, to produce habitual disquisitions on the "Types of Mankind." The natural order of man was divided, hierarchical, organic. Questions about the respective influences of environment and physiognomy had been mostly decided in favor of the latter. By 1850, few quarreled with the view that race was, somehow, one of the most compelling explanations of things, and this was stated in a new way. The older science of the Enlightenment had classified nature with an air of puzzled detachment. The new Romantic science eagerly saw the diversity of creation and rushed to its cruel judgments.

Yet race was unstable. Intended to demonstrate order, race had a gift for creating intellectual disorder, not least in being unclear about how many races populated the world. Most contentious was polygenesis, because it focused on several issues: the authority of the Scriptures, the age of the earth, and the unity of mankind. The idea of polygenesis itself had been around since the mid-eighteenth century. As long as science accepted the biblical definition of the earth's age, the idea of multiple origins would not go away. Shortened time, many species (human and otherwise), a single Creation, little evidence of mutation during the historical record, a resistance to the inheritance of acquired characteristics, all left a devastating problem of explanation, which homilies upon the sons of Noah offered a scant chance of resolving. Before Charles Lyell expanded time, Charles Darwin posited the evolutionary mechanism of natural selection, and the Bible slipped off the scientist's laboratory desk, polygenesis was the skeptical man's obvious choice. The unity of man was the uneasy position of the Christian conservative, diversity of origin the confident assertion of the radical modernist.

Proving the point is Josiah Nott, a doctor who had grown up in South Carolina and been educated in New York, Philadelphia, and Paris in the most progressive and empirical of schools, before ending up in Mobile. He became a man who laughed at Revelation, mocked priests, had his eye on the main chance, and became a polygenist, since it was the latest thing. He first entered these disputes in 1843 by arguing that mulattoes were hybrids, short-lived and tending to infertility. This was a step toward making whites and blacks into separate species, since fecundity defined a species. Inter alia, Nott observed that, while it was unclear whether all five races were separate creations or merely varieties, he was sure that "*the Anglo-Saxon and Negro races are, according to the common acceptation of the terms, distinct species, and that the offspring of the two is a Hybrid.*"[9] A little later, he was invited to give two lectures in Mobile and chose to turn his new interest in race into a more incautious exposition. One should not pay much attention to the Bible, he explained, because modern science had disproved much of it. The Ark? Not big enough, too many species. Adam and Eve? Only one creation of a human species was insufficient. The biblical chronology? Too short, probably by several thousand years; Moses and Bishop Ussher would not do. One human race before God? No, blacks were a separate species, separately created, intermediate between Caucasians and apes, possessed of smaller brains. To mingle races created only sterile hybridity and social degeneration, while environment explained little.

Nott liked the ensuing uproar and, in time, he would make himself a world expert on race. It is arguable that he was the most famous Southern intellectual of his day, insofar as Northern and European reputation defined celebrity. In the great roaring torrent of anthropological racism, Nott roared with the best or worst of them. His book with George Gliddon, the *Types of Mankind* (1854), went through ten editions before 1871, and Nott acquired honors of satisfyingly intercontinental scope. If one examines the English translation of Blumenbach's *Treatises*, published by the Anthropological Society of London in 1865, one will find a list of the Society's honorary fellows. They include Louis Agassiz, Paul Broca, Charles Darwin, Charles Kingsley, Charles Lyell, and Ernest Renan. There is also "Nott, Dr. J. C. Foreign Associate of the Anthropological Society of Paris. *Mobile (Alabama, C.S.A.).*" Broca, though he disagreed with much that Nott wrote, nonetheless acknowledged him as "one of the most eminent anthropologists of America."[10]

Nott was less popular in the South. His *Two Lectures* fell to Moses Ashley Curtis, naturalist and Episcopal minister, to review in the *Southern Quarterly Review*. Curtis, unlike Nott, needed a way to reconcile Scripture and science. He did so by loosening up both Scripture and science, and so had to concede ground. He granted to Nott the notion that there had been several creations, some unmentioned in the Bible; he admitted that there were animals now on earth different from those existent before the flood; he waved aside the option of incessant godly intervention; he acknowledged that the Bible's chronological information was vague and broken, though he saw little reason to believe that the discoveries of Egyptology falsified it. As for the flood, modern geology was in confusion and Nott was overconfident in asserting that it insisted upon a multiplicity of floods. All this was shrewd of Curtis. Nott's tactic had been to assert that science's conclusions were firm and decisive while the divines were muddled. Curtis returned the compliment by showing how science was controversial even among scientists. While it was easy for Curtis to show that Nott had a modest command of the Scriptures, it was more pointed (and as accurate) to indicate that Nott's science was often haphazard. As to Nott's ideas on mulattoes and hybridity, Curtis was dismissive, because the world was full of mixed races, all propagating to good effect. So, by moving subtly between scientific authority and those moments where science was divided, Curtis strove to gain the leeway where biblical difficulties might be regarded charitably. Much was doubtful, he seemed to say. Nott's radicalism was unnecessary, on both scientific and religious grounds.

To this Nott replied in two installments, then Curtis replied. Both found their allies, and passions ran high. The veracity of the Scriptures, the authority of science, chronology, nature, environment, these topics agitated nerves. Explicitly, the social subjection of Africans to white Southerners' control was almost the least important issue embroiled in these disputes, and this omission will seem curious, since almost all these Southern controversialists were slaveholders. But race was a great international concept, a cosmopolitan idea. Southern scientists sought to engage others beyond local boundaries. While race was everywhere, slavery was only in a few places, so they could not make the latter central. A Southerner might think naive the opposition of Blumenbach and Gobineau to slavery, but a Southerner might know, conversely, that slavery did not need rigorous racial concepts. Such ideas helped, but they were not essential, and that help would not have compensated for the isolation which an explicit proslavery argument would have imposed upon the Southern scientist wishing to engage in the discourse of race. To jump from race to slavery meant embattlement, a barrier between the South and the world.

Further, scientific racism wandered into infidelity, and, forced to choose between a proslavery God and an antislavery scientist, most Southerners chose Jehovah as the weightier endorsement. Slavery was comprehensively effective, an iron curtain between them and us. By contrast, race was fluid, uncertain, contentious; it pitted white against white, infidel against cleric. Later, with slavery gone, racism became more urgently necessary for segregating masters from servants in a differently fluid world. Then, Southern racism made sense not only in Richmond but in New York, Berlin, and Calcutta. Which is not to say that the Old South lacked the simpler prejudices of color. "We" were white, more or less; "they" were black, more or less. But color prejudice had existed in Elizabethan England, as in colonial Virginia, and would survive into the twentieth century, when the science of race was discredited.

It will be evident by now that the unstable complexities of the word "race" makes it easy to misread many antebellum writings, the more so as Southerners themselves did not always know what they meant by the word. The modern reader sees the words "black," "colored," "African," "race," and runs them together into something coherently called "race," something different from ethnicity, or family, or class, because peculiarly unyielding. Antebellum discourse was more loosely jointed. Race-as-ethnicity coexisted with race-as-biology, and the latter gave ethnicity a harder edge, to the point that in 1860 William Falconer of Alabama could argue that Northerners and Southerners qualified as races. By then the language of scientific racism had leeched into the wider discourse. "Race," "blood," "body," "mind," these were harder words in 1860 than 1800. No more in the American world could one say that, as Blumenbach put it, "all do run into one another, and that one variety of mankind does so sensibly pass into the other, that you cannot mark out the limits between them."[11] The world had became a place full of unyielding forms, peopled with tribes which demanded a fierce allegiance, delimited by barriers. This came to be so especially of the idea of the sexes, which seemed to demonstrate Tocqueville's pessimism with even more precision. But, whereas scientific racism had a way of driving people's minds away from slavery, sex had the opposite effect. Thoughts of women's bodies seemed to prompt a consideration of slaves' bodies.

THE SOUTH HAD MANY intelligent women who had the delicate task of mediating between the liveliness of their intellect and the deadening expectations of their society. This problem began in childhood. Before the 1820s, girls tended to be educated at home by a mother, a maiden aunt, or an elder sister. While boys had to be educated, for girls such things were optional. So, in 1810 the debate had hinged on whether a girl needed education at all. By 1830, the point was conceded, but it was unclear what should be taught, for how long, and for what purposes; the usual answer was to make wives who were ladies. By 1850, matters had progressed to concede the reality, if not the necessity, of female higher education. Hence, gradually the number of female schools had proliferated and their curricula went beyond what the late eighteenth century had offered. By 1839, the Methodists had established in Macon the Georgia Female College, which was not only the South's first college for women but precedent to anything else in the rest of United States and (it is claimed) western Europe. By the 1850s, thirty of the thirty-nine female colleges chartered in the United States were in the South, and in some states female colleges outnumbered those for men. From the beginning, they took male education as a standard to be emulated. Their scientific education was often equivalent, their teaching of modern foreign languages perhaps better, and their attention to the fine arts (painting, music) was superior. Many prescribed texts were identical to those used in male colleges.

Missing from female higher education, however, were the debating societies which trained men for public life. Women might read manuals of rhetoric, but they concentrated on advice about letter-writing, not the forensic arts. Since female colleges were usually sponsored by religious denominations, religion tended to be prominent, the more so as religion fitted, too easily, into the arts of the private realm, where women were supposed to be confined: conversation, dancing, singing, playing the piano, even the making of wax flowers. In general, it was presumed that a woman's education was practical and her vocation was the home or (if a husband was unforthcoming or delayed) the education of other young ladies. In this spirit, compared to the rough spartan quality of male colleges, their female counterparts had more comforts, to foreshadow how a home should be arranged.

Southern society told young women to be very conscious of their bodies. Minds and eyes were full of the curve of a neck, the clarity of a complexion, the thinness of a waist, and many women were close and anxious students of what to wear and how to carry themselves. High society licensed an awareness of sexuality and authorized some of its arts, the teasing flirtatiousness of the drawing room, even if religious society did not. But even high society was formally puritanical about sexuality itself, which was forbidden beyond marriage and little discussable within it. Sexual transgression meant social death, if discovered. Marriage was intended to be a finality, divorce being extremely rare, though separation informally undertaken was more common and the precedent death of husbands was usual. Some never married, but this was a hard road. The single woman was regarded with condescension, and society offered little by way of a profession (except being a teacher or governess) for such a person, which might free her from dependence upon the world of married people, who took themselves to be the center of the social universe. Even to be married but childless was to invite knowing sneers or, worse, pitying advice.

On the whole, Southern men feared the dangers posed by women's bodies more than their minds, or rather felt at ease about the minds because the bodies were imprisoned. It was true that the domestic realm, for a Southern woman who was born or married well, could be a great domain. A plantation was a business in which wives and mothers participated actively, and there knowledge and shrewdness was useful. Nonetheless, the expansion of female education was, potentially, on a collision course with the adult role of women, because a Southern woman's legal position was drastically constrained. A single woman and a widow controlled her own property (a one-third dower was usual), but a married one conferred all on her husband and lost the power of independent contract, unless an equity court made a special exception. This was somewhat softened in the late antebellum period, especially in the western South, and Louisiana's Napoleonic Code had long given more discretion, but in general the law discouraged female economic independence and action. Except as an informal adviser, a woman was denied almost all the public realm (the franchise, officeholding, juries, religious office). Most of the informal realm of public culture—libraries, conversation clubs, and debating societies—was also forbidden or inaccessible. No woman was allowed public speech if her body was present (no sermons or orations, except student ones); she was permitted a public voice only when her body was absent, as in the printed word.

In general, Southern men felt little pressure for a readjustment in the civil standing of women. During the Virginia State Convention in 1829, it was idly mentioned that women were often thought to be men's equals and were certainly superior to slaves, Indians, or foreigners. Why should they not have the vote? Samuel Moore had an answer: "The women have never claimed the right to participate in the formation of the Government, and that until they do, there can be no necessity for our discussing or deciding upon it." These were burdens they did not want and were "unwilling to bear." Besides, "their interests are so completely identified with our own, that it is impossible that we can make any regulation injuriously affecting their rights, which will not equally injure ourselves." Did they not have "unlimited confidence in our sex"?[12] On the last score, Moore was egregiously misled, since it is evident that many Southern women thought of men with less than confidence, in fact often with contempt. But, on the first score, Moore was not wrong. There were no suffragettes picketing the Virginia Convention, and no antebellum Southern woman chained herself to a iron railing or threw herself under a horse at the Washington races in Charleston.

This is not the place to consider all that women wrote or thought about, which can be assessed at the other places in this book where their contributions to fiction, poetry, social criticism, or autobiography are considered. Rather, it is a place to consider what sorts of women found a foothold in intellectual life, and what they said about sex when they spoke of it.

Social configurations made it extremely difficult for any woman who was not well born to become a writer. This was in some contrast to the experience of men, among whom modest origins were common. Society leaned against the literary woman; she tended to need affidavits of respectability or the confidence that social standing conferred to hazard her opinions. Hence many female intellectuals were the wives or daughters of notable men, usually of means, if often self-made men; most, too, had children of their own. As for the novelists, they offer a slight variation; though often well born and usually married, they were not infrequently harried into print by adverse financial circumstances, the death or incompetence of husbands.

It was very unusual, therefore, for a Southern female writer to break free from matters of gender as understood from within the household (love, courtship, disappointment, marriage, religion, education, and death) and write on the genres of public matters (history, politics, economics), except by imbedding the latter into the former. Louisa McCord is probably the only Southern woman who managed to do so, and even she often turned such essays into a meditation upon the family. Hence female writings provide a very partial understanding of women's understandings in their culture, because many women were poor or unmarried or childless. But, as the writings of Sarah Grimké show, even the unmarried could be drawn to speak of the family as normative and of motherhood as the center of a woman's meaning.

To sample the antipodes of Southern female thinking on gender, it will be helpful to look briefly at Sarah Grimké and Louisa McCord. The former stood for defiance of the old ways expressed in exile, the other for defense from within slavery's heartland. But both offered a grim assessment of men's ways and power.

The story of the abolitionist Grimké sisters has often been told, if seldom in books about the South, yet their thought was indelibly formed by their Southern experience and their words often were aimed deliberately at the community of Southern women, whom they were among the first to define as a community. For our purposes, Sarah's story is more salient, for she came closest to feminism. While Angelina tended to see the problem of women as subsidiary to that of slavery, Sarah moved beyond that to a sense that women had their own problems, mission, and need for social thought. The latter's story was, in outline, simple enough. She grew up in a prosperous judge's household in Charleston, had the usual half-education, went unhappily into society as a belle, and nurtured the impossible ambition of being a lawyer. In time she became religious and, after coming to live in Philadelphia, a Quaker. There in 1829 she was joined by Angelina, the sister who (being thirteen years junior) was in many ways a surrogate child. Angelina had come to antislavery and Quakerism by her own route, more marked by revulsion at slavery's violence and the unsettling experience of being formally tried for religious nonconformity.

Sarah advanced to abolitionism, the more so after 1838 when Angelina married Theodore Weld and the sisters continued to share a household. In truth, Sarah's experience of both South and North was disquieting, because in the latter she and her allies were vilified for their advanced opinions, while in the former her antislavery views made it dangerous for her to visit. After they became abolitionists, neither woman was ever to see Charleston again, for no one was sure that even the Grimké household would be proof against a proslavery, antifeminist mob. As such, Sarah's mature writings sought to learn from but transcend both places. Angelina was, in many ways, the bolder spirit when it came to public performance, but Sarah was the deeper thinker and more adventurous intellectually, though each saw beyond the problem of slavery to that of racial prejudice, which was further than many abolitionists saw.

The vital text is Sarah Grimké's *Letters on the Equality of the Sexes and the Condition of Woman* (1838). It is a work part theology, part comparative ethnography, part memoir, and all sermon. During its composition, she was still a Quaker, and the spirit of that religion informed the book because she was anxious to be plain and modest, and to mistrust sexuality. (Her greatest complaint against slavery was its habitual sexual abuse.) Being religious, she was preoccupied with a quarrel with biblical exegesis, by arguing that Genesis showed God making man and woman equal, that Adam and Eve shared in a fall from innocence "*but not from equality*," and that the old charge that Eve was delivered into inferiority by her temptation of Adam was unfounded.[13] For Sarah, the growth of male dominion grew illegitimately.

Grimké's idea of separate spheres was complicated. At one level, she was its fierce critic. She insisted that women ought to have a public role, that history (Semiramis, Queen Elizabeth) proved their competence. "Intellect is not sexed," she boldly asserted, nor "strength of mind." Did this mean that, as

Margaret Fuller was to assert in her *Woman in the Nineteenth Century* (1845), spheres might dissolve, that women might be sea captains, that Grimké would "have every arbitrary barrier thrown down . . . every path laid open to woman as freely as to man"? On this, Grimké was slippery: as fathers and mothers, husbands and wives, each sex had different duties, but these "do not attach to them as men and as women, but as parents, husbands, and wives." She glimpsed possibilities: she praised Harriet Martineau for writing, working to improve lighthouses, and knowing various languages; she trumpeted Madame de Staël as "intellectually the greatest woman that ever lived." She knew the old order was wrong, deeply resented the scoffing condescensions of men, and detailed the mortifying legal and financial disabilities of women, but her sense of what the new order would look like was shadowy. Women will be free to choose; "they will regard themselves, as they really are, free agents, immortal beings, amenable to no tribunal but that of Jehovah."[14] She wanted them to have the right to be preachers, for example, to reassume their old sacerdotal roles as priestesses.

But, on the whole, she was tentative. "There is a vast field of usefulness" for women, she said, but what was in the field was a matter of some obscurity. In Grimké's *Letters* women seem often to choose something like the old roles, as parents and wives. As one might expect, her vision of marriage was rooted in her theory that God had made men and women equal. She tried (with little success) to show that the Bible did not sanction patriarchalism, and, inter alia, she afforded herself the easy luxury of abusing the wretched Saint Paul. Nonetheless, she seemed to oppose divorce and wrote that, God having establishing marriage, man had "no right to annul it."[15] And in 1838, she was not claiming the suffrage, as she would do later in life, or the right to sit in legislatures, but only (as Angelina asserted elsewhere) the right of petition. What Sarah wanted, above all, was the right to be heard, the freedom to choose, the ability to control her life, but she was too close to the eighteenth century in which she was born to choose anything drastically radical. Or so she seems from a later perspective. Seen from Charleston in 1838, she was radical enough, indeed a moral impossibility.

The Grimké sisters were abolitionists before they were advocates of women's rights; they became "feminists" (to use the anachronistic term) partly because of the hostilities from the Northern public they had encountered as antislavery activists, partly because the abolitionist community liked to restrict them to being Southern women. For talking about slavery bound them, in memory, to the South. It was their utility as testifiers from within the citadel of the Slave Power that made them useful to the abolitionists, and, like Frederick Douglass who wanted to be more than a fugitive slave, the

Grimkés wanted to be more than cultural refugees. To be a reasoner upon women in general was to become more than a Southern woman in particular, and the *Letters on the Equality of Sexes* touch only glancingly upon Southern matters. Nonetheless the Grimkés used their Southern experiences habitually, scathingly, both as women and as ex-slaveholders, and their mature writings can be read as autobiography.

There is only one reference to the Grimkés in the writings of Louisa McCord. In her 1852 essay on the "Enfranchisement of Woman," she speaks of women's rights activists and mentions Angelina Grimké Weld, whom she mocks as "the gentle" and "the fair," someone who would be wise not to contest with the crudity of men in the public arena.[16] Yet they came from the same, small South Carolina, and it is improbable that they did not know of each other, since theirs was a world of gossip and the Grimkés, at least, were notorious and McCord was the daughter of fame. They shared much: powerful fathers and troublesome brothers, the discomfort of being awkward belles, the witness and consciousness of men's violence, the meditating upon God and suffering, the idea that slavery offered a key to a woman's self-understanding. They agreed, in fact, on a lot, except the crucial thing of how a woman should respond to the pressure of a harsh world; above all, they disagreed on the cogency of hope.

Most of McCord's published writings on gender were written in response to the ideas of northern and European theorists. Superficially, she did not like them, but as with most conservatives she came to know what she wished to conserve in dialectic with those who wished to reform her world. She was among the earliest Americans habitually to use the word "conservative" to describe her ideology and to say "we, of the conservatives."[17] Her earlier writings, especially her poetry, were deeply inflected by the matter of women, but they did not formally engage the many texts and ideas (from Mary Wollstonecraft to Margaret Fuller) that might have come her way. Much was impelled into clarity by the problem of slavery, since she became engaged by the problem of gender in the same year (1852) she read and abused *Uncle Tom's Cabin*.

In general, Louisa McCord had little sympathy with hope and reform. While she conceded that mankind, though not perfectible, was capable of improvement, little proposed for that improvement met her approval. Scorn was her usual response to a world growing dangerous with "free-soilers, barn-burners, anti-renters, abolitionists," threatening social anarchy. The proponents of women's rights fell easily under this rubric. But her disagreements can be readily misunderstood. In fact, she shared many of their presumptions; it is even possible that her understandings were partly derived from reading them, that McCord was a sort of wayward Grimké, with the same contempt for silks and belles, and the same sense that woman's condition needed improvement. If anything, her estimate of men was more scathing. "When have the strong forgotten to oppress the weak?" she asked, and knew the answer in woman's case. She was willing to own that most women were "out of place, unappreciated, having their talents and powers not only hidden under a bushel, but absolutely thrown away, while she becomes either the slave or the toy of men." She spoke of men's "brutal superiority," of a world without women's influence as "a wrangling dog-kennel." She even forcibly acknowledged the analogy of woman and slave: "In every government, and under every rule, woman has been placed in a position of slavery—actual, legal slavery." This was not so perfect a slavery as that experienced by "our negroes" but was still "a very decided state of bondage," because it involved the deprivation of rights, from which arose hardship. "Many a woman of dominant intellect is obliged to submit to the rule of an animal in pantaloons, every way her inferior."[18]

Why then so conservative? McCord saw no alternative. She blamed God for the cold facts of female submission. She had no interest in gender as a thing socially constructed. She believed in the reality of sex, because she believed in the compulsion and fate of bodies. McCord's criticism of the women's rights advocates rested on her sense that they merely succeeded in becoming a "*third* sex" or "unsexed," unable to be men, ceasing to be women. McCord saw women's bodies as enforcing upon them duties, sensibilities, and feelings. Among God's creatures, women were mandated to endure, suffer, love, and nurture, that is, they were charged with Christ's mission. So they had no place in the public sphere, no claim upon power in the ordinary sense. "The *world of action* must to her be almost entirely a closed book," she once said. Corporeal weakness and nature's bargain meant women needed men's strength for protection, however ugly was that strength. But McCord unquietly expanded this meek sphere. She was adamant that a woman's duties were not confined "to shirt-making, pudding-mixing, and other such household gear, nor yet even to the adornment of her own fair person." She placed intellect within woman's sphere, as well she (the author) might if she was to retain any sense of personal rationale. She insisted that woman was not inferior, merely different, and she flirted with asserting superiority. She thought that if mankind was to improve, it was by the intensification of woman's mission to man. The millennial ambition McCord mocked in the socialist she was willing to grant to the woman "in her true place," which was "the quiet, unwearied and unvarying path of duty, the home of the mother, the wife, and the sister, teaching man his destiny." For men might be powerful, but they were confused: "Her duty is always clear, while *his* may be doubtful."[19] By this logic, McCord was inverting the order of gender in her society. She lived in a world where men were self-confident of their manliness and she called them doubtful, and she took Southern woman's doubtfulness and tried to purify it to her own especially tense commitment.

Her own history casts a complicated light on all this. She worshipped her father and probably did not have a happy marriage to David James McCord, the most likely candidate for the "animal in pantaloons." Her references to her own mother, including the letter in which the latter's death was announced, are few and matter-of-fact. Yet nothing in her mature life mattered more to Louisa McCord than being a mother, especially to her son, Langdon Cheves McCord. She wished to be for her woman's sphere what she romantically believed her father was to the public realm, an influence for stability and good in a world full of the less prescient and less competent. But this does not quite capture the complexity of her views, because Louisa McCord was not unlike her own mother, whom she once described as leaning trustingly on a man's arm in a moment of danger. McCord's surviving correspondence shows her tacking between these two impulses, to demonstrate the fearsome strength she took to be necessary and which others habitually discerned in her, and to seek out protection. "I like a woman who *leans* a little," Dexter Clapp of Savannah once observed, and it will seem odd to observe that McCord could be such a woman, if sometimes against her will. It was her misfortune that during her life she needed strength more than she was satisfied in being protected, because after her father, the men she knew intimately seemed often to have been violent, weak, or inadequate. Over them she had powers of persuasion, but not power. Power was the mother's prerogative, including the power to protect, just as it was understood to be the prerogative of the slaveholder over the slave. "You believe the negro to be an oppressed race, while we believe him to be a protected one," she once told Henry Carey.[20] Part of McCord's incomprehension of abolitionism was that she did not understand why anyone would wish to forfeit protection for freedom, if freedom meant danger.

The complexity of her position is most starkly exposed in the story of her father's long dying, which casts a bleak light on what was possible for even the strongest of Southern women in a man's world.

Langdon Cheves grew old, and, after a stroke which occasioned partial paralysis, his mind started to become "constantly confused, constantly restless, constantly changing." So, in the middle of the winter of 1855–56, his daughter took him into her Columbia house. This was awkward, as it usually is between generations. She was a widow in possession of her own household, while he was a patriarch accustomed to command. It rapidly became clear that he would not accept living in a house not his own and talked often of returning home. "I do not think it will be possible to keep him here, unless he could get the impression that this house belongs to him," she saw. Her father needed controlling, but would not take it from a woman. So, as he grew more senile, she strove to give him the illusion of mastery. She gave up "my whole lower story to him except one small back room" and kept away her friends. Later she was driven to building a second, small house on her town lot, where she could hide herself and her children, thus leaving her father with the belief that he lorded over the main building. Consistently, she protected him from bad news, especially that his son Hayne was dying in Florence. She often had to lie, to flatter his self-importance, and to deal with his slaves (who clashed with her own). She was central to the events, yet, being a woman, marginal. She came very close to despair, until eventually the crisis eased. The old man grew too weak to express his wayward will, became "helpless almost as an infant," and a woman was, after all, permitted to deal authoritatively with infants. He grew sufficiently oblivious that she could put him in the new cottage and return to her own quarters. He died in June 1857.[21]

This experience was a stark commentary on McCord's version of the separate spheres. It confirmed her hard assessment of woman's difficult lot and man's brute insensibility. But she had liked to think that the boundaries of the spheres were distinct, that everyone knew his or her place. It was not so. Keeping place required effort, a repression. "Although I have been pushed back in every possible way," she said in 1848, "and have myself endeavoured for many a long year to crush my own propensities, there has been a struggling consciousness of something which has goaded me on." Necessity half dissolved boundaries and compelled different fictions, a blurring of his and hers. "I think he will be much happier when he sees something of a house getting up on *my* lot and will feel that *this* is *his*," she observed at one point of her father. This was the "concocted falsehood" of the doctrine of separate spheres. Everyone was told what they must be, but it was seldom possible to accomplish this, because reality was too fluid, "constantly confused, constantly restless, constantly changing."[22]

IT WAS TO BECOME customary later for white Southerners to speak of their unity of origin. By 1900 Southerners were supposed to be all Anglo-Saxons, blessed with a providential English heritage, which elsewhere in the country was being corrupted by immigrant floods of greasy Italians and darkly gabbling Jews. But antebellum Southerners had a different view. In 1890 Boston was ethnically more complex than Charleston, but once the reverse had been true. Distinctions of ethnicity, later swept away, were powerfully relevant in the earlier South, when it mattered whether one's forebears were English, French Huguenot, Sephardic, or German Lutheran.

The South was a polyglot culture. Spanish cultural influence lingered and was reinforced by the annexation of Texas in 1845, while in Louisiana the French language powerfully competed with English. There were Jewish communities which used Hebrew and Spanish and German-speaking groups such the Moravians of western North Carolina. In 1860 half of the adult white males in Savannah were of foreign birth, and of these, 70 percent were Irish, many Gaelic-speaking. There were all the native American languages: the varieties of Algonquian spoken by the Powhatans; the Iroquoian of the Cherokee; the Siouan of the Osage. In addition, 30 percent of the Southern population was of African descent; many spoke an English inflected by African survivals, and some spoke a Creole language of their own, compounded of African languages and, variously, English, French, and Spanish. So, perhaps only a bare majority of the population of the southeastern United States spoke English as a first language.

Ethnicities had their institutions: the St. Andrew's Society, the Hibernian Society, the Hebrew Harmonic Society, the Deutschen Gesellschaft, and their like. Militia companies might be ethnic, as with the Irish Jasper Greens. In addition, religion refracted ethnicity; synagogues for Jews, Episcopal churches for the English, Methodist chapels for the Welsh, African Methodist Episcopal churches for Africans. All these had congregations where one would meet people of reassuringly similar background and experience, where a Peyre might meet a Porcher, a Cheves encounter a McCord, where cultural memory and ritual might be shared; here the battle of Culloden was invoked, there a Mandingo word.

Except when they involved white supremacy, many of these institutions evolved toward the inclusive. As the lines of ethnicity began to blur, it became an emphasis more than an indispensable qualification. The German Friendly Society of Charleston, for example, had been founded in 1766 with the mandate that only Germans or their children could be members and that all had to be German-speaking. But the latter rule quickly lapsed and the former was often ignored. Benevolent societies, founded for the care of this group or that, often came to spread their philanthropy eclectically. Intermarriage between ethnicities was so extensive that exclusivity was hard to sustain. As between "white" ethnicities, almost everyone was mongrel and pride in origin was selective.

There are many ways to measure the implications of ethnicity for intellectual life, but one way lies in examining the writings of the historian Charles Gayarré (1805–95), a man who betrayed an acute awareness of these issues of origin and culture, because his ethnic background was richly complicated. His father had been a Spanish royal functionary in New Orleans and his grandfather (who brought the boy up) a French plantation owner. By the early 1820s, Gayarré had come into a wealthy inheritance of land and slaves, which he retained until the Civil War impoverished him. He lived most of his life in New Orleans, while studying the law in Philadelphia in the late 1820s and living in France and Spain for eight years after 1835.

As a historian, he began his literary career in French, his first language. Among his earliest publications was the *Essai historique sur la Louisiane* (1830–31), which Gayarré hoped would be useful for "cette partie de notre population pour qui le Français est encore la langue maternelle," and later came two volumes of the *Histoire de la Louisiane* (1846–47).[23] Gayarré was to publish nothing substantial in English until "The Romance of Louisiana History" appeared in *De Bow's Review* in 1847, when he was forty-two. So Francophone was Gayarré that it was others who proposed to publish an English translation of his writings. And no one doubted, even when he migrated into writing in English, that his writings were a vindication of Creole culture.

Gayarré published the four volumes of his *History of Louisiana* in stages. The first two volumes, *The French Domination*, and the third, *The Spanish Domination*, came out in 1854, while *The American Domination* did not appear until 1866. Collectively, the series was a study in cultural tension. The titles of the volumes were eloquent. It was customary in places like Virginia to speak of the colonial period as the preface to the nationality inaugurated by the American Revolution, but Louisiana had no share in this process. She had not experienced the American Revolution and her inhabitants had never claimed their independence; they were in the Union only because in 1803 Thomas Jefferson thought it prudent to acquire more land and people, and Napoleon needed ready cash. A Creole could stand before the New Orleans city hall on 30 November 1803 to observe the Spanish flag being displaced by the French tricolore and then return three weeks later to see the French flag replaced by the Stars and Stripes. Seeing three imperial flags hoisted and lowered, he knew that his preference had not been consulted. In Gayarré's lifetime, only once were Louisianans asked to express a preference about their membership in a polity, which in 1861 they asserted should not be the United States. In 1865, as in 1803, this was to make little difference. Gayarré knew this: in his later work, all of Louisianan history is colonial; France, Spain, and the United States offered but a series of dominations.

Discriminating among these dominations, Gayarré was most generous to the French and Spanish. No doubt in this he was influenced by his great-grandfather having been a Spanish colonial administrator who commenced generations of ethnic intermingling. But the originating Gayarré had been from Navarre and had entered Spanish service as a soldier, so cultural diversity had been a European as well as a Louisianan experience. Knowing this, Gayarré the historian leaned over backward to be generous to the Spanish and called upon his contemporaries to assert that there was scarcely an elderly Louisianan who had experienced Spanish rule "who did not speak of it with affectionate respect, and describe those days of colonial rule as the golden age, which, with many, was the object of secret, and with others, of open regrets."[24]

To this verdict he had promptly added: "Such a government would, of course, have been insupportable to us, but it is not hence to be inferred that it did not suit the tastes and feelings, and deserve the gratitude of our ancestors." This was being not only historicist but also polite to American democratic ideology. In his antebellum writing, Gayarré could sometimes show the instincts of a sometime American politician who knew about the Fourth of July, even if his ancestors in 1776 had not relished its significance, except as a blow to Britain. In this spirit, he observed of the Louisiana Purchase that it was "the most important treaty perhaps ever signed in the nineteenth century," and that, among its consequences, might be numbered "the extension of the area of freedom, an immense accretion to the physical and moral power of the great American republic, and the subsequent acquisition of the Floridas, Texas, California, and other portions of the Mexican territory."[25] By the standards of eagle-screaming, this was modest. What differed in Gayarré was that he seldom showed other than contempt for democracy, except when in an election, and he usually respected power for its own sake. In his own eyes, he was a gentleman, a seigneur, a don. In his history, he reveled in the gaudiness of brave inceptions. The opening pages of his first volume are full of pleasure and romance, chivalry and pomp, Andalusian chargers and Castilian roundelays. By contrast, the opening pages of *The American Domination* are marked by darkness, and, for Gayarré, the passage from feudalism to bourgeois democracy was no movement into the light.

The American Domination dealt mostly with Louisiana's years as a territory of the United States and the few years between its admission as a state in 1812 to the battle of New Orleans in 1815. It is a study in cultural mistrust, which began in gloom and advanced to misunderstanding, in which the Americans were the misunderstanding outsiders. Much hinged on the figure of William C. C. Claiborne, who appears as an uncomprehending despot, governing a population "of which he knew nothing," speaking neither French nor Spanish, and introducing common law to those who found it comically incomprehensible. With indignation, Gayarré narrated the debates in Congress, by which the principles of territorial government were established. He pointed to hypocritical congressmen (and a president) who spoke of Louisianans as a conquered people without rights, a population little above the level of slaves, unable to be trusted because so long the subjects of despots. This was in contrast to the narratives of other Southern historians, who were not Creole. John Wesley Monette's *History of the Discovery and Settlement of the Valley of the Mississippi* (1846), for example, praised Governor Claiborne for his assiduous devotion to arduous labors, by which "the eagle of Liberty . . . extended its flight to Louisiana" and covered "its virtuous inhabitants with its protecting wings."[26]

For Gayarré, local habits were too little regarded and Creole honor slighted. Even his celebratory narration of the battle of New Orleans was prickly about those incidents where the Americans were insensitive to Creole needs, contribution, or custom, though Gayarré did recognize that New Orleans was rife with "conflicting opinions, wishes and feelings."[27] On balance, Gayarré disliked the British more than the Americans, though he was aware that the diehard French party could be as obtuse as the Americans, and this was not a contradiction. The Creole mistrusted loyalties beyond the local, whether to France or Spain or the United States, which by such logic never became local. Gayarré had two candidates for *us*, Creole Louisiana and the South. True to this, the *History of Louisiana* had been kinder to Americans when they appeared as Southerners. America was *them*, but the South was *us*, and this sense of Southern comity was influenced by slavery and race.

Gayarré had begun to write *The American Domination* in 1859 and he continued after 1860. It is unsurprising that the experience of secession and war deepened his skepticism about membership in the United States and cynicism about the imperial hypocrisies of Washington, both in 1804 and 1863. Though the book was published in 1866, he left in the passages, written at various times during the war, which denoted his anger, although he did so against the wishes of his New York publisher. *The American Domination* ended its considered narrative in 1815 but has a "supplemental chapter" of sixty-one pages that runs, helter-skelter, over the years to 1861, and here Gayarré's bitterness about "Federal injustices or neglects" was unbridled.[28]

That the Creole, with reasons to keep a distance from Americans, found slavery to be a connection to other Southerners shows a truth. Slavery helped to dissolve the singularities of ethnicity by offering a shared experience, which amended other cultural traits resistant to assimilation. Membership in Southern culture could appeal to those who regarded themselves as culturally marginal and thought they might work inward toward a center where lived the unalienated, the real Southerners. It is unclear whether there were, in fact, many such people in the middle of the Southern world, though the minority who were the descendants of the English were the obvious candidates.

The matter of England was in dispute, especially among Virginians. On the one hand, Virginia had been preeminently the colony which had most received English immigration and had thought itself another England, as much so as (perhaps more than) the Dissenters who had given their settlement the name of New England. On the other hand, the revolutionary generation had spat on England's name, had violently forced a separation, and created a brisk Virginian tradition of Anglophobia.

By midcentury, however, some Virginians had drifted toward a mild Anglophilia, bound up with a growing skepticism toward the Jeffersonian tradition and helped by the receding of Anglo-American political animosities, evidenced by the Webster-Ashburton Treaty of 1842. While slavery was a running sore, since Britain had made itself the great antislavery power, this was a mild vexation compared to British troops burning Washington. Literary people, many of them associated with the *Southern Literary Messenger*, felt a comity with Dickens, Thackeray, and Tennyson, who offered a side to English culture which was far from the wars of the eighteenth century, was both sentimental and modern, all at once. For many, clubbable jocularity offered a surcease from the incessant politics of the American scene. This encouraged an often-satirical interest in manners and customs, which seemed to point backward to an eighteenth-century Virginia of periwigs and drunken conviviality, hospitality, and courage.

Contentiously, there emerged the notion that Virginia was English and Cavalier, in contradistinction to New England, which was English and Roundhead. This seemed to explain both the seventeenth and the nineteenth centuries, because the warfare of sectionalism in the Union was thereby just a continuity with Marston Moor. It was also a form of ethnic identity for Virginians. Clearly, being English tout court offered them no singularity, for Massachusetts could claim as much, perhaps more. But being English and Cavalier seemed to offer grounds for distinction.

The eighteenth century in Virginia itself had not given sympathetic thought to Cavaliers. Robert Beverley's *The History and Present State of Virginia* (1705) disavowed the notion, and Jefferson was innocent of the idea, which was as well for a man of Welsh descent. The notion crept forward only in the opening decades of the nineteenth century, and its groundwork was laid by those often not English or Virginian, who were contemplating as outsiders the decline of Virginian preeminence and sought an explanation. William

Wirt, whose *Letters of the British Spy* (1803) commenced the exploration, was born in Maryland of a Swiss father and a German mother. George Tucker, whose *The Valley of the Shenandoah* (1824) advanced matters, was from Bermuda. John Pendleton Kennedy, whose *Swallow Barn* (1832) came close to the heart of the matter, was born in Baltimore and had a father from northern Ireland. William Alexander Caruthers, whose *The Cavaliers of Virginia* (1834–35) sealed the process, was born in western Virginia, but he was of Scotch-Irish descent and was living in New York and Savannah when writing his novels.

These are books that will bear examination for many reasons. Here it is relevant only to note their description of a colonial and revolutionary gentry, who could be fitted into a Cavalier myth. Wirt's book, following upon the model offered by Montesquieu's *Lettres persanes*, assumed the voice of the outsider, which for Virginia was someone British and spying. A differentiation between the native Virginian and the old country was the book's presumption, and there was nothing of the Cavalier myth in it. There was, however, a suggestion that there was something aristocratic about Virginia, and aristocracy was a predicate of subsequent mythologies. The spy, for example, describes the occasional "stately aristocratic palace," surrounded by the "log cabins of poor, laborious, ignorant tenants," who "approach *the great house* cap in hand, with all the fearful, trembling submission of the lowest feudal vassals, [but] boast in their court-yards . . . that they live in . . . a land of equal liberty and equal rights."[29] Wirt's 1817 biography of Patrick Henry makes clear that colonial Virginia had been marred by aristocracy, against which Henry had led a liberty-loving struggle. But there was no suggestion that this aristocracy was anything other than homegrown from a migrant population of lesser folk, no hint that boatloads of silken Cavaliers fleeing from Cromwell had founded the colony.

The next step both weakened and strengthened this assertion. On the first score, George Tucker's *The Valley of the Shenandoah* (1824) introduced ethnic cross-currents. As a book about western Virginia and not the Tidewater, its early pages were preoccupied with the valley's unpretending inhabitants, not often English but Germans ("a pains-taking, plodding, frugal people") or Scotch-Irish ("ardent and impassioned" but "often idle, indolent, and improvident"). However, the novel's second volume did stray toward the east, where Tucker portrayed the sensual amiability and agrarian ease, the mansion houses and horse races, and the "lively jests and urbane suavity" of a dying order.[30] But these were not proud aristocrats, surrounded by cap-doffing tenants, but a slightly scruffy gentry, primus inter pares. Certainly Tucker's portrait was a half step away from Walter Scott's *Woodstock*, where

Cavaliers were amiable, unpretending, good-natured, and losing ground to the modern world. Nonetheless, Tucker himself never took that half-step. As late as 1837, when sketching colonial Virginian history, he saw no reason to mention Cavaliers.

Kennedy's *Swallow Barn* (1832) was, in some essentials, a duplication of Tucker, in others not. The plantation of Swallow Barn itself is portrayed as sitting on the James River, the white ethnic complexity of western Virginia is absent, and a character speaks unambiguously of "our English ancestors." While Tucker was close to being an eighteenth-century rationalist, the younger Kennedy was influenced by Scott and Washington Irving, whose *Bracebridge Hall* was a model. Hence Kennedy spoke of "the gentlemen of Virginia," who lived hospitably "surrounded by their bondsmen and by their dependents," their "congregated household and . . . numerous retainers," who together afforded "a tolerable picture of feudal munificence." Much was made of decay and decline, of "dilapidated buildings" "desolation," and the "mouldering wharf." Throughout, Kennedy referred to Virginia as "the Old Dominion" and, in this vein of antiquity, the state was described as old enough to be Gothic, a place where a traveler might wander during "nights as dark as pitch, over commons, around old churches, and through graveyards." In short, Kennedy went in for what, in the furniture world, is called "distressing," the forging of not-so-old things as antiques by the application of faked varnish and carefully placed dents.[31]

The book ends in an old library, where a character leafs through heavy folios and comes across a book about John Smith from the 1620s. In the ensuing disquisition, it is lamented that "we have nothing to record the early adventures and chivalric virtues of the good soldier," whose character was "moulded in the richest fashion of ancient chivalry." This trembles on the edge of a Cavalier myth, a possibility reinforced by the earlier chapter titled "Traces of the Feudal System," in which it was asserted that Virginia's "early population . . . consisted of gentlemen of good name and condition, who brought within her confines a solid fund of respectability and wealth." But, in fact, Kennedy carefully noted that Smith had been born poor, however much he may have demonstrated "many of the points of a true knight."[32]

So, although *Swallow Barn* was not quite there, it was a bare step away from a developed Cavalier myth. A final step was made in historical literature by Henry Augustine Washington, who in an 1848 essay asked the novel question, who were the Virginians? This was asked by a complacently modern man, because Washington was a great admirer of François Guizot's *General History of Civilization* and Thomas Carlyle's essay "On History," an advocate of social history, and a skeptic of histories which concerned themselves only with governments. For Washington, the Virginians were "men of Anglo-Saxon descent," accustomed to dependents, which they acquired in the form of "African slaves, or European serfs." These "lords of the soil and masters of slaves" were, to a considerable extent, "Cavaliers, and [the] younger branches of noble English houses," and Virginia society was "a *continuation* of English society."[33] Washington did not assert this to praise Virginia, since he adduced a Cavalier origin to explain a strength which became a failing. As he saw it, the isolated conditions of a plantation life sealed off by slavery, and the absence of cities, led to powerful ideas of individualism and liberty among the Cavalier Virginians, which made the American Revolution possible. But isolation contributed to a debilitating absence of ideas of communal responsibility, without which a modern civilization of material and moral improvement was difficult to achieve. This was the standpoint of a modern Whig, an admirer of Macaulay, and a proponent of the middle class and the national debt. In short, Washington doubted that Cavaliers were fit for the modern world, and such doubt was characteristic of the Whigs, who wanted ballast against the storm of American modernity and often turned to ethnicity and Anglophilia as a store of experience which might teach the trick of continuity and survival.

This Cavalier theory, something warm and reassuring to carry into a future which Virginians had every reason to mistrust, was vulnerable to evidence. More exact historians than Washington were not convinced. Hugh Blair Grigsby, to whom all Virginian historians were inferior in knowledge, never accepted the idea of the Cavaliers and was insistent that Virginia was settled, rather, by "thousands of Cromwellians—the bone and sinew of the British people, who gave that colony its peculiar cast." In Grigsby's case, ethnicity endorsed political ideology; he was of Scottish descent and a Jeffersonian. For Grigsby, Whiggery would not do, because too elitist. Virginians might be chivalrous, not because they were "the miserable offshoots of the British aristocracy," but because of their experience as slaveholders and tobacco planters.[34] The Cavalier myth was, irreducibly, a condescension to those not Cavalier, and such pretensions deeply irritated Grigsby. Rather, he was convinced that there had been a great historic struggle of the plain folk of the Anglo-Saxons with the Norman yoke, which had been transferred to American soil. At least for Grigsby, to be Anglo-Saxon was something different from being English, a thing older and truer.

Hence aspects of Southern intellectual culture were structured by ethnic loyalties. But it would be wrong to overstress the burden of this. Few felt ethnicity to be a bounded thing, which demanded exclusive loyalty. One might know one's heritage, but this need not circumscribe one's self. You might inherit the language of one's family, but it was good to know other languages, too. Intellectual culture was peculiarly associated with multi-lingualism, with fluency in ancient and foreign tongues, whose acquisition was the serious business of anyone aspirant to the life of the mind.

Southern culture, for example, amply furnished instruction in the ancient languages, and the place was full of people who knew the gerund, the ablative absolute, and *oratio obliqua*. On the whole, Latin was more prominent than Greek, though a surprising amount of the latter was normal, and faintly prestigious, especially to those ignorant of it. There was, to be sure, dispute over the utility of the ancient languages. Thomas Grimké strenuously argued for their diminution in education, and undergraduates habitually found them overrated, though the classics were defended to them as necessary preparation for the learned professions. Of the two, Greek had less utility to the lawyer or doctor, though it did vaguely instruct in republicanism and honed the skills of oratory. The experience of reading Greek was thought to be aesthetic, even sensual, though also (the uninformed did not always realize) vulgar, because it was a literature which waved phalluses. While Latin was thought to inculcate rigor, Greek was thought to prompt sublimity. The consequence was that the teaching of Greek was often imprecise, since the rigor of a meddling intellect might despoil the exquisite passion. It was usual for the South's classicists to deprecate the classical training which had produced them. Still, Hugh Legaré, James Warley Miles, George Frederick Holmes, Thomas Caute Reynolds, William James Rivers, all were serious classicists. Basil Gildersleeve was the greatest classical scholar produced by American culture in the nineteenth century, the founder of its professional philology. Dozens were knowledgeable about the language and literature of the ancients, without any pretension to scholarly precision. Thousands more were influenced by the classics, saw them as a touchstone for their culture, a measure by which it might be judged.

Beyond the ancient languages were the modern. French mattered most, but Spanish and Italian were surprisingly common, and German grew in importance. French was considered a necessary civilized acquirement, even beyond its practical value in a society which embraced Louisiana and a culture which sent many people to Europe, for diplomacy, business, or pleasure. With so much Latin and Greek in curricula, however, little time was left for other languages, and even French was not always standard. Italian tended to be acquired by those who planned to visit Italy, as a byproduct of neoclassical enthusiasms. Among serious scholars, Italian literature had still a high reputation: Tasso, Ariosto, Dante, Machiavelli were supposed to form a part, albeit minor, of the armory of the accomplished philosophe. But, as the fourth or fifth language, it could be easily squeezed out. Increasingly, German displaced it and came to challenge French itself, because the number of Southern intellectuals who came to cultivate German, its language, literature, and philosophy, was remarkable. Robert Henry wrote on Goethe and worked at a translation of Niebuhr. Legaré self-consciously took up the study of German while he was chargé d'affaires in Brussels in the early 1830s, the better to understand German classical scholarship and literature, and, as has been shown, a large number of Southerners went to Germany to study, formally and informally. But others, though they seem never to have visited Germany, made a serious study of the language, including James Henley Thornwell, Moses Ashley Curtis, George Frederick Holmes, Basil Manly Jr., and John Young Bassett.

All these foreign words allowed Southerners access to a wider world. When we come to consider libraries and print culture, it will become clearer what proportion of intellectual life was formed by languages other than English. But even the exogenous could be used to comprehend what was indigenous and local, the topic to which it will now be useful to turn.

AMONG SELF-DESCRIPTIONS, the sense of coming from a locality loomed large. When Henry Augustine Washington looked at the Virginian world inherited from the colonial period, he saw localism as its characteristic. Virginia was but a "a number of little societies scattered through the country, each with a distinct organization," a colony which "proceeded upon the principle of leaving each of these little societies all the power which could abide there, and carrying to the great central society only so much as was absolutely necessary to the ends of social order." A decade earlier, John C. Calhoun had said of Daniel Webster: "I do not censure him for his local feelings. The Author of our being never intended that creatures of our limited faculties should embrace with equal intenseness of affection the remote and the near."[35]

Locality took many forms. There were states, regions, counties, and cities. Of these, most important was loyalty to a state, because it was in states that law, culture, and manners most powerfully intermingled. States had widely different origins, and all were idiosyncratic, something of which their residents were acutely aware. The Marylander was conscious of Catholic toleration, the Virginian of Jamestown and George Washington, the South Carolinian of Francis Marion and Charles II; each state had its peculiar mix, an awareness of which the antebellum years enriched.

Whatever else a state was, it was a legal fact. It had a constitution and laws which defined rights and obligations, controlled property, including that of slaves, possessed a politics, structured marriage and divorce (or the lack of it), monitored many of the rules of finance and trade, provided higher education, and represented its citizens to the nation and the world. As between state and nation, the state was incomparably the more influential upon the life of citizen and noncitizen alike. As Abel P. Upshur put it, "In all the daily business of life, we act under the protection and guidance of the State governments. . . . There is nothing dear to our feelings or valuable in our social condition, for which we are not indebted to their protecting and benignant action."[36]

In the years before 1860 an intellectual's life could begin to be occupied with attending and speaking to state historical societies and agricultural societies, undertaking state geological surveys, running state Bible societies, giving sermons to state denominational organizations, and writing textbooks for state schools. A large number of periodicals began to be published: religious magazines like the *Kentucky Missionary and Theological Magazine* (1812– 14), agricultural journals like the *Virginia Farmer* (1829–33), educational journals like the *North Carolina Common School Journal* (1856–57), literary journals like the *Arkansas Magazine* (1854), historical journals like the *Virginia Historical Register* (1848–53), and journals dedicated to medicine, science, and the law, like the *Maryland Medical Recorder* (1829–32), the *Georgia Botanic Journal and College Sentinel* (1847–48), and the *Carolina Law Journal* (1830–31). Such insistent cultural affiliation strengthened a sense of mission and belonging, a mystical obligation that informed even those who had left the state.

The ritual discourses, by which many of these periodicals and state societies were launched and confirmed, provide clues as to their meaning. William Cabell Rives, speaking to Virginia Historical Society in 1847, showed how state history undertaken in a federation could be a matter for anxiety, because it might legitimate what his friend Legaré had once called "centrifugal tendencies." On the one hand, Rives complained about the "false glare of *national* honors" which led Virginians to forget a duty to their state. On the other hand, he insisted that Virginia retained a stake in "our glorious confederacy." He squared this circle by imagining it was "a law of our moral nature" to begin with the local attachment, which, if adequately strong, radiated outward. To states were given the great tasks of modern development—internal improvements, schools, factories—whose strength at home would lead to enhanced influence abroad. Hence "state patriotism" was an instrument of "progressive improvement." With this, William Henry Trescot in 1859 mostly agreed. "If an American be asked abroad of what country are you," he said, "his first impulse is to answer, I am a New Yorker, a Virginian, a Massachusetts man, or a Carolinian, as the fact may be. Whatever his pride in his nationality, his home instincts and affections are bounded by State lines." But, for Trescot, states were the main power in the land, predominant even in Washington. A president had to consult state representatives in matters of patronage; a senator was only efficacious insofar as he was "the expression of his State."[37] Nonetheless, Trescot had also a sense that history, locality, and self were interwoven. In this he concurred with Rives, not least in worrying about declension. Localism was often a jeremiad; it lamented loss in order to urge improvement.

Though the state was an intellectual and moral focus, state governments themselves were only perfunctorily interested in sponsoring the institutions of intellectual and cultural life. A formal charter, the odd room, the occasional tiny appropriation, the donation of a reluctant librarian was as far as they ever went. Unlike the federal government, states had almost no patronage for intellectuals, they could offer no embassies and consulships, no customs houses. An intellectual society needed different attachments, and best was a prosperous civic culture which could provide a reliable audience, a merchant class for subventions, a series of institutions which might assist the life of the mind, such as a club, a lyceum, a reading room, an archive, and a library. In most cases, a city provided the base and a state, it was hoped, would provide an audience.

The language used to describe a state was familial, and usually feminine. Grigsby was profligate of maternal imagery for Virginia: "Behold our beloved mother! How beautiful she seems! Pure as she is beautiful, good as she is great!" Of course, mothers could be demanding, could suffer at the hands of her wayward children, might be abandoned by the expatriate, and there might be sibling rivalry. Being humanized, states could seem individuals who might think with a single mind, and thereby a state became more than the sum of its citizens. "*Virginians* will cooperate. But not Virginia. The *mind* of the State will act," Beverley Tucker once said to James Henry Hammond.[38] A state, like any individual or family member, might acquire a nickname—the Old North State, the Old Dominion, the Palmetto State—and be an object of love and service, and might even stand in a relationship to God, by being blessed by the deity, or cursed, or admonished.

These were heavy burdens of obligation, fashioned to strike at an individual's most vulnerable emotions and loyalties. In a Romantic age, the state might be enlisted to confirm emotional richness, alienation, and complexity. Sometimes there was anti-cosmopolitanism, as when in 1843 George Frederick Holmes reflected on those who disparaged local attachments. Speaking against himself (born in Guiana, educated in England, living in South Carolina, soon to move to Virginia, later to teach in Mississippi), Holmes hazarded that the rooted man was a better citizen "than he whose fancies are ranging all around the compass, and whose estimation of his place of abode is measured invariably by the amount of rice, cotton, tobacco, or corn, which the adjacent fields will produce."[39] Since so many did migrate, it was helpful deliberately to promote local feelings, to undertake the work of invention by way of invigorating selves, by older states riveting loyalty, by new ones creating it.

For modern nations, most of the elaboration of their iconography, symbol, and ritual was a product of the late nineteenth century. In Southern states, a little was done in the earlier part of the century, though only a little. Each state had a coat of arms and a militia (with the attendant heraldry of arms), but only Texas had an official flag before the Civil War, an inheritance of its brief career as an independent republic. A few states acquired symbols, the pelican for Louisiana and the palmetto for South Carolina, but these were informal and vernacular. The natural foci of iconography, the state capitals, were often migrant in these years, as cities struggled for possession of their symbolism and patronage. In states which predated 1776, the concrete imagery of a more ancient history stayed in the old capitals like Williamsburg and were mostly British and royalist (statues of William Pitt and the like), while new places like Baton Rouge had to commence de novo. In these latter, there grew up a modest collection of architecture, statuary, and portraiture, which gave the state some meaning for the eye. But, in general, antebellum Southern states were niggardly, reluctant to spend money on artists, and the statehouses themselves were ambivalent statements of state identity. Their styles were cosmopolitan: Jefferson's statehouse in Richmond was modeled upon the Maison Carrée in Nimes, that for Kentucky in Frankfort was in the Greek Revival style, and that for Georgia in Milledgeville was Gothic. Hence iconography sent mixed and often federal signals. The Georgia statehouse had "nine full-length portraits of early state and national leaders," and "national" was characteristic, since George Washington was popular throughout the South, in Richmond carved in modern dress, in North Carolina in Caesarian armor and cloak.[40] Rather, concrete expressions of state pietas often came from individuals and voluntary associations, as with an 1859 statue of Henry Clay which was commissioned not by the Commonwealth of Kentucky but by the Ladies' Clay Association of Virginia.

When states began to mandate public schools in the 1850s, there developed an increased market for school textbooks, that instrument of state patriotism. North Carolina, intellectually among the least regarded of Southern states, had been most energetic in this effort. In 1851 Calvin H. Wiley published *The North-Carolina Reader*, before becoming the superintendent of the new North Carolina public school system and after having been a lawyer, newspaper editor, and historical novelist. The book was a hybrid, partly intended to help students with their reading and life by laying down rules for pronunciation and dispensing assorted bits of moral advice. ("When you are alone, think of your faults; when with others correct those faults.")[41] But it also provided chronologies of historical events and inventions, an almanac, a glossary of popular terms, and a list of common foreign phrases. Further, it had literary selections, many of them of North Carolinian provenance, but others not, notably in the section on poetry, which had pieces by Whittier, Pope, Longfellow, Milton, and others.

Wiley's main purposes were patriotic, even mystical. If North Carolinians only darkly understood themselves, he thought them partly at fault for lacking common feelings and turning to wayward cosmopolitans, who taught only self-contempt. For such cosmopolitans, "the schools, the books, the fabrics of their own country are not worthy of their patronage; and the idea of permitting their children to learn to read in the work of a North Carolina author, and which does not treat of far off places and foreign customs, cannot for a moment be tolerated." This deference to books and authors who shared a silence about North Carolina ought to end. Identity, not alienation, was the solution to despair. North Carolina was "sacred," a compact of generations.[42]

For the rest, the book benignly toured the state's landscape, furnished a history from Walter Raleigh to the end of the American Revolution with only a brief glance after 1789, and offered selections from various North Carolinian writers. Throughout, Wiley spared no pains to impress upon the young reader his Whig philosophy of internal improvement, especially the value of a public education system. Wiley's vision was of a diverse North Carolina, with a complicated flora and fauna, and "a great variety of people, of all classes and professions, of all trades, and of almost every kind of genius."[43] The state must resolve into harmonious diversity what might otherwise occasion strife, and, in this endeavor, landscape and climate conspired to help. All was various, yet mysteriously all was one.

Wiley was frankly xenophobic, but his dark "foreigners" were not necessarily Europeans or Yankees. He seemed mostly to indict other Southern states, those to the west who were drawing away the sons of the Old North State, those to the north and south. (The despising of North Carolina was a hobby of Virginians and South Carolinians, so this was a natural reaction.) North Carolina was "a land between extremes; it knows not the rigours of a Northern winter, and it is free from the tornadoes and earthquakes of the South. Equally exempt it is from the gloomy fanaticism and chilling selfishness of the north, and from the bloody scenes and blazing passions of the South." Such animosity was not uncharacteristic of the antebellum years. Even Andrew Jackson noticed it: the social diversities of the different states, he once told Congress, were "greatly exaggerated by jealousies and that spirit of rivalry so inseparable from neighboring communities."[44]

"Louisiana is not my country," John Randolph observed firmly in 1814. "I respect as much the opinions of the people of London as of the Western States." The western South was scarcely unaware of such opinions, nor lacking in its own contempts. Oscar Lieber went geologizing in Alabama in 1851 and wrote of an encounter: "S.C. has . . . not many admirers here. The other day a blacksmith accosted me, 'Capt. I say, now you'se from Sou Calina, is you? Well maybe you can tell me vot she's a kicking up such a dust about? Seem's to me as long as I can remember, an I aint young nether, she's bin a kicking up about some G- d- thing or other. Now you see I's a unedicated man stranger. I cant read a d- lick, to save my life, but my daughter can, and she reads the bible to me pretty near all day, be Gad. &c &c I believe as how God has some respect for unedicated people.' "[45]

In fact, there were relatively few occasions for states to come into formal competition, except in Washington. This was not the case for intrastate conflicts, which were the currency of state politics. But the idea of sub-regions (the word itself was not yet in use) was not as highly developed as it became in the late nineteenth century, when local color novels reified the identities which existed before the Civil War, when nomenclature was fluid. Then there were east and west, Tidewater and backcountry, Tidewater and western country, low country and west, upland and lowland, or middle country. The old usage of "backcountry," common in the eighteenth century, had begun to be superseded in the 1790s, but Basil Manly could refer to a "back-country use of [a] phrase" as late as 1834. Wiley's *North-Carolina Reader* divided the state into small chunks: the Albemarle region, Nag's Head, a vague "region south of Albemarle," the Pamlico country, the Cape Fear country, the Upland regions, the midland districts, the mountain region.[46] All Southern states, especially the older ones, had these nuances, tending to diminish to the west because there the states were so recently settled that such tribalisms had yet to refine.

As for counties and parishes, they had some force as sites for loyalty. They, too, might indicate a people, and a man might be denoted as being from this county or that. The historian J. G. M. Ramsey was "of Mecklenberg County," just as David James McCord was "of St. Mathew's Parish." This might have ancient English resonances ("Randolph of Roanoke"), or it could mean little beyond a postal address. The seasonal migrations of planters weakened this form of identity, even as it provided occasions for its expression, because in the urban drawing room someone might be introduced as being "from Horry" or "from Ascension Parish." At colleges, students came from counties, rather as in medieval universities undergraduates had a *natio*. However, it was rare that a county was a focus for writing, far less so than in the twentieth century. But it did happen, most remarkably in a piece written by Frederick Porcher for the *Southern Quarterly Review*. His "Historical and Social Sketch of Craven County" (1854) is the ancestor of the Yoknapatawpha novels as well as the descendant of *Tom Jones*, an affectionate elegy written from somewhere else, wherein the city dweller looks back on the countryside of youth and pronounces it better than the anomie of the boulevards.

In being skeptical of the city, Porcher was not as typical of Southerners as modern opinion, fed upon a more dramatic relationship between town and country, has had it. Many in the South could quote "O fortunatos nimium," and some even believed it, but the imagery of Vergil's *Georgics*, the contrast of the farm and Rome, led more into benign celebrations of the rural, less into assaults upon the Southern city. For, with the great exception of New Orleans and the partial one of Charleston, no city was large enough or sufficiently insulated from the life of its countryside to generate the sharp differentiations of city and country found in European discourse, ancient and modern. The Southern city was full of country people, the country full of city people, and the contrast was a differentiation within the experience of a migratory individual, less often between two opposed groups of people who never met. It was more common among Southern intellectuals to find assaults upon the tedium of rural life or small towns. In this the South was the inheritor of a European tradition which celebrated the civic. Athens, Rome, Venice were models and warnings. Almost no one aspired to duplicate London, but Edinburgh, with its modern intellectual achievement, was another matter. Every three months, a new copy of the *Edinburgh Review* would show up to remind everyone what an energetic provincial city might accomplish.

So cities could offer a powerful instinct of identity. "I was a Charlestonian first, Carolinian next, and then a southerner," was how Basil Gildersleeve remembered the hierarchy of his antebellum loyalties. The dispersion of culture across so vast a territory as the South posed a problem, even as it suggested a mission. Would the city's culture be strong enough to direct the countryside? Or would its voice be lost in the voiceless tracks, the bayous, the coves? The Society for the Advancement of Literature and Science in the State of Tennessee thought that such a mission might succeed, but Edward Johnston doubted it. He thought emigration from the Atlantic states to the West impoverished "intellectual improvement." In "thinly peopled communities" there was too little a "spirit of society . . . to give grace and elegance to the understandings that it controls." Hence, "a separate class . . . cannot be found, that occupies itself with letters alone; nor is it possible that we should possess, in such a state of things, a single one of those more determined scholars, patient and quiet toilers in the mine of thought, who obscurely dig out for others the deep treasures of the intellect."[47] In short, there was no one to talk to.

Curiously, the city was less often the subject of discourse. William Gilmore Simms published *The Charleston Book* in 1845, with selections from fifty-eight authors associated with the city, but none of the pieces concerned themselves with Charleston itself. Still, there were things, here and there. There are memoirs like Charles Fraser's *Reminiscences of Charleston* (1854), a handful of tourist impressions like Albert J. Pickett's *Eight Days in New Orleans* (1847), and a very few histories like John Peyton Little's *Richmond, the Capital of Virginia, Its History* (1851). But almost all of the histories of Southern cities are postbellum; the earlier years show little to compare to the bittersweet elegance of Grace King's *New Orleans: The Place and the People* (1895). There were some antebellum guides, as with *Norman's New Orleans and Environs* (1845), and novelists liked, sometimes, to set their stories in cities. Though Simms's mind more often ran to narratives of rivers and states, as with *The Yemassee: A Romance of Carolina* (1835), he also wrote *Marie de Berniere: A Tale of the Crescent City* (1855). On the whole, however, it is more striking that Southern writers, sitting in their town houses, walking to their law offices, resting on their piazzas, coming home from their literary clubs, seldom bothered to narrate what surrounded them but looked past the city to the valley of the Shenandoah, or to Swallow Barn, or to rustic taverns where men's eyes were gouged out.

AS SHARPLY AS ANY Americans, Southerners knew that the world had its social distinctions. But they were clearer about how class worked than how it might be defined, because they inhabited a fluid world. Race and gender seemed to have some fixity, even to gain in focus as the century progressed. Ethnicity was looser, as was locality, since people might intermarry and migrate. But social status was most profligate of confusions. The word "class" itself offered little hope of clarity, for it meant little more than classification. A "class" might be any group of people who shared something: the "senior class" of a college, a "class of readers," a "class of editors & politicians," even what elsewhere might be designated as a race. In 1831 Moses Ashley Curtis shuddered at news of the Nat Turner revolt and observed: "No class of beings I ever heard of take such vile advantage of favors as the blacks."[48]

A reluctance to reify the idea of social class was partly an inheritance from the eighteenth century, which had spoken eclectically of social divisions, and later Southerners would be equally miscellaneous, mostly because they were caught by the conflicting usages of various discourses layered in their minds.

First, they had inherited from early modern England the conception of "orders," which had itself supplanted the medieval conceptions of "estates." To be sure, Southerners no longer spoke of "sorts of men" or of "degrees," and all manner of English ranks had disappeared: cottagers, burgesses, husbandmen. But "freeholder" and "freeman" remained, as did "gentry" and "gentlemen" and "ladies." The term which most powerfully survived was "master," so much so that its old referent, "servant," was transmitted to those who were more than servants, being slaves. ("Servant" was the usage of the domestic realm, "slave" of the public realm.). Piled on these terms, second, was the neo-Harringtonian language of interests, sharpened by the political economy of Adam Smith, which suggested that society was divided into economic groups. This conception, in turn, was influenced by the categories of professions: a poor lawyer and a rich one, a wealthy planter and an indigent farmer, a bishop and an itinerant preacher might share a class, even if they did not share an income. Third, by the late 1840s, there began to develop the Victorian conception of a threefold, horizontally divided class system (upper, middle, lower), in which the middle class was regarded as possessing moral primacy by being the respectable guarantor of social order and progress. Little wonder, then, that critics might run discourses together. In 1858 Thomas C. Reynolds used language which was simultaneously early modern, Harringtonian, and modern, and even hinted at the postmodern: "It is but natural that men should stand by their interests and their 'class,' whether high or low in our fictitious social scale."[49]

Nonetheless, there was a tendency to define a social continuum from high to low, often broken sharply in the middle. In 1855 the white society of colonial Virginia might be explained as "divisible into two classes: an order of proprietors who owned the larger and more valuable estates, which were cultivated by slaves, and a much more numerous class who owned few or none and derived their support in part or wholly from the labour of their own hands."[50] This twofold division could be explained, as here, solely upon economic terms. But others saw moral issues, if one reasoned that prosperity encouraged probity and poverty taught crime. In this case, the continuum was severed, because the division between virtue and vice, productivity and idleness, was thought to be abrupt.

If one followed this continuum from high to low, however, one encountered many contradictory perceptions. There was, for example, a notion that there was a Southern "aristocracy," though Northerners tended more frequently to believe in this. For Southerners themselves, the construct was becoming tenuous and ironical. The South had no House of Lords, no orders of chivalry, no formal legal differentiations, no primogeniture, none of the rules which marked genuine aristocracies. All these had been proscribed by the American constitution, endorsed by its Southern and Northern drafters alike. In London and Paris, rich Southerners tended to feel discomfited by liveried servants and armorial markings emblazoned on carriage doors. In the South itself, there was a reluctance officially to certify and measure rank. There was no Southern *Debrett*, not even the equivalent of the listings of best families which was beginning in New York. Francis Lieber, a Prussian acquainted with the European meaning of aristocracy, was right to observe of wealthier Southerners, "They are arrogant indeed but not aristocrats."[51]

The political language of the American Revolution powerfully militated against candid pretensions of rank. In the language of Jacksonianism, aristocracy was a lively target, but so it was in the language of Whiggery, which aimed its arrows at "King Andrew." Almost everyone abused aristocracy, and very few identified with it. As George Fitzhugh put it in 1859, "In America everybody is ashamed of low ancestry because it is low, and everybody, almost, ashamed of respectable parentage, and afraid to acknowledge it, lest he should be slandered and abused as a 'rich aristocrat.'"[52] The only exceptions were those who lamented aristocracy's disappearance as a reproach to a leveling democracy, people safe in the knowledge that what they admired was no longer available.

What there was, rather, was not an aristocracy but rich people with powerful kinship networks, who owned large houses, many slaves, and oil paintings by Thomas Sully, who wore new fashions from Paris, and who poured their China tea from delicate silver into fine porcelain. Such people lived apart. Not a few among these "gay and fashionable" confessed a pride in their superiority.[53] Nonetheless, it was widely acknowledged that good manners might exist independently of high caste and that arrogance could disfigure the reputation of even the lofty. Hence caste was informal and, so, was not caste. This only partially served the interests of the socially mobile, because it made social distinctions not unimportant, only subtle. Insiders could judge, approve, or reprobate the quality of the parvenu by the skill with which the aspirant learned the arcana.

Families got most points for being wealthy, especially if wealth was expressed tastefully. One got a few points for having longevity of affluence, but the antebellum South was little interested in genealogy, not entirely from indisposition, mostly from the lack of the antiquarian infrastructure necessary for the hobby's pursuit. Sustained habitation of a particular house or plantation meant very little, uncommon enough to be notable. There was a presumption of mutability. Hugh Legaré once complained of this indifference to place: "We have no local attachments, generally speaking—nothing bears the *pretium affectionis* in our eyes. If an estate, a residence in town, a country seat, rises a little beyond what we are accustomed to think its value, it is sold without any hesitation."[54]

Good blood lines might forgive a small shortage of ready cash, but not for very long, while a great amount of money excused almost any amount of obscure birth, as long as the new man acquired some taste. Singleness of ethnic origin mattered little. Having a famous member in a family helped; politicians were acceptable (if they were successful), but Founding Fathers were best. Merchants were fine, though planters were a touch better, while having both in a family was advisable, as insurance. Professionals varied in standing: lawyers were respectable, doctors were very little so, while ministers were, only if their denomination had status. Religion was of some consequence, though there was little sense in the higher reaches of society that a family was required to pray together. As Caroline Gilman once indicated, there was a pecking order for Protestant denominations, which was, in descending order, Episcopalian, Presbyterian, Methodist, Baptist, and then assorted evangelical sects. (In Louisiana, the prevalence of Roman Catholicism changed these rules.) Early in the century, a casual indifference to religion was something of a mark of social elevation, but by 1860, as evangelicalism colonized the heights of society, this had abated.

Some lofty people, if of Federalist instinct, spoke freely of "the mob." But such language could be heard lower down in the social scale, too, because it only marked off those who thought themselves independent and well-behaved from those deemed to be indisciplined and malleable. Yet mobs and beggars were hard to find in the South, which had little reason to fear a jacquerie of the dispossessed. (Slaves were another matter). Since unemployment was very scarce, this mob worked, yet its members were not known as the working class, and very seldom even as the laboring class. When in 1845 William Gilmore Simms used the term "working classes," he meant slaves, and they lay in apposition to "the wealthy proprietors of the soil."[55] Rather, Southerners spoke of the "lower classes" or "the common people." They were the Paddies who dug ditches for railroads, or the tavern keepers who dispensed whiskey, or the men who shifted dung in public stables, or the white prostitutes who wore rouge. The lower classes were those from whom gentility recoiled, those who dressed badly, smelled worse, spoke in obscenities, and fought with their bare hands. These were never numerous, but their numbers grew with urbanization. Since Southern cities followed the old pattern in being unsegregated by class, rich and poor lived cheek by jowl and saw each other constantly. The genteel person abroad had often to keep a handkerchief to a nose. Habits of condescension were a means of moral insulation, when physical isolation was hard to achieve. In the countryside, too, were lower classes, differently estranged. They were those in the hinterland, away from the great commercial zones of Southern agriculture. They lived amid clay hills, in swamps, in a quasi-mythical Lubber Land, and were troublingly remote, in need of annexation to a world which might civilize them.

The power of this vision of upper and lower classes meant that the Old South had an impoverished conception of a middle class. There were those lower than the higher, higher than the lower, but few who were middling. This omission was not unusual. England in the early modern era had been innocent of the idea, and only after the 1790s did it come falteringly into use. Much hinged on the French Revolution and the coming of industrialism. Edmund Burke argued that a middle class was a bulwark against Jacobin excess, and Karl Marx hazarded that a bourgeoisie might be the vanguard of social transformation. However, the South, feeling relatively little pressure on its class structure—its Peterloos concerned slavery, not class—felt little need to develop such a conception. By the late 1840s, however, there is some evidence that a quasi-Victorian idea of a middle class was beginning to develop, such a class being defined as urban, respectable, and a guarantor of social order and progress. But this idea was inhibited by the porousness of the distinction between rural and urban in the South, and by the prevalence of ideas about gentlemen and ladies. "In this country every man considers himself a gentleman, no matter what may be his social status," Daniel Hundley was to complain.[56]

In 1829 Thomas Dew suggested that it was the "moral disadvantage" of manufactures that "they have a tendency to divide society into two distinct classes, capitalists and labourers, who are separated at too great a distance from each other," and that "there is no middle class to form the link between the highest and the lowest, and whose example and instruction always operate most beneficially on the latter, and exert, too, a very salutary influence on the former." This was close to the mid-Victorian moral ideal of the middle class, but Dew was not describing anything around him in Virginia; in fact, he was arguing that even modern industrial societies lacked such a body of people. In his Southern world, there were other terms of reference, such as "plain, humble, unpretending people," or even just "the others." These other people paid their bills at the local merchant, went to church and sat near the back in the cheaper pews, and had a few items in their homes which showed a respect for gentility, not a pianoforte but a few pieces of lace.[57] They might or might not own slaves, but they always owned some property. They were distinguishable because, being respectable, they might mix with their betters, who granted them hospitality, though not without congratulating themselves upon their latitude.

Such plain folk might become less plain, two slaves might become eight, a pianoforte might appear in a drawing room, a wife might withdraw from candle-making, a son might go to college. Southern society did not have a name for them, except those with "respectable pursuits." Such respectability might blend into gentility, the quality of being a gentleman. In theory, any-one with good manners might be a gentleman. In practice, one had to be very well off. One of "the other people" was almost never gentle, one of middling rank might be, and a person of the best society more or less had to be, if place was to be honorably sustained. The cynical truth of this some understood, some denied. In 1846 Lieber tried to sketch the "character of a gentleman" and offered an ideal portrait of someone honorable, self-possessed, refined, honest, and courageous. William Grayson smiled at this earnestness. There was, after all, scarcely a principle ascribed to this cardboard figure uncon-tradicted by experience, he observed, for honorable men forgot to pay their debts, swore, gambled, and drank excessively, all without losing their status as gentlemen. So what was honor? As William Paley had observed, it was the observance of "the conventional code by which men of the world seek to regulate their conduct." The acknowledged gentleman revolved around, rather than embodied, this Protean quality. After all, these were "men of the world."[58] One was supposed to do one's best, but lapses did not disqualify, if here and there a respectable number of these demands were met and a few were not. Gentlemen, who ratified each other's standing, understood this laxity. Honor understood the fallibilities of dishonor.

So the Southern social structure had its peculiarities, its own language, though nothing that a stranger who had been in London or Boston or Cincin-nati would have found unintelligible. Still, things were afoot in Friedrich Engels's Manchester that were little visible from Alabama. Laboring classes were becoming proletariats, middling ranks were becoming a middle class, "capitalists" were being freshly described. European books and articles came into Southern culture, which, as a result, sometimes saw itself with foreign eyes. The new discipline of political economy, written in the wynds of Edin-burgh, the arrondisements of Paris, and near the cloisters of a Cambridge college, was seeking to make new sense of society and, thereby, came to reify concepts of class even for societies which Smith, Sismondi, and Malthus never saw.

Few Southerners, in fact, wrote about social structure. They produced reams about race, gender, politics, and religion, but class did not often seem worth a sustained analysis. The great exception was Daniel R. Hundley, who published in 1860 a book called *Social Relations in Our Southern States*. He wrote as a quasi-outsider, because, though he came from Alabama and was educated mostly in the South, he ended up in Chicago, where he wrote his book as both satire and analysis.

Hundley divided the Southern world into eight classes, all of them defined by males: gentlemen, the middle classes, Southern Yankees, cotton snobs, Southern yeomen, Southern bullies, poor white trash, and Negro slaves. Several of Hundley's categories—middle classes, Southern Yankees, bullies— were very little to be found in antebellum discourse. Poor white trash was very unusual, though less abrupt versions occur in the late antebellum years when rapid economic growth exacerbated social tensions. At one level, this means that Hundley is an unreliable guide to how antebellum Southerners saw their world. At another, it suggests that contemporary usage was so unfixed that categories might be invented, *ad libidinem*, in an attempt to freeze the fluidity of things.

Hundley's categories fell, more or less, into pairs, in which one was bad, another good. In the upper reaches of wealth, there was the gentleman, who was shadowed by the parvenu cotton snob. In the middling, there were the good middle classes and the crass Southern Yankees. At the bottom, there were worthy yeomen and (here things doubled up), bad bullies and poor white trash. Beyond the bottom were the slaves, an undivided mass with almost no good qualities. What distinguished these pairs were morals and manners, ancestry and physiognomy, issues profoundly connected in Hundley's imagination. For him, virtue was not arrogated exclusively to any one class. This judgment distinguished him from those nineteenth-century social commentators who exalted the virtue of the middle class and complained about the upper and working classes, or, for that matter, those socialists who exalted the working and damned the middle and upper class. For Hundley, there was a line sweeping vertically downward through a horizontally segmented society and dividing the moral from the immoral. Hence he was remarkably uninterested in class antagonism; his classes sat next to each other, with a curious detachment. In this he sat squarely in an American tradition; Jacksonians especially had argued that one might have classes without class warfare.

A respect for the body, for the ancestral, marks a gulf between Hundley's time and our own. Modern sociologists and historians tend to see social behavior as contextual. Biology is little, because we have learned to fear those for whom it is everything. Not knowing of Auschwitz, Hundley did not usually explain society by circumstances, but by physique. He devoutly believed that "[t]here is a great deal in *blood*. Who ever yet knew a Godolphin that was sired by a miserable scrub? or who ever yet saw an athletic, healthy human being, standing six feet in his stockings, who was the off-spring of runtish forefathers, or of wheezy, asthmatic, and consumptive parents?" This language of *blood*, which has now dwindled to unfelt metaphor, was vivid to Southerners; it explained many things. Grigsby saw people on his Southern travels and observed, "When I see a handsome Carolinian, I am apt to enquire if he thinks he has any *Scotch* blood in his veins."[59] Hundley's question, "Who ever yet knew a Godolphin that was sired by a miserable scrub?" offers a partial explanation for this instinct. The South was a culture which bred horses and studied pedigrees, and examined a slave's teeth when buying. Blood was a part of class understanding.

In the multifarious categories of social groups, it was unclear whether those who gave much of their lives to expressing thought constituted a separable group, designated by themselves or others. The term "intellectuals" did not yet exist, nor did "the intelligentsia," though the noun "intellect" and the adjective "intellectual" did. By the late eighteenth century, the adjective denoted a quality roughly equivalent to "rational" or "pertaining to the understanding"; it was often used by those influenced by the psychological categories of Scottish commonsense philosophy. Thus Grigsby might write that a debating society was "well designed to whet the intellect and amuse the fancy of those who composed it," and thereby he distinguished separable components of the mind. Professions thought peculiarly to require rationality, especially the law or the academy, were distinguished by a larger admixture of such intellect. By extension, a country might have an intellect, that is, a significant quality of rationality in the conduct and comprehension of its affairs. The South being increasingly regarded as a cultural nation, it, too, might have such an intellectual quotient. So, by 1847, one might write of "the activity of Southern intellect."[60]

In later years, Southerners came to insist that the antebellum South had despised the thinker. The cases of William Gilmore Simms and Edgar Allan Poe were often adduced as evidence. And it is true that both of these suffered indignities, but they suffered less for being writers, more for being socially awkward. Poe drank too much and tended to fall on the floor. Simms talked too much, not always with as much knowledge as impetus, which was a fault of his writing too. In general, there was nothing vulgar about being a writer; it was a condition which neither gave nor detracted from status. The modern notion that writers are a breed apart, usefully unaccountable to ordinary behaviors, little existed in the South before 1860, though it was beginning to be available; they admired and knew about Coleridge and opium, after all. Simms himself especially knew that men of letters, elsewhere, were often thought to be marked by genius, the reputation for which might earn them the delicious sensualities of being lionized. But Byron, the exemplum, was a suspect model, and Hugh Legaré had delivered the verdict of his culture by insisting that Walter Scott was a genius, like Byron, but a gentleman, admirable for his probity and regularity of habits.

If a writer was anything socially, he or she was usually supposed to be a gentleman or lady, because a thinker was believed to need qualities necessary for gentility, hence it was common to see gentility adduced as evidence of intellectuality, and vice versa. In 1853, John Pendleton Kennedy wrote a letter of introduction to Washington Irving for the editor of the *Southern Literary Messenger*, John R. Thompson, whom he described as "a very worthy gentleman, and a man of fine literary talent and acquirement." Likewise, George Frederick Holmes was a "gentleman and scholar," a person of "manly intellect and sound scholarship, as well as experience and true judgement."[61]

Learning did not automatically confer gentility; these were overlapping, not identical categories. A college professor might be a gentleman, and it helped as a qualification for election. Edward Johnston, angling for a chair at the University of Virginia, thought it helpful to announce that "I am a gentleman, not a learned blackguard." But not all professors earned the grade. M. J. Williams of South Carolina College thought "that the opinion seemed to be current in S C that a Mathematician could not be a gentleman," and even those not mathematicians could fail the test.[62] But failing to be a gentleman and refusing to be one were clean different things. Many failed, but very few tried to fail, in order to prove that they possessed intellectual and moral originality superior to the pedestrian and genteel.

Still, intellectuals were deeply committed to the idea of differentiation, hierarchy, and rank. Being more learned, wiser, shrewder, and so better was what justified them. Intellectuals were above "the common mass," but they dwelled in that part of the uncommon empyrean which their broader social status conferred.[63] Some resented this, most did not. But, being firmly in society, they were partly formed by the structures of society, which not only suggested ways to classify men and women but prescribed how it might be possible to talk, write, and publish.

3 · A Volley of Words

Even when writing is done alone, intellectual life can depend on conversation. Yet talk is hard to reconstruct. However imperfect the answer, the question is worth asking. How did Southern thinkers converse?

Solitude and society was a problem, because the South had many acres and few people. In modern urban societies, alienation defends against the press of bodies and minds, but antebellum Southerners' difficulty was the other way, so they were inclined to disparage solitude and fear loneliness. The occasional Catholic ascetic might praise "la vie solitaire et contemplative," but he did so in the knowledge that he was surrounded by those who saw no point to "les mortifications volontaires." Rather, Southerners reached out to one another, and good talkers with ideas were a prized possession, while those lacking the gift were deprecated. Calhoun was especially deficient, as Louisa Preston once observed: "If he had asked how your family were, and you had answered . . . one of the children is ill; Mr Calhoun would have exclaimed—'Ah, but as I was saying, the concurrent majority,' etc., etc., & neither you or yours would possess his ear or heart one minute." But the sarcastic wit James Louis Petigru, the gadfly critic Littleton Waller Tazewell, the harrumphing eccentric John Randolph, the learned questioner Mitchell King, these and others were famous for their conversation, which was regarded as an influence. Hugh Blair Grigsby, especially, liked to set down table talk, "rich, various, and overflowing," and acted the Boswell for more than one Johnson. Most of their words have evaporated, but some were to survive. Petigru's remark that South Carolina was too small to be a nation but too large to be an insane asylum has, rightly, passed into legend. His mock expostulation, when hearing of the secession of Louisiana, deserved a similar fate for its succinct command of the illogicalities of constitutionality: "Good Lord . . . I thought we bought Louisiana."[1]

Even writers might be good conversationalists or compelling monologists. In the older generations, Thomas Cooper was notable enough that David McCord felt impelled to write down in a notebook Cooper's stories of days during the French Revolution, of Brissot and Robespierre, and of those who dined with Pitt and endured "the vacant stare of genius." In a later generation, William Gilmore Simms had a similarly hypnotic effect, at least on his literary juniors. "I can hear his voice," Paul Hamilton Hayne was to remember, "rolling in jovial thunder above a murmurous sea of conversation."[2]

Conversation has a social context; it is structured by patterns of when people meet or are kept apart. During an ordinary day, Southern urban men of letters might have several opportunities to talk (morning visits, dinner, evening parties, clubs), while women had fewer. However, there were few occasions for men and women not sharing a household to talk together, and almost none for both sexes that were formally dedicated to intellectual discourse, except for the sermon in church. Even at evening parties, men and women tended to drift into separate groups, except when the exigencies of flirtation or courtship pressed. A consequence was the absence in the South of a great institution of intellectual life, the salon. Women of mind and social presence who might otherwise have presided there—Louisa McCord, Susan Petigru King, Mary Chesnut—fared otherwise, were called masculine or fast when they hazarded informed opinions. This concerned them, and even some men worried about it. Thomas Dew, in writing about the French Revolution, talked of salon society with enthusiasm, though also looked upon it as a strange and gilded phenomenon. But many men, who preferred their women frivolous, were unworried by the salon's absence. Even Southern men who in France would have presumed the capacity of a woman for erudition might not in America. Such condescension was occasioned partly by fears that debauchery was the price of salon life. Southern men and women alike concluded that in abjuring the salon what was lost in female brilliance and influence was compensated for in female virtue. This had been Jefferson's opinion, despite or because of his flirtations with Maria Cosway. It was further presumed that, by reducing women's social and intellectual range, their enhanced virtue would improve the men, even when the men were not with their women.

So there were barriers to talking. As for the sounds of Southern speech, one can get some sense from Southern fiction, since the growth of dialogue as a way of telling stories and conveying meaning (until in William Faulkner there came to be little else) is a crucial fact of the South's literary history. But early works like Wirt's *Letters of a British Spy* (1803) have very little dialogue, and there is only a little more in Tucker's *Valley of the Shenandoah* (1824). To a modern ear, talk in the latter seems stilted, too precise in its diction, too much like an elegant quadrille. In early Southern fiction, voices were seldom permitted to give meaning. The author's narrative established the pace, which no single voice was allowed to disrupt, but only to illustrate. Evenness was all. This was no mere literary convention but a reflection of how higher culture saw conversation, as a reconciliation, a courtesy, a flowing outward from what was already decided, which was a person's character. To speak without knowing who you were was deeply undesirable to a Southern mind formed before 1820. So, in Tucker, exuberance was gently deprecated, even regarded as sinister. This is one reason why, in Tucker, only the language of the poor possessed exclamation marks, because the ill-educated were thought to be more heart than head.

Later, everyone was to have exclamation marks and there was among the voices a widening differentiation. Tucker had given his slaves better English than his Germans, for the former often spoke like gentlemen and ladies. In Simms, dialect became full blown, diminishing and differentiating, as with, "'Hi, missis, hi! Da me! Da Jinney! I jis' want for know od dem black people gone.'"[3] As for white people, there came to be a calibration of grammatical manglings, multiplying as one sank in the social scale or ventured into marginal ethnicities. Such amiable hauteur complicated what might otherwise be regarded as a growth of realism, since there is no reason to doubt but that the South was, in Simms's day, as it had been in Tucker's, alive with different voices, multiple accents, patois, and one can understand this more fully in Simms's fiction than in Tucker's.

In the seventeenth century, in the Anglophone world, there had been little disposition to standardize grammar, pronunciation, or spelling, though rather more (after the foundation of the Académie Française) in the Francophone. In Britain, this began to change by about 1760, with teachers of elocution making a living by erasing Scottish and Irish accents, and with books of grammar conducting a long siege against the premodern Babel. One justification for learning Latin had been its utility in putting a grammatical backbone into an English language deemed unhappily random compared to Cicero's Latinity. In time, there would be the order of the Oxford English Dictionary. Some of these regimenting impulses drifted to the South. Grammar was studied, though schools could be haphazard and colleges had often to take up the slack. However, correctness of grammar was more prized than pronunciation. Hugh Blair, the rhetorical guide used in colleges, when giving advice on pronunciation, intended mostly to instruct in matters of emphasis, pausing, audibility, pace, and modulation. Scot that he was, he was wary about reeducating accents and advised that, in speaking English, one should "follow nature."[4]

Few doubted there was a group of Southern pronunciations, though no one felt an obligation toward standardization. Equality of accents as between places was accepted, though caste and class were different matters. Louisa McCord, who reproved Harriet Beecher Stowe for making her characters in

Uncle Tom's Cabin speak like New Englanders, in contradistinction to "the idioms of our Southern tongue," confined her remarks to "Southern language in select society." Moreover, she made such subregional and class distinctions as to be conscious that "Mrs. Stowe . . . has certainly never been in any Southern state further than across the Kentucky line at most, & there in very doubtful society." So there was a sense of "Southern" as word usage, and this sense was notably articulated in the debate over Americanism in language. Some Southerners, in the neoclassical party of order, were anxious to preserve the language of the Augustans as a standard for American speech, not in order to prevent Americanism, but to preserve American society against centrifugal provincialisms and prevent reaching a point where "the Mississippian and the Virginian shall be as diverse as were the Athenian and the Macedonian." On the side of disorder were people like Simms, for whom vitality in language emerged from social mobility and migration, which occasioned transient difficulties but offered cultural gains. This was a vitality from which the writer ought to draw strength. As Simms put it, "to write *from* a people is to *write* a people."[5]

Many used new coinages like "improvement" and "demoralize" as a way of cocking a snoot at English Toryism. Others endorsed Noah Webster's campaign for Americanism in language and licensed "labor" not "labour," "traveled" not "travelled," though practice was inconsistent. In theory, Webster himself had been suspicious of localism, though he was often reproached for mistaking New Englandism for Americanism. So it was not straightforward where any Southern distinctiveness of language might fit into any notion of the American language. In general, Southerners had two options: they might see Southernism as the persistence of older English usages, or they might see it as one among many American divergences from English usage, not a reinforcement of a classical standard but an inventive defiance of *The Spectator*.

Speaking and writing were different things. The prose and poetry of the South were similar to those written in Boston or London in style, grammar, and tone. The eighteenth century had worked very hard to achieve such evenness. Few imagined that the vernacular should structure writing. Such a bifurcation was then the familiar condition of the English-speaking writer; Coleridge had a broad Devonshire accent, but did not strive to embody this in his writings, for all of the brave words in the preface to his and Wordsworth's *Lyrical Ballads* about the language of every day. Southerners presumed there were standards of correctness, even when (especially when) the vernacular was being portrayed. In the first edition of *Georgia Scenes*, Longstreet skittishly reinforced this point, that the reader should not take amiss "the coarse, inelegant, and sometimes ungrammatical language, which the writer represents himself as occasionally using; *that it is language accommodated to the capacity of the person to whom he represents himself as speaking.*"[6] The moral weight of intellectual society, when it came to the written language, lay with propriety, which was a recent and hard-fought possession, like the gentlemanly status of authors.

Viewed from the standpoint of slaves, free blacks, and those like Frederick Douglass who had freed themselves, the matter of language was differently complicated. It seems the case that the closer slaves were to the household of masters and mistresses, the more they were forced or wanted to speak "correct" English. The gentlemanly accents of slaves in Tucker and Kennedy's novels might not have been inaccurate transcriptions. Douglass, when speaking to abolitionist meetings, resented the pressure on him to speak as Northerners presumed a slave would speak. For reformers, the moral authority to denounce the crime of slavery was reinforced by (what they thought were) the manglings they heard in black English. For Douglass, wanting to be more than an ex-slave was of a piece with a command of a pure English, which might signify his membership of a greater, intellectual community. Besides, as he said, he had grown up more with white children than field hands and his English was less Creole than his Northern audiences imagined. Like any parvenu, he had to speak better than those whose world he was joining, to prove his worth. For free blacks in the South, it seems likely that a similar logic applied.

Not all talk was informal. There were, for example, debating societies. Young men went off to college, wandered home, drifted into a profession but had time on their hands, and they gathered together in upstairs rooms and formed debating societies, in an ephemeral effort to extend their youth. They did this mostly in lesser places. To these ends, constitutions and manifestoes were drawn up. So, "Several gentlemen, of Petersburg Virginia, actuated by a desire of improvement, as it regards their minds and morals, or in relation to all those endowments by which our Creator has distinguished man from every other being that exists in the world; having agreed to join in an association, the exercises of which to consist of composing and debating; and having determined to hold a meeting for the purpose of organizing such an institution, met at the store of Mr. Allen James, in a room procured for the purpose, on friday evening the 21st. September 1821."[7]

Southern young men were supposed to aspire to gentility and propriety. This marked their societies off from the debating societies which had crowded the gin-sodden, sawdust-bestrewn public houses of London in the late eighteenth century, into which all manner of men and women had jostled, from a "noble Lord" to "bar-maids or Strand girls" and "even men in women's clothes."[8] Rather, Southern debating societies were training for oligarchy and so were closer to the old world of Jeffersonian caucuses where gentlemen debated behind closed doors than to the new world of the Jacksonian hustings.

Characteristically, a day and hour were assigned for meetings, a limit was set to the length of speeches, the number for a quorum was fixed, fines were specified for un-parliamentary behavior, essays might be required from members, and the election of officers was prescribed. Subject matters seldom touched on local matters, for debates were intended to extend minds beyond the immediate sphere. So they spoke most about national affairs, international politics, and morally vexatious historical events. Should the United States go to war with Britain? Should Ferdinand and Isabella have expelled the Moors? Contemporary controversies were not shunned, they being the lifeblood of vigorous debate, and even slavery was discussed. But sectarian religion was generally avoided, though morality was everywhere debated, especially those issues which affected a young man's career. (Should a lawyer defend a bad cause?) The looming prospects of domesticity were seldom far from minds, since the debaters were not far from being children and close to becoming parents. So, "which has more influence upon society, the father or mother?"[9] Such matters were more common that abstract philosophical issues, though one group did wonder whether *Don Quixote* or Locke's *Essay Concerning Human Understanding* had done more for the improvement of mankind.

Debating societies were for young men. The older found their way into conversation clubs, a specialized division of an abundant landscape of Southern clubs, male and female, by which persons gained amusement, society, and instruction—jockey clubs, hunting clubs, agricultural clubs, sewing circles. In olden days, masculine gatherings had been determinedly drunken, but latterly clubs came to admit grave pastors and temperance advocates, and some of them to acquire ambitions of serious discourse. In Charleston in about 1807 was founded the Literary and Philosophical Society of South Carolina, modeled on the American Philosophical Society and its numerous eighteenth-century companions. It lasted until about 1836, when it seems to have lapsed. Of its proceedings there is little evidence, except that it varied between public lectures and papers given in private. Some of these were to find their way into the pages of the *Southern Review*, some into pamphlets, while others remained unpublished. It was revived informally by Mitchell King in about 1842 and survived until the Civil War, during which time it was known as the "Conversation Club" or the "Charleston Literary Club" or, more simply, "the club." There were many such organizations, which formed part of the experience of traveling men of letters, because such clubs made it their business to entertain interesting strangers.

The Charleston Conversation Club had a formal membership, as many as forty, to which one had to be elected, although guests were habitual. Women were forbidden, though it seems that meetings might be held in a house presided over by a hostess. Since admission was by consensus, membership tended to eliminate the awkward and difficult man, and this earned the club a reputation for being "a stiff-starched assembly of old fogies."[10] Members did tend to be older, with the young attending first as guests before advancing to admission, and almost all were planters, merchants, and professional men. Of these, some made a habit of publishing thoughts aired before the club, some published only occasionally, and some never hazarded print. Silence mattered less then. Southern society in 1850 was closer to that losing world where it had been as important to know as to do, where the term "scientist" had been as freely granted to those who read about science as those who performed its experiments. Still, even by such standards, some members were amiably below the intellectual salt, because they not only wrote nothing but said little.

The procedure of the Charleston Conversation Club was unvarying. During the season, which ran roughly from November to May, each week, sometimes each fortnight, a club member would act as host. A subject was announced at the preceding meeting so that members might read up. Unless an outside guest was speaking, the host himself gave the paper, but the proceedings were presided over by a separate moderator. Discussion ensued, the whole taking about two hours, whereupon the gathering adjourned to a simple supper. Topics were various: political, moral, economic, and historical. Porcher observed that the club avoided religion and politics, though judging from what is known of their topics, by this he seems to have meant partisanship and sectarianism. In the 1849–50 season, for example, there were sessions on the unity of the human race, the Dorians, the sources of South Carolina history, and "inspiration." The next year provided a memoir of Mary Elizabeth Lee and discussions of Mohammed, swamp drainage, authorship as a profession, and immigration. No doubt the civilities of society often muffled sharpness of debate, and the civic diversity of the members precluded technicality of discussion. This was an urbane intelligentsia, not a workshop of experts with a professional jargon. Still, the club encouraged modest dissent and often structured proceedings to generate debate, though sharp views were expected to be expressed in soft voices.

Porcher left the best evocation of the club and its habitués, a portrait both severe and affectionate. He knew that human frailty and pretension did not prevent or vitiate useful conversation, and in its own way the club contributed to the life of the mind, even as it served exclusivity. Of the two possible qualifications for membership, learning and geniality, only the second was indispensable. As Porcher rightly observed, "The Club did not require learned men, or eloquent men but it did require genial men, social men, men who would take an interest in it." Yet learning was not infrequent, intelligence scarcely less so, and seriousness a purpose. Porcher's general verdict was grateful: "The constant intercourse with men of high intelligence on all sorts of subjects gave an activity to thought which was a great advantage to one whose course of life had hitherto been so sluggish, and I gradually and imperceptibly acquired the power of expressing myself freely and without embarrassment."[11]

AS A MOBILE PEOPLE, Southerners were often divided one from another by political service, commerce, education, or migration. Their great medium of connection was the excellent postal service, which even a zealous states' righter might agree justified the federal government. To write a letter was one of the most common, sometimes more intellectually exacting obligations that fell to a literate Southerner. They came to be good at it. John Pendleton Kennedy thought that, next to political writing, Southerners were better at the epistolary arts than anything else and this ought to be represented in any anthology of Southern literature.

Letters had once been a prime form of discourse between early modern intellectuals in Europe and its colonies. The "republic of letters" had been precisely that, a community which exchanged letters. For many, this "manuscript culture" was not merely a proving ground for ideas which might find their way into print, but a means of discussion which made print superfluous. Print was often regarded as vulgar and uncontrollable, while manuscripts might be contained within the charmed circle of cognoscenti. Such men and some women saw themselves as in a separate realm, there equal to one another but above locality and the petty obligations of church and state. A remarkable number of the chefs d'ouevres of what is now called, anachronistically, colonial Southern literature remained in manuscript (as their authors wished) until the modern era, which finds such inaccessibility an affront to the suzerainty of print.

That William Byrd's *Histories of the Dividing Line Betwixt Virginia and North Carolina* was first published by Edmund Ruffin in 1841 shows that the impulse to turn colonial manuscripts into American print commenced in the antebellum years. By the mid-nineteenth century, belles lettres had all but abandoned itself to print culture. For a thought not to be printed came to seem the mark of a thought's marginality. But correspondence stood as it once had. Thomas Jefferson, who published only one book in his lifetime, exerted much of his intellectual influence and spent most of his waking hours, especially in retirement, in the writing of letters. Thereby, he did not think he was contributing the less to the life of the mind than he had by publishing *Notes on the State of Virginia.*

As with conversation, letter writing was driven by the scattered isolation of the intelligentsia. Scientists, in particular, had long since developed ways to remedy these immurements by fashioning a cosmopolitan tradition of epistolarity, with learned societies encouraging "correspondents." The elder Stephen Elliott worked in this way, as did his Southern successors. To write letters and get replies was to register membership in the wider community of mind. Indeed the most avid correspondents were often those most insecure about their intellectual standing, people who needed a physical reminder that they belonged on the landscape of ideas. A letter admitted distance, but built a bridge.

The antebellum South stood at a distinctive moment in the history of correspondence. The form was, of course, ancient. Cicero's letters began to be published soon after his death (43 b.c.); the Middle Ages had ventured treatises on the art of the letter; and the Renaissance had seen a revival of interest. Petrarch's letters first appeared in 1492, and Erasmus in the *De Conscribendis Epistolis* (1522) had argued that letters should be free to express individuality. By the mid-eighteenth century, the intimacies of the private letter had become a literary fashion, not only by the publication of its supreme exponent Madame de Sévigné but with the invention of the epistolary novel. By the nineteenth century, learning how to write a letter had become a household duty, since family letters helped to hold domesticity together, and venturing a correspondence involved the inheritance of a complicated, self-conscious tradition poised between the public and private realms. The premise was that a letter was a private thing, a confidentiality sent from one person to another. But correspondents were conscious of writing for more than one eye, because letters were often shared within a household and read out, while a letter writer engaged by the life of the mind might write with a still-sharper sense of watching eyes, because there was the potentiality of print. Here the range of options was great.

There was the genre of the letter on current controversies, such as Hammond's *Two Letters on the Subject of Slavery, Addressed to Thomas Clarkson, Esq.* (1845). Such a form varied from a conventional publication about public affairs only by being brushed with the sense, thought to be inherent to a letter, that the author was speaking with more candor, was revealing more of a private mind, and was in turn hoping to reach the private sensibility and convictions of the recipient. By a polite fiction, the public letter suggested that the reading public was but an eavesdropper, accidentally engaged by a purloined thing.

Next were travel letters. Anyone who traveled was expected to report back to those at home, who would read out the exotic missives. Such letters were an aide-mémoire to the traveler himself, a literary equivalent of the photographs which choke modern drawers. They were sometimes handed over to local newspapers, and this tradition was later to become the occasion for Mark Twain's satire in *The Innocents Abroad*. Commonly the traveler published a volume, too, in which the epistolary form was preserved, as with Randal MacGavock's *A Tennessean Abroad; or, Letters from Europe, Africa, and Asia* (1854). A specialized form of the travel letter was the genre initiated by Montesquieu's *Lettres persanes*, in which "under the mask of a foreigner, a satirical view is given of the manners and customs of a country."[12] The Southern prototype was Wirt's *Letters of a British Spy*, but the genre was still alive with Joseph Holt Ingraham's *The Sunny South* (1860), which pretended to be letters from a Northern governess on a Tennessee plantation.

Next in self-consciousness were letters which, though private, were written with an awareness that they might eventually be printed. By the early nineteenth century, the posthumous publication of letters was an established genre, as well as a mark of celebrity. Byron's correspondence set the new standard, which moved things from the sententious moral traditions of Sévigné and Chesterfield to the irresponsibly seductive. Byron, however, complicated matters. It was the promise of Thomas Moore's *Letters and Journals of Lord Byron* (1830) that the letters' casual and exuberant intimacy showed what had been the private, the real Byron. It followed that, in writing intimately but with a premonition of fame, a writer might hope to structure posthumous understandings, might trick those who felt that the formal things (poetry, fiction, philosophy) should be understood through the informal (the letters). Within this logic, Southerners began to edit the letters of other Southerners, mostly politicians, more rarely novelists and poets. Many of the letters of the revolutionary generation were printed in these years, although all had seen some of their correspondence, not always with their own connivance, printed in their lifetimes. But scholarly editions were done later of Jefferson, Madison, and Washington. Of later generations, pickings were thinner, since many were not yet dead in 1861. On the whole, politicians were more vulnerable to this posthumous rifling, because they commanded a greater celebrity in the culture than "authors." Nonetheless, Wirt wrote of Patrick Henry and used his letters, and Wirt's "life and letters" was in turn written by Kennedy, whose own letters were liberally scattered through Henry Tuckerman's 1871 biography of Kennedy himself.

Before sketching the landscape of correspondents, it will be helpful to say something about changing epistolary conventions, observed by ordinary and intellectual Southerners alike. One consequential change was physical. Until the late 1810s it was customary to write on a single folded sheet of paper, so there was a natural limit to the length of letters. When envelopes come into general use, this limitation was removed and letters could become as discursive as the writer wished, which matched in the private realm the blowsiness which cheap printing was bringing to publications.

Superscriptions and subscriptions did not change much, though a little. In 1810 as in 1860, the address of the writer was placed at the top of the first page and, by later standards, was inexplicit. Mail was collected from post offices, so it was necessary only to signify "Charleston, S.C." As to terms of address, there was a modest decline in formality. Early letters might begin, "My Dear Son," but it was common to begin as though writing an essay, in which the name of the correspondent was elegantly enfolded into the narrative. "Behold me on entering the breakfast room presented with your anxiously expected letter, and on breaking the seal and finding the enclosure, stopping not even to read the kind and considerate entreaty with which it commences. What my dear brother could be more polite," is how an 1816 letter from Rachel Mordecai begins.[13] Likewise, subscriptions were often made to flow from the final sentence. By 1860, this eighteenth-century art of inviting the recipient into the continuous flow of talk had declined, especially at the beginning of letters, and the modern stiff routine was more common, in which recipient, narrative, and author are rigorously separated and punctuated.

By modern standards, signatures were formal, not only between strangers but between family members, even husbands and wives. Letters took care to denote a precise relation. "Dear Brother" begins an 1858 letter from Louisa McCord to Langdon Cheves Jr., and she signs herself "Most affectionately Yr Sister Louisa S. McCord."[14] To modern eyes, this looks odd, as though she thought he might forget she was his sister, that they were so strange that she needed a surname. In fact, none of these implications were relevant. The individual who was Louisa McCord was not stripped down to "Louisa," but her reality was associated with her surname and hence her marriage and with the registering of her relationship of "sister" with Langdon. For relationships and surnames mattered a great deal, Christian names very little, and initials were stubbornly important. There was sometimes more familiarity in the use of a surname or initials alone.

As to the functions of letter writing in intellectual life, they were manifold. They dealt with business, with authors writing to editors and others of their ilk, which kept the great business of print moving. They bantered trivial, friendly, or malicious gossip about ideas or people, which bounced backward and forward across the landscape. (Samuel Gilman called this "all the juice of information and opinion.")[15] They gave advance knowledge of books or decoded intentions and opinions, masked in print. They admitted failures, confessed to hopes, or solicited puffery.

To be sure, there were those who seem to have had no gift for or interest in the genre. George Tucker's letters are laconic and functional, as are those of Thomas Dew, who mostly wrote about his business affairs. Mary Chesnut's few surviving letters show little aptitude for the form, Petigru's letters show little of his wit, and Poe (harried and wary) was but briefly self-serving. Like most politicians with great power who were harassed by office seekers, Calhoun tended to be businesslike and lofty. De Bow seems to have corresponded little, which is odd for an editor, a fact which has handicapped the understanding of his periodical. John Bachman is scraps, Bledsoe intermittent, Fitzhugh nearly invisible. The epistolary voice of many others was or became, either through their uninterest or the loss of their papers, all but mute.

But many others have substantial bodies of intellectual correspondence, which are sometimes the better for not being very intellectual. For esprit, there are the letters of Trescot to his contemporaries, which strike a tone at variance with the cold, precise, and analytical manner of his published writings and show what pleasure there was in being young and clever, loose among the ladies and the folios, telling jokes about cuckolds and vaginas, and worrying about the Whigs. For an understanding of a working evangelist's life in town and country, there are those of the elder Manly, often sententious and humorous, aware of the tricks of his trade, and passionately committed to his religion and his South, not always distinguishable to him. Among historians, Grigsby's correspondence shows the deepest care for the shape of historical knowledge, plots an aging process from wide-eyed student days to stubborn old age, and is striking for the anxious letters which passed between him and his often-ill wife, for whom he showed a sensitive if bewildered care. Louisa McCord's letters have little of the qualities of her published writings— violence, bitter irony, passion—but show other sides, her anxious vulnerability and great competence. Of them all, Francis Lieber and William Gilmore Simms were preeminent for the scope of their correspondences. Both were ambitious men who craved company and influence, who wanted to place themselves at the center of things. This was easier for Simms, though he did not think so; as an editor, as a man of letters, as a mediator between Southern and Northern writers, as the guru of young writers, as a dispenser of hospitality, he flung out letters the way he did everything else, profligately. As Paul Hamilton Hayne suggested, Simms did things best when he gave little premeditation to it, and letters fell into this category. Sitting at the center of his web, which kept breaking, he spun and spun; mostly he kept cheerful and dispensed cheer. Along the way, he would tumble out his experience, his hopes and fears, often rendered melodramatically. (If he had been an actor, Simms would have been a ham, more Donald Wolfit than John Gielgud.) And he corresponded with so many people, North and South, young and old, to each of whom he turned a slightly different face, because his range was very great.

It is conventional to say that Simms was the South's first professional man of letters. Whatever the dubious merits of that claim, he did work at the life of the mind from day to day, from year to year with barely wavering commitment, and knew how the machinery of his business worked. More, on the whole, he knew what he was good at, where he was weak, and did not care who else knew it. He seems to have thought it was more honest, perhaps preemptingly shrewd, to own up to accomplishment and failing alike. He wanted to be liked, hoped to be respected, strove ceaselessly to make himself matter, and mistakenly thought this might be best achieved by essaying everything. At one level, his gifts were at war with his ambitions. He wanted to survive, to have a literary posterity, to be timeless as he imagined genius had to be. But he was so sensitive to the moment, so fluid and chattering, that his works only make sense to those who care for his moments or those of his culture. These people are more numerous than he feared, when he died impoverished and neglected. But in reading old letters, posterity agrees to immerse itself in past moments. Though he tried least to capture the future by his correspondence, there he probably succeeded best.

Lieber's letters were different. Simms sat, like the thinking man's Mr. Pickwick, in the middle of a world he belonged to, however much he grumbled that he was alienated. But Lieber sat alone, as the emissary of a foreign world, with which his letters maintained a connection vital to his sense of self-esteem. He was the stranger, reserved to those around him, though he liked company, which is why Columbia was such a trial to him. A few there he came to trust: Henry Nott, William Campbell Preston, David McCord (but not Louisa), the young Charlotte McCord. And, though he made little of it, Lieber not infrequently corresponded with Southerners, usually politicians who might support his various causes. But mostly he stuck to his wife and family, his students, his library, his writings, and his letters to friends in the North and Europe. Letters were his conversation, he told George Hillard in 1853, at a bleak moment: "I never felt lonesome in prison, but I do feel so in the midst of men here. I walk about with my lantern not to find a man but a soul. Nay more—I have been walking about for years, and now I have blown it out and hung it up."[16] Yet he was fascinated by what was around him, which he described in his letters. Lieber had both a systematic mind and a talent for minute observation, and in his letters these gifts achieved a balance. His publications sometimes suppressed the latter, to their loss, which is why Hillard thought them inferior to Lieber's conversation and correspondence.

Because Lieber was a cosmopolitan, his strength was a wideness of vision, which he worked hard to sustain by his traveling. (By comparison, Simms knew no one beyond the United States and his letters are studies in the Americanism he espoused.) Lieber's letters are not only from the South but to it, since he wrote back to his family and friends in South Carolina when he was in the North and Europe. So his angle of vision was constantly shifting, and his letters are crowded with people unaccustomed to sharing a literary space: Tocqueville and Calhoun, Frederick William IV and a slave called Betsy. Though he wrote most to men and many of his letters are like over-hearing someone at the Athenaeum Club, he was unusual in writing to women with freedom, and with only a little condescension, despite having no time for newfangled feminisms. His correspondence with his wife Matilda is as good as anything else he wrote, which is rarer among husband and wife exchanges than one might imagine or hope.

Like many men of his time, Lieber was oblivious of weather, clothes, flowers, and landscape, but he saw people clearly, both as types and as individuals. Like Simms, he had enormous vivacity, though a greater calculation, an awareness of his correspondents' needs and usefulness, which was a natural thing for a man between worlds, wanting escape and worried about survival. Still, he was often prickly and tactless without quite knowing how, and this isolated him. Such bluntness was a strength for his letters if not his life, because he could seldom hide his moods, which fluctuated between blank depression, cool analysis, and wide smiles.

In short, letters were the means by which writers confessed their humanities, sought out those of others, and grasped the personal realities behind the formalities of cold print. They helped to create patterns of friendship and enmity across a landscape broader than physical contact alone could sustain. For some, these epistolary exchanges were one among many intellectual connections; they worked alongside clubs, dinner parties, periodicals, and bookshops. For others, solitary either by temperament or by location, they were close to being intellectual connection and life itself. George Frederick Holmes, awkward and rusticated for many years in the Virginia mountains, lived through his letter books, as did James Warley Miles, who palely loitered in Charleston and Berlin.

Correspondence achieved social connection unevenly. In descending order, the landscape of intellectual correspondence in the white community was dominated by men writing to other men, then by women writing to other women, and lastly (by a considerable distance) by men and women exchanging letters. Blacks and whites almost never corresponded, except as masters and slaves, and a proslavery intellectual never wrote to a fugitive slave like Frederick Douglass, only to an abolitionist like Thomas Clarkson. Though much has been lost or misplaced, there are few sustained adult and intellectual correspondences between men and women, except rarely as husbands and wives, more often as parents and children. There are no Horace Walpoles and Madame du Deffands in the South. More strikingly, there are relatively infrequent instances of accomplished love letters. One can find a few written during courtship or flirtation, almost none outside the bounds of marriage, but more by those who managed to sustain love after the wedding. In the last category, the letters of Sarah with John Gayle, Francis with Matilda Lieber, Basil with Sarah Manly are notable.

As has been observed of the epistolary novel, letters were a form without closure. Their importance to this culture says something about its willingness to tolerate, even to rejoice in, fragmentary pieces of knowledge about people and ideas, tossed backward and forward between times and places. Letters written by intellectuals tended to function as places to scout and test ideas, and many of them (being untidy and awkward) were later lost or repressed in published works. Because often the best of a culture is found in its disorder, in the South's letters can be found a lot of what is freshest in it. Conversely, there is little of its darkest side, the brutal matter of slavery, the institution whose prisoners flit palely and harmlessly through Southern letters only as "servants."

In the world of print, in the early nineteenth century the epistolary novel began to be replaced by the novelistic diaries of ennuyées, country parsons, and itinerant actresses, and journalizing came into vogue. Over time, as a form the diary acquired conventions: the affixing of a date, the rehearsing of recent events, the interrogation of the self. In practice, however, its form was uncertain. Diaries might be only journals, a daily record to keep bare track of the weather, the crops, or the beaux, and (even as diaries) they often got tangled up with letter books, or commonplace books, or ledgers, or lecture notes.

It was a Puritan tradition to use the diary as a way of studying one's relationship to God and man. In this spirit, Thornwell ventured one in 1836; it begins, "I have this day commenced to keep a journal of my personal history with a view chiefly to my growth in grace."[17] He was then young and this was typical, because diaries were a rite of passage. Young women alone on plantations like Elizabeth Ruffin took up diaries as a means of polishing their education, of examining what was peculiarly fascinating and fluid (themselves), and of pleasing their friends and relatives. Changes in attitudes toward the nature of youth, especially a belief in its evanescent specialness, encouraged this impulse to set down memories, which might be available later to be hugged to the diarist's old or middle-aged breast. Youth was felt to be peculiarly subject to temptation, and a diary was a moral aid. Writing entries required discipline, regularity, and so virtue, which might spill over into the rest of a life. But the official obligation to be virtuous necessarily kept vice on young diarists' minds.

As a result, diaries are among the best ways to enter into the minds of young Southerners. Although it was, in practice, the case that diaries were often intended to be read by other eyes, this was at the discretion of the diarist, who might choose privacy or, when writing, forget the prospect of publicity. And the rhetorical form of a diary, which often compelled the writer to talk to himself or herself, eased the way into confessional. This usually stopped far short of intimacy. Diaries dealt in venial not mortal sins, and grave matters (especially sexual) were touched upon only in repressed allusion and codes, often now impenetrable. Miscegenation, brothels, murder, bigamy are seldom the subject matters of diaries (and homosexuality never), even those written by adults, except sometimes when it was an experience someone other than the diarist had had. Madaline Edwards, who kept a diary in New Orleans in the 1840s when she was in her twenties, had lived a life which invited confession. Divorced parents, marriage at fourteen, four dead children, one separated or divorced husband, a possibly bigamous marriage, an affair in Vicksburg, a lover and patron in New Orleans, illness and literary ambition, all might have prompted intimate self-reflection. But her diaries are discreet, oblique, allusive. Her lover came and went, and she made note of it, of what was said, and of what gifts he brought, but the hours or minutes of their essential relationship, the welcome sexuality of their traffic, is a silence.

Yet diaries could license honesty, which letters often did not. The latter had an immediate audience, a fact which mandated wariness. But a diary's opinions could be expressed, because the diarist need not worry it might be promptly read. Nonetheless, diarists were often unable to be honest with themselves. The possibility of prying eyes was one reason for stopping short, but there was a deeper dissimulation. Ella Gertrude Clanton Thomas's confusion on this point was typical: "A Journal—Defined to be a book in which one writes their thoughts and actions. If such be the case this volume of manuscript will only have partially have accomplished the purpose of a journal. My thoughts! Write those!"[18]

So the diary was often a formative thing, which assisted self-invention. Most young people had modest ambitions: happiness, piety, erudition, little more. The culture of slavery might encourage such a sense of limitation. But the South was an imperial culture not lacking in millennial expectations, which could lead to greater extravagance. The diary of Henry Hughes, the Mississippian proslavery writer, is a perfectly formed Romantic (even Nietzschean) document, written to prove a destiny. "I will place myself upon a throne from which I can look down on Alexand[er], Caesar, Cicero, Bonaparte, Washington" and "I will be the President of America and Europe," these were not the usual sentiments.[19] Few young Southerners aspired to be Napoleon, Fourier, and Byron all at once. Perhaps none but Hughes. On the whole, the imaginations of young Southerners were delicately entrapped within ambitions not meant to shatter worlds: to be a graduate, a lawyer, a president, a mother, a saved soul. In using a diary to probe and make a self, Hughes was conventional enough. However, once a self was made, it was common to stop keeping a diary, since the task was either done or, if undone, too exasperating to complete. Very few kept up the habit.

Here there is a fissure. Like the letter, the diary was a democratic literary form. Elizabeth Ruffin, Ann Hardeman, Thomas Miles Garrett, and many others survive only for their diaries, which stand alone as their contribution to the written word. More than a letter, however, the diary might intimate a bashful interest in posterity. The diary first appeared to young Southerners as printed literature, and then it became a private manuscript, kept in the desk drawer. So the diary might be a literary form for those who diffidently wanted to be famous, they having more pain or vanity than they liked the world to see. This may explain why most who went on to sustained intellectual careers and produced the South's social philosophy or belles lettres seldom kept a diary, or few that survive.

Nonetheless, there are diaries by the South's literati. Hughes went on to write an eccentric work of social philosophy, which built on the reveries of his diary. Like him, several kept diaries when young, then abandoned the form: Francis Peyre Porcher, James Johnston Pettigrew, Charles Gayarré, and several others. A few more kept up a lifetime's habit: Hugh Blair Grigsby, John Pendleton Kennedy, Mitchell King. Still fewer, notably Edmund Ruffin, took up the habit in later years. Many of these diaries have value. The usefulness of Kennedy's and King's journals are mostly for their faithful, if not very imaginative, logging of the minute trafficking of Southern intellectual networks: what was read, who dined with whom, what was published, who wanted what job. Kennedy, on the whole, was too interested in being urbane to be greatly self-aware, which was a venture too risky for a cautious Whig. King's jottings were, more strictly, memoranda; only when he grew old did they become sharply self-conscious.

The liveliest of Southern diaries may be those of William Henry Holcombe of Natchez, which are mostly confined to 1855, when he was thirty, married, with a baby. Like ministers, doctors often kept diaries, and Holcombe was partly following their custom by reviewing the condition of his patients. But Holcombe was no ordinary doctor; he was a homeopath, a Swedenborgian, the son of a Virginian antislavery man, nothing if not different. His diary is, by turns, learned, breezy, modest, funny, unafraid of being judged. It may be that in diaries, as in fiction, the Southwest bred freedom of expression. Holcombe's effort was paralleled, if not matched, by several others, written by breezy men knocking around the hinterland, "far from the haunts of men, where [one] can lead the life of a hermit, commune with my God, woo the Maids."[20] It was good not only to be shifty in a new country but also to keep diaries.

Back in the old country of Virginia, Edmund Ruffin looked very differently on the world, which to him was not new and had no joy. He began a diary in 1856, when he was sixty-two and had just given over the ownership of his plantations to his children and so found time more on his hands. Ruffin's diary has been most used, and not incorrectly, for its insight into the mind of a secessionist and the cumulating drama that led to Ruffin's firing upon Fort Sumter and his bitter suicide in 1865, after having written a letter of defiance to the Yankees. It has equal value as the anatomy of a seasoned older mind, coping with "degenerate times."[21]

Edmund Ruffin was not a worldly man and inept at diplomacy, quick to judge, someone who wore his passions on his sleeve. He had long wanted influence but had been disappointed and concluded that his learning had borne some responsibility for this. Nonetheless, Ruffin was conscious of having done important things in the company of important people. At the end of his life, he summed up his achievements and pronounced them good. But he was acutely conscious of a gulf between learning and action, in which self-knowledge was a mixed blessing. This helps to explain the broad shape of the diary. Until 1861, it was mostly an interior document. It documented his reading and thoughts about books, referred to his writings and travels, and discussed public events. Ruffin was on the utmost fringes of power and very unsure that public events would move his way, the way of a Confederacy. Because Virginia seemed timidly Unionist and South Carolina most likely to act, he moved toward the latter like a moth to a flame. Until 1860, that is, his was the diary of *un emigré de l'intérieur*. Thereafter, it became an almost exclusively public document, as he observed with excitement and passion the crushingly swift events which turned his Virginia from an irrelevance to a battleground.

The Ruffin of earlier years, though never at ease, had been an energetic observer, an analytical busybody, constantly reading, thinking, watching. His judgments had been crisp, those of an old hand used to forming critical opinions. So he finished *Little Dorrit* and concluded that it had merit, "but like most of Dickens' novels, there is a great deal of wretched poor stuff." He liked *The Scarlet Letter*, "a strange book, by a powerful writer." He read Fitzhugh, "a profound thinker, though a careless writer." This pattern—the description, the judgment, the generalization—was habitual for Ruffin and applied as forcefully to those whom he met as to the political events he monitored. Among Ruffin's objects of curiosity was himself, but not as in a young man's diary, where self was thought to be plastic. Ruffin's self was long made and intractable. He knew, for example, how he wrote, and he knew that certain kinds of writing were now impossible, however desirable. His problem was not only that his self was made but that it was beginning to slip away. The surrender of his property and the beginning of his diary were a preparation for death, not imminent but coming. He saw that his hands now trembled and that his memory was beginning to fail. This fumbling was important because it helps to explain the later, Confederate diary. Secession and nationhood gave Ruffin and Virginia back a purposeful self. This exoskeleton held him together until 1865 when he knew that the public world had brutally failed him and he was left with little private self with which to survive. At the end, he had only his diary, the shred of self, in which to set down his final testimony and write, "The End."[22]

THERE IS A CYCLE in the creation and dissemination of the printed word. A reader becomes an author, a book is printed, readers read, and some become authors. One can break into this circle at any point and it is wrong to privilege the author as the originating agent, some authors assure us. Nonetheless, in the life of any intellectual, reading precedes authorship. So three topics serve as a necessary prolegomena to understanding the ways in which, in the South, a manuscript passed from an author to a publisher: how books were sold, how they accumulated in private collections, and how libraries worked.

If one lived in a major city, it was easy to buy print, but it was more inconvenient for the rural person, who depended greatly upon colporteurs and book agents, those most diligent, unreliable, and unfortunate of men. They trundled along rutted, muddy roads with carts or buggies freighted with popular books; they stopped at farms, approached plantations, peddled at railroad depots, called upon bookshops, sold periodicals and tried to collect money for them. These itinerants were so common that there was a prejudice against them, or so Lieber believed: "In our thinly settled country . . . there is the strongest anti-pedlarism and anti-book-agent disposition. We are here so pursued with agents, and people have been so often deceived in books or maps, for which they had subscribed, that they will no longer nibble at the fly."[23] Such tension arose partly because agents might illicitly pocket some of the money they had collected and partly because customers might be equally dishonest. In short, the relationship between peddler and reader was unsatisfactory, though in a thinly settled place like the South, grimly necessary.

In the towns, book stores took two forms: the specialist bookshop which occasionally became a publisher; and the general store which sold the latest popular literature on the side. The former were common and the latter ubiquitous: between 1804 and 1824, New Orleans had "at least fifty-six different persons or firms . . . concerned with bookselling," most ephemeral. Both sorts of stores would place advertisements in local newspapers to inform the public of newly available items. (Publishers did not yet advertise on their own account.) In these the specialist bookshop might be specific about titles, authors, prices, and bindings, while the general store might speak only vaguely of "a small lot of new novels."[24] By comparison with modern techniques of marketing, which tends to privilege a few favored titles, these older advertisements were undifferentiated. The latest novel from Southworth or Dickens might occupy no more space than an edition of Cicero, a law journal, or a school primer. The shelves and tables of the bookshops themselves were similarly serendipitous.

One can get some sense of how the minor stores operated from 1845–47 daybook of Richard Elward of Natchez. It shows that, mostly, he sold stationery and sundries (pens, paper, candles, cigar cases, and the like) but also books and periodicals, which he could bind. In these two years, he had about a hundred different customers, of whom a fifth were women, mostly young female students buying textbooks. His Natchez was full of Roman Catholics, to whom Elward supplied missals, editions of Thomas à Kempis, and novels about Ireland. The town had many professionals who needed law books, congressional proceedings, political periodicals, medical works and journals. As for binding, women's orders were almost exclusively confined to musical scores, with a sideline in "lady's books." Otherwise, trade was eclectic; a volume of *Travels to Russia*, an atlas, pamphlets, Smollett's *History of England*, Lockhart's biography of Scott, an American almanac, dictionaries, a "Flower Book," Vergil, poetry, novels from Cervantes to Scott. Periodicals were frequently bound and ran the gamut from *Blackwood's* from abroad to *Graham's Magazine* from the North. Of major Southern periodicals, only the *Southern Literary Messenger* appears in the daybook, but many ladies journals are vaguely mentioned, with *Godey's Lady's Book* being probably among them.

Elward was in a small town, which numbered only 4,680 people in 1850, including slaves. He sold ordinary books in small numbers, nothing unusual, nothing rare, and his business did not survive for long. More ambitious was someone like William T. Berry in Nashville, whose shop lasted for forty years (from 1835 to 1876). He had several investors, a steady income from schools, colleges, and the state library, and a prime downtown location. The store was handsomely appointed, with a well-furnished room which served as a circulating library and a gentleman's club; briefly, the Tennessee Historical Society met there. He stocked not only the usual books but expensive editions, since Berry liked fine printing, having been apprenticed to the trade. He would travel to the eastern United States and to Europe to acquire stock. And he was more than a salesman, for he had intellectual preferences of his own, wrote for local newspapers, and did a very little printing, most ambitiously several volumes of the works of Philip Lindsley, president of the University of Nashville.

Berry's combination of bookselling, librarianship, and printing was not singular. Sometimes, as with Joseph Gales in Raleigh, to these pursuits were added the publishing and editing of newspapers. Entrepreneurs of Berry's ambition and ilk were a focus for the various aspects of the printed word, aspects which a later, more specialized culture would disperse to various industries. That it was common for booksellers to be printers and, hence, rudimentary publishers made the South's publishing trade closer to the world of Edmund Curll and Alexander Pope than to our own.

A bookshop which exemplified this synergy was that of John Russell in Charleston, most famously settled at No. 251 King Street, where customers encountered an "ample entrance and handsome plate-glass windows" and found a remarkable service.[25] It would not be too much to say that, at Russell's, the Charlestonian could eventually find almost whatever modern book he or she wished, for Russell provided Charleston imprints and American publications, as well as works from European publishers. The shop was a place where fashionable society of the younger set liked to be seen, while Russell and others made it a focus of intellectual life, too, even beyond chance meetings. Most famously, a group began regularly to meet in the store's back room, where Simms presided over the younger generation of poets and novelists, though older people came, too. These meetings often spilled over into debates in private homes, and, out of this, developed *Russell's Magazine* (1857–60). Hayne was its editor, with Russell as its financial backer and publisher; after a few issues, he became the assistant editor. This periodical was a logical extension of Russell's established role as a publisher, which had begun with a volume of Simms's poetry, then advanced to Smyth's and Miles's theology, Fraser's memoirs, Grayson's poetry, Holbrook's ichthyology, among other works. For the most part, Russell was publishing his customers, because he very seldom ventured beyond Charlestonians and South Carolinians. *Russell's Magazine*, by contrast, though it published the Charleston set, drew upon contributors more widely dispersed, even to the North.

Russell was following a well-established pattern for Southern booksellers-cum-publishers. J. W. Randolph of Richmond, for example, published several score imprints, books, and pamphlets, many of them canonical works by Virginian authors. The difference between Russell and Randolph was that the latter published music and had access to the official publications of church and state, the mother lode of publishing, besides which (as far as earnings went) the literary accomplishment of a community was a minor consideration.

While many Southerners bought books from such urban bookshops, they would buy from the North, too. If one lived remotely, it did not matter whether a book came by mail from Philadelphia or New Orleans. In addition, there was a tradition of importing directly from European booksellers, sometimes through intermediaries. The net result was that the South was a place into which torrents of print poured. Hence some intellectual Southerners had private libraries of considerable scope. The tradition of "public" libraries being relatively weak, to acquire such a personal collection was almost necessary. These varied greatly in size and quality. Thomas Jefferson, in his day, had set the standard of Southern bibliomania; in 1815 he founded the Library of Congress with a sale of 6,487 volumes, and, upon his death, a further thousand were willed to the University of Virginia. Subsequent generations matched and, sometimes, overmatched this.

The greatest collection was that of Thomas Smyth, whose library consisted of some 20,000 volumes, housed in his Charleston home. Next in size were probably the libraries of Simms and Mitchell King, at about 12,000 volumes apiece. When he died in 1843, Legaré's library was about 6,000 volumes, which was roughly comparable to Grigsby's. Four-thousand is a conservative estimate for Lieber's library in his Columbia days, and a catalog of Thomas Cooper's library shows about 2,400 volumes. By itself, of course, size meant little. That Smyth, Legaré, and Simms had large collections was significant, since the consequences can be traced in their writings. But a library need have no consequence other than the pleasure of the reader or the vanity of the property owner. One of the South's largest libraries was that of Alexander Augustus Smets, a Savannah merchant, who had perhaps 8,000 volumes, an assembly of sufficient celebrity that visitors called to examine it. It was, in fact, remarkable in extending to incunabula, medieval documents, modern literary manuscripts (Addison, Sterne, Scott), and even Oliver Cromwell's Bible. Yet Smets's books need little trouble the intellectual historian, because it is unclear whether he read them. Many items listed in his catalog have the bleak notation, "*in parts, uncut.*"[26]

It is more instructive to study what categories of books composed libraries. Self-evidently the shape of a personal library was most governed by the tastes of its owner. St. George Tucker had many law books, John Holt Rice much theology, Legaré many classical works, and so forth. But Thomas Cooper had a taste for most things, and his 1838 catalog breaks down roughly into the following percentages: history, biography, and Americana, 18 percent; science, travel, and economics, 31.5 percent; classics, 18 percent; belles lettres, 19 percent; philosophy and theology, 11.5 percent. Comparing this with the catalog which Stephen Elliott devised for the Charleston Library Society in 1826 and using categories comparable to Cooper's, one sees history, government, and law, 32 percent; belles lettres, 29 percent; geography and science, 25 percent; philosophy, theology and ethics, 10 percent. Cooper read more science than most, and Elliott doubtless augmented the society's holdings in natural science, though library catalogs from elsewhere suggest by not much. Adjusting crudely, one might hazard that the ordinary secular intellectual spent about a third of his time on history, politics, and the law; somewhat less than a third on fiction, poetry, and rhetoric; an eighth on philosophy and theology; and about a fifth on science, embracing travel and geography. Among these, the classics distributed among these genres probably accounted for about 15 percent.

As to where these books came from, one can get some idea from the Charleston Library Society catalogs of 1826 and 1845. The first may be said to summarize the legacy of the eighteenth century and the first fifty years of American independence, while the second provides a snapshot of the mid-antebellum decades. They show, as one might expect, a shift. In the 1826 catalog, about 61 percent of the imprints were English, 6 percent French, 3 percent Scottish, with smatterings from other cultures. Twenty-six percent were American, mostly from Philadelphia, New York, and Boston, with very little from anywhere in the South other than Charleston. These numbers are, however, slightly misleading. The English share is exaggerated, since London was a literary entrepôt and many of its publications were of Continental origin or were editions of classical texts. Further, many Northern books were pirated editions of foreign works, and perhaps a third of the American imprints were not, in origin or culture, American. Such an adjustment would reduce the American cultural presence to about 18 percent. Things look very different for the imprints which found their way into the library between 1826 and 1845. Then 78 percent were American, mostly Northern but more Charlestonian and some (though not many) Southern. England had dwindled to 16 percent, France was little changed, Scotland was reduced to less than 1 percent, and the rest were trifling. In these numbers is evidence of how the publishing world had changed. The American trade was now at full throttle and, even if one discounts a third of its imprints as pirated from Europe, this still left a very great growth in the representation of American print culture. Scotland was lessened, its intelligentsia assimilated to London. The eighteenth-century Irish pirates were gone. The abolition of censorship in France had curtailed the Swiss and Low Country publishers, who had once offered refuge to Voltaire. Moreover, the 1845 catalog shows an great increase in the number of pamphlets. About a third of the items were pamphlets, almost all American, since they were political speeches, sermons, and government documents.

What libraries own and what readers borrow are, notoriously, different things. The former expresses what a culture wishes itself to be, the latter what it is. The records of the Savannah Library Society help in understanding the gulf. In 1839 its librarian calculated that, from its foundation in 1809, the society had accumulated 3,799 volumes, though he could find only 3,304. He devised categories for them, in addition to listing how many volumes were, at the time of his report, checked out or missing. From his numbers, one can calculate what percentage of the library's holdings in each genre was in the hands of readers (and pilferers). These were, in descending order, romance and novels, 42 percent; natural history, 24 percent; biography, 23 percent; history, 23 percent; physical science, 23 percent; agriculture, 17 percent; chemistry and physics, 16 percent; law, 12 percent; drama and poetry, 12 percent; political science, 11 percent; philosophy, 8 percent; philology, 8 percent; travels, 6 percent; geography and ethnography, 5 percent;

medical science, 2 percent; and then astronomy, mathematics, rhetoric, technology at zero.

These are raw numbers. One can get a more sensitive understanding from the Savannah Library Society ledgers, several of which show what individual readers were borrowing between 1822 and 1826. Seven of the 131 different individuals in the ledgers are women, who seem to have been allowed informally to borrow as a courtesy, as the relatives or friends of the library's shareholders. Over five years, these 131 people checked out 3,890 items, which means the average reader checked out about six items a year. But, as one might expect, discrepancies were great. Fifteen people used only one item over the five years, while the library's greatest user checked out no less than 225. No one else used more than 200, but seven readers exceeded the century, eighteen used between 50 and 99, fifty-six between 10 and 49, forty-nine below 10.

Looking through the whole Savannah ledger, one gains the impression that the society's members read mostly British and American fiction, history, and biography; even the not-infrequent studies of European culture and history were usually written by English speakers. There was surprisingly little poetry read, not even Byron, and almost no drama. Travel literature was extensive, and a Savannah reader did not seem to mind whether the travelers in Egypt or the Arctic were English, American, or French. Almost all reading was modern, though readers often went back to the mid-eighteenth century, which was, after all, in 1825 still modern. But they seldom ventured earlier, and the medieval was almost completely absent. About 7 percent of the items in the borrowing ledger were written by authors not English-speaking, and most were in translation, so reading foreign languages was relatively rare. Of these alien works, 151 were French, 35 Latin, 28 German, 23 Italian, and 19 Greek, so French literature preoccupied over half the non Anglo-American quotient. It will be little astonishment, especially considering the earliness of this ledger, that very few items were about or by Southerners. About 86 such items are apparent, with 22 different titles, which was barely over 2 percent of the borrowings.

It will be useful to look beyond the numbers to the institution, by way of commencing a discussion of the landscape of Southern libraries. The Savannah Library Society had been founded in 1809 with a charter from the state. It was, like its Charleston predecessor, a corporation in which the public might purchase a membership and pay an annual subscription. In origin, it was an association of gentlemen, a standard feature of learned bodies. The length of borrowing privileges was defined by residence (a country member had twice as long as a city one) and by the size of a book (a folio for four weeks, but a duodecimo only for one). There were fines for writing in a book, being the cost of replacement and suspension of membership for a year. There was supposed to be an annual oration by a member, and it was expected that members would donate books, as well as decorative or useful things, a bust of Brutus or a "map of the world on rollers."[27] But the collection grew with only modest steadiness, about three books every two weeks, and this was all the economics of the society permitted, considering only about a hundred members, the cost of books, the expense of a librarian and rent, and negligence in paying subscriptions. In the long run, the venture proved impractical, and, by the late 1840s, it was merged with a younger, more energetic organization, the Georgia Historical Society.

As far as libraries went, the Savannah Library Society was following the eighteenth-century pattern and had many peers. In South Carolina, at least forty-one society libraries were founded between 1748, when the Charleston Library Society was founded, and 1837, when the James Island Library Society appeared, all but three being started after 1800. In Kentucky, seventy-nine existed before 1861. Very few developed any intellectual energy. In small places they testified to a community instinct: rules were drawn up by well-intentioned citizens, a room was found, a few hundred books put in it, and the society library drifted into a desultory existence or extinction.

In time, the corporate pattern of the social library proved insufficient because it was too narrow and too genteel, and matters diversified. Southern cities and small towns acquired libraries aimed at specific constituencies: an Apprentices' Library Society, a Mercantile Library Association, a college library, a college society library, a legislative library, a Female Library, a historical society library, a denominational or Sunday school library, a medical library, an educational and scientific library. In addition, there were circulating libraries, which were commercial ventures. Baltimore had seven of them between 1800 and 1835. These, like library societies, were joined by annual subscription, but they catered to a wider social audience; one need not be a gentleman to join and you might even be not a lady but a woman, if you were able to spend four dollars or six dollars a year. Unlike library societies, circulating libraries stocked more resolutely popular works and were usually owned by single proprietors.

Very frequently, libraries shared premises with other institutions, with which they might merge, to be transmuted into athenaeums or lyceums. In 1871, an antiquarian examined a book which had been knocking around Louisville libraries for the preceding half century and found upon it the marks of seven institutions. In this, the South was worse than some American regions. In New England, social libraries lasted on average for thirty-five years, while in the Midwest it was half that, and the South was certainly closer to the latter.

In terms of scale, Southern libraries began to lose ground during the early nineteenth century. In 1830, Harvard had a far larger collection than any other college, but the better Southern institutions were comparable to most Northern colleges, and there was a roughly similar pattern among social libraries. The record of the next decades was mixed. The Northwest did about as well or bad as the South, despite their disparate social systems, but the Northeast moved decisively ahead, with the Boston area developing into the richest concentration of printed matter in North America. In the 1850s, a prosperous South regained some ground, at least in its college libraries, whose number of books doubled. The Northern improvement had come mostly from philanthropy by alumni and business leaders, while the South benefited less from this, though it was not unknown. Rather, whatever modest strength developed on the Southern university library scene came from governments, especially South Carolina and Virginia, both of which were generous, but especially the former. If one looks at the amounts provided to colleges by governments and university administrations, none did better than South Carolina College at midcentury, and hardly anyone came close. Yet the college was still falling far behind Harvard, and the difference lay in philanthropy.

For all these reasons Columbia, South Carolina, was the richest place in the South to be placed for books. Nowhere else were there other than isolated collections, good, bad, or indifferent. In Columbia by 1860 the college library, the legislative library, and the theological seminary had accessions amounting to about 60,000 volumes. If to Columbia one adds Charleston— the cities were conjoined worlds—the region furnished libraries which held about 90,000 volumes, perhaps more. This density of printed matter alone helps to explain why this area produced so much of significance to Southern intellectual culture.

Of college libraries, only that of South Carolina College, however, fumblingly moved away from serving only undergraduates to being a research library after the German fashion. One reason for this failure of imagination was that books were more valued than librarians, who might plan and achieve great collections. Library catalogs were haphazard or nonexistent, classifications idiosyncratic. Moreover, books were often inaccessible. This was especially so in colleges, where suspicion of the destructive power of the young was deep-seated. At Charlottesville, at first the Rotunda was open only an hour on each weekday, and on only one of those days could a student borrow anything, and then only with the written permission of a professor. At the University of Georgia there was no librarian, at all, and at Chapel Hill, it was unreliably said, David Swain kept the library in an attic and for twenty years never added to it. Consequently, the wardens of these little empires, the librarians, were a sorry lot, sorry for themselves, underpaid, marginal, and indifferent.

So, the accessibility of printed words in the South show a variegated pattern, fairly good for private individuals of ample means, less good for those who depended upon public institutions. Much depended on where in the South one lived, and as much on one's social standing. An apprentice boy in New Orleans might pick from a few hundred volumes, whereas the son of a rich planter in Columbia might have access to a hundred thousand. As will be seen, the ability to move from being a reader to being an author was also an unstable and inconsistent business.

THERE WERE MANY ways for Southern authors to give printed words to a reading public, Southern or otherwise. These included newspapers, pamphlets, periodicals, and books, which might be done by local, Northern, or European publishers. None of these options was satisfactory, but they were sufficiently multiplied that no one had to remain silent in the South, if they could but summon the desire to publish and fashion the words to be printed.

On the whole, newspapers were unimportant for intellectual discourse. Most were broadsheets of four or six pages, of which more than half consisted of advertisements, while the rest consisted of reprinted news items, assorted financial news, political speeches, letters to the editor, and pieces of doggerel or satire. Perhaps only for political discourse were newspapers significant, for many politicians wrote in them.

Next were pamphlets. These were usually emanations of local events and locally published: a sermon, a Fourth of July oration, a speech to an agricultural society, or an intervention in a controversy. They might contain thought of the highest seriousness, though the ubiquity of pamphlets had a way of disguising significance. As Lieber observed in the late 1830s, "In the United States . . . the country is deluged with pamphlets, but on a thousand different and very frequently wholly uninteresting subjects."[28] The printed oration, at least, was a hybrid form, since it was often written with an awareness that printing was to follow, because the orator who spoke extemporaneously and declined publication was rare.

Above the pamphlet was the periodical, compared to which nothing was more fundamental to Southern intellectual life. As Thomas Dew observed, the "periodical press is now the organ of communication, and the potent engine that controls the popular will."[29] This was a highly specialized but very large and unstable world. A bibliography lists about 850 different periodicals as being established in the South between 1792 and 1860, with about 675 of them coming in the three decades after 1830. So there were periodicals for many tastes and interests: religious, professional, local, commercial, urban, rural, sporting, ethnic, foreign language. Somewhere, for a while, someone's taste was catered to.

In general, what happened was that an individual or a group would wish to vindicate a political, religious, or literary position. Founding subscribers who might form a joint-stock company were solicited. Then local or regional networks were solicited for annual subscriptions, which might begin encouragingly. An editor was appointed, and he or she occasionally owned the periodical but usually was paid by the founders or the publisher, unless (as was common) his or her services were gratuitous. Agents were appointed to solicit and renew subscriptions, which were inclined to falter. Appeals were issued, patriotisms encouraged, the tide might turn, or it might not and the periodical died. So the *Southern Review*, the *Southern Literary Journal*, *Russell's Magazine*, and the *Southern Quarterly Review* were born and died. Only the *Southern Literary Messenger*, the *United States Catholic Miscellany*, and *De Bow's Review* lasted from their foundations until past the outbreak of the Civil War.

Of major regional periodicals, one might focus on four as expressive of a range: the *Southern Review* (1828–32), the *Southern Literary Messenger* (1834–64), the *Southern Quarterly Review* (1842–57), and *De Bow's Review* (1846–80). Among their pages can be found most of the region's major intellectual figures and much of its significant discourse.

The *Southern Review* was sponsored by a group of South Carolinian grandees, in response to the crisis which would eventuate in Nullification and as an attempt to articulate and influence Southern opinion. It was intended as an imitation of the *Edinburgh Review* and, secondarily, of the *North American Review*. True to that format, it carried scholarly articles on contemporary political and social matters, as well as on natural science, classical scholarship, and philosophy. On average, it had about nine articles per issue, with each number having about 250 pages. It had three editors in succession, the elder Stephen Elliott until his death, then his son briefly, and lastly Hugh Legaré, but only one publisher. Relatively little is known of its financing or circulation except that its annual subscription was $5 and it needed about nine hundred subscribers to meet annual costs of $4,500. Since it went out of business after four years, it is probable that this number was not reached, or at least that the number of paid-up subscriptions proved inadequate. There seems, however, to have been an initial underwriting, both financial and literary, in the sense that various people agreed to contribute money and others (sometimes the same people) agreed to write essays. The three editors' services came free.

The *Southern Review* depended upon a small stable of regular reviewers, willing to write or to be enlisted when others failed to produce copy. These were Legaré (about 25 articles), Elliott (12–16), Thomas Cooper (about 12), and Henry Junius Nott (about 10). This small circle of friends contributed a little under half the essays. They had a range of interests, with all but Nott dealing with politics. Otherwise, Legaré specialized in the classics, the law, and modern Anglo-American belles lettres; Elliott did natural science and travel; Cooper, geology, medicine, and ethnography; and Nott, modern French literature. So the review had many interests, but politics had created it and sustained its most insistent debates. In the cacophony of South Carolinian struggles, though the periodical's editors were Unionists, they took care to admit the voices of Nullifiers and, in this, were less partisan than the *Edinburgh Review*.

As gentlemen, the editors of the *Southern Review* were untypical of editors elsewhere, who often came from the unstable world of journalism, but might come from elsewhere. John Milton Clapp of the *Southern Quarterly Review* had been editor of the *Charleston Mercury*, but Benjamin Blake Minor of the *Southern Literary Messenger* had run girls' schools, and J. D. B. De Bow of *De Bow's Review*, who never made a living at editing, survived by having academic posts, practicing law, and working as a statistician for the United States Census Bureau. Such people varied between being gentleman proprietors and hired help, but editing was not steady work. The *Southern Literary Messenger* was perhaps the most stable: its editor was usually the proprietor, it was always domiciled in Richmond, and it had only three editors over a span of twenty-four years. Still, its financing was eleemosynary. By contrast, the *Southern Quarterly Review* had a byzantine history of ownership and publication, with four civic bases, seven different publishers, and six different editors.

The motives for being an editor were mixed. The elder Stephen Elliott and Legaré were men of high social and intellectual standing, for whom editing and writing expressed noblesse oblige. They also had a passion for writing and filled their pages with their own words. This was a common motive, because to edit was to guarantee oneself a forum. By contrast, De Bow needed to make a living, though he also had a messianic dedication to advancing commercial society by informed journalism. Thornwell took up editing as a public duty, Simms as a literary obligation (though the money was important, too). For Thompson, it was something of a lark, since he was "a man partly *litterateur*, and partly dandy," and dandies did not customarily trouble themselves with balancing books, which was as well, because there was little money in owning or editing a periodical, and only a little éclat.[30]

Payment to contributors was fugitive. The *Southern Review* paid $2 a page, while the *Southern Quarterly Review* sometimes paid $1, which Thornwell raised to $3, a generosity with some bearing on his periodical's demise. All editors took contributions without payment, if a writer did not ask for it, and some would browbeat others into refusing payment on the grounds that there were enough free articles to fill any issue. It was usual to appeal to patriotism. "As yet we cannot promise to pay contributors," begins a typical letter, "and we believe there is plenty of dormant literary talent in the South—men who [are] public spirited enough to write articles for one year without pay."[31] In this, the South was like most of American publishing. The *North American Review* gave $1 a page to only a few of its contributors, and this was usual practice for quarterly reviews. Only literary magazines of broader appeal did better; in the 1850s *Graham's Magazine* was paying between $4 and $12 a page, though this was above the norm.

It is unclear how much editors troubled themselves to edit, other than in discharging the task of assembling and refusing contributions. George Frederick Holmes, who worked as Daniel K. Whitaker's associate for a while, asserted that the latter did little editing: "He is much more out-door-clerk and beggar-boy than editor."[32] On the other hand, Simms was unusually interventionist and, when at the *Magnolia*, rewrote both prose and poetry without authors' consent.

The model for editors was Francis Jeffrey of the *Edinburgh Review*, who saw his role as being a sort of literary stage manager and hence not someone who told the actors how to say their lines or interpret the play, just someone who made sure that the actors turned up for the performance. Like Jeffrey, the Elliotts and Legaré for the *Southern Review* found reviewers and subjects, stayed alert for controversies, and filled a gap if one occurred. But there is less evidence of their arguing with contributors over matters of substance or style, little sign that they threw in (as Walter Scott put it of Jeffrey's practice) "a few lively paragraphs or entertaining illustrations."[33] Discrimination seems to have lain in soliciting contributors and braving whatever consequences flowed from giving patronage to an opinion; once asked for, a contribution to a quarterly review, since both editor and essayist were gentlemen, seems to have been printed automatically.

The extent of circulations is hard to establish, though there is scattered evidence. Caroline Gilman in 1833 said that the *Rose Bud*, her children's periodical, had 735 subscribers, and this constituted a flourishing condition.

It seems probable that the *Southern Literary Messenger* had the greatest circulation, perhaps around 3,000. According to various unreliable sources, the *Southern Quarterly Review* had 2,500 subscribers in 1845, 2,000 in 1846, 1,700 in 1849, 800 in 1853, but 1,600 in 1854. In 1848, *De Bow's Review* listed 825 subscribers, of whom two-thirds were said to be in arrears. By comparison, *Graham's Magazine* in 1842 was printing 40,000 copies a month. The comparable figures for British periodicals are somewhat more flattering to the South, however. *Blackwood's* varied between 5,750 and 10,000 copies, the *Edinburgh Review* managed as many as 13,000 in its early days, but shrank to 4,000 in the 1840s. Considering the disproportion of population between Britain and the South, remembering the severity of competition from "national" periodicals and cheap American reprints of British journals, and recalling differing literacy rates (higher in the North, lower in Britain), the circulation of Southern periodicals was not especially discreditable to the curiosity of Southern readers.

In 1846 the *Southern Quarterly Review* tried to shame its delinquents by publishing a list of its subscribers, with their place of residence attached. From this, one can gain some sense of the geographical distribution of its paying readers. Of these 840 people, 43 percent were in South Carolina, 17 percent in Alabama, 14 percent in Georgia, and nearly 8 percent in Louisiana. Around 4 percent each were in Tennessee, North Carolina, and Mississippi. Surprisingly, Virginia managed only 3 percent. Maryland shared with the Northern states about 1 percent. The rest dribbled away into four subscribers for the District of Columbia, and one apiece for Arkansas, Texas, and Kentucky. So the periodical pointed more decisively to the Lower South than to the Upper, it addressed the non-South hardly at all, and its audience was mostly urban.

Unsurprisingly, a home base mattered. The *Southern Quarterly Review* had 43 percent of its market in South Carolina and did well in the eastern South, while *De Bow's* had 37 percent in Louisiana, and reached the Southwest with more efficiency. Neither periodical did well in the Upper South. There are no parallel numbers for the *Southern Literary Messenger*, but it seems plausible to extrapolate that its main market was Virginia, that it did far better in its former colony of Kentucky, probably fared better in Maryland and North Carolina, had a considerable market in South Carolina, but began to fade the farther south and west one got, with Mobile and New Orleans forming small islands of readership. That is, periodicals had circles of influence which overlapped in a few urban areas and most robustly in Charleston. But it is striking how incurious was Virginia about the region to its south, which would eventually drag the commonwealth into secession and war.

But what of authors in these journals? Of the *Southern Review*'s thirty-six contributors, 86 percent were in the immediate orbit of South Carolina, nearly 95 percent were Southerners, and only about 5 percent were Northerners. In short, when the quarterly's editors looked up to find contributors, their gaze seldom went beyond the state, even beyond Charleston and Columbia. Hence this was a South Carolinian, not a Southern, localism. There were only three contributors from other Southern states, being two from Virginia and one from Maryland. If you lived in the North, or were a Northerner or foreigner living in South Carolina, your chances of finding your way into the pages of the *Southern Review* were better than if you lived in New Orleans or Mobile, and better even than if you lived in Virginia.

Look a few years later at the *Southern Quarterly Review*, and Charleston has tilted somewhat inward and westward. Rough figures suggest that, of the 109 contributors who have been identified, South Carolinians constituted 51 percent, the rest of the South, 40 percent, and the North, 7 percent, so there had been a reaching-out to the rest of the South, though some of this was to a South Carolinian diaspora. Nonetheless, the evidence suggests that state localism had been modified, regionalism strengthened, and (curiously) sectionalism diminished. The proportion of Northern names in the *Southern Quarterly Review* had risen, perhaps to the norm of the hospitality offered to Southerners by New York and Philadelphia journals and far above that of Boston, where the *North American Review* managed only one Southerner for every hundred authors.

In 1870 Charles Dimitry of Louisiana put the matter of Southern periodicals harshly: "Their epitaph may well be written: Died of an indisposition to disburse, and of an infliction of immature intellect."[34] This was a half-truth, on both accounts. In general, there were too many bad authors and too few good ones, who were appearing in too many periodicals, which were chasing too few readers and still fewer paying subscribers. A disciplined literary order might have had one or two quarterly reviews, a few evangelical journals, and perhaps two literary magazines. These would have adequately provided for the region's talented authors and been comfortably sustained by the subscription base in the society, which was simultaneously (and sensibly) contributing to the sustenance of national and international periodicals. A Southern author's payments might thereby have been more regular and generous. But the South did not have that sort of literary order, but a pell-mell entrepreneurial one. For the alert reader, the effect was not so unhappy. What was needed appeared, though it was scattered hither and yon.

For a writer, this system had advantages and disadvantages. If you wished to make a living from it, it was useless. Writing for the journals could make a peripheral addition to an income, but no more. Simms worked the system and himself to death, but he could not have survived without other income from books and, not insignificantly, the plantations he acquired upon marriage. Poe, who oscillated between the more munificent Northern periodicals and the *Southern Literary Messenger* fleetingly made decent money, but usually did not.

Naturally, many found this exasperating, but complaints misunderstood the purposes of the system, if it was a system. It was designed not for professional authors, but for the convenience of readers and those authors for whom writing was an avocation, and so was intended for openness, not professionalism. The middle men, the publishers and editors, exploited free contributions to stake a place in a highly competitive literary and intellectual marketplace. They did this for a bare living, vanity, and influence. So this was not the oligarchical system preferred by an intellectual elite, where the hoi polloi are excluded, experts are well-rewarded, "standards" are enforced, and the intellectual world is rendered manageably small.

Hence Southern periodicals lived in a Jacksonian world, with some nostalgia for Federalism. Many eighteenth-century European periodicals had been pell-mell affairs, inclusive and undiscriminating, full of snippets. This tradition did not vanish and carried over to the United States far into the nineteenth century, but it had been the accomplishment of the *Edinburgh Review* to attempt a reform of such tatterdemalion abuses. As befitted a High Whig organ, it was oligarchical and paternalistic, evidenced by the drastic cutting down of the number of articles, which by 1810 had been reduced to about twelve per issue. As its opening announcement proclaimed, it wished "to be distinguished, rather for the selection, than for the number of its articles."[35] In effect, Francis Jeffrey said to the reader that the realm of knowledge was too large to be encompassed, that much was unworthy of serious attention, and that he would undertake to sift through the knowledge, find the gold, and discard the dross. What was left would be subjected to sustained and discursive analysis, undertaken by a small, self-selected, elite group of politicians, historians, clerics, and scientists, none of them specialized, all of them men of affairs.

These were the presumptions of the *Southern Review*, too, which was likewise oligarchical, paternalist, constricted, and presumed no small erudition in a reader. However, its successor, the *Southern Quarterly Review*, weakened this tautness. More reviewers of different social origins and locality and of more dispersed intellectual interests presented a fuzzier image of Southern culture; under the autodidact Simms, the commitment to erudition palpably weakened. In the *Southern Literary Messenger*, things were still murkier; it offered yet more voices from within and without the South, speaking in more various genres. In these ways, the reader was given more of the freedom which had been natural in the eighteenth century and falteringly snatched away in 1830.

In all this, the role of the contributor was significant, because the system existed for his or her convenience. The creation of 850 periodicals in about fifty years alone indicates that writing was a popular venture. These writers expected access to the media of expression. They did not mind that, the further up the scale one went, there might be rejections. These were not so frequent nor so brutal as to be incommoding. It was the pious sentiment of the age that the press was the medium of a democratic culture, but it was a sentiment that came close to a reality, and this not by accident. Voices were raised, words were printed, people read, discriminations were made, and everyone expected the right to be printed and heard. They did not expect a committee of scholars and experts to rule that a mind was too incompetent to be allowed articulation. So a lady or a young man might write poems about nightingales, the cleric might denounce German skepticism, the planter might advise on how best to plant sugar, the classicist might construe a line of Homer; all these were not created equal, because readers made their discriminations, but they were allowed to sit in their libraries, write down their words, take or mail them to an editor, sit back and wait for the printed word to appear.

This ideology of accessibility had variously arisen. There was the old republican presumption that the citizen had the right of independence, hence of thought, and hence, too, of expression. There were Jacksonian presumptions, which presumed entrepreneurial opportunities in the printed word, careers and pages open to the talents, by which some would rise, some fail, but all would have the chance to gain the spoils.

Hovering around this matter of openness was the issue of authorial anonymity. In the *Southern Review*, in imitation of the *Edinburgh*, all contributions had been unsigned. This was a mild variation on the habits of the eighteenth century, when most reviews had published anonymous contributions while favoring pseudonyms (Publius, Plain Truth). The *Southern Review* adopted anonymity, out of the modern hope that it would ease freedom of speech, especially for the scathing and witty. Edinburgh and Charleston were both intimate worlds and anonymity, though it could not provide invincible disguise, offered modest protection. It was a way of deflecting blunt confrontation.

It was said of the *Edinburgh Review* that anonymity protected a writer's reputation from the taint of Grub Street. At the beginning, this may have been so, but the influence and celebrity of the *Review* became so great that few authors were pained, other than by way of gentlemanly affectation, for any chance discovery of their contribution and hence of their critical importance. The same was true in the South. Moreover, it was a pleasant game to guess at contributors, though a game harder to play the more remote a reader was from an author's world.

In Grub Street, anonymity had disguised the profligacy with which needy authors had spun prose by the yard. This, too, in a modest way, served the interests and reputation of quarterlies. It would have looked impoverished, if a candid table of contents had revealed—as was the case with the August 1828 issue of the *Southern Review*—that three of its nine articles were by Legaré, and perhaps another three by the elder Elliott. Anonymity thus disguised narrowness of authorship by highlighting breadth of subject matter.

It will seem odd that members of a Romantic generation should have opted for anonymity, when Romanticism made so much of originality. Yet Wordsworth and Coleridge had published the *Preface to Lyrical Ballads* anonymously, and famously, Walter Scott, "the Great Unknown," had disguised his authorship of *Waverley*. In the United States, neither Irving nor Cooper put his name on his title pages until the 1840s. Curiously, for an age which mingled gentility with self-absorption, anonymity could liberate the confessional mood. When in the pages of the *Southern Review* Legaré mused on Byron's club foot, he could speak of his own deformity without the glare of abject publicity. Such disguise also, curiously, helped to establish a voice of authority. The anonymous voice spoke, not for itself alone, not merely for the poor, shrunken body of Hugh Legaré, but for the review, the times, and the domain of literature. There was an imperial ambition in the use of the word "we."

Anonymity, however, did proclaim a distance from the profession of authorship because it abjured advertisement and implied that opinion, not the opinion-maker, mattered. George Frederick Holmes always declined to have his periodical contributions assigned to himself and, when pressed by a New York editor who spoke of a personal bond between author and reader which anonymity prevented, responded that intellectual understandings went beyond personal credit and were belittled by prying intimacy. In this, gentility was involved. Professional authors like Simms might resent the hegemony of gentlemanly amateurs, but the struggle of Francis Jeffrey's generation had been to turn authors from the companions of pimps into gentlemen, rather as Henry Irving was later to elevate actors from the status of cads into knights, and eventually, by Laurence Olivier's day, into peers.

This view of things was never unanimous. The logics of Romanticism did demand self-regard, prized originality, and invited sympathy. Interest in celebrity did grow, which began to affect how anonymity was preserved or abandoned. So it is unsurprising that the *Southern Literary Messenger* was more muddled on the question of authorship and voice than the earlier *Southern Review*; some of the former's contributors were anonymous, some were pseudonymous, some had initials, some had initials with a place name, some were pseudonymous with place names, and some plainly signed their names. It seems editors often allowed contributors the freedom to represent themselves as they wished. But a literary magazine was more random and carried less authority than a quarterly review. When the *Southern Quarterly Review* was started in 1842, it took up where the old *Southern Review* had left off, with firm anonymities. With odd and inconsistent lapses, most articles remained anonymous until the October 1849 issue (Simms by then was editor), in which nine out of eleven articles were subscribed by initials. Thereafter the practice grew increasingly common, even usual. All this denoted an ambivalence about authorship.

Simms was an energetic proponent of the profession of letters and liked to argue that literary skill required specialization, even to the extent that authors should concentrate on a single genre. Conscious that he himself dissipated among many genres, he pleaded that, in America, writers were obliged to be jacks-of-all-trade to get by, and this would be so "until literature shall arrive at the dignity of a profession among us."[36] But he knew the old Ciceronian argument which held that the writer should mix with the world, know its affairs, and gain the wisdom which experience alone might give. Only to be an author gave the writer little to say. A century later, Allen Tate would complain that Southern letters in the early nineteenth century had been impoverished because thinkers had been drawn into politics. For many antebellum Southerners, this view would have seemed obtuse. Authorship and the public realm needed one another.

For some, being an author did mean sharing modestly in the benison of fame. To be Judge Longstreet was one thing; to be "the author of Georgia Scenes" was something else, mostly better. On the other hand, it might be worse, since the sins of the author might impugn the man and celebrity might bring notoriety and humiliating criticism. "Happy indeed is the author if he never has suffered martyrdom in the press," Caroline Lee Hentz later observed, not only of a "he." Worse even than this, an author might risk moral imperilment: "Fiction stands naturally opposed to fact," a reviewer of Dickens once insisted, "and story-telling, in popular estimation, is only another name for deceit."[37] So it might be wise for even a professed author to be unobtrusive, since this reticence might mitigate the inward perils of dishonesty and deflect the outward blows of critical hostility. Certainly putting yourself in a narrative was a risk. Byron had done so and had abandoned his wife, kept mistresses and monkeys in Venice, and boys in Greece, and some of these disreputable facts could be learned in Thomas Moore's biography.

Many feelings about authorship were focused by the debate over copyright, which flourished most in the late 1830s and early 1840s, partly because the Panic of 1837 had thrown the book trade into crisis. The United States had its own copyright laws, which protected the interests of American authors publishing at home. But foreign authors were not extended the same protection, so a great piracy fattened the profits of American publishers who took the latest Bulwer Lytton romance, which sold for $5 in London but might be peddled in Poughkeepsie for $2 or less. In the scramble, a cheap Dickens novel squeezed out an expensive, copyrighted book by John Pendleton Kennedy, or, more to the point, Kennedy was forced to take a profit near to that of Dickens in America, that is, none. The most famous of American authors, like Washington Irving and James Fenimore Cooper, could ride above the storm, but the more marginal could be driven to the wall. To remedy this situation, lobbies converged on Washington: the large lobby of the publishers and the small one of the authors appeared, while the public, which benefited from such systematic cheapness, looked on with indifference or a preference for the present order.

Various Southern writers and politicians were interested in the problem, on both sides of the debate. Henry Clay introduced four copyright bills between 1837 and 1842, all unsuccessful. But other Southerners were affected by the arguments that were to defeat international copyright: that the public was served well by getting its literature cheaply rather than expensively, that the publishing trade employed many workers who would suffer if copyright enforcement contracted business, and that no true-blooded American would want to line the pockets of the condescending British, anyway.

Simms entered this argument in 1844 with four articles in the *Southern Literary Messenger*. They were fiercely nationalistic, anxious to foster American literature and diminish the influence of foreign ideas, especially the British. According to Simms, only in recent decades had American literature awakened to itself, despite the handicap of sharing a language with perfidious Albion. Insofar as he thought a foreign literature relevant to the American experience, it was the German, for the sake of its liberation from French intellectual tyranny. Further, Simms was adamant about the merits of professionalism. Until 1834, he argued, American literature was the domain of literary amateurs, who wrote "at leisure hours, as a relief from other labors, or while preparing himself for other avocations," men who were content to publish small editions at their own expense or for "a trifling gratuity." Simms thought that American literature had struggled briefly into hopeful life, only to be stunted by cheap foreign reprints and the self-interest of American publishers, which "would seem to lie in discouraging as far as possible, the pretensions of the native author."[38] So he described a betrayal: he imagined that it had been the rise of American literature which had created a taste for reading in the American public, which in turn had been improperly directed into a taste for cheap foreign books.

Simms was painstakingly acquainted with the economic facts of American publishing, and his letters were (and are) a good introduction to how things then worked: the prices in London and Philadelphia, the different kinds of paper and binding, the techniques of stereotyping, the size of editions, and the significance of these conditions for the parties involved. He seems to have regarded his letters as a contribution to "the trading history of Letters in this country."[39] But, mostly, he wanted to reform a system which he regarded as hurtful to everyone but the American publisher, and that perhaps damaged even him. By this status quo, the American reader lost a native literature and was corrupted by the alien, the American author lost a living, the foreigner lost an income.

Simms was conflicted in that he was arguing that British authors should be paid American money and, further, that international copyright would serve as protectionism for an American domestic industry. He was an energetic free trader and an Anglophobe, and the combination caused him difficulty. In truth, however, he staked his case upon something which transcended nationality, because he clove to individualism. "It is individual life and property which needs and claims protection," he claimed. Copyright was, for the author, what the legal guarantees of property were for the citizen participating in the social compact. In this argument, Simms was driving away the view of the author as one artisan among many, a view current in early modern Europe, which had seen a book as a physical object made by many hands: the writer, the papermaker, the printer, the publisher, and so forth. Simms was dismissive of this cooperative vision. For him, as for many Romantics, a book was an author's creation: "He is as peculiarly the thing he makes as the spider is of his web of gossamer; spinning from his brains and his sensibilities, as the latter from his bowels, the structure which he endows and inhabits."[40]

These contentions were a powerful mix. Simms was a Jacksonian democrat who appealed to the logic of the age by speaking of the rights of property, the compulsions and benefits of competition and struggle, the suspicion of the Old World and the intoxicating promise of the New. Above all, he saw society and government as creatures of the acquisitive, possessive individual. But this individual was an author, a mystical original, a thing "*above*," a little less than God but more than man. He was the alchemist, who might "convert his genius and industry into a means of support." Of his intellectual property "*[he] is . . . creator*, and he sends it abroad, even as God sends light, and air, and sunshine, for the benefit and the blessing of mankind."[41]

Some of the arguments deployed in the copyright debate were transferable from the Anglo-American cultural controversy to the dispute between Northern and Southern society. The South, too, felt itself flooded by the cheap imprints of an alien culture, considered its nativity stunted, and imagined its originalities denied. The problem might affect all generations, but those who were thought to be most vulnerable were schoolchildren. (The antebellum South lived in the age which began to trouble itself about the culture of children.) In 1842, in the midst of the copyright controversy, the *Southern Quarterly Review* regretted that so many books used in Southern schools came from the North, "containing . . . oftentimes open declamation against the South and Southern institutions." Spelling books and reading books must be policed, as the young mind was easily swayed. In 1852, *De Bow's Review* published an article which passionately advocated the marginalization of textbooks that "*originate* in the North" and the substitution of publications which reflected "southern life, habits, thoughts and aims."[42] By 1853, Southern commercial conventions began to have similar opinions, which became a piety by the late 1850s.

Such animosities or hopes led to some action, but not much. The facts of publishing were stubborn. When a Southern author wished to publish a book, juvenile or adult, a Northern publisher was usually the better of two bad choices. This was not because the author made more money in the North, but because on balance a book published outside the South reached more readers, perhaps even in the South. So one could publish in the North, have more readers, and be indigent, or one could publish in the South, have fewer readers, and still be indigent. Vanity tended to dictate the former option, even if patriotism might urge the latter. (Vanity is usually the stronger force for an author.) In the choice of Northern venues, Boston was least common, not only for its abolitionist tendencies, but for its introspection. New York was the greatest publishing center, though Philadelphia was more sympathetic to Southerners.

Only the most marketable of writers could expect even mildly favorable terms. For a book in which they had some confidence, publishers might agree to share the profits, but most authors made little or nothing. One exception to this rule of poverty were lady novelists in the South, who often did nicely.

It was an empirical fact, which famously irritated men like Nathaniel Haw-thorne and Simms, that women came to engross more of the landscape of fiction, from about a third of it before 1830, to half in the 1850s, to three-quarters in the 1870s. E. D. E. N. Southworth was preeminently successful, not only among Southerners but among all American writers, so popular that she earned, at her peak, about $10,000 a year. Augusta Evans's *Beulah* (1859) sold 22,000 copies in its first nine months. Caroline Lee Hentz's *Linda; or, The Young Pilot of the Belle Creole* (1850) had thirteen editions in three years. And others did well, writers like Caroline Gilman, Maria McIntosh, and Mary Virginia Terhune. Below the likes of Southworth, below the lesser likes of Simms, things were tougher. And the descent depended partly upon genre. Novelists were best off, travel writers got by, scholars fared badly, and poets were lost souls. Trescot was put heavily into debt by the publication of his *Diplomatic History of the Administrations of Washington and Adams* (1857), which was done by Little, Brown of Boston. Paul Hamilton Hayne published his *Sonnets* in 1857 with Harper & Calvo of Charleston; these were printed at his own expense, in an edition of three hundred, of which he still had one hundred copies in his library in 1859.

One alternative was to collect subscribers, who paid for the book in advance, a practice that went far back in publishing history. But John Wesley Monette of Mississippi, publishing his *History of the Discovery and Settlement of the Valley of the Mississippi* (1846) with Harpers, was to find this process both disgruntling and exhausting. He not only had to write the book at no small expense but also had to collect the names of the subscribers, write and print a circular, prepare notices for newspapers and periodicals, distribute them, and send copies to his publishers (not the other way around), travel to New York to superintend the printing and proofreading, and employ an agent to peddle the book (who seems to have run off with some of the money). For the absence of these services, Harpers received half the book's profits and neglected to keep track of what ought to have been paid to Monette from both the first and second editions. Still, the practice of subscription was common enough. It was, in its own way, the last faint, cheap vestige of aristocratic patronage, because subscribers could flatter themselves that, by laying down two or three dollars, they were advancing the cause of literature.

As to where authors chose to publish, a few patterns are dimly visible. Some border state authors like Kennedy published exclusively in the North, while Simms in good times went North and in bad stayed closer to home. Others wandered hither and yon. John Taylor used Philadelphia and Peters-burg, Richmond and Washington; George Tucker appeared in Baltimore, Georgetown, and New York; David Ramsay in Charleston and Philadelphia;

Louisa McCord in Philadelphia and New York; Gayarré in New Orleans. Just to confuse the issue further, many books were published simultaneously in different cities by different presses. In general, unsurprisingly, the more local the topic, the more likely an author was to resort to a local publisher, but what defined "local" was often idiosyncratic, since some local topics were thought to transcend locality. Simms published his *History of South Carolina* in Charleston, but Campbell his *History of Virginia* in New York. Simms was by far the more notable figure, but South Carolina occupied a more provincial place in the national imagination than the Mother of Presidents. Much depended on chance knowledge, friends, stray meetings, fleeting reputations.

How far social ideology structured the access of Southern authors to Northern publication, or determined them to refuse the opportunity, is unclear. In the early days of American publishing, the Southern market was of great consequence for Philadelphia publishers especially, and they treated the South with consideration. Even as late as 1845, a publisher in Philadelphia excised antislavery poems from a collected edition of Longfellow, lest the South be offended. But the depression of 1837 had hit the South badly and led to the cancellation of many debts, some of them owed by Southern booksellers to Northern houses. So the latter grew wary. More important than ideology, however, was economics. The development of a railroad system, which reached the Northeast and Midwest with more efficiency than the South, deepened a growing sense that the Southern market was dispensable, that one could make very tidy sums of money without it. The success of *Uncle Tom's Cabin*, moreover, intimated that anti-Southern books might be a positive advantage on a publisher's list.

For the most part, though, the more aggressively "Southern" a book was, the less likely it was to be published in the North. This was partly a matter of self-selection. A Southern writer who wanted intellectual autarchy was likely to disdain non-Southern readers and Northern publishers. So most proslavery writing was locally published. But the rule was not universal; Lippincott's of Philadelphia was hospitable to such books. Moreover, one should not make too much of a Northern imprint as evidence of a connection to Northern culture. Often a publisher like Lippincott's took manuscripts from Southerners and returned them to the South as books, without making a significant connection with Northern readers; in that sense, that Lippincott's was in Philadelphia might be incidental.

Beyond the North, the last possible stop was publication or republication in Britain, France, or Germany. Such European dissemination happened to very few books by Southerners, and almost all of these were first published in the North, where publishers had established links with the Continent. Though no American publisher was compelled to pay anything to a British publisher for the republication of a British book, many of the former did pay for advance proofs as a way of beating their American rivals to the act of piracy. Thereby American houses acquired regular links with London, which might express itself in the British reprinting of an American text. Kennedy's *Swallow Barn* and *Horse Shoe Robinson* were both reprinted by Richard Bentley of New Burlington Street, who specialized in American authors. A few American publishers had both an American and a London imprint. This carried a number of Southerners across the Atlantic: Caroline Gilman, George Henry Calvert, Simms, Brantz Mayer, and Josiah Nott. However, the majority of books by Southerners published in Europe were picked up from Northern publishers and issued under a single imprint. Further, there were some Southerners who were expatriate or traveling who dealt directly with European publishers: Washington Allston and John Izard Middleton in London, Henry Lee in London and Paris, Adrien Rouquette in Paris, Thomas Smyth in Edinburgh and Glasgow.

However, only a few Southern authors ascended to cosmopolitan standing. In the earliest generation, there had been David Ramsay, who of all Southern authors probably reached the furthest. Most of his books were published in London, were sometimes pirated in Dublin, and had Dutch, French, and German translations. Next to Ramsay in reach was Poe. His works were routinely pirated in London, but in Paris the partisanship of Charles Baudelaire was to make him into the preeminent American Romantic for the French. Baudelaire, however, was unusual among Europeans for being sensitive to local distinctions among American writers. Except when slavery was directly at stake, the English, French, and Germans tended to muddle Americans into much of a muchness. The Leipzig publisher Tauchnitz ran even English and Americans together. To these Germans, at least, Washington Irving and James Fenimore Cooper were British authors, and so had no chance of being Yankees distinguishable from Southerners. Partly this was obtuseness, ignorance, and indifference. In the Southern case, it arose partly because the representation of Southern culture finding its way eastward across the Atlantic was severely filtered. A Southern author usually needed to be waved through by several cultural gatekeepers in Charleston, New York, London, or Paris before he or she could land on a European library table. Such filtering tended to export the softer side of Southern culture expressed in its fiction, as well as the harder racial theory so congenial to European tastes. But the process excluded the South's proslavery sentiment and permitted little even of its political theory. William Harper, Thomas Dew, George

Fitzhugh, all had no European reception, and even Calhoun was seen as a politician not a thinker, at least until Lord Acton noticed him. Poe, however, made it triumphantly over these divides. To be sure, he was in part preferred because he was, in many ways, a postcolonial writer and cast his themes in a rhetoric which seemed invitingly a mix of the strange and familiar. For his scenes were set in "a misty-looking village of England," "at an obscure library in the Rue Montmartre," "in the dreary district of Lofoden," amid "a thousand vague rumors of the horrors of Toledo," and only infrequently "near the western extremity, where Fort Moultrie stands, and where some miserable frame buildings, tenanted, during summer, by the fugitives from Charleston dust and fever, may be found."[43]

4 · The Shape of a History

In the first half of the nineteenth century, historical literature expanded as a species of knowledge deemed to explain the human experience. It came to engross a greater share of Southern culture than before or since, even though its standing was not unmixed, being thought by some trivial, by others an entertainment for ladies. As an undergraduate, James Henley Thornwell read philosophy in his serious hours, but "Saturdays," he wrote, "I amuse myself with history."[1] Still, historical writing mattered deeply, so it will be important to look at how Southerners defined the canon of historical literature, explained the philosophy of history, organized the infrastructure of historical research, and wrote its various forms, which can be taken to encompass history, biography, and autobiography. It will also be important to examine how Southerners conceptualized and practiced "literature," as critics, poets, and novelists.

First, the historical canon, which was still influenced by eighteenth-century tastes. One still read the ancient historians. Among the Greeks, Thucydides was most common, Herodotus standard, Xenophon unexpectedly usual, though Polybius rare. Among the Romans, Livy was a civic duty, Suetonius a closet taste because scandalous, Sallust uncommon, and Josephus mined by the pious. Tacitus was thought relevant by republicans wary of decline and of the savagery of human nature, despite his "dark, pregnant and startling" style, and disproportionately read for the fragmentary *Germania*, which nourished the discourse of race.[2] As for medieval historians, almost none were studied, though the Italian historians of the Renaissance did better because of their importance to classical republican theory, and Niccolò Machiavelli was pondered, at least for *The Prince* if not the history of Florence. Matters began to pick up with the English historians of the early modern period. In general, the canon of English historians began with the Earl of Clarendon and, rarely, Gilbert Burnet for his study of the English Reformation, though both were seen as old and musty. They were superseded by the elegant discursiveness of the ubiquitous British historians of the eighteenth century, David Hume, William Robertson, and Edward Gibbon. Below these, Smollett, Ferguson, and Goldsmith were read as popularizers. By the late 1820s, however, others had become conventional, notably James Mackintosh and Henry Hallam.

Among French historians, Jacques-Bénigne Bossuet was unusual and Voltaire standard for his biographies, while Charles Rollin, the ancient historian, was commonplace. With minor exceptions (Paul de Rapin de Thoyras, René Vertot, François de Mézeray), however, surprisingly little French historical literature was read, unless one counts Montesquieu. As for German historians, very few before Barthold Niebuhr made it into the Southern canon, except Johann Lorenz von Mosheim, the ecclesiastical historian, and those students of the ancient world like Christian Gottlob Heyne and Johann David Michaelis, who were more philologists than historians. Any single reader, of course, could and did read beyond this canon, but these embodied the common knowledge which dwelled in curricula and in cautionary letters sent from parents to children.

In addition, there was a small canon of American historians who were little part of curricula but were read privately. There were historians from the colonial period, who were usually deprecated, when rare copies could be located: John Smith, Robert Beverley, William Stith, Hugh Jones, John Lawson, and Alexander Hewat. Even more peripheral were the Northern historians, such as Thomas Hutchinson and Jeremy Belknap. More common were the first historians of the new republic. For his dull biography of George Washington, John Marshall was honored and even sometimes read, though John Daly Burk's history of Virginia was racier. For most people, however, David Ramsay's works *were* American history, since he had written the most influential account of the American Revolution and his history of South Carolina was the best colonial and state history. By comparison, Hugh Williamson's *History of North-Carolina* (1812) and Hugh McCall's *History of Georgia* (1811) were poor competitors. With the possible exception of Ramsay, however, no educated Southerner in 1820 or so would have been regarded as uneducated who had read none of these American works, whereas not to have read Thucydides, Hume, and Gibbon would have been reprehensible.

It followed that the Southern historical consciousness had a powerful sense of connection with times and places beyond itself. Ancient, medieval, modern, European, colonial, American, these terms offered a sense of place and ventured an explanation of a social self. In this historical succession, the non-American crowded out the American, let alone the Southern. It was to require much effort to disrupt and reverse this narrative and thereby to create the South as no longer the last and minor stopping point for history but its beginning.

The presumptions of the Enlightenment had seen history as, in Bolingbroke's paraphrase of Dionysius of Halicarnassus, philosophy teaching by example. Human nature was thought to have stability across time and space. History was "the register of the crime, follies, and misfortunes of mankind" but also of human accomplishments. Historians told the stories which clarified the lineaments of a mixed human nature and thereby showed what was possible and likely. Hence Thucydides, Livy, and Machiavelli told historical tales of trans-historical significance, whose value was to encourage the morally great and to warn against the immorally forceful, to balance philosophy against experience, to construct institutions and elaborate ideas which might maximize happiness and minimize misery. It was, in that sense, a guarded discipline of modest confidence in human progress. Gibbon wrote of "the pleasing conclusion that every age of the world has increased, and still increases, the real wealth, the happiness, the knowledge, and perhaps the virtue, of the human race," but there was hesitation and irony in that "perhaps."[3] A progression in virtue was harder to prove than an accession of knowledge, but even the skeptic tended to grant that Christianity had had some role in clarifying virtue's meaning. An American philosophe, whether Federalist or Jeffersonian, might concur in seeing the American Revolution as a decisive improvement in the human prospect. Yet both had seen Americans as connected in tension to the wider human condition, discernible in historical evidence from Rome, Florence, and Westminster. The idea of exceptionalism, the premise that Americans and Southerners had leapt free of flawed human experience, was, under these intellectual circumstances, hard to establish, but possible.

Historicism, the self-designated revolution of historical thinking which began with Johann Gottfried Herder and a rediscovered Giambattista Vico, changed matters. It became arguable that human nature was not stable but assumed different forms in different times and places, and hence it was proper to be skeptical of natural law. Human personality and behavior were formed by membership in a nation or race, to which individuals owed a moral responsibility. History, philology, and literary analysis captured the process of change in national character, so that students might distinguish the ephemeral from the essential. With these presumptions, historians were thought to possess a critical method which was scientific but distinct from natural science, because historical composition required an act of sympathy and imagination. It came to seem that there were no values outside of history, though many that God had placed within the stream of history. Beyond these beliefs, historicists differed widely. Some stressed the state as the fulfillment of history's progress and purpose, others resented the state as a tyrant; some dwelt upon the people's will and destiny, others saw society as a collectivity of myriad individual biographies; some thought race transcended national boundaries, others treated nations as races; some stressed inner biological compulsions, others a dialectic between nature and nurture. But, however the paradigm was manipulated, the intellectual tendency was to split time and humanity into fragments, though each fragment was deemed to have its own coherence.

In time, Romantic historicists would become condescending toward the eighteenth century and exaggerate the immobility of its historical understanding. But even cautious Southerners thought themselves in the midst of a promising transformation. To Mitchell King, discoursing in 1843 on "the qualifications and duties of an historian," history seemed a progressive science of experience, recently making headway in concert with political theory and political economy. Institutions like the Georgia Historical Society were the laboratories of this moral science, which focused on the historical experience of peoples, states, and nations. Historians must study economic conditions, literature, and philosophy, while commemorating contributors to the welfare of mankind, including scientists. Mostly, historians must study chains of cause and effect, the dependence of future upon past. As to qualifications, King stressed self-knowledge, hard work, and wide knowledge (philosophy, geography, chronology, style). Because history was "a store of moral experiments," the historian must love truth and disdain sectarianism, both religious and political, though not to the point of tactlessness. At least, the historian should regard his own and others' creeds with sympathy. Patriotism did not require the hiding of a country's faults, nor did piety excuse a religion's ill effects. Prejudice, then, must be eschewed, because it could distort. Gibbon, for example, had been marred by his hostility to Christianity, marred, too, by pride in himself.[4]

This was a formidable list of qualifications, more taxing than anything Samuel Johnson had in mind when he observed to James Boswell: "Great abilities are not requisite for an Historian; for in historical composition, all the greatest powers of the human mind are quiescent. He has facts ready to hand so there is no exercise of invention. Imagination is not required in any high degree, only about as much as is used in the lower forms of poetry."[5] Mitchell King, on the other hand, was insistent that historians had been placed far too low on the rung of literature. Great historians were rare, because their task was so exacting. The fact that history had been written for so long and by so many cultures and the list of its eminent practitioners was so short was alone evidence enough to show the loftiness of the venture.

King was a serious Presbyterian and more priggish than most Southern philosophers of history. And he was no preacher of a pure historicism, with its central doctrine of the separateness of times and places, its tendency to remove the philosophical historian from a skeptical perch above history and plunge him into the complicit rivers of time. True, King was anxious to praise historians like Niebuhr who can safely be regarded as historicists. But there was a stronger whiff of Edinburgh than of Bonn about King. In this, he was behind his Southern times, which were moving rapidly in the 1840s toward a full-dressed historicism. Preeminently George Frederick Holmes documented and criticized those who had changed matters: Vico, Herder, the Schlegels, Niebuhr, François Guizot, and Jules Michelet. For these, the past might be different, but it was knowable, capable of reinvigoration by means of a human imagination. By 1820 skepticism had moved far enough to demolish Hume's easy assumption that human nature was universal, but not so far as to assimilate Hume's difficult proposition that reliable knowing was impossible. And so a historian like Niebuhr was a metaphysically safe model, a man praised not for deconstruction but for reconstruction, and peculiarly influential on Southern historical literature, far more so than Leopold von Ranke or Jules Michelet. This standing was, partly, the natural respect from an intellectual culture where antiquity remained a crucial point of cultural reference, and readers tried to keep up with ancient historians. But respect for Niebuhr ran deeper than this; he was thought to have opened "a new era for all history."[6] His name was scarcely ever mentioned without an accolade that stressed his centrality to the philosophical *and* practical accomplishments of historical literature since Gibbon. The importance of control in a slave society helps to explain this pertinence. Niebuhr was a Prussian conservative, one of the many who were trying to put the genie of the French Revolution back in the bottle. He seemed to prove that human intelligence could establish control, create order, from the most refractory of materials, from even broken columns and crumbling palimpsests. Above all, he was thought to have reconciled imagination and science, while according to each its own sphere.

It was a paradox of the historicist revolution that what began as Christian, utilitarian, and conservative in both metaphysics and politics ended up as agnostic, aesthetic, and radical. The early historicists, like Herder, began to see the past as another country, and, eventually, this broke the link between past and future, whose manipulation people like Mitchell King saw as the crowning accomplishment of the historian. But human nature itself broke into shards, for some beyond even imaginative recreation, for many beyond utility. The frankly utilitarian disciplines like economics, sociology, and even anthropology drifted away from history, when historians could no longer confidently assert that things in the past could be known and then deployed in what Robert Henry called "regulating the conduct of mankind."[7] As we shall see, male Southerners from Thomas Dew to William Henry Trescot went further along in this journey than has been recognized, but not all the way. Mary Chesnut was to know more, but then she lived through a great war which shattered the illusion of control.

Thomas Dew fashioned the best account by a Southerner of the wide scope of human history, because each year he gave lectures to the undergraduates of the College of William and Mary on matters since the Creation. These were printed posthumously as *A Digest of the Laws, Customs, Manners, and Institutions of the Ancient and Modern Nations* (1853), a book divided into two sections, with the transition coming at the fall of Rome and the rise of feudalism. The ancient world is discussed in eight chapters, although the first six are very brief and fragmentary, before two long chapters on the Greeks and Romans. The section on modern history has nine chapters: on feudalism, chivalry, the rise of Christianity, urban development, the revival of literature, the growth of royal power, the Reformation, the development of the English constitution up to 1688, and the French Revolution.

Dew's earliest pages are skeptically respectful toward the biblical account of creation and most committed to Christian belief when non-Christian cosmogonies lent support to Moses. In this, Dew was influenced by the Neptunian school of geology, and, on several occasions, he cites its advocate William Buckland. Otherwise, Dew gives an account of ancient tribes rooted in the discoveries of modern ethnography, while being quietly dismissive of polygenesis and insistent upon man's common origin, because modern scholars of language had shown that all languages had diverged from a common root. Nonetheless, Dew gives a short account of the ancient Jews, with an emphasis upon their tribal divisions and patriarchal system of governance, and with praise of their literary accomplishment as (in Herder's way) "purely national."[8] As for Egypt, his estimate is polite if unpreoccupied, mostly anxious to deny Herodotus's awkward claim that the Egyptians were Negro. As for ancient Asia, he followed the standard modern line that it was a land of despotisms and nomads. In general, his case for European superiority and imperial expansion is what one might expect of a Southerner whose culture was itself imperial, the more so as he deployed racial explanations for this success.

Dew's approach to the Greeks was sympathetic if anthropological, since he inclined toward Hume's contention that their myths expressed primitive irrationalities. As a first principle, Dew believed that polytheism was natural to early societies, while being conscious that Greek religion (unlike the Egyptian) had not been the exclusive possession of priests and this quasi-openness had encouraged a sense of humanity. Still, Dew was careful to insist that monotheism was superior, if difficult to grasp, and to ensure that his enumeration of the multiplicity of ancient cosmogonies should not incline his undergraduates to relativism. Rather, the main ground of Dew's sympathy for the Greeks was their decentralization of governance, which had created disorder and vitality alike. As was common among the Romantic historians, he deprecated the Spartans for conservative rigidity and praised the Athenians for democratic initiative. Unlike his authorities, however, Dew was sanguine about the beneficial consequences of slavery. Athens, above all, was a shining moment for liberty and republicanism.

Dew on the Greeks mingled several intellectual influences. There were his Romantic themes, that the Greeks had more imagination and less reason than the moderns, a more sensual and tactile sense of materiality, which expressed itself in the crude licentiousness of their drama. But Dew was never more than a half-hearted Romantic and was as likely to cite Voltaire as he was to quote the Schlegels. Thus he often alluded to the Scottish stage theory of social development and argued for philosophy's independence from religion. Moreover, Dew displayed a restless sense that social forms have a transhistorical significance. In his narrative, one could jump from Attica to modern America, from the Agora to modern Italian music, and usefully compare Philipp Melanchthon with James Madison.

Unusual was Dew's preoccupation with the historical role of women. In one sense, this arose from his interest in social and economic history, and was partly inspired by the various dissertations on the "progress of the female sex" to which the Scottish Enlightenment had been prone. But Dew seemed impelled by a restlessness about exclusively male worlds and was deeply interested in the power of sex. The young men of Williamsburg must have leaned forward in their desks when their college president launched into a long disquisition on Greek courtesans, wherein he happily dwelt upon how their corruption had been matched by their allure and intelligence.

More broadly, Dew offered an explanation for the decline of Greece, which self-evidently mirrored his American prognostications. Athens, he argued, had too greatly restricted the franchise, had made citizenship into a caste, and so become the tyrant of Hellas. Further, Greece was plagued by a racial division. Athens came to lead the progressive and democratic Ionians, Sparta the conservative and aristocratic Dorians, and between the two no reconciliation proved possible. Hence the tragedy of the Peloponnesian War.

In general, Dew's view of the ancient world was influenced by Benjamin Constant's contentions that the problem of antiquity was the overweaning power of the state and that the distinctiveness of modernity was the primacy it gave to the individual. From statism had flowed Greece's incessant warfare, absence of gentility, abrupt ostracisms and confiscations. Like Constant, Dew made some exception for Athens, which never acquired modernity but whose democracy mitigated the stifling implications of state power. Dew stressed the value of risk: better a turbulent Greece than "all the barren annals of Chinese history for thousands of years past."[9] The trick was to find a middle ground between the ancient and the modern. This, too, had been Constant's liberal message, which in Dew's Virginia translated itself into a Whiggery keen to navigate a course between Jacksonian democracy and proscriptive aristocracy. For the Virginian student, the value of Greek history was its offering a laboratory in which to study the varieties of political experience, wherein one could see the value of balancing energy against order and the wisdom of giving small commonwealths the freedom to create innovation, while also giving a federal government the power to restrain anarchy.

Fashionably Dew made less of the Romans than the Greeks and was interested in the tribal origins of the "early Italian races." After Niebuhr, Arnold Heeren, and Thomas Arnold, Dew stressed the wise process by which the governing oligarchy of Rome had admitted the plebs into citizenship and reformed the early republic. Only later, when the plebs were reduced to dependency, did they become the feared rabble of legend, at which time an impassable gulf developed between patrons and clients, a gulf unmediated by a middle class, and thereby Rome became subject to "continual convulsions."[10] For Dew, Rome acted most wisely when it assimilated strangers and lost distinctions of race, most unwisely when insisting upon rank and exclusivity. Nonetheless, Rome was able to gain an empire through the peculiar force and coherence of her political system, though that empire brought both an enlarged civilization and the temptations of imported vices. Dew thought that one should only judge Rome's probity at the expansive moments when it was seriously tested, not when in narrower republican times. On the whole, however, Dew's account of Rome is a chronological survey of its wars, in which he found little to admire. Even the Antonines, whom Gibbon had invited the world to admire, were given only a grudging approval, Dew noting the empire's prosperity but also its moral littleness. Certainly, unlike Gibbon, Dew did not blame Christianity for the fall of Rome, but then its continuance mattered less, if one did not admire the empire.

Dew was not without the Enlightenment's mistrust of the Middle Ages, which he consented to call "*dark*."[11] He debated, for example, in what medieval century one should locate the nadir of European history and offered as alternatives Robertson's claim for the tenth century and Guizot's for the seventh. Nonetheless, he did not locate the origins of modernity in the Renaissance, as Jacob Burckhardt would later do, but in the Middle Ages. No doubt it was an anarchic period, but it saw the emergence of chivalry, the vernacular languages, modern literature and manners. In the aristocracy, the carriers of the idea of liberty, there began to be a concept of individualism which in time would trickle down to the masses. Notable, too, is that Dew located the significance of Christianity not in the story of the ancient world but in the birth of the modern.

In Dew's account, the Crusades are a brutal and coarsening education in massacre and persecution, but a venture that promoted an understanding of the non-European world and produced a spirit of nationality in Europe, because the Italian city-states, which (after Sismondi) Dew saw as vital sponsors of commercial modernity, had been stimulated by the new trade with the Levant. In medieval Italy Dew saw the conditions of ancient Greece reborn: smallness of scale, turbulence, initiative, and energy. Again, he argued (not very clearly), the great change from the eleventh to the fourteenth centuries had been a shift from the local to the national. More, the cities had impelled the emancipation of the serfs, which Dew saw as an advance. This assertion was, of course, an awkward insight for a slaveholder, so Dew had to make his distinctions, of which the greatest was that modern Southern slaves (unlike Renaissance serfs) were of a different race. Moreover, he argued that the economic expansiveness of the Italian cities had enabled them to absorb the emancipated serfs, which was not the American situation, and that the European climate had not required a labor force peculiarly fitted for subtropical conditions. In time, however, the Italian republics duplicated the errors of ancient Rome; they expanded, conquered, and sought control, while their citizens learned supine acquiescence to an overweaning aristocracy, and so, in "the strong language of Sismondi, Italy appears struck by the hand of death" by the seventeenth century.[12] The implications of this for a South, expanding and seeking control, were troubling.

By the seventeenth and eighteenth centuries, as Guizot had suggested, the political dynamic of modernity, which lay in the interaction of government and people, had been fashioned. But, before discussing how the power of the people began to countervail centralization, Dew turned to the Reformation, which for the Protestant Romantic was conventionally understood to be a major source of modernity. It is notable that Dew diminished the Protestant content of the Reformation and made it more of a piece with humanism; both are seen as ventures which liberated intellectual inquiry, at a time when the invention of the printing press and the voyages of discovery unraveled the tight authority of the medieval church. Still, Dew was in no doubt that Protestantism had marked an advance, observable in the material progress of Protestant countries compared to the laggard enervation of Catholic ones.

Dew next turned to the two great political traditions of modern Europe, the British and the French, the one leading to 1688 and 1776, the other to 1789. His history of the English constitution was conventional, except in leaning toward the proposition that the origins of English liberty had lain less with Anglo-Saxons and more with the Anglo-Norman aristocracy, which had evolved an alliance with the people as a means of resisting the monarchy. (This was not how Jefferson had seen the matter.) The evolution of parliament was central to Dew's account, and he highlighted the process by which parliament acquired complexity and depth of representation. For the most part, he was persuaded that this occurred for fiscal reasons, partly because no one social class could monopolize power and wealth. He did not, however, see popular uprisings as the cause of political revolution. Rather, he suggested that the English populace had been conservative, even legitimist. Further, he argued as a principle that "the great revolutions of modern times have been brought about principally by the agency of the propert[ied]."[13]

Dew was more impressed with a religious explanation for the English civil wars. The Puritans may have been "ridiculous and unamiable" but courageous and competent, too, and only religion persuaded ordinary people to support the Parliamentarians.[14] Otherwise his narrative was sharply aware of contingency and unintended consequences, and unusually conscious of the historiographical debate. He was not enthusiastic about either the older Whig historians (John Oldmixon, Catharine Macaulay) or the older Tory ones (Clarendon, Hume). Instead, Dew favored the new generation of Guizot, Hallam, and Thomas Babington Macaulay. To trust Macaulay was to be a modern Whig, and Dew's Whiggery was businesslike, even Victorian in tone. The constitutional adjustments of 1688 were doubtless important for liberty, but more significant for balancing king, aristocracy, and commons. Less usual was Dew's insistence that this balance was completed not in 1688 but later, even under Sir Robert Walpole, and he skipped over 1688 in barely a page, benign but unpreoccupied. His Burkean argument was that propertied people sorted things out in a gradualist fashion. Unlike Burke, however, Dew admired Oliver Cromwell, and his praise is significant, because it exposed a tension. In his narrative of English history, Dew had tended to lose touch with his heritage as a Virginian republican, but in this regard for Cromwell, he recovered himself.

Dew's English history was fashioned in the light of his understanding of the French Revolution, as most recent accounts were, and his position on the

American Revolution came from weighing French against English history and putting the American experience on the English side of the ledger. Upon this logic, the English had had an experience of contingent liberty and, undeluded by abstract theory, had found no temptations in agrarianism. Considering all that had gone before in the *Digest*, Dew's version of the French Revolution is unsurprisingly Burkean. His ancien régime personifies corrupt centralization, his revolutionaries demonstrate the temptations of radical liberty, his middle classes do good work. He stressed the unfortunate role of the philosophes, who were impractical men of utopian disingenuousness. Still, Dew did not go all the way with Burke and, amid his Anglo-American complacency, did acknowledge the value of the French Revolution for its modern reenactment of the ancient lesson of Greek history, which was that a polity needed to find the middle ground between liberty and anarchy, diversity and centralization.

This précis does not do justice to the complexity of the *Digest*. For one thing, it is almost best for its Tocquevillean gift for instructive details and its un-Tocquevillean fondness for humane anecdotes. To read Dew is to be told that history makes sense and has lessons, but not always the lessons habitual to the moderate Whig-cum-bourgeois tradition, to which he belonged. His libertarian argument was sufficiently emended by his preoccupation with the problems of centralization and property, and by his concern with the status of women, to make Dew more than just a rehash of Niebuhr, Hallam, and Macaulay. Dew was interested in matters beyond political society. Because of his training as a political economist, he went further than his eighteenth-century exemplars (like John Millar) in worrying out the problem of society, in trying to see some relationship between how men were governed and how they lived.

As a slaveholder sympathetic to racial theory, Dew added touches alien to Bonn and London. On the whole, however, it is striking how little the *Digest* made of slavery's role in history. Dew seemed to stir himself to discuss slavery and race only when he knew the thought of their relevance would have arisen irresistibly in the mind of his readers. In the *Digest*, in contrast to Dew's review of the Virginia emancipation debates of ten years earlier, slavery was seen as too intermittent an institution to be made an analytical centerpiece. Slavery, in 1842 as in 1832, was subject to the criterion of practicality: if it worked, it should live; if it failed, it should die unregretted. Slavery was but a facet of the great historic drama of liberty and centralization, of risking freedom and needing order.

Thomas Dew's *Digest* was the most sustained account of the scope of human history written by a Southerner, but its scope was not singular. There was a large body of wide-ranging history in the periodicals and in books. While most of this writing was lame, no little was competent. There is substance to and even original research in works like John Izard Middleton's *Grecian Remains in Italy* (1812), Henry Lee's *Life of Napoleon Bonaparte* (1837), Thomas R. R. Cobb's *Historical Sketch of Slavery* (1858), and David Flavel Jamison's *Bertrand du Guesclin* (1864).

When David Ramsay published his *History of the American Revolution* in 1789, there was no chair of history in the South, no historical society anywhere in the United States, few archives, and no historical profession. Though history was taught in colleges, and had been so since the beginning of higher education in North America in 1643, the first chair of history in the South was created at the University of Maryland only in 1813. But the subject was commingled with belles lettres, or the classics, or moral philosophy, and, even when released from these affiliations, it was often only to proclaim an attachment to political economy. However, most of those who instructed adolescents in history did not trouble publishers and most history was written outside the academy.

The institutional structures which underpinned historical literature were unimpressive. The first American historical society had been started in Massachusetts in 1791, but the South had no such organization until the Tennessee Antiquarian Society in 1820, which combined the functions of a historical with those of an archaeological and anthropological society, with a dash of interest in zoology and geology, seasoned with the uplift of an educational reform movement. In time, other historical societies emerged, all enterprises of gentlemen, since women were deemed to have no stake in any history which merited an organization. These societies varied greatly in scope, robustness, and permanence, but most concerned themselves with collecting the historical records of their state. A few had connections with state governments, many did not. Several, notably Georgia, Virginia, and South Carolina, published documents, sometimes after emissaries had been sent to catalog the sources available in Britain. In each case, there was a sense that such societies might help to create a state's feeling of self-worth. There was a sense, too, that the South had catching up to do.

The weakest historical societies were those in Alabama, Florida, Mississippi. Missouri, Kentucky, Louisiana, and North Carolina, most of which convened irregularly, were undersubscribed, and did little by way of accumulating libraries and archives. Stronger were Virginia and South Carolina (chartered in 1855), and strongest were Georgia and Maryland.

The Virginia Historical and Philosophical Society was organized in Richmond in 1831, when its membership was by election not subscription. A volume of *Collections* was published in 1833 and anniversary discourses appeared in the *Southern Literary Messenger*. After 1838 the society became moribund, but in 1846 its meetings revived, and it acquired an endowment, accumulated manuscripts, and started publishing. Alone among the societies, it ran a periodical, *The Virginia Historical Register*, which published six volumes between 1848 and 1853, when it was succeeded by a more limited annual, the *Virginia Historical Reporter*.

The Georgia Historical Society dated from 1839. Its speciality was invited speakers, whose lectures were habitually published; most were Georgians and many only casually historians. A committee of the society, consisting of a bank cashier, a diplomat, a doctor, and a chemist would invite a judge to speak about historical matters, in order to promote "State interest and State pride."[15] In addition, the society published volumes of its *Collections*, three of them before 1861, and commissioned William Bacon Stevens to write a history of the state. A building was constructed in 1848, in which was deposited a library of about five thousand volumes.

Even more robust was the Maryland Historical Society, founded in 1844 by assorted Baltimore literati "to collect, preserve and diffuse, information relating to the Civil, Natural and Literary History of the State of Maryland, and American History and Geography generally."[16] In 1845, it formed an alliance with the Library Company of Baltimore, and (after raising $45,000 in only three months) constructed a new building to house itself. It procured documents from London and published a little, notably the *Journal of Charles Carroll of Carrollton* (1845). For a historical society, it proved unusually popular with (by 1858) a membership of five hundred, attracted by the society's active and eclectic lecture program. Its annual dinner was an occasion, attended by celebrities, often available because of the proximity of Washington.

The men who wrote, not the history of the South (which no one yet wrote), but of the states which made it up, were habitually the sons of the Southern governing classes, usually too wealthy to need a job but too retiring to venture politics. Of these, Albert James Pickett of Alabama was typical. In 1847 he decided dutifully to write a history of his state. Planting engrossed little of his time, he disliked politics, he had no profession, and so he "determined to write a History," only to be surprised at how much work and expense was involved. Out of his innocence, Pickett wrote to various gentlemen experienced in state histories to announce his intentions, ask advice, and enquire about the location of documents. From them he got counsel about archives, documents, books, and amanuenses (to copy documents), and acquired a sense of the network of historians. Jared Sparks counseled that "your facts should be derived from original sources; that is, from the earliest writers or manuscripts," while William Bacon Stevens advised the wisdom of collecting "every book—pamphlet & document which will throw the least light upon your subject."[17] Such advice made the writing of history an expensive business, confined to gentlemen of means.

For such a history, documents had a special gravity, because hard to obtain. To a surprising degree, however, state historians relied upon oral testimony and narratives often derived from the memories that gentlemen (very rarely ladies) were willing to share. These amiable sociabilities left little room for the tone of skeptical subversion which is the standard trope of modern historical writing, the more so as these exchanges might ascend to the mystical. Those old people, soon to die, who had experienced the American founding told stories which seemed sacred. Narratives might betray a breathless care for the true witnesses of the holy moments, even its minor episodes.

This led to haphazard research. A bookseller might or might not have the book the historian needed. It might be convenient to examine documents in New Orleans, or their owner might be away. Copyists might be careful, or they might not. For the most part, despite the view that a historian needed to be a sort of circuit rider, the sources came to the historian, more than the historian went to the sources, and the adequacy of a personal library went far to define what history could be written. A historian was, preeminently, a man of means alone in a study, and historical writing attracted those who could bear being alone. As Charles Campbell once remarked of his labors, "These pursuits have been solitary."[18] Hence history attracted more than its share of the shy, who sometimes reached out for a sense of membership in a guild, but were often disappointed. Within the intellectual communities of cities and states, matters were often sour and camaraderie seemed to flourish in inverse proportion to distance.

Of the men and no women who wrote such local history, perhaps the most knowledgeable was Hugh Blair Grigsby of Norfolk, Virginia, where in the 1830s he owned and edited a newspaper. Marrying late to a woman who brought him a large and valuable tobacco plantation, he was little engaged by planting but preoccupied himself with literary and aesthetic pursuits, especially with collecting books. Grigsby conducted a large correspondence with fellow historians, Northern (George Bancroft, Henry Adams) and Southern (Charles Campbell, David Swain), though, like most Virginians, his links with the North were better than with the Lower South. For all that, Grigsby wrote sparingly: a few articles, some reviews, a few orations, a little fiction, a youthful imitation of Montesquieu and Wirt, a eulogy of Littleton Waller Tazewell, and two brief studies of the Virginia constitutional conventions of

1776 and 1829–30, with a third upon that of 1788, which was published posthumously. He let others write general histories of Virginia, even though they were his inferiors in intellect and knowledge, perhaps because he lacked the physical stamina which sustained historical composition required. Fragments suited him better.

To be an intelligent Virginian of lively historical awareness, born in 1806, was not easy. Virginia was full of great men, growing greater in legend, such that the young might feel incapacitated by the burden. True, Norfolk itself had been peripheral to fame, though not to events, and there the American Revolution was palpable and the British came to burn things as late as Grigsby's seventh year. Politics and the making of government was the Virginian pastime; a young man was supposed to learn the art of it. Grigsby seems to have done his best. He studied widely, learned the law, entered the legislature, and thought about putting pebbles in his mouth. But, like Henry Adams later, he lost the ambition of politics in the study of it. Grigsby became a sort of permanent younger son of Virginia, who sat at the feet of the great, listened to their stories, tried to make sense of their personalities, and wanted to hold the tradition together so that it might be transmitted. Thereby he might belong to the procession and his ashes might be "mingled with the ancestral mould."[19] Yet Grigsby was no slavish acolyte: he knew enough to distinguish between accomplishment and pretension. Still, he was a court historian, even if he knew that the court might have many lesser men, and more who were unscrupulous or incompetent.

Grigsby's intellectual career was made by his brief engagement with political power, especially the moment when he attended the Virginia constitutional convention of 1829–30. He went first as a spectator, then became a delegate, and there began a sketchbook, in which he was more drawn by the men, less by the issues. In the disputes of the convention, however, he was a moderate conservative who leaned toward the slaveholding oligarchs but understood the force of the western democrats. This was odd in a Jacksonian from a commercial city, but he was an easterner, young, and under the sway of Tazewell and John Randolph; more, as a student of the past, he was reluctant to break with it. The Virginian political tradition and the men who made it thereby became Grigsby's great theme, though it was to be a quarter century before he published his discourse on the convention. There he returned to fuller portraits of Madison and Marshall, before descending to the lesser figures. By Grigsby, Madison is seen as the urbane maker of the Union, the backroom boy whose voice did not carry but whose intelligence and stamina were crucial. By contrast, Marshall is rough, self-made, solitary, robust. Insistently, Grigsby located meaning in personality. "The history of these names is the history of the period," he said of the period from 1789 to 1801, but he could have said this of any period or narrative of which he was capable of writing.[20] By Grigsby, the reader is asked to pause, to look around the room of Virginian history, to hear the men talking, now in oratory, now in half-shadowed cabal. Though he verged on eulogy, Grigsby had the gift of distilling character.

It would be easy to neglect that Grigsby had general views of Virginian history. He had, it is true, small sense of the "history of morals or manners," and even the history of slavery barely existed in his narrative, because these were to be found outside his rooms of hair-splitting politicians.[21] Still, he did offer a periodization for the political history, at least, of the early republic: 1789 to 1801, the time of organization; 1801 to 1806, which saw the high water mark of Jeffersonian retrenchment and reform; 1806 to 1815, when the struggle with Europe occasioned a politics of crisis; 1815 to 1829, when matters settled down and ancient disputes (as over the national bank) were inconsistently reconciled.

The *Virginia Convention of 1776* (1855) forcibly stated many of Grigsby's preoccupations. On the meaning of the Revolution, it was conventional enough, at least for a Jeffersonian. While the Revolution of 1688 was mis-called, being but a dynastic shift, that of 1776 taught "a far more imposing lesson." It legitimated the people as the source of power, made government a trust, validated personal worth over the hereditary principle, abolished primogeniture, and created freedom of religious conscience and practice. But Grigsby had more idiosyncratic themes. As noted elsewhere, he was scathing toward the Cavalier myth and those historians who romanticized "the acts of the beggarly governors who for a century and a half were sent over to fatten on the revenues of the Colony." Grigsby understood the Virginian revolution as class warfare and a three-way civil war between Anglophile baronial planters, young professionals defensive of their rights, and radicals of moderate means from the interior who were jealous of the colonial oligarchy and church hierarchy, and resentful, too, of growing taxes. Grigsby was enough of a postrevolutionary man to ask for understanding, even for Tories or timid Whigs, who had helped to keep together the fabric of society "when a civil war was raging in the land." The moral heart of the book is Grigsby's apostrophe to the Virginia Declaration of Rights of 1776. He did not blush to elevate it above the Declaration of Independence and the Petition of Right, because the Virginia Declaration laid down with exquisite concision "the principles on which all good government ought to rest."[22]

In the book, Patrick Henry is shown as great if misunderstood, while George Mason and Jefferson share the honors of heroism. As Grigsby saw it, there was nothing inevitable about the creation of a republican system embracing religious toleration, disestablishment, the abolition of primogeniture and entail. Jefferson had grafted these on to the new order and made them seem natural, though the hostility of other Virginians showed that they were not. Grigsby's admiration for Jefferson was profound, though touched with a sense that there was undue precipitation in Jefferson's reformism, an instinct useful in the Revolution when boldness was necessary, but of more dubious efficacy on other occasions. As a Norfolk man, Grigsby was most skeptical of the embargo. Defending Jefferson in 1855 was delicate work, not least because of his deism, and was best done by removing him from party passions into the quieter realm of analytical history.

Throughout, Grigsby's Virginian patriotism vied with his skepticism. In a complex story with a varied dramatis personae, it was possible to be critical, but Grigsby was too much committed to the inspirational centrality of Virginia to national history to do more than insinuate doubts. Individual men died, but "our beloved Virginia is immortal," a fertile mother of beauty and generosity to all her children. To honor her, Virginians should make of the state a more perfect family: "Shall we not seek by a mild and wise policy to undermine the loathsome jail and the fearful penitentiary, and rear on their reeking ruins the school-house, the college, and the church? Shall we not seek by physical means as well as moral, by the railway and the canal as well as by the school-house and the church, to connect in pleasant communion all the parts of our territory, all the children of one family?"[23] This was a kind of belonging for a man who had lost his father, was not brought up by his mother, was separated from his wife, had quarreled with his in-laws, and could hear the world only through an ear trumpet.

BIOGRAPHY WAS AN ancient form which had commenced as the praise of famous men, but autobiography was a modern form, and many were puzzled to know whether old narratives like the *Confessions* of Saint Augustine belonged to this newly self-conscious genre, which conflated "confessions" and "memoirs." To later generations, it came to seem self-evident that biography and autobiography were mutually reinforcing, but that the genre of biography existed for millennia before the invention of autobiography shows that no such mutuality is essential.

Southerners grew up with biography as an intellectual staple. Plutarch, at least, was an indispensable former of youthful sensibilities, though medieval lives of the saints meant little and Giorgio Vasari little more. James Boswell, however, meant a lot. George Fitzhugh in 1860 thought the *"Life and Anecdotes of Dr. Johnson . . . the most fascinating book in the English language."*

In general, Southern biography tended to the public and outward glance, though this tendency began to weaken in later antebellum years. That the genre commenced with lives of the Founding Fathers encouraged this distance. Great men and greater deeds required formality, because the young were watching and were not supposed to see clay at the feet of marble statues. If the marble was cracked, one applied what William Wirt called "plaster of Paris" to restore the civic illusion.[24] Nonetheless, the genre did mutate in the decades before the Civil War. The importance of understanding a childhood grew, character became an explanation for a life and no longer a commentary, domesticity became allowable, and eventually even the possibility of failure and madness was glimpsed. These developments are evident if one considers the sequence of David Ramsay's life of George Washington (1807), William Wirt's biography of Patrick Henry (1817), George Tucker's life of Thomas Jefferson (1837), John Pendleton Kennedy's life of Wirt (1849), and Hugh Garland's biography of John Randolph (1850).

Ramsay wrote of Washington with the utmost formality, such that the man disappeared into the public realm. In Ramsay's account, Washington's childhood barely occupied two pages, mostly on ancestors. This brevity was explained as arising from an absence of evidence, but there is little suggestion elsewhere that Ramsay would have been drawn by the revelatory story. Rather, his narrative was a condensed history from the French wars to Washington's retirement from the presidency, mostly filched from John Marshall's life. In Ramsay's pages, what the United States became and Washington was were little distinguished. As was the custom for Plutarchan biography, summary of the subject's physiognomy and character was left to the end, where the reader was told that Washington had been tall, strong, wise in judgment, and so forth. After having established these private qualities, Ramsay could thereafter explain Washington's political principles and public service, before reaching an exordium that showed how Washington's life afforded "the brightest model for imitation, not only to warriors and statesmen, but to private citizens; for his character was a constellation of all the talents and virtues which dignify or adorn human nature."[25] Such severity was, perhaps, an intentional reproof to Parson Weems, who had rushed out his own life of Washington soon after the man's death and had been untroubled by the absence of evidence, since invention could supply the deficiency. In principle, Weems had promised to portray Washington as a private man, but, apart from inventing the story of the cherry tree, did not deliver on his promises. In truth, both Weems and Ramsay shared the standpoint that nothing in the public and private realm could conflict. This explained narrative structure: deeds were narrated before character was explained, because the latter was but a gloss on the former.

Many biographers later than David Ramsay have found trouble breathing life into so stiff a man as George Washington. Patrick Henry was a more complex opportunity for William Wirt, sufficiently so to test the latter's patience. Evidence was scanty and contradictory, not all was glory, much was dull, more was insignificant. Still, Patrick Henry had changed the world, or so all right-thinking Virginians believed, and this justification from the public realm had to carry the biographer over the pettiness of the private. Nonetheless, the private was awkward, so Wirt decided to make the best of a bad job, to admit the problem but explain it away. The young Henry might have been coarse, slovenly, and lazy, but he was a child of nature who "ran wild in the forest." Thus was genius undefiled by the artificiality of society or education, but instead was rooted in an instinctive "knowledge of the human heart."[26] This proposition could be harnessed to a wider, more sincere thesis that Patrick Henry embodied the natural movement of society from English thralldom to American liberty, by coming out of the yeomanry to free Americans from deference.

Wirt's *Henry* broke with the formality of Ramsay, since more was conceded to human frailty, and even culpability was admitted. Patrick Henry was portrayed as morally strict, a good husband, father, and master, but vain, cheap, and mean-spirited, too. To be sure, Wirt politely cast doubt upon these lesser qualities, but the reader was not really expected to doubt their veracity, merely to respect Wirt's courtesy. Only upon Henry's laziness was a charge of guilty unambiguously rendered. But even this was used to point toward Henry's quasi-literacy, which expedited the triumphant verdict that, unencumbered by learning, Henry had studied "the great volume of human nature."[27] Further, such common sense had been decisive in Henry's reading of the political situation, which impelled the American Revolution. So, somehow, the creation of the republic rested upon Patrick Henry's being too lazy to read. William Wirt, it is worth remembering, was a lawyer. His biography was a brief, he pled his case, he got his man off, more or less, because few wanted Henry to be found guilty.

In another sense, Ramsay and Wirt were close. For both, public and private marched together. Washington was all great in both realms, Henry was mingled good and bad in both. In neither case was there dissonance, for there could not be, if human nature was true all through and explained the world. This remained the standpoint for George Tucker's 1837 life of Jefferson, which, though published later than Wirt's *Henry*, is morally its elder, because Tucker had the even tone of the philosophe and little interest in evoking cataracts and impulses from vernal woods. Again, the public realm predominated. But Jefferson was a case middling between Washington, whose greatness no one doubted and whose private life was unexceptional, and Henry, whose greatness was dubious and whose private life was suspicious. No one doubted Jefferson's greatness, but there was dispute over his worth in the public realm, and his deism had bred doubts about his private character, especially for those godly who saw a contradiction between morality and a man who edited down the Scriptures. Tucker's solution was a coolness and dispassion, which Henry Randall was to complain was but ice trying to understand fire.

With Kennedy's life of Wirt, biography became an echo chamber. Wirt had written of Henry, in turn Kennedy wrote of Wirt, and later Kennedy would be portrayed by Henry Tuckerman. Wirt and Kennedy were both lawyers, men of letters, politicians, inhabitants of Maryland and Virginia, and so men much of a muchness. Neither was great, just notable, and so the anxiety that troubled Wirt when undertaking his life of Henry lessened for Kennedy trying to understand Wirt. Being of the type, Kennedy judged Wirt as a type, which was the American public man of letters. But here a tension emerged. Kennedy was a novelist, even a sentimental one, and was writing late enough to be interested in domesticity. This impulse humanized Wirt, made him one of the boys, someone with whom to break open a bottle. On the other hand, Kennedy was interested in Wirt as a professional specimen, as a model for how men of his sort began life, progressed, and managed. So Kennedy's *Wirt* was more personal than Wirt's *Henry*, but more abstract, because Henry had been a singular force of nature while Wirt stood in a group daguerreotype.

Humanity was conveyed in the many private letters, reprinted by Kennedy, that Wirt wrote to his family and friends. These disposed the reader to like him. "If you should chance to come in the Christmas holidays, you will find me at home here, when we shall be delighted to eat mince-pies and drink champagne with you," is how one read.[28] Ramsay's George Washington had eaten no mince pies, but such munching made Wirt amiably accessible. However, Wirt's professional and literary life was more sternly judged in a book interested in male rites of passage. Always there was the counterpoint of what happened to Wirt's sort of man, and what happened in particular to Wirt as he was advised by his peers about the moves of life (becoming a chancellor, participating in the trial of Aaron Burr, going into politics, becoming attorney general, running for president). At each moment, Kennedy judged how well Wirt had played the game, how hard it had been to get it right, and how many anxieties had been attendant.

It was the mix of public man and author which had attracted Kennedy to Wirt, so Wirt's thoughts about American authorship were especially debated, above all his consideration of whether it had been sensible to be an author at all. In general, Kennedy's admiration for Wirt the writer was cool. The modern reader "will express his surprise that the public judgment should have given such weight to a production so unlabored, and so desultory" was how Kennedy introduced the *Letters of a British Spy*, and a very mixed judgment was rendered on Wirt's other writings, too.[29] Biographer and subject were at odds. Kennedy aspired to urbanity, a neat handwriting, the deadline met. By contrast, Wirt was irritatingly anxious, confessional, raw boned. For all his doubts, however, Kennedy had liked Wirt, his cheerfulness, stories, honesty, and competence. And if Wirt could not be praised, what hope would there be for Kennedy, in his turn, and young lawyers seeking honorable fame in bookshops?

These biographies celebrated the civic virtues. In them, private character had, finally, to be publicly useful. John Randolph's life was harder to adapt within this logic. Misanthropic, perhaps mad, puzzlingly bachelor, Randolph was a man who could not be fitted in. On the whole, Hugh Garland took a way out that the intellectual culture of 1850 made possible by turning Randolph into a Byronic hero, the wise madman in the attic. But Garland wanted to plough the old furrow, too, and make Randolph conventionally Virginia's "wisest statesman, truest patriot, and most devoted son."[30] It was not clear that a biographer could have it both ways, but he could try.

The book begins with a description of Randolph's birthplace, by which is evoked a disused order of cavaliers and old retainers inhabiting decaying mansions, a world of melancholy occasioning nostalgia. Garland was au courant in thinking that childhood was the key to character and so to biography. Wordsworth, that "wise poet and philosopher," was duly quoted on the child being father to the man. By such logic, "personal identity" (Garland uses this deceptively modern phrase) was shaped by youthful experiences and then inescapable. However, there might be a gulf between what men were and what they seemed. The external might be only a masquerade, since a man might want "to seem what he is not." The outward man might be false and only the inward man "true and worth knowing," for without the inward "we know nothing," except useless facts and dates.[31] This was far from the biographical principles of David Ramsay and such a newfangled attitude made biography fascinating, but frustrating, because the biographer sought secrets tantalizingly beyond reach.

In fact, Garland's taste for secrets was constrained. An obvious question about Randolph had long been, why did such a man, so conscious of family, ancestry, and posterity, never marry? Why was he a beardless man, thin voiced and angry? Garland alluded dramatically to "a tragedy in the life of this man, more thrilling than romance." At this prompt, the reader leant forward to listen and be thrilled. Today such a reader would not be disappointed of the secret. 1850 Virginia was not like that. "This is a subject not for us to deal with," wrote Garland; "we promised not to touch it more; let it go down to the oblivion of the grave, and there sleep with those who, in life, endured its agonies."[32]

So, the dictum became: if the secret be too unsafe, be true to the mask. In his own clumsy way, Garland was. He showed Randolph in most of his moods, the man of Bizarre. He even flirted with the notion of Randolph being mad, when the latter was most solitary, sleepless, irritable, lovelorn, and imaginative. But Garland never connected this deranged Randolph with the public man, who was portrayed conventionally, if erroneously, as a steady Burkean conservative of states' rights persuasion, a proponent of "a wise and masterly inactivity," a prophet of the resistance to "that centripetal tendency which was rapidly destroying the counterbalance of the States," a man whose early religious skepticism was superficial and rightly replaced by a more natural religiosity.[33] Rationality and madness lived in different chapters and paragraphs of Garland's biography; he could not conceive of a whole man simultaneously reasoning and raving. The nearest Garland came to such an understanding was his argument that solitude had driven Randolph into madness, but in the public arena Randolph had been different, not sober but less misanthropic, because more conscious of being useful. This had not been, it must be said, the impression of those who had shared the public arena with Randolph.

IN EUROPEAN AND American usage, autobiography was a latecomer, whose naming was even uncertain. At various times, around 1800, it was called autobiography, self-biography, and periautography, and idio-biography would have been most consistently Greek. The Germans had begun speaking of *Selbstbiographien* and *Autobiographien* by the late 1770s or early 1780s, and Friedrich von Schlegel discussed the genre disparagingly in 1798, when he hazarded that autobiographies were written by egocentric neurotics like Rousseau, self-deceivers anxious to leave the world with commentaries on themselves. As for the French, despite Rousseau, they took more slowly to the usage of *autobiographie*, which did not acquire significant usage until the 1830s and was then regarded as an Anglo-American term, inferior to the indigenous *les mémoires*. But even in Anglo-American usage, there was overlap between memoirs and autobiography, with the distinction slow to develop that memoirs looked outward from the self toward the world experienced by the individual, while autobiography looked inward. Many works which subsequent times came to categorize as autobiography were then called memoirs.

That confusion existed between memoir and autobiography was partly because many early autobiographies were skittish about self-revelation. John Randolph once said that "he was not in the habit of always talking of himself and of his own concerns," though, in fact, he was. Even as late as the 1860s many such narratives were beginning, with words like: "I come now to reminiscences of my poor unworthy self, in inserting which in this book I have no intention of disclosing those inner workings of the soul, which should be reserved for God."[34] Instead, many wrote of the self as an author might write of others, and thus made the biographical and the autobiographical nearly equivalent.

It has often been suggested that the purer form of autobiography began among the marginal, among women and the culturally disadvantaged, who were unencumbered by the civic inhibitions of public greatness and had only themselves upon which to found significance. Yet only one Southern white woman published a memoir or autobiography before the Civil War and asserted the importance of her own life, however often in the private narratives within diaries and letters such assertions were made. And Caroline Gilman did so briefly, with ambivalence. On the other hand, for fugitive or rebellious slaves, autobiography was an essential form, which worked as a political weapon. Since they were formally denied the public realm but were cruelly mastered by it, their private realm became public property, sometimes with their consent, often as a way of mastering their selves.

Black autobiography existed mostly in the specialized form of the emancipated or fugitive slave narrative, established as a genre from the mid-eighteenth century, and encouraged by the antislavery movement as proof of slavery's cruelty. The partial exceptions were the confessions of rebels like Denmark Vesey and Nat Turner, which contained the vestiges of an autobiographical instinct, though extracted in the shadow of the gallows and set down by white amanuenses. And there was a handful of memoirs by Southern free blacks, though none published in the antebellum South and only a few in the North, with most appearing after 1865. For the rest, the standard bibliography lists about a hundred book-length "autobiographical narratives and slave narratives dictated or written by persons of African descent" between 1760 and 1861, though these can be multiplied many-fold by the inclusion of briefer published or manuscript texts.[35] Of these, many concern Europe, the Caribbean, or the North, and far fewer directly touch the South, though they include many that are notable. Of these, only one book was by a

Southern black woman, the *Incidents in the Life of a Slave Girl* by Linda Brent, the pseudonym of Harriet Jacobs. Since it was common for slave narratives to be ghostwritten or intrusively edited by white writers, these works were a negotiation between what an ex-slave wished to say and what an abolitionist permitted to be said. But even those, like the works of Frederick Douglass and Jacobs, whose narratives were "written by himself" and "written by herself," were profoundly influenced by what a white readership expected, though this fact scarcely distinguished their works from those written by any American author, black or white.

The conventions of the fugitive slave narrative were strict. There was an engraved portrait, intended to show a person of gravity and propriety. There were testimonials from white abolitionist patrons, which proclaimed the veracity of the narrative. A first sentence began, "I was born" in a certain place, though an uncertain time. Then parentage was vaguely specified, usually racially mixed, filled with rumor. The cruelties and incidents of slavery were described, with stress upon the hypocrisy of Christian slave-holders, the viciousness and suffering of mistresses betrayed by lascivious husbands, the opposing strength of a single strong slave, often of pure African descent. Patterns of life—food, work routines—were narrated, including slave auctions and the wrenching separations of families. Then there was the escape, perhaps first unsuccessful, then a glad arrival in the North, the welcome of friendly antislavery people, the assumption of a new name and identity, and concluding general remarks upon slavery. Hence, though the particular experience of a slave was under reflective scrutiny, the generality of slavery mattered, too. Charles Ball or William Wells Brown might disappear as utterly into the exemplum as George Washington vanished into the differing category of Father of a Country. Like a medieval morality play or *Pilgrim's Progress*, people appeared as types—the slaveholder, the slave trader, the field hand—even when they had names. This convention had the effect of creating great narrative drive, because every small thing and event was pregnant with the larger story, the quest for the grail of freedom.

In accomplished hands, the slave narrative came closer to intimacy than anything in Southern white discourse and was more modern in its confessional scrutiny. The Southern white man assumed his self, had it freely conceded by all, and did not need to earn it. The slave had the task of self-invention, against the odds. Calvin Fairbanks once told the story of sailing down the Ohio River and seeing "a strapping darky, an ax flung over his shoulder, jogging along on the Virginia bank." "Halloo, there! Where are you going?" Fairbanks called out. "Gwine chopping in de woods!" was the answer. "Chopping for yourself?" was asked, to which the man replied, "Han't got no self." "Slave, are you?" Fairbanks asked, taking the point. "Dat's what I is." In the slave narrative, small things mattered, the glance of an overseer, the sneer of a mistress, footsteps in a wood. Since it was hard to claim that God was on the slave's side, except in a heaven or a society to come, easy pieties were less available, though Victorian sentimentality was not uncommon. The autobiographers were almost invariably honest, godly, domestic, resistant to vice, even though surrounded by its temptation. But this sentimentality was acidly laced with cold realism, and, in general, it is a rule that passages of high-flown rhetoric in such narratives were the interpolating work of white editors. For Douglass, this realism led to a frank grappling with the relevance of violence to manhood; for Jacobs, with the dilemma of sexuality for slave girlhood turning into womanhood. At its best, the slave narrative was a triumph of the plain style. "I was born in Tuckahoe." "The woman did not die, but it would have been the same if she had." "Sometimes I woke up, and found her bending over me." "I will now mention a few things, that I could not conveniently bring in, as I was going along with my story."[36]

Above all, the slave narrative rammed home the centrality of the "I." Everything was seen from the position of an observing, thinking, feeling self, who was unsure of what was to come, poised and anxious, scheming and afraid. Public history mattered little, other than the facts that the South was a slaveholding prison, the North and Canada a haven. Africa, the American Revolution, the idea of centuries, the term of a president, all were unimportant. Landscape was irrelevant, except when it mattered to an escape. Architecture went unnoticed; New Orleans was a place with an auction block, not a filigree balcony. What mattered was grandmother, the master's son, the lost child, the location of a jail, and voices that shaped events. So dialogue was very important: " 'They are going to give you hell.' 'Why?' said I. He said, 'This is a note to have you whipped, and says that you have a dollar to pay for it.' "[37]

It is no paradox to observe that black autobiography, being rooted in the hardest of facts, was free to reach toward the techniques of fiction, which might capture truths and even contrive introspection. On the other side of the divide, white Southern autobiography retained a connection to the public realm so powerful that the invention of self was inhibited. This helps to explain why there was relatively little white autobiography before the Civil War, and that little was usually familial, a thing addressed to relatives by men confident of their own importance and posterity. Vulnerability was not a Southern trait, at least for white men, at least before 1861. More was to be released later. Then William Grayson and Frederick Porcher, these and many others felt the public realm disappearing beneath their feet as the Confederacy faltered and disintegrated. The old, neat congruence of self and society fractured, and it was necessary to ask what was left, what self might mean, in a world that could no longer propose a workable conjecture of order.

SOUTHERNERS WERE AMONG those in the nineteenth century who began to accept the modern notions that there is something called the imagination, which expresses itself in poetry and fiction; that such an imaginative litera-ture is a distinct venture of the mind, to be understood as a commentary on the culture which produces it, as well as a transcendence; and that hence it is plausible to speak of "Southern literature," and even desirable to write it. But there were many steps in the coalescence of these ideas, all contentious, many slow to be taken. For most of the antebellum period, "literature" retained its old, eclectic meaning of the written word, not merely the novel and poetry.

To understand this process, one must begin where Southerners them-selves began, not only in their nineteenth century, but in their individ-ual lives. Prescription began in youth with those rhetorical manuals which Southern colleges gave to young men. Among such works, preeminence was shared between Lord Kames's *Elements of Criticism* (1762) and Hugh Blair's *Lectures on Rhetoric and Belles Lettres* (1783), both Scottish texts dealing mostly with ancient authors and only glancingly with moderns. In time, these manuals began to be displaced by the German school of Romantic literary criticism, though more beyond the classroom than in it.

Kames's *Elements* exemplified the Scottish desire for a "science of man," the enterprise of Adam Smith, and was a Scottish civil lawyer's book, in that Kames believed that one should first establish principles and then apply them in the comprehension of experience. He was influenced by David Hume's account of human nature and, more remotely, by Hobbes. As Kames put it, his book drew "the rules of criticism from human nature, their true source." For him, literature was but one among the arts and the critic's task was to discern how art created states of mind and feeling in a reader, listener, or viewer. A respondent might weep or laugh, but only because an artist had intended this reaction and learned the technique to achieve it. Since Kames presumed a "common nature of man," which was "invariable not less than universal," it mattered little to him when, where, or for whom an artist had performed, though, like most Scots, he had a sense of the evolution of society through stages. In general, Kames preferred the orderly to the disorderly, tranquility to passion, while knowing that passions drove the will and had to be redirected "to just and rational ends."[38]

Mostly, Kames was interested in the small matters of composition, in soliloquies and hyperbole, apostrophes and metaphor, allegory and comparisons. Only late in the book did he come to genre, epic, and drama, and to Aristotle's three unities. Here the details of his views matter less than his supremely self-confident tone. Kames was profligate of words like "general," "universal," "rule," "principle," "certain." His book did not invite dissent and presumed a "we" who shared presumptions. In an important late chapter, he interrogated the proverb "that there is no disputing about taste" and asserted that there were, in fact, canons and principles to settle controversies.[39] On the whole, for him, literature existed to create a polite civil society, which wished to be edified, improved, and moved. Moreover, Kames wrote from the reader's standpoint not the author's, or at least presumed that reader and author were committed to a partnership which fostered civilization.

Hugh Blair's book was different, but he, too, preferred liberal humanity, refined taste, and the impulse to "apply the principles of good sense to composition and discourse."[40] However, Kames affected to be a metaphysician, a lofty office which Blair understood to be above his own mark. Belles lettres and criticism moved on a lower plain, and this made possible a certain homeliness. While Kames spoke to adults, if clumsily, Blair was an urbane pedagogue concerned to train young minds to good habits, a man who patiently explained how to write a letter, form a sentence, speak from a pulpit, or write a poem.

Blair had critical preferences. He hated ostentation, cunning, and technicality, and stood for the plain style against the baroque. He had a greater sense of history than Kames, partly because he was more preoccupied with the achievements of the modern age, especially with Augustan advances over the rougher language of earlier English writers. But Blair, too, thought belles lettres conduced to civilization, if only by giving busy men an agreeable way to spend their leisure and prevent them flying to "the riot of loose pleasures." And, like Kames, Blair reprobated the notion that taste might be anarchic and imagined the possibility of someone whose senses were so exquisite and whose reason was so sure that he "would, beyond doubt, be a perfect standard for the taste of others." Absent such a paragon, there was the accumulated judgment of men in time, which "overthrows the illusions of opinion, but establishes the decisions of nature."[41]

For Blair, languages had a historical and social context, as well as an internal logic, which enabled or disabled them from envisioning dimensions of human nature. In general, primitive languages began with few words and were expressively poetical, but later the understanding gained ground on fancy and imagination. Hence languages matured, just as children became adults: "Language has become, in modern times, more correct, indeed, and accurate; but, however, less striking and animated; in its ancient state, more favorable to poetry and oratory; in its present, to reason and philosophy."[42] So Blair was a historian of language and he was sensitive to the strengths and weaknesses of different languages, in vocabulary, syntax, and grammar. For the most part, he regarded English as fecund but hard to discipline, a fact which explained the necessity for his own book, which might help to train a purer, more metropolitan diction.

One difference between Kames and Blair was generational, the first having been born in 1696 and the second in 1718. Kames roamed eclectically from society to society, from time to time, and scarcely noticed disjunctions. Blair was close to being a late Enlightenment figure who worried about context and knew that history made language and therefore the possibilities of speech. What distinguished Blair from the early Romantics was that, finally, for him genres were rooted in the needs of human nature, which were invariant even under the shifts of social context, and he believed one could distinguish critically between good and bad, order and disorder, classical and "romantic and unnatural situations," and could know which to prefer, not just for oneself but for civilized society.[43]

What marked off the next generation of critics was not the impulse to use history as a way of explaining the evolution of genre but the need to make that impulse central to the venture of criticism. There came to be a higher respect for the primitive and original, while order ceased to be thought natural, but was regarded as an artificial shackling of the human spirit. Mostly, these critics were German, above all the Schlegel brothers Friedrich and August. But there was also Madame de Staël, whose *D'Allemagne* was widely read, and the Germans' English followers, Samuel Taylor Coleridge and Thomas Carlyle. These names began to surface in Southern critical writing in the 1820s and, by the 1840s, competed with the Scots in the curriculum. However, Kames and Blair lingered past the point when even the schoolmasters ceased to accept all their arguments, because the Scots were pedagogues who taught firm rules. The Germans were harder to use in class, partly because the Romantic critics wrote, not from the standpoint of readers, but from that of authors, and rarely gifted authors at that.

Most accessible and influential were the lectures given by August von Schlegel in Vienna in the spring of 1808 and translated into English in 1815 as *A Course of Lectures on Dramatic Art and Literature*. This book was to inform

Hugh Legaré's discussions of literary Romanticism, was quoted approvingly by Edgar Allan Poe, and appeared familiarly among the reading lists of later Southern undergraduates. Though his lectures were ostensibly confined only to the drama from the Greeks onward, Schlegel offered a gloss on the new critical thinking about Romanticism, a concept (at least as an adjective, not yet a noun) he and his brother did more to establish than anyone else. Unlike the Scots, Schlegel located universality, not in making order out of the heterogeneous, but in achieving an empathy for the diverse. The ancients were admirable, but chiefly for having had the courage to be themselves. The moderns must learn to do likewise, though being different, they would make a different world.

Though he was diffident about the terminology, Schlegel resorted to "romantic" as the appropriate adjective for what was modern, not to denote its identity with the romance, but to show how "modern civilisation is the fruit of the heterogeneous union of the peculiarities of the northern nations and the fragments of antiquity." For Schlegel, the classical was plastic and joyous, while the modern was religious and otherworldly, made conscious by Christianity of failure and the need for salvation. Since man had been expelled from Eden, he had sought vainly to return, and, because of this awareness, the modern was habitually unfulfilled and found earthly enjoyments fleeting and illusory. In particular, while the Greeks had worked for harmony and balance, the moderns were conscious of "internal discord . . . and hence the endeavour of their poetry is to reconcile these two worlds between which we find ourselves divided, and to blend them indissolubly together."[44] The very clarity of the classical tradition signified its infidelity to the messiness of diffuse reality.

So Schlegel had as master units of analysis, the ancient and the modern, but he further argued that modern cultures differed one from another. He explained the mutations of genre by the exigencies of time and nationality, first by looking at the Greek and Roman drama, then by examining the theatrical traditions of the modern European cultures. He was conscious that such a typology underestimated "reciprocal but fluctuating influences" between cultures, but found each to have had such a differing pattern that a particularist analysis was the truer method. As one might expect, Schlegel was hostile to Aristotle, deprecated the French theater for its neoclassical imitativeness, saw signs of life in the Germans with Schiller (on Goethe he was cool), and recommended the Spanish and English theater as most original. If his book has a hero, it is Shakespeare, master of a romantic spirit which "delights in indissoluble mixtures; all contrarities; nature and art, poetry and prose, seriousness and mirth, recollection and anticipation, spirituality and sensuality, terrestrial and celestial, life and death . . . blended together in the most intimate combination."[45] In fact, Schlegel was to have an influence on how even the English came to understand Shakespeare, especially when the German was used and plagiarized by Coleridge. Always Schlegel leaned to the national, original, and peculiar, to passion over regularity. It was not that Schlegel was against order, merely that he thought all parts of creation had their own differing organic orders, which it was the business of art to discern and express.

Many of these passages Hugh Legaré was to quote in 1831 when discussing the relative merits of the ancient and modern. He conceded that the historical case for the distinction had been persuasively put by Schlegel, even though Legaré preferred the neoclassical. Still, for good or ill, the modern was inescapable. Legaré's friend Thomas Grimké, the proponent of the Reformation, natural science, and the modern, had few such contradictory inhibitions. His long essay on the origin of rhyme, published in the *Southern Review* serially in 1828 and 1829, showed how the Romantic critical revolution was advancing in Southern culture, because he put together his argument from the body of late Enlightenment and early Romantic literary history and criticism, from Thomas Warton and Jean François de la Harpe, Schlegel and Sismondi, and Scottish social theorists like John Millar and Adam Ferguson. This added up to a body of concepts and knowledge which made it possible for Grimké to make the central claim of historicism, that ancient and modern were discontinuous.

Grimké's argument that rhyme did not exist in the ancient world but emerged in the Middle Ages is less important here than that he asked the crucial question which arose when literature was understood socially and historically: "Whence has arisen this state of things . . . *to whom, to what age, to what country, do we owe*" a particular form of literature? Moreover, Grimké had been molded by a critical discourse in which ideas of nationality, especially concepts of North and South, had been crucially deployed. He wrote freely of "Northern and Southern nations," he used the concept of the indigenous to understand a literary sensibility, and he spoke of the "stern and hardy Europeans of the North, and their refined neighbours of the South."[46] However, Grimké was uninterested in transferring these ideas to the United States, to seeing American literature as divided in sensibility between Northern and Southern. Nor was Legaré, though he comprehended the intellectual currents which would legitimate such an apprehension.

This critical legacy was double-edged. It legitimated the notion of a literature formed by culture and society, offered the categories of North and South, but it insisted that being "Southern" was a mixed blessing. The Southern was deemed to be sensuous, spontaneous, lazy, resistant to rationality; in Europe, innovation came from the north. One could solve this problem, as Frederick Porcher did in 1852, by identifying all Americans with northern Europe, but this was drastic. Many Southern intellectuals identified with southern Europe, which meant that they were conscious, in aspiring to literary accomplishment, of working against the grain. In this lay an origin of the Southern habit of literary self-contempt, since it became characteristic of appeals to create a Southern literature to speak of the need to transcend enervation. "The Sunny South is not propitious to the products of literature," Charles Campbell, typically, observed in 1847.[47]

The pages of the first *Southern Review* were innocent of a developed concept of "Southern literature." Its chief mover did have a notion of "the literature of the South," that is, he knew there was a South which ought to be a literature.[48] But it did not follow that anyone there had an obligation to take the South as a subject matter. So the beginnings of an appeal for Southern literary accomplishment was closer to the logic of Edinburgh, where David Hume was an adornment to Scottish literature, but no one thought him obliged to write about taciturn crofters. By the same token, Hugh Legaré might be an ornament to Charleston, but he was not thereby expected to write less about Demosthenes and more about the Cooper River. It was the generation below Legaré's, reared upon Romantic presumptions, who made the shift, though their opinions did not surface before the early 1840s. The editor of the *Southern Quarterly Review* in 1847 was accepting as a premise that the "people of the Southern States are so far a peculiar people, that their forms of social life differ from those of other States here and in Europe," and this affected views of literary obligations, though even he still thought that Southern intellect should be dedicated to many topics, "to physical science, to natural history, biography, classical learning, to literature and science in all their forms, to historical, moral and *religious truth*."[49]

By 1851, however, the category was sufficiently established that William Gilmore Simms was suggesting "a History of [the] Art & Literature of the Southern States." There is no evidence of what might have been included, but, if Simms's *The Charleston Book* (1845) is a guide, it would have opted for the miscellaneous definition of Southern literature, that is, any literature written in the South, on whatever subject. Still, by 1858, Archibald Roane in *De Bow's Review* might familiarly make the connection which Legaré and Grimké had been uninterested to make in 1830 and used the arguments of Schlegel to predict William Faulkner. Southern books, he wrote, had started to improve as "reflexes of Southern thought, Southern feeling, Southern manners, customs, and peculiarities" and had become more rooted in the

Southern soil and less imitative of the exogenous. This lesson England, Germany, and Spain, too, had learned, and, in them, literature had grown as "a vigorous and hardy plant fresh from its native soil."[50]

Throughout this progression, doubt was persistent. Most did not confuse prediction with accomplishment. Almost everyone was self-lacerating. Politics was habitually blamed for intellectual distraction, or migration might be at fault, or inadequate schools, or a lackluster reading public, or the weather. And many were unsure about the wisdom of the Romantic venture, which slashed away the classical tradition and even the English literary tradition, and made Shakespeare an unavailable foreigner. Was it wise for the American or the Southerner to begin de novo? Was not literature a wider thing? Legaré had insisted that it was and, though he assumed that American literature would grow with its language, did not see the need for an introspective cultural nationalism, but preferred a comparative scholarship and literature, which made available the classical and the modern, the European and the American.

Even later, the awkward question would not go away. Henry Timrod, as interested in the South and as Romantic a writer as one might wish, was aware of the shortcomings of the Southern scene and did not want to be confined in the prison house of patriotism. In 1859, he trotted out the familiar Simmsian lament that no one loved a Southern author and blamed old fogeys who still praised Pope and read Kames. This self-interested jeremiad was not, however, one which accepted the category of Southern literature as a way to describe Timrod's own work, because Timrod quarreled with those (including Simms implicitly) who had transferred over from the campaign for "Americanism in literature" to another for "Southernism in literature." By this last phrase, Timrod understood the proposition that "an author should confine himself in the choice of his subjects to the scenery, the history, and the traditions of his own country." For Timrod, nationality mattered, but subconsciously; it expressed itself in "those thousand nameless touches, which are felt rather than expressed." It was not that Timrod thought it wrong to write about Southern things, just that the demand only to write of these was "a narrow creed."[51] As will be seen, this expansive vision was easier for the poet to embrace than the novelist, for by critical convention the one was thought to be universal, the latter to be local.

IN THE SOUTH nothing was more common than to write poetry, especially when young. Elderly cognoscenti lamented that such verse lacked rigor. Good poetry required a skilled technique and a wide culture, but Romanticism had made the rules looser, while licensing self and locality (two things everyone had or could invent), with the result that poetry became a demo-cratic medium, a career open to the ill-talented and gifted alike.

Poetry in the colonial South had been sociable, with verse written for clubs or friends in a tone bantering, witty, and metropolitan. It had also been often civic, with odes celebrating empire and commerce, revolution and war. These traditions did not die. The Fourth of July and commencement days still called out their awkward verses, new buildings needed poetical dedication, great men required eulogy, and gentlemen still thought that ladies liked acrostics. (And perhaps they did.) But, in general, poetry became a solitary and apolitical business, a meditation on human nature, a conversation with selves often disguised in the form of magical spirits. These were devel-opments viewed with misgiving, and there were grave discussions about whether poetry could survive a modern age designed for prose. Poets became misanthropic and depressed. From being glad to pass a few dozen manu-scripts from hand to hand, they grew gloomy to have a few hundred copies of printed verse stockpiled in their back rooms. They had been beguiled by promises that, in choosing solitude, they might transform the world. They became disappointed to discover a world incuriously resistant.

William Crafts, born in 1787, followed the old route of a lawyer who casually rendered up light and familiar verse to friends and community. Once such poetry would have been amiably praised, but it was a sign of the times that, when Crafts died young and his friends published a memorial selection of his writings, Hugh Legaré brutally demolished the gazebo of Crafts's ac-complishment, dismissed as "a heap of ephemeral rubbish," which might be encountered "at any time" in "the 'poetical corner' of a fashionable news-paper." For Legaré had the newer Coleridgean conception of poetry, which stressed sublimity, beauty, and pathos. Such verse could be prompted by "Alpine precipices and solitudes," human sympathy, and the "mysterious connexion between the heart of man and the forms and beauties of inani-mate nature."[52] This required more than scrawling ditties on the back of tavern bills.

Washington Allston was a friend of Coleridge and an acquaintance of Legaré, so one might have expected from him something better, because the painter was a poet who pondered formal aesthetics. If philosophical clarity could help make a poet—and Coleridge had said it helped—then Allston was advantaged. He leaned to allegory, as philosophical poets did. He rode on horseback through the Milky Way, slept and dreamt "within a desert cave," and was transported over fabulous landscapes. There he conversed with "the Sylphs of the Seasons," who explained how time and variety of experience would change him, how he might "with rare combining skill, / With new-created worlds fill / Of space the mighty void."[53] This was Allston's habitual preoccupation, how art made the world.

Self-consciousness about words and meaning was Allston's strength; he tried to put his experience into verse. So there were sonnets on looking at paintings by Michelangelo and Rembrandt, a poem on the cultural differences between Britain and America, a valedictory sonnet on Coleridge's death. On the whole, the poems show a man struggling to give vivacity to a melancholy temperament. In them, people touch only rarely and "the living presence of Another's mind," the realization of sympathy which Legaré celebrated as the quintessentially poetic task, was a "deep mystery" seldom grasped, still more seldom by the less than great, which Allston knew himself to be.[54] In his verse, therefore, he meditated on his sense of failure as a painter, the sense that would eventually freeze him over the giant canvas of "Belshazzar's Feast," when he came to live in Massachusetts.

A fondness for fairies, demons, sprites, and talking Emotions became a characteristic of Southern poetry. In this, Edgar Allan Poe was typical, though he abominated the Lake School doctrine that poetry should be philosophical. For Poe, poetry concerned beauty not truth, and should be indefinite, musical, and brief. This argument had wide appeal, though his insistence that the rhythms of meter were attributes of the human body and poetry spoke a universal language which might resonate for Bantus and English alike did not. Nonetheless the latter argument was typical of Poe, who was a devotee of logic and regularity, a man who preferred the universal to the local, myth to history. Allston's fairies were but humans who could do surprising things, but Poe's condors transported his readers to unknown realms, in order to show patterns indifferent to the idiosyncrasy of human experience. Poe insisted that beauty was the poetic principle and strove in his own poetry to locate beauty in sound, while he roamed free "out of space, out of time," in a dreamland, "with forms no man can discover." Even when, in his verse, an unfortunate human wandered among the archangels, ghouls, or golden thrones, it was seldom to fare well, but usually to be dead in a sepulcher, an inert object around which winds blew, bells rang, waters lapped. Where Poe differed from his contemporaries was not in invoking the mythological but in his ingenuity and originality, the qualities that his critical times had come so to prize. Mostly Poe differed in his chilling capacity to find beauty in what was beyond nature. There was little warmth of landscape in Poe, much that was silent, shadowy, "like starlight on a pall."[55] He liked stars and graves, the cold things. In his hostility to the philosophical, he permitted few subjects in his poems to think. Most only felt. In his own miserable lifetime, opinion differed over the merits of Poe's verse, as it has since. Baudelaire was entranced by it; others found it jangling and bizarre. But Poe was certainly the only antebellum Southern poet whose works passed into the popular imagination and made a world of its own, which even Poe could not bear to inhabit and at which others were fascinated to peer, at a safe distance.

The Southern poet who came closest to Poe's bleak fairyland was, surprisingly, Louisa McCord, that most vigorously commonsensical of women. In *My Dreams* (1848), the reader is introduced to "phantom fiends," a smiling Fancy, a "spectre-haunted pillow," and a houri. But McCord's poetic world, unlike Poe's, is humane. She wanted to understand her womanhood, especially the experience of being a mother, and she had a powerful sense of generations and declension. In her cosmological poem "The Voice of Years," a transcendent voice speaks of an individual's passage from birth to death, of hopes blighted and joys flown, and her central poem, "The Fire-fly," features another inhuman thing telling lessons of evanescence, of the doom of regret, of restlessness, and being "crouched in dust" when imagining heaven.[56]

McCord was to become an anomaly as a woman who spoke forthrightly on slavery, political economy, and secession, but her poetry predated that phase. It was religious and vulnerable, when later she was silent about religion and more concerned to expose the vulnerabilities of others; its diction was even, whereas later she was Carlylean, violent and angular; it was allusively individual, whereas later she was intensely social. In *My Dreams*, society was lost in loneliness and instructive sorrow. A sort of transition can be seen in her play *Caius Gracchus* (1851), which is fascinated by politics. Its main argument was that the state is man's realm, that women can only act secondarily through sons and husbands to limit the state's brutality. Thereby the drama insisted that the world's life is not man's alone but for men and women together, with women contributing the mettle to compel men to act. It is a pitiless doctrine, the personal is political, but it led McCord from the disembodied sprites of her earlier poetry to the bully pulpit of the Southern periodicals.

In general, the poetry of Southern women was bleaker than the men's. Mary Elizabeth Lee of Charleston, to be sure, had special reasons for being unhappy, since she was often ill and was to die young. Unlike McCord, whose religiosity was a speculation, Lee found in Christianity a warm consolation and truth. This softened her modest verse, which dealt with death, life's brevity, and health's elusiveness. But Lee was not only a student of her own pain. Allston, Poe, McCord, all abjured their place and time and wrote allegorically in landscapes vaguely Transylvanian, Alpine, or English. But Lee had poems on Virginia and George Washington, on the coronation of Queen Victoria, and on American freedom and Bertrand du Guesclin, as well as assorted Charlestonian civic verse. In one particular she was singular: she was almost the only white Southern poet who fashioned an image of slaves and blacks. (Grayson was the other, but very differently.) To be sure, most of these figures move through her verse as devoted retainers, but they do appear as sympathetic, human, and capable of pain. Lee even noticed black Christianity, had her whites and slaves bend down together in prayer, and acknowledged that slaves, too, had a stake in heaven.

Elsewhere in Charleston, another single woman was writing poetry with more force than Lee, but equal eclecticism. Penina Moise was a reform Jewish schoolteacher who wrote hymns and in 1833 published *Fancy's Sketchbook*, which betrays a sensibility concerned to bridge traditions, Jewish, Christian, local, and cosmopolitan. Moise was preeminently a poet of ideas. The first few poems of *Fancy's Sketchbook* indicate her range; in subject matter, the first is Jewish, the second Shakespearian, and the third Philhellene (with echoes of Byron and Lessing), while the fourth is Popean in style. Lee was not afraid to be political and she once wrote a half-serious, half-mocking poem which came out against the tariff and complained about the Nullification controversy. No doubt her collected verse contained the usual collection of flowers, trees, and sylphs, the customary groping for human allegory in the natural and unnatural world. But Lee was not especially bleak, her verse has an engaging bounce to it, and she was remarkably unafraid and venturesome.

However, most Southern poets, at least the men, seemed to have felt that poetry offered a refuge from politics. Richard Henry Wilde literally gave up a political career to go to Italy and become his own Byron. Albert Pike, who became an Arkansas politician, did not write about elections but love, travel among the Navajo, prairies, and canyons. Alexander Beaufort Meek of Alabama, too, though he had the odd poem in eulogy to dead politicians, was preoccupied with love and landscape, birds and climate, which were only implicitly political. The preface to Meek's *Songs and Poems of the South* (1857) explains that "the poetry of a country should be a faithful expression of its physical and moral characteristics," that "its imagery . . . should be drawn from the indigenous objects of the region." So there was nothing Gothic in Meek's poetry, but rather sunshine, verdancy, gentleness, extolled by a poetic antecedent to Henry Grady. That Alabama had a "delicate clime" was not evident to its residents, including Meek himself in prosaic moments, but, in his verse, it was always spring, the breezes blew softly, the mockingbirds sang, there were magnolias and honeysuckle, and Alabama was a rose whose thorns damaged only the tyrant. Meek was the most self-consciously Southern of poets, the bard of an "imperial land." Conquest was what freedom was for, landscape enumerated possession, and the Forest of Arden had a master.[57]

Meek was a cruder version of Simms. In the latter's poetry, there is the same sense that landscape is overlain by history, especially a succession of peoples, Indian and European. Simms, too, has verse on "the sunny, sunny South!" with "myriad flowers that bloom and fade." But Simms had a greater range and a better technique and he posed less. In practice, he wrote as a relaxation from the demands of prose, though he did believe with Shelley that "the Poet is a Seer" and poetry "*winged thought*." Simms was an exponent of a theory of literary alienation, almost a proponent of the avant-garde. This was not merely a historical and social argument, the idea that men of genius saw more clearly and earlier, were scorned, might die in indigence and failure, then have their truths posthumously recognized. Simms did believe all that, so much so that he relished and even invented evidence of his disparagement by society as evidence of his gifts. But he also saw alienation as personal history, as the story of how the gifted child grew up. Many Southerners had such Romantic theories, but few managed to translate them into effective poetry, to make the Ashley River work as well as Lake Windermere. Simms did not manage it often, but sometimes he came surprisingly close, by his usual profligate process of hit and miss. In truth, his verse touched on most things, and, in it, Indians and the Spanish are frequent, rivers flow and mountains stand, but woods are preeminent. On the whole, he abjured the ghostly, though few Southern poets could entirely omit "cold phantoms," because they were the symbols of memory.[58] When he ventured the epic strain, the effect was seldom compelling, but he was better at colloquialism, in the way of Thackeray and the lighter side of Byron, and he had many verses, ephemeral but pleasing.

His most characteristic poem, "Boy Lost in the Woods" (1828), enacts Simms's philosophy. Its imagery (trees, gloom, the helpful woodsman) was a variant on the brothers Grimm, a bildungsroman arguing that pain and self-awareness make a worthwhile man. Still, it was humorous, when such narratives tended to be earnest, and its language refreshingly tactile. Simms was conscious of sentimentality, but its absence, too. Not many Southerners were then willing to admit that families might be unhappy and a boy might benefit from experiencing cruelty. No doubt he stopped far short of disillusion. Simms liked to look on the bright side of despair. But Simms, unlike Meek, knew there was a problem in the human condition and found a way in his poetry to state it, partly by noticing that the world was both magical and ordinary, full of "plates and dishes, cups and clinking saucers."[59]

Oddly, Simms's protégés, Henry Timrod and Paul Hamilton Hayne, who carried the reputation of the South's poetry in the mid-nineteenth century, in this regard were a retrogression, though they were more dedicated to the craft than Simms, and were among the first Southerners to put themselves forward as poets pure and simple. They became pre-Raphaelite and Tennysonian, began to grow interested in chivalry, maidens, and flaxen hair, while struggling with the messianic role of the philosopher poet. Timrod was the better of the two, which Hayne himself acknowledged, though because Timrod died young soon after the war, it was Hayne who survived to make himself into one of the preeminent bridges between the Old and the New South. But both bore a responsibility for spreading the legend of Southern literary debility, because for them life was pointless unless it possessed futility, spurned love, languid emotions, conditions "yet so hopeless, yet so cureless."[60] In their poetic worlds, there was repose but little satisfaction, in part because both repudiated the enervating world of nature without accepting the bustling world of commerce, so life hung inadequately between the streets of New York and August in the Low Country.

To William J. Grayson, such verse was sickly and silly. He was briskly neoclassical, he leaned to common sense and Lord Kames, and he knew that what made poetry was rules. "We may . . . define poetry to be the expression, by words, of thought or emotion, in conformity with metrical and rhythmical laws," no more, no less.[61] In the 1850s, Grayson published *The Hireling and the Slave* and *The Country*, both poems self-consciously Augustan. The former was most noticed, and has been most deprecated subsequently for its proslavery argument, that the African slave in the South lived better than the industrial worker employed and unemployed in Europe and the North. In this thesis Grayson was little original. Indeed it was part of his stance that he did not need to be original, for all truths were old. Further, he believed that political economy was a fit subject for verse, because poetry and prose shared the whole domain of ideas and sensibility, and hence poets should not be confined to conversing with peddlers, or to observing daffodils and pots of basil. What mattered was technique, what oft was thought but ne'er so well expressed. By these standards, *The Hireling and the Slave* has a reasonable claim to being the best poem written in the antebellum South, for its Augustan wit, range of allusiveness, and taut language.

The argument of *The Hireling and the Slave* was complicated, more than a proslavery apology, though it was indignant about New Englanders who profited from the slave trade and the Duchess of Sutherland who, as Louisa McCord elsewhere said, preached Christian philanthropy while pocketing the revenues of Highland Clearances. Grayson did say that the lots of the slave and the hireling had been historically miserable, though he deprecated this and his was not a straightforward apology for any master class, especially the European. This stance was typically Augustan, because in that tradition the objects of satire were bishops, lords, politicians, profligate sons, and rapacious merchants. What distinguished an upper class was hypocrisy, the plundering use of others' lives. But Grayson was an American Augustan, which complicated matters, since he had to consider whether the New World had changed anything, when the *Beggar's Opera* moved west. This problem lay at the heart of the poem. *The Hireling and the Slave* is mostly a poem about migration, about the convergence of two different migrants, the European and the African, on the American strand. In general, Grayson argued that America had made a difference: his bleakest passages concern the Old World, William Hogarth's England as well as Africa, because he did not prettify the slave's migration. It is the poem's thesis that America had improved the human condition; it had not abrogated the cold fact of human inequality, but it had found a more humane way. This was partly a religious argument. As his autobiography was later to show, Grayson took pleasure in boisterous eighteenth-century ways but stiffly accepted that the growing piety of the nineteenth century had been a step forward, that it was better to sit soberly in a pew than to lie vomiting under a table. So the great gift of America to the African was Christianity, which taught truth, discipline, and gladness in being an efficient laborer. By the same token, the master learned kindness and philanthropy.

Beyond that, Grayson was lovingly interested in landscape. For him, there was value in the American land, though it is unclear what, because it had not saved from near extinction the Indians, who linger in the poem as ghosts admonishing the slave not to risk unsupervised freedom in competition with the white man. A lot is made of Providence, and a little of prophecy. The poem ends with a vision of former slaves returning to Africa, there to create a modern, progressive society, a vision ironically similar to that then being articulated by black intellectuals like Alexander Crummell and Martin Delany. Here, in fact, lay the poem's failure; it tried to be millennial and Augustan, all at once. This fudging was connected to Grayson's liking for his own place, which he celebrates elsewhere in *Chicora* and *The Country*. He was fascinated with how men interacted with nature in history's progress; he was an ecological poet and veered dangerously close to the abominated Wordsworth in writing of Nature and "deep, mysterious things, / Dim shadowy visions, half discerned." Living as he did on a Sea Island and the edge of the continent, Grayson often pondered the moment of first contact, of what was lost and gained in the time after the Indian first looked out and saw "great canoes, / Broad-winged, like winter cranes that fly," disgorging "a hideous crew." In this view, the European was masterly, a member of a conquering and imperial race, which made a world while destroying another. Nature's "subtle spells and plastic powers" were needed for the white man's salvation, too.[62]

Having written verse and being learned about its history, Grayson felt entitled in 1858 to ask, "What is Poetry?" According to him, poetry is not inspiration or soothsaying, but technique alone. "Because tastes are different," he asserted, "therefore poetry assumes a diversity of forms, applies itself to all subjects, addresses itself to all minds, and becomes, like them, multiform in shape and character." This being so, Grayson was entitled to his own tastes. He did not like border ballads, thought "The Ancient Mariner" repulsive in its putrescent imagery, was neutral about Shakespeare, praised Milton, but was vitriolic about Wordsworth. "He looked on nature as a kind of poetical milch cow, which he never tired of milking—a mass of raw material to be made up into metrical dresses," is one of Grayson's milder complaints, which hinges on the sense that Wordsworth had used nature to make a living as a poet, had been "mechanical," even industrial in his commercial exploitation.[63]

To all this, Henry Timrod took passionate exception. He defended Coleridge and was indignant about Grayson's "caricature of Wordsworth." Plausibly, Timrod insisted that Wordsworth, too, spoke from the heart, and he scattered long quotations from "Tintern Abbey" and other poems to prove it, as though no one reading them could doubt. With this, Grayson was unimpressed. In his autobiography, he remembered with amusement Timrod's rejoinder: "I said . . . once [that Wordsworth was mechanical] and was nearly annihilated by an indignant admirer who overwhelmed me with quotations to prove how much I was in error. The quotations did not change my opinion."[64]

It has been customary to see in this controversy a struggle between Timrod the modern and Grayson the antiquated. In fact, it was Grayson who was the modern, Timrod the conservative, because Timrod was uttering the conventional wisdoms of Southern poets, who had been reading Wordsworth and writing Romantic verse for at least forty years. Timrod, in fact, began his rejoinder by appealing to public opinion, to "the general dissatisfaction occasioned by [Grayson's] article." Grayson, conversely, knew that he was heterodox. The preface to The Hireling and the Slave defends its metrical form as offering variety to "poetic forms that are almost universally prevalent" by returning "to the more sober style of an earlier period," as an "experiment on the public taste." "May we not imitate the poetry of Queen Anne's time as well as the tables and chairs?" Grayson asked.[65] At a later time, this instinct would come to be called postmodern, the sense that taste and standards are intrinsically various, no authority deserves to prevail as an orthodoxy, and intellectual preferences come and go historically.

Grayson's easy eclecticism, surprisingly, mirrored how poetry was dispersed in Southern culture. Many eras sat cheek by jowl, in shifting esteem. Beyond the ancient poets, Chaucer grew in importance, Shakespeare persisted, Milton was honored if seldom read, the Augustans were known, many eighteenth-century poets of sensibility were surprisingly popular, and the Romantics were deeply influential (Byron most in the early days, then Wordsworth and Coleridge, Shelley somewhat, Keats least.) Perhaps only the metaphysical poets were a rarity.

Grayson laconically noted that he made no money from his verse, and Timrod did the same, with resentment. Both were gentlemen, with ample notions of fit living. It is a paradox little observed that the only person who made his living as a poet in the South was George Moses Horton, a North Carolinian slave who began in the 1820s to sell verses (acrostics, love poems) to students in Chapel Hill, verses which at first he did not know how to write down, but dictated. In time, he became a famous curiosity with white patrons who helped to publish his poetry, first in Raleigh as *The Hope of Liberty* (1829), pirated in Philadelphia as *Poems by a Slave*, then in Hillsborough as *The Poetical Works of George M. Horton, the Colored Bard of North Carolina* (1845); two further poems appeared in the *Southern Literary Messenger* in 1843.

Most of the themes of Horton's poetry are indistinguishable from those of his white, free contemporaries, which is less surprising if one recalls that many verses were written on commission. So he spoke to his muse, invoked landscape, heard singing birds, knew a bonny belle, and saw eagles soar. But Horton guardedly spoke of being a slave, too, though more of the general condition, less of his own sharp experience. He was clear that freedom was preferable to slavery, that without liberty he lived on a "vile accursed earth" and endured "drudg'ry, pain, and toil," and that he was thus condemned "because my skin is black."[66] Understandably, liberty was seen as a blessing and an asylum, and Horton's verse was often religious and spoke of embracing death with gladness. In the white community, however, poetry seldom reached toward the political and social imagination. Not the least of Grayson's heterodoxies was the writing of political verse, especially about slavery, a topic about which usually Southern poetry was silent.

THERE WAS A troubling illegitimacy in fiction. A South Carolinian debating society deliberated in 1842, "Are the advantages of novel reading sufficient to warrant us, in recommending them to others?" and decided not. The sybaritic experience of reading fiction, the "lounging on a sofa & reading the last new novel," seemed to trouble a Christian people.[67] This was understandable, considering that the novel had prospered in the eighteenth century with Samuel Richardson and Henry Fielding, who had written of rutting farm boys and the lascivious consumption of fruit, and it had flourished in France with Pierre de Laclos, who had described rakes writing hypocritical letters on the backs of naked whores. That fiction indulged invention and so untruth was another accusation. Even the friends of fiction might be uneasy, because this perspective affected reputation and honor. The timid Albert James Pickett, when choosing between writing history and fiction, wondered whether venturing the latter might lead many "to doubt the authenticity of my late historical work."[68]

Fiction divided into two genres, the novel and the romance. The distinction was that a novel portrayed human life but did not offer "a metaphysical anatomy of the human mind," while a romance permitted the unnatural and extravagant.[69] Strictly speaking, or so Simms argued in 1835, only the romance was the heir of the epic, because it pushed credulity beyond limit so as to show the potentialities of human nature, whereas the novel plainly stuck to what was more or less normal. This was a distinction hard to sustain in practice. *The Castle of Otranto* might plainly be a romance, because men are seldom flattened by huge casques, but *Gil Blas* was less clear, for in it nothing happened that might not happen to a man, however improbably events occurred in such swift succession. The ordinary world was sufficiently full of wonders to make even Simms lose his grip on the distinction. The American Revolution might offer, at once, the opportunity of a history, romance, or novel, and a historian like Charles Gayarré might cheerfully think romance a prerogative of his craft, while the author of a romance might insist that historical knowledge was a prerequisite of his.

Fiction written in the South began in the late 1790s at about the same moment as elsewhere in the United States, but there was little enough thereafter until the 1820s, when it began to be habitual. In general, the genre's development was from the Gothic and satirical, to the domestic, then to the romantic, which was a movement from skepticism to commitment, from the apolitical to the political. One can plot these movements by a brief look at authors and texts from each moment, though these were not mutually exclusive categories.

Students of William Faulkner may be pleased to learn that one of Southern literature's earliest stories concerns incest. John Izard Middleton's "The Confessional: A Tale" (1810) is set in a Roman church in the Trastevere. A novice nun sings in the choir and glimpses a melancholy man, wrapped in a cloak. Noticing that he goes into a confessional box, she sits in the priest's place and hears how he had come from a noble Spanish family, and how as a youth he and his adopted cousin had begun to feel illicit attractions. On the eve of his departure for university, an earthquake had struck and, in its confusion, they had tumbled together on the floor, "lip prest to lip." Later, at university, he had received a letter from his father which announced the dishonor of the cousin, the father's killing of her, and his own impending suicide. The father had laid upon the son the duty to kill the offender. Anguished, the son had wandered the world and come to Rome, where the nun's singing had recalled his lost, scandalous love. By this point of the narrative, the nun has fainted away. After various harrowing incidents, the nun dies of convulsions and the man goes mad, eventually flinging himself into the Tiber. This is told in a narrative that is cool, atmospheric, and gloomy, and evincing a repressed sensuality that is almost pedophile.[70]

Such Gothicism, the remote heir of Elizabethan and Jacobean drama, with its bubbling cauldrons and Spanish revenges, persisted in Southern fiction. In Allston's *Monaldi*, the scene is likewise Italian, and there, too, can be found betrayal, violence, bitter wandering, and a "wild mixture of reason and madness."[71] *Monaldi* is *Othello*, except that Othello and Desdemona survive to madness and regret, finally to reconciliation at Othello's deathbed. In Poe, too, the Gothic bleakly flourished, though he leaned more to decaying cities near the Rhine than Trastevere churches, more to Protestant than Catholic nightmares, but everywhere in Poe pestilence stalked, pendulums sliced, and orangutans murdered, and there are "assumptions and aspirations which mortality had never before known."[72]

The Gothic appealed to the late Enlightenment sensibility, to those who had first thought reason sufficient, who were then troubled by passions and failure, and who thereafter sketched visions of extremity, often sexual in nature. Blame for failure is shifted to villainy or madness, and adulthood is refused by violence. The genre, being concerned about the loss of mastery, appealed to Southern sensibilities, though less so by midcentury, when late Romantics became more confident about their turbulent emotions, sometimes came to enjoy life's bumpy ride, and worried less that falling might kill them.

In the Gothic tale, the narrator was usually an aristocrat and cool, the historian of madness and mayhem, and spoke de haut en bas. It was similar to what is superficially a genre remote from the Gothic, that is, the tradition of southwestern humor, which began with Augustus Baldwin Longstreet and eventuated in Mark Twain. The locale was different, western taverns instead of Roman churches, and the response likewise, humor instead of guilty astonishment. But the structure was similarly Federalist; the civilized narrator looked out on an unsafe and uncontrollable world disfigured by passionate license and moral discord, occasioned by the pell-mell pace of social mobility and change. The chaos never reached him, but he knew about it, had stood on the scene, and so thought it important to tell the monitory tale. This genre had many antecedents other than the Gothic: English sporting tales of the eighteenth century and colonial writings on Lubber Land, for example, and even Joseph Addison. And the class element was different from that in the Gothic form: the narrator was not an aristocrat but usually of middling rank, even a Christian minister, and so was uncomfortably closer to what he deprecated. The genteel was only fragilely superior. Later, by Mark Twain's time, the vernacular came to be accorded some respect, but earlier the leitmotif was amused condescension.

In this tradition, writers were often startled by boisterous ruffians and social differentiation was conveyed by the standard English of the narrator juxtaposing the impertinent dialect of the vernacular heroes, who tended to have grotesque names like Sharp Snaffles and Ovid Bolus. Their native wit was oddly respected, insofar as they tended to prosper in their various rogueries, but the reader knew that they were indifferent to right and wrong. "IT IS GOOD TO BE SHIFTY IN A NEW COUNTRY" was the empirical motto given by Johnson Jones Hooper to Simon Suggs. As frontiersmen, they were doomed to be overwhelmed by civility's progress and, as such, worked like Scott's Highland eccentrics, victims of history's dismissive stages. Because, in their reprobate world, the natural ethical order was suspended, it often followed that the rules of physical nature, too, were intermittent and the frontier was a place of surreal legend and tall tale, where invulnerable bears calmly chose when to be killed and Mike Fink lived in "the *mythic* haze" of the Mississippi River.[73]

The authors of these stories tended to be rambling men, Southerners from the east who went west, or Northern-born men rattling through different parts of the Mississippi Valley in pursuit of the main chance. So, unsurprisingly, the genre was relatively indifferent to the North-South divide, but was more sensitive to what was East and West, what followed rivers and penetrated forests. It was very interested, therefore, in the scenes of travel, in steamboats, taverns, and strangers talking. Everything moved, and the world was made intelligible by story. Or, to be more precise, a man's world was made intelligible. Women never wrote these stories, and they little appear in them, except as eccentrics who might limp and howl "like a full pack of wolves," because women belonged in the kitchen not the bear hunt.[74]

Satire in the mode of John Pendleton Kennedy's *Swallow Barn* took up a different, if connected, stance. While southwestern humor laughed jaggedly in fear of the future, the plantation novel smiled in regret for the past. Kennedy was not a rambler, but was corporate, Whig, metropolitan, and quietly antislavery. On the whole, he did not greatly fear change, because he thought people like himself could handle matters. But he was sadly conscious that homogenizing change flattened out the distinctions of different social worlds and was creating a standardized American-European world, in which the city came to dominate the countryside. For Kennedy, the story of America was not of being colonially English, then growing toward an American difference; it was of being rurally American and growing toward an urban transatlantic culture. What seemed especially to have troubled Kennedy was the sense that the old order had conferred a recognition of individuality but the new was impersonal in its bustle.

As with Scott and Irving, Kennedy offered a sincere but not a serious elegy for lost worlds, and he was lighter than Oliver Goldsmith on the deserted village. Kennedy wrote of the anachronistic last days of the old order, and laughed at what he regretted. Moreover, *Swallow Barn* was an allusive tour of the mannerisms of eighteenth- and early-nineteenth-century literature, where one bumped into a little Fielding here, some Irving there, a dash of Scott, an imitation of Peacock; it was, to use a recent term, a very *writerly* book. In Kennedy, little was ominous, history was not a nightmare, lightness was almost all. His narrator is an outsider writing to a friend in New York, so that the former is free to be amused at everyone and might be uncommitted. He sees the Virginia plantation world (now vanished) as amiably uncosmopolitan, unlike himself.

In the Gothic tradition, women were sexual objects of guilty male predators; in the southwestern, stage props; in Kennedy, they were central because the plantation was a household transmittable by marriage and so courtship mattered. Certainly, the novel became a form attractive to female writers and readers, in part because it could describe the domestic scene where they were immured. Caroline Gilman's *Recollections of a Southern Matron* (1837) is only technically a novel, since it had little plot; rather, it was a series of scenes intending "to show the habits of Southern domestic life." In it, a young Charleston woman lives in her father's family, witnesses sundry incidents, is courted, marries, has children, and with that, the book stops. Even with nearly twenty years of Southern residence after a New England youth, Gilman wrote often as a an outsider, because everything was seen by her comparatively, as this and not something else. A home existed in a world of other places, though in Gilman, the shutters and doors of that home were open, so that people came in and out. As such, *Recollections of a Southern Matron's* emphasis on the South's sense of community—"I write in my paternal mansion" are its first words—was an observation from someone for whom the condition was not instinctive.[75] An odd consequence of this is the unwonted importance of slaves in *Recollections*, because, unlike native Southerners, Gilman was estranged enough to notice them. Though all her slaves are conventionally loyal, they appear as individuals, with special needs, voices, and mannerisms.

Gilman wrote as a mother and the editor of a children's periodical. Education, of which language was the medium, was a preoccupation, and her scenes of Southern life worked like posters tacked to the wall of a classroom; her reader sat at a desk and was instructed by a kindly schoolmistress, who pointed at the illustrations of life and said, see how slaves talk, this is how you do needlepoint, there is merit in simple folk, this is how you can cope with death. Death is a feature of Gilman's world, as it needed to be if she was to be faithful to the scything down which marked ordinary domesticity. People die in her book with gentle regularity, and, for Gilman, managing grief was a household task. Bodies had to be dressed, flowers arranged, coffins secured, ceremonies ·ordered, and monuments erected. Her language insistently spoke of wild emotion fiercely contained, of "the shrieking voice within" which did not emerge.[76] Conventionally, she sought the consolations of religion but knew the possibility of their absence, of what it might be like to face death without the comforts of Christianity. Like most Christians, Gilman saw the atheist as unnatural but knew nature permitted the unnatural.

For the rest, the rhythms in Gilman's book were inexorable, as was essential to domestic fiction: childhood, school, courtship, marriage, birth, death, all happened in their turn. Life was not the less emotional for this patterning, and the unexpected was part of the rhythms. It was not easy to experience the ordinary. Still, for Gilman, the home offered the best hope of getting by. She was inclined to mock the belle and the bon ton, and to mistrust society. If it is true that Southerners located self in the regard of others, Gilman remained a New Englander. For her, the woman was the peacemaker, who smiled through pain, who was a hypocrite for the sake of morality, who "rises to a high moral elevation, and looks calmly down upon the angry passions that are floating beneath."[77]

There was little in Gilman which was political, though her sympathetic vision of the South was, for a New England woman married to a Unitarian minister in Charleston, a political gesture. Much changed in Southern fiction after William Lloyd Garrison spoke and Nat Turner rebelled, notably in the creation of the Southern political novel. Neither George Tucker's *Valley of the Shenandoah* nor Kennedy's *Swallow Barn* had been other than implicitly political. But Beverley Tucker's *The Partisan Leader* (1836) commenced a new form, by offering a futuristic tale of 1848–49, in which Martin Van Buren had secured a fourth term and corrupted the American political and legal system into a quasi-monarchical oppression, the Lower South had seceded, and Virginia had tried to follow but been compelled into a guerrilla war against the Union. The novel explored divided loyalties in a Virginia family, so it was *Waverley* moved from the Highlands to the Appalachians, from the past to the future, and stripped of Scott's ambivalence about Jacobite and Hanoverian, because Tucker used the novel bluntly to expound his political and economic views. The book was founded in a very old political vision, being the Commonwealth tradition reenacted, but was also a response to Jacksonian politics, to Nullification and the tariff, to the Whig revulsion from "King Andrew" and the maneuverings which secured the presidency for Van Buren, that man of suspiciously pliant principles. There was but one slight and fleeting reference to "the poor negroes that the Yankees pretend to be so sorry for," but otherwise the book was indifferent to slavery.[78] Tucker's book, oddly, shows that it was easier to evade slavery in male political fiction: there need be no slaves in scenes where politicians argued, judges were bought, or guerrillas were killed. But, as Gilman showed, it was hard (though not impossible) to speak of Southern domesticity without representing household slaves, so it is unsurprising that the Southern novelists who responded most sharply to *Uncle Tom's Cabin* were women.

The Massachusetts-born Caroline Lee Hentz was the most notable of these, especially in *The Planter's Northern Bride*. Liminal women in the South seem to have been more interested in defending slavery than those who were Southern born and bred, though Hentz lived more on the margin than Gilman. The former was married to a volatile French émigré called Nicholas Hentz, who was only intermittently employed, and they moved around very often, eventually to Florida. With children and debts, she earned needed money with her writings, which were various, short stories, novels, plays, and poetry. The controversy over Mrs. Stowe's book was an opportunity, beckoning with sales. In Hentz's writing, intersectional harmony had been a theme, natural not only to a Northern-born woman but to someone who lived on the edge of the South.

The plot of *The Planter's Northern Bride* is simple enough. A Southern planter visits the North, where he falls in love with the daughter of an abolitionist. The bride moves to her husband's plantation, where she learns the benignity of slavery and the limitations of Africans. There are crosscurrents, but the burden of the novel is the successful marriage of a strong Southern man and a pliant Northern woman, an event which Hentz suggested should instruct all those not blinded by malignant animosity. Her slaves are cruder than Gilman's, being not individual but stock characters, and Hentz was more didactic, more racist, and spoke of smells and revulsion, the "shudder of inexpressible loathing." The book was almost more an argument for racial hierarchy than for slavery, which makes sense, when one remembers that Hentz was concerned to find ground upon which Southerners and Northerners could stand together. So *The Planter's Northern Bride* was a bleak book, despite its often glowing language, because fearful. Hentz wrote of "the bondage of poverty" and, though this was partly the typical Southern vision of Henry Mayhew's Stygean London, it was more the anxious glance of a struggling author and mother, not sure where sustenance was to come from. Both Hentz's women and her slaves accepted a planter's mastership because it offered safety, a thing of greater moment than freedom, which was regarded with skepticism. Hentz was unashamedly partial to wealth, and her enthusiasm for the South was connected to its prosperity. For Hentz, wealth meant possibility and the South seemed wealthier, at least then. She portrays New England, not as the springboard for modern industrialism, but as a crabbed, isolated world of unworldly village provincials. The bride's wedding journey from North to South is a movement into a world of greater complexity, movement, and sophistication. In this way, Hentz was implicated in the discourse of moral landscapes, of the North as a constricting "cold dream" and the South as warmly vivifying.[79]

Hentz's book only occasionally varied the standard beliefs of what was her chosen culture. Its most striking contribution was to find a voice for Northerners drawn to the South by its wealth, who understood that slavery was essential to its opportunities, and who made their peace with its ideology, while remaining anxious not to be despised by their distant relatives. Being New Englanders, they needed morality, but being Americans, they sought prosperity, hence they made of the South's gleaming fields a vision of both. So, in Hentz, the benediction from the North was important. In *The Planter's Northern Bride*, the bride's father comes around to his Northern daughter's Southern life, her mistresshood of a slave community and her birthing of a young master, and convinces himself that slavery is a missionary venture, a means of turning African pagans into Christians.

The obverse of Hentz's worldview can be seen in William Alexander Caruthers's last novel. For Hentz, the domestic scene offered a microcosm of the political realm; for Caruthers, domesticity was enfolded dialectically within a larger politics, masculine and violent. Few novels more neatly narrate the imperial vision of Southern culture than *The Knights of the Horse-Shoe* (1841), whose scene is set in 1714 and Virginia, from which its governor,

Alexander Spotswood, led a military expedition to the brow of the Appalachian Mountains, in a plan to dispossess the natives and push aside the competition of France and Spain. Caruthers was clear that morality resided in this projection of power, because Spotswood was the pathfinder of the "glorious and magnificent scheme of conquering an Empire," which was to reach a consummation in Caruthers's own day.[80] Equally clear is that this was an American not a British achievement, the harbinger of what a postcolonial South would later accomplish.

In the novel, what is worthwhile is caught between two dark forces, Indian savages to the west and corrupt Europeans to the east. In the Old World, there is narrowness of vision, religious skepticism, and war, and Europe sends forth both "human swarms" and death.[81] An opening scene shows the governor secretly burying the body of his half-brother, beheaded as a Jacobite and smuggled out of England to be honorably interred in Virginia. Equally, American natives offer dishonor and massacre. Suspended between these two ominous worlds is Virginia, a place of sweet domesticity. Caruthers was interested in the ideology of separate spheres, and, as such tales required, he made much ado about lovers lost and found, virtue rewarded and vice punished. Even more powerful was his sense of a feminized landscape, possessed by masculine energy. Like a woman, landscape had natural power, and, like a virgin, it needed despoiling. When possessed, however, land created domesticity and, eventually, Caruthers's own Southern home.

Nonetheless, Caruthers did not intend his allegory to bestow an unmixed blessing on the project of empire. He was a Whig and hence a man caught in the middle, with some sympathy for oligarchy, but some interest in the people. He lived at a time when Virginians were troubled by decline and depopulation, when the Chesapeake was being deserted. He liked to imagine that, in time, the descendants of migrants would return to the land of their fathers and restore it. For this to happen, people would have to learn the merit of stability, see the value of the old ways, which unusually combined "social aristocracy and public equality."[82] To make a future, Virginians would have to restore the past. This was a proposition to which the political theorists were elsewhere giving thought, not only for the sake of Virginia. Like Caruthers, their confidence was touched with misgiving.

5 · Pride and Power

In many genres ventured by Southern intellectuals, they were interpreting the innovations of European thought, but political thought was different. The pertinent interpretation had taken place in the late eighteenth century, when readings of canonical political thinkers had been collated with the indigenous experience of British colonials, American revolutionaries, and constitution-makers to form what was then the modern world's most original body of political thinking. Southerners were conscious of this preeminence, fashioned partly by their forebears. The events of 1776 "had opened a new area in the science of politics," and to this had been added nearly a half century of turbulent constitutional history, generating its own texts. Together, these formed an ambivalent tradition. Some Southerners came to see themselves as lesser men grappling with an overly powerful legacy, while others felt at ease with their status as heirs. All knew, however, that this legacy required husbanding by "an incessant vigilance, a sleepless jealousy, and a promptness of resentment," all marks of a serious republican, because any complacent sense of completion would signal the end, even the moral bankruptcy of, what 1776 had commenced.[1]

In the twentieth century, it was to become usual to speak of an older tradition of Southern political thought which was decentralist, conservative, and skeptical of democracy. This was a better description of how that tradition stood in 1900, since then Southern politics (battered by the escalating revolutions of Reconstruction, the establishment of segregation and disfranchisement, and a failed Populism) did acquire such characteristics. It may seem a paradox to observe, considering slavery, that in 1840 Southern politics for whites were more democratic than those of 1900. Antebellum political thought covered a fairly wide ideological spectrum, though stopping short of socialist philosophies which mistrusted property. Merely to observe that the South had John Marshall, Andrew Jackson, John Taylor, John C. Calhoun, and Beverley Tucker, very different men, is to see how fissiparous was the debate and how variously the problems of power, equality, democracy, and rights were there analyzed. Thomas Carlyle once spoke of the "constitutional battle of the Kilkenny cats," and the Southern scene answered to the description.[2]

Little was settled, beyond the presumption of republicanism. Secession in 1860–61 was, in part, an attempt to resolve ambivalences grown intolerable. The fierce certitude which characterized Southern writings on the state arose from a knowledge of incertitude. As Beverley Tucker observed of the Founding Fathers, "So anomalous is their plan, that, to this day, the ablest expounders of the constitution are not agreed upon its fundamental principles, and so little does it resemble any other government, whether past or present, that all attempts to illustrate and explain it by analogies to them, are sure to lead to dangerous mistakes." Calhoun called it "Our present peculiar, complicated, and remarkable system of governments."[3]

Of necessity 1840 expressed a revisionist view of what had happened in 1776 and 1787, even though antebellum Southerners believed in their continuity with the Founding moment. This revisionism was assisted by the dark complexity of the American Revolution, which had had many reasons for obscuring its constitutional understandings. Madison and Jefferson had left a confusing legacy, about which even they themselves were unsure. To be a Jeffersonian often required taking sides with Jefferson against himself, to appeal from Philip drunk to Philip sober, if one could but reason out when he had been in his cups.

One thing, however, was clear. There was continuity back to the Commonwealth tradition of James Harrington, John Locke, and Algernon Sidney. In political conventions, orations, and essays these names were ritually invoked, and cognoscenti could judge how well the old texts were being expounded. No one was more an expert than John Taylor of Caroline, a revolutionary and a Jeffersonian, who late in life offered a running commentary on the early years of the Constitution, especially in his *Inquiry into the Principles and Policy of the Government of the United States*. It was a book begun in the 1790s but not published until 1814, and was simultaneously a quarrel with the Hamiltonian program, a meditation on the American future after 1812, an intervention into the debate over the French Revolution, and a retrospect upon the growth of English state power during the eighteenth century.

In many ways, Taylor was a conventional Commonwealthman. He mistrusted power, especially the corrupt interpenetrations of government, patronage, and wealth; he disliked the metropolitan and preferred the countryside; he abominated standing armies and liked a militia; he was a watchful republican who excoriated aristocracy, monarchy, and established religion. But much in Taylor was unconventional, closer to modern liberalism. Among other things, he put little faith in *virtù* as the preservative of liberty, was impatient with too many references to ancient Rome and Florence, and doubted that the past demonstrated a fixity in human nature and society. In opposition to John Adams, his bête noire, Taylor believed in the plasticity of human nature and hence in the possibility that the United States might have inaugurated a *novus ordo seclorum*. Taylor was a late-Enlightenment philosophe, which is easy to forget because he wrote so badly. Yet he did speak of living in an "enlightened age," had a fondness for stage theory, spat upon "Gothic ignorance," and possessed a Herderian consciousness of the confused richness of the human record. This last standpoint made him pull back from the enormous condescension of posterity, since he was unconvinced that modernity was always doing better. Still, he understood his political theory as a venture in discerning and promoting a Linnaean order in the political realm. As he put it, "Unity, harmony, and proportion, are as necessary in politicks, as in the drama, musick or architecture."[4]

Taylor disbelieved in man's "natural depravity," because to believe would make man's case hopeless. He was anxious that the lesson of the French Revolution not be pessimistically overinterpreted. Man was matter and mind, and while the former mandated constraints, the latter conferred freedom. Free men made the world's institutions, which in turn structured how men's potentialities were realized. As Taylor believed, "forms of government mould manners," men were "both virtuous and vicious," but they had the "power of regulating motives, or electing principles," which had an effect upon virtue and vice.[5] There could be more to man than self-interest, and this was not the less true because history suggested otherwise. Circumstances and human will together might make a difference, and, on both scores, the United States was peculiarly blessed, because intellectually enlightened and physically advantaged. In so thinking, Taylor insistently fought off the ideological tyranny of the "natural," which he took to be acceptance of a barren stoicism, and he refused the tyranny of history. This was why he rejected John Adams's insistence that a limited diet of political forms (monarchy, aristocracy, democracy) was ineluctable. This rejection made Taylor into an American exceptionalist, who stressed that American moral insight, being grounded in American circumstances, was not exportable.

Perhaps no Southern thinker was more radically invested in the idea of individualism than John Taylor: "Society must be composed of, or created by individuals, without whom, it can neither exist nor act."[6] For him, society was a reification, whose form could be altered by the decisions of individuals. He raged at Adams for thinking that men naturally combined into "orders." In Taylor's worldview, men—women did not exist for him—were alone, freely choosing and acting, and a wise polity offered them no inducement to combine with others, because it was by such combinations that greed and power were encouraged. Wisely, then, dividing men one from another was a principle of the American polity. However, Taylor saw the case differently from James Madison, who had thought that, men not being angels, a wise polity should balance self-interests and dispel animosities by a dissipating but permanent tension. To this pessimism Taylor opposed a very guarded optimism; he believed that the principle of division dialectically improved human beings and served to prevent the emergence of factional passions. Still, both Madison and Taylor endorsed the heterodoxy that, in the operations of government, sovereignty was divisible; its only resting place lay with the people, who originated the compacts of government and monitored their operations. However, for Taylor, the people were only so many individuals, whose deliberations and free moral decisions happened to sponsor political volitions.

The practical implications of this analysis were, on the whole, straightforward. The presidency should not become a monarchy; Congress should abjure Hamiltonianism; there should be no standing army; the Supreme Court had no right of judicial review; religion should be disestablished and tolerated; freedom of speech must be axiomatic and education encouraged; democracy must be resisted and the principle of representation acknowledged; parties were a bad idea.

The individualism inherent in Taylor's political theory gave him a special standpoint on the issue of the United States as a social and political compact. It became important to later Southern political thinkers to argue that the Constitution of 1787 was a revocable compact, by which the people of each of the thirteen states had, by a sovereignty expressed in conventions, licensed participation in the polity called the United States; and that, consequently, there had been thirteen American peoples, who kept a reserved right of withdrawal from the Union. Because of his individualistic "atomical philosophy," Taylor saw this question differently. For one thing, he did not see Virginia as any more natural than the United States, because all societies and governments were fictions. Hence Taylor declined to see the movement from the individual to society, from society to the state, from the state to the Union, as the appropriate sequence for grounding any theory of the compact. The individual was real enough, to be sure, but all else was invention. So he spoke of "the whole herd of fictitious compacts between the people and the government, or between the states, or the states and the Union" and asserted that "none of these governments had any agency in their own creation." This was not an idiosyncratic idea. Thomas Cooper saw it similarly: "Every nation is composed of its individual citizens: the terms nation, state, community, are words merely—they do not denote any thing separate from the individual members whose aggregation and association has received these names."

Hence, for Taylor, the federal government was doubly made, by individuals directly, and by the states which were "moral beings" also made by individuals.[7] This was a merit of the principle of division, that it multiplied the complexities of political connections. It followed that no state had the single prerogative of dissolving the Union, because that would only invoke one of the lines of connection between the atom that was the individual and the federal government. It seemed to follow, too, that the individuals acting through states, and the individuals acting as citizens of the Union, had a double right to dissolution or reformation, by seceding as states, or by acting in a general American convention. In both cases, Taylor shared the premise, crucial to later Southern thought, that the constitutional convention was the means by which the sovereignty of the people must be exercised, and that courts, legislatures, presidents, and constitutions were mere instrumentalities, revocable as intellect, will, and circumstances dictated.

The *Inquiry* is a turbulent book of Jacobean vividness, wherein Taylor stated and restated, circled and fumed, excoriated and praised, chopped off the Hydra's head of aristocracy in a plenitude of ways and paragraphs, and always wore his heart on his sleeve. He made phrases better than he made chapters, though he could be incisive. "We lose truth in names and phrases, as children lose themselves in a wood, for want of geographical knowledge," is a satisfying sentence. But the *Inquiry* is a very long book, and many readers lost their way. "For heaven's sake, get some worthy person to do the second edition into *English*," John Randolph advised.[8] Others wondered about a mind which strangely mixed the disillusioned and the hopeful.

Nonetheless, many of Taylor's ideas were to circulate widely. The Jacksonians took much from him, especially in their individualism, optimism, and suspicion of banks and paternalistic government, and the Nullifiers had studied their Taylor, too. Calhoun saw Taylor as an ideological mentor, one of "the political fathers of the Republican school."[9] Taylor himself survived until 1824 and published several more works which monitored the fate of the republic, celebrated agrarianism, commented on Marshall's court, and observed the revived Hamiltonianism which came to be associated with Henry Clay. Throughout, his achievement had been to find a way to transmute the anti-Federalist tradition of the mid-1780s into constitutional and social thinking which might work within the framework set up in 1789. He taught antebellum Southerners that one could not reason *only* within that constitution. Unionism was only enough if it addressed the fundamental problems of man's individual and social existence. And, if the Union proved inadequate, there could be no more sovereign obligation than to kill it.

A more complex legacy lay in Taylor's revision of the Commonwealth tradition. This had once been a cosmopolitan intellectual project, which had gathered its evidence eclectically across time and space as a way to comprehend the human condition, understood as (on the whole) a constant. Taylor was close enough to this tradition to play the game. He spoke of the Spartan constitution, debated Machiavelli, and set Montesquieu against Bolingbroke. But he did this partly to prove the inutility of the old game and to show, instead, the peculiarity of the hopeful American experience. In time, this standpoint would come to encourage a falling away of the old knowledge as an irrelevance. Southerners would come to measure the abstract problem of humanity against the concrete record of the United States, especially its founding moment, and speak less of the Petition of Right or the Amphictyonic Council and more of what was said in that hall in Philadelphia. A sense of singularity bred a habit of self-absorption. That is, Taylor made political thought into a problem of an American historicism. Further, he reinforced the custom of seeing political thought as a jeremiad, which set standards so high as to ensure incessant occasions for observing defalcations. They were so lofty that he was conscious that men might become negligent and fail to notice signs of danger. In *Tyranny Unmasked* (1822), he offered tests by which tyranny, coming masked like Scaramouche to a Venetian ball, might be discerned. Thereby Taylor indicated how subtle might be the problem to all but the political scientist, the bravo watching the canals.

Political thought drew upon those moments of crisis and pressure when stray thoughts about David Hume's essays were compelled into hard choices about the franchise, apportionment, or tariffs, because power was at stake. One such moment was the Virginia Constitutional Convention of 1829–30. It was not singular. A restlessness about constitutional forms distinguished the Southern experience in the nineteenth century. But Virginia furnished the most sophisticated seminar on the Southern understanding of political science held between the Revolution and the Civil War.

At bottom, the issues were straightforward. Virginia had formed a constitution in 1776 which had little changed the political structure of the colony, save in attaching a resonant Declaration of Rights. The new state had defined a franchise confined to white male freeholders, and seats in the state legislature were apportioned by a system of county representation, which gave to each county an equal weight irrespective of its population's size. But Virginia's western population had grown quickly while the eastern had remained almost static, with the result that the Tidewater had counties with few white people and many slaves but a preponderance of political power, while the west had many white people (most nonfreeholders), fewer slaves, and less political power. Westerners wished to make the system responsive to a changed demography, as a matter of equity and to gain the leverage which might change policies, especially in encouraging the internal improvements to which the Tidewater was hostile. Expediency was connected to principle, too, which had been ambiguously expressed in the Declaration of Rights of 1776. Should the suffrage be confined to "all men having sufficient evidence of permanent common interest with, and attachment to, the community," which meant property? Or should one respect the dictum that "all men are by nature equally free and independent"?[10] And what was nature, what was a community, what was freedom, anyway?

The delegates came to Richmond and assembled on 5 October 1829 in Jefferson's Capitol building. He was three years dead, but Madison, Monroe, and Marshall attended, and their presence colored the task of reassessing the legacy of 1776. Those who had been born when Virginia was comfortably a part of the British Empire debated with those born in the shadow of the Revolution, and those who would outlive the Civil War.

The practical upshot of the convention was a few concessions to the west, with the east maintaining most of its power, a result surprising when one notes that Andrew Jackson was then in the White House, but less so when one recalls that the convention was elected under the old rules. Those with power had to consent to give it away, and they did so only sparingly. More pertinent are the intellectual presumptions on display. Four themes ran contentiously through the debates: the nature of the social compact, the relationship between abstraction and experience, the problem of progress and democracy, and the possibility of social disorder and schism.

A few matters were claimed to be consensual: free government best promoted human happiness, sovereignty lay with the people, and representation was an essential principle. But delegates were also conscious of "many conflicting and various principles."[11] Once there had been Mr. Jefferson's glad confident morning of self-evident truths, and eventually there would be the verities of democracy, but in between the Virginians of 1829 endured fluidity. The useful illusion of a constitutional convention was that it stopped history, considered fundamentals, and gave the people and their representatives the prerogative of reconsideration. At such a moment, self-evidence was unlikely. Hardly any one seemed safe from criticism, not Locke, Montesquieu, or Jefferson, and names once thought invidious (Burke, Filmer, Hobbes) were puzzlingly praised.

The most lucid expositor of young conservatism was Abel P. Upshur from the Tidewater, who asked the fundamental question. Upon what right did the proponents of reform ground their claim that majority rule was a self-evident truth? It could not be located in nature, because nature was a Hobbesian world of naked self-interest and violence. In the beginning, perhaps all in the world (men, women, children, Africans) were equal, but the social compact had discriminated, decided who was to rule, who was ruled. Egalitarians could not have it both ways by insisting that they had natural rights but others did not, that men did and women did not. In fact, the idea of majority rule, even of the state itself, was but a translation of the principle of numbers, coupled with force, and it followed that rights were a matter of social expedience and invention. Free to choose a principle, Upshur chose that which suited his condition. Land, slaves, and slaveholders required the extra weight granted them implicitly in the old Virginia constitution, since they were the guarantors of social order. Since government mostly acted upon property, property had a stake in its decisions. In short, Virginians needed less of what in 1826 Upshur had called the "childish fripperies of natural rights" and more history. Virginians were not standing naked at the beginning of time, whimpering on the fields of praise, but at the end of their shared, self-defining experience. So Upshur urged that Virginians go for experience and practicality and disdain "speculative systems."[12]

This was a newfangled conservatism. Though Upshur did argue that property seemed intrinsic to an ordered society, he was otherwise radical in his thinking. Little but violence was natural: all else was human invention, which necessarily enforced inequalities, mandated who was in and who was out, made of government and rights a tautology of social power. Upshur made no Burkean appeals to an ancient order of nature but stood only on what Virginians had invented and, as he saw it, had made to work. As such, he was poised between those who mistrusted the abstract and those who understood only expediency, because Upshur was too dismissive of the idea of the natural for the latter, and too interested in discussing theory for the former. Fear of the abstract ran very deep in the convention. Denouncing theory was a mantra which validated practicality, because all liked to say, as even John Randolph improbably did, "I am a practical man."[13] In fact, the convention took pains to consider theory and did so as a first order of business.

In general, reformers were more trusting about the idea of the natural and self-evident. John R. Cooke tidily squared the circle of abstraction and practicality by asserting that what "might have been called an abstract principle, in Europe, in the time of Locke and Sydney . . . became *practical* in Virginia, in 1776." The conservatives saw men as wolves and tigers, but Cooke found this a libel. To the contrary, man was "an *affectionate*, a *social*, a *patriotic*, a *conscientious* and a *religious creature*," closer to the person described in Adam Smith's *Theory of Moral Sentiments* than anyone in Hobbes's *Leviathan*. Cooke could unblushingly speak (as Upshur never could) of improvements in the "science of Government" and even of "the march of intellect" and "progress." As tellingly, Cooke made mock of the conservatives' fears, what Philip Doddridge called their disposition "to look altogether on the dark side of things," their expectation that property would be despoiled, anarchy let loose, despotism established. Was there not, near the heart of the conservative case, a contradiction? They urged that men were not to be trusted, yet they themselves asked to be trusted and even boasted of the wisdom and sufficiency of their stewardship of the state's affairs since 1776. They asked why anyone would wish to alter so happy a condition and were annoyed when it was even hinted that there had been moments of "misrule."[14] This contradiction expressed a profound disagreement over the shape of Virginia's history, which crossed the conservative/reform divide. Some thought reform would be but a consummation of the principles of 1776, while others knew that 1776 had deliberately circumscribed the idea of equality and that Virginia had emerged from the eighteenth century as a flawed polity, in need of ideological and political transformation, which might fit her for a modernizing world.

Much hinged on this problem of confidence. That Virginia had once been great and her political system had had a role in that, hardly anyone disputed. A glance toward James Madison would suffice to settle the insight. That Virginia was changing, hardly anyone doubted, either. But would change forfeit greatness? Or had greatness gone already, only to be restored by judicious change? The conservatives offered little reassurance that the continuance of their power would reverse history. At best, they promised only a slow descent into the maelstrom. They said, as John C. Coalter frankly admitted, "I confess I am afraid," and the reformers reassured them that change would not occasion "tumult and riot." The conservatives felt a connection to an older history and thought Virginia embedded in a longer narrative. A reformer like Doddridge, to the contrary, let the past go and offered, instead, an American historicism. He was tired of being "incessantly lectured like school-boys" about ancient republics and wanted to adhere to "the Virginia sense" of republicanism.[15] He gestured toward the West and indicated that all would be well, perhaps even greater. And, somehow, the conservatives were not persuaded. They were not reassured by the thought of Ohio.

In all this, little regarded were the subjects of slavery and democracy. The former was only obliquely germane to how the convention saw its task, or so at least the delegates claimed, though Madison discerned a "morbid" and "violent" disinclination to broach the subject. Nonetheless, when the matter was raised, there were no explosions occasioned by disagreement. Some thought slavery a moral evil, others that it was happily marginal in the west, others that it was happily growing in the west, others spoke glowingly of the master-slave relationship. For the most part, slavery was enfolded into the broader issues of wealth, property, and interests, and the internal social dynamics of the institution little detained debate, though westerners frequently invoked an unsubtle racism in speaking of "this principle of negro representation" and denouncing the weight given to slave property in calculating representation. And it was not uncommon to suggest that slavery might be responsible for the east's decline, though one did not need to be a westerner to say this. Most glumly agreed with Monroe when he said that they were stuck with "the evil" of "the slavish population," that there was no way out, because emancipation would bring only "disorganization . . . and perfect confusion."[16]

As for democracy, no one spoke up for it, which says a lot about Virginia's ways, because elsewhere in the South the topic was common. True, the reformers spoke for adult male suffrage, but they accepted the older definition of democracy as the direct rule of the people, and, like the conservatives, deprecated this "visionary and impracticable" idea and preferred a representative republic, "the principle of intermediate elections" in "a great, extended, populous community." Reformers had the premises of a democratic ideology but not a willingness to make good the tainted word. Still, they did repel the contention that majority rule was unrepublican and insisted that "the people" meant the whole people, not just "qualified voters." And they were tempted into the discourse of class animosity, as when Alexander Campbell spoke of those who "at home, or when they return from Congress . . . have negroes to fan them asleep."[17]

Fear of political schism ran deep and subtly interwove state and federal politics. Here the preoccupations of 1787 and 1861 met, and to this matter slavery was deeply pertinent. William Branch Giles was blunt: "The forcible separation of Virginia, must and will lead to a separation of the United States, come when it will." This was so, because the representation of Virginia and the Southern states in the federal Congress was determined by the principle that slaves counted as three-fifths of a person for the purposes of determining the size of a population. To abandon principles within the state which gave sanction to this might leave the state ideologically defenseless within the Union. What gave eastern Virginia power within the state gave Virginia power in Washington, or so the conservatives argued. Further, there was the fear of class division, of the landed being pitted against the unlanded, of slaveholder opposing nonslaveholder, in what might become a "Trojan War between the two great parties of the State." The powerless nonslaveholders might reach out to others of their kind. As Benjamin Watkins Leigh saw it, one path led toward a United States "consolidated into one vast empire, without any reference to existing boundaries." Another led to a moment "when this great political Confederacy shall be broken up, and separated into its original atoms, and new political beings shall rise out of its ruins," which he guessed might be four smaller confederacies, "one Government North of the Hudson, another between the Hudson and the Potomac, another in the South, and another in the West."[18]

So the convention, not obsessively but often, commented on the nature of the Union. Perhaps curiously, on this score there was little disagreement, though the westerners had more to hope from an active United States which might offer internal improvements, and the easterners feared tariffs and protectionism. But the discourse of social compacts flowed naturally into a reading of 1787 as another moment of compact. Such an approach saw the Union as a thing invented to serve Virginia's purposes, and something whose instabilities grew from those inherent in Virginia's own situation. If Virginia succeeded, so might the Union; if not, not.

Less usual was the view which enfolded the fate of Virginia into that of the South. The incessant theme of East and West tended to limit the competing vision of North and South, as did the greatness of the Virginian past, whose existence (literally so in the presence of Madison and Monroe) created a fiercely proud introspection. There were, to be sure, moments when the tariff or the antislavery movement was discussed, which were the moments when the idea of a coherent slaveholding South with shared interests was most relevant. In general, however, the convention's intermittent habit of comparative constitutional analysis did not favor the South over other states. Some might point to South Carolina's constitution, but others to New York's. Most looked inward, because the lares and penates were compelling.

Melancholy Virginian introspection contrasted with South Carolinian energy in the 1820s, partly because the latter had settled its internal constitutional argument in 1808, was more cosmopolitan, and over the years came to gain rather than lose political influence. The Virginians, long skeptical of the Constitution, were less disillusioned by its shortcomings than the South Carolinians, who had been more convinced Unionists and wanted the history of the Union to prove their case, to demonstrate that they had rights *within* the logic of 1787. By contrast, Virginians had often taken their stand upon extraconstitutional grounds and natural rights.

The driving force of South Carolinian political thought in the 1820s was money, that is, the tariff, internal improvements, and banking. Between the election of John Quincy Adams and the Compromise of 1833, South Carolina hammered out a critique of the Union, which was not original in its essentials and surprisingly consensual, and concentrated on the proposition that "the Federal Constitution is a bond of Union for distinct and independent commonwealths."[19] The difference between Unionists and Nullifiers, who nearly went to civil war with each other in the early 1830s, lay not in presumptions but in varying judgments of the urgency of the economic and political crisis, and whether that crisis justified the theory of Nullification.

Though Calhoun became the champion of what Thomas Cooper called the "South Carolina Doctrines," Cooper himself had defined them, most effectively by turning an economic into a constitutional analysis. In 1823 he had critiqued the tariff as economically ill-advised though not necessarily unconstitutional. In 1824 he argued for "the *independence* and separate sovereignty of each state of the Union," and contended that, even at the convention of 1787, a federal government had been established not as a supreme but a subordinate authority. For Cooper, the political history of the American republic since 1789 had been the attempt of consolidationists to extend federal authority, augment the military, extend patronage, interfere in European politics, and turn the United States into "a great and energetic nation, one and indivisible," chiefly by using the Supreme Court to control states.[20] To an old English radical like Cooper, this project was a conservative and antidemocratic movement, hostile to the principles of the French Revolution. His analysis suggested, too, that opposition to increased federal power could be conservative, liberal, or radical indifferently, because the crucial issue was why local power was desired and how it was exercised.

Mixing radicalism and conservatism was characteristic of Cooper. He was often unsympathetic to the Commonwealth tradition, though he was a devotee of Paine's *Rights of Man*, and cheerily tossed aside most theories for justifying political authority, whether divine, patriarchal, nationalist, or hierarchical. Rather, he thought that power derived only from the people, whom he understood to be "an aggregate of individuals." But Cooper was a utilitarian, who believed that "the greatest good of the greatest number, is the polar star of all good government," so he was more sympathetic than John Taylor to majority rule.[21] For Cooper, the individual consented to be governed but only to be well governed, government was only provisionally sanctioned, and rights adhered to the private realm which no government could touch. But who were the people? Surprisingly for an English radical and immigrant, they did not include the stranger, the resident alien, and the poor, but only the propertied. In the struggle between Paine and Burke, Cooper had been on Paine's side, though he saw propertied people as instruments of change, not as guardians of inert prejudice, and presumed that freedom would incessantly transform the nature of the state.

Cooper was a proslavery thinker, in contradiction to his younger self, and his arguments of the 1820s were to become staple fare: antislavery was hypocritical; slavery was an ancient fact sanctioned in the Bible, as well as a modern fact practiced throughout Africa; American slaves lived better than the British laboring classes; free blacks were idle and debauched; African slaves flourished as labor in hot climates where whites died; Northern wealth depended on Southern slavery; and emancipation would turn ex-slaves into vagabonds and lead to race war. More particularly, Cooper made a case for the constitutionality of slavery and its compatibility with republicanism. In bringing these two things together, the problem of civil government and the fact of slavery, Cooper was a little heterodox, since usually Southerners left slavery to the specialized genre of the proslavery argument, which was carefully separated from political thought.

The story of South Carolina's movement toward Nullification has been well told elsewhere. Here what matters is that what began as a constitutional quarrel ended up as a cultural assertion, that skepticism about the interpretation of the Constitution of 1787 became a quarrel with the emerging discourse of American nationality, and that eventually a state like South Carolina came to be understood as itself a nation. The logic became inexorable. High tariffs were thought to be bad for South Carolinians, and so, since the Constitution was being construed to facilitate protectionism, it followed that one needed to illegitimate the institutions of the Union and legitimate the countervailing power of states. The Supreme Court lay at the heart of the matter, because John Marshall had asserted the right of judicial review and aggrandized the federal government's competence over economic and legislative concerns. It was not difficult to demonstrate that judicial review had nowhere been explicitly ceded to the court, not in the 1787 convention, not in the text of the Constitution, not during ratification, not even in the *Federalist Papers*, and so the court was not "the tribunal of dernier resort."[22] It was more contentious to argue that the states were the judges of constitutionality, because this meant strengthening the states and this would violate the Madisonian premise that stability lay in divided sovereignty. In this way, the South Carolinians showed themselves more interested in possessing power than in denying its necessity.

From Massachusetts, Daniel Webster had argued that the Constitution was the creature of the American people in aggregate, the Supreme Court served as its constitutional arbiter, and hence the locus of sovereignty rested with a branch of the federal government and was not diffused throughout the federal system. It was simplest to attack this logic at its starting point, the premise that the American people were one people, so many South Carolinians refused the idea of American nationality. They were insistent that the United States were (not was) a federation or league, but not a nation. This was not, however, a refusal of nationality but its relocation. As Cooper said, in 1776 there had been "thirteen distinct communities or nations." Even after 1789, civic allegiance was only to "our own *Sovereign State*; which was such before the federal government was created; which is so still; and which will be such when the federal government is altered or dissolved."[23]

Calhoun designed Nullification as a way of steering between the Charybdis of Cooper's radical idea of state nationality and the Scylla of Henry Clay's Unionism. Calhoun wanted state sovereignty *and* the Union, whereas Cooper insisted the state was finally supreme over the Union. This desire to have it both ways was characteristic of Calhoun, who was not a newfangled conservative like Upshur, who saw little generality in human experience. Calhoun was easier about the idea of "an universal and fundamental political principle," despite his recognition of "the great diversity of the human intellect."[24]

While Cooper had said that the arbiter of sovereignty was the individual state, and Webster said it was the Supreme Court, Calhoun said it was a tribunal of the states, sitting in perpetuity and charged with monitoring the evolution of the American polity. From this proposition flowed all the logic of Nullification: that, if a federal law was thought repugnant, a state could summon a state convention elected by the people and nullify, but such a nullification might be repealed by similar conventions in the other states of the Union, if three-fourths of them agreed. Under such circumstances, state sovereignty did not exist as a matter of principle, though the procedure was so improbably extended that, in practice, it did. Nonetheless, Calhoun did concede that, though South Carolina might nullify the tariff, if eighteen other states told it otherwise, South Carolina must rescind its nullification. So sovereignty had been bargained away in 1789, though it had passed not to the federal government but to the states collectively, standing in perpetual alliance as the guardians of constitutional virtue. For many, Calhoun's was an unintelligible compromise. Nathaniel Macon saw no difficulty about nullifying a federal law or even secession, but presumed the former put the state out of the Union and made it a foreign power.

Calhoun's reasoning was premised on a broader understanding of man and government, which might be summarized by saying that he envisaged a Hobbesian world with Queensberry rules. Man was selfish, but it was possible to regulate the baleful consequences of selfishness. In the Union, there was a "dissimilarity of interests," and this unevenness of selfishness occasioned "the great difficulty of forming, and preserving free institutions." Slavery was one such interest and, since slaveholders were a minority, a reason for mistrusting majority rule. John Taylor solved this problem by denying significant power to government and majorities. But Calhoun had a different solution, which was to grant power to all, since he believed that such grants created the conditions for making civility and *"that moderation and justice so essential to harmony and peace, in a country of such vast extent, and diversity of interests as ours."*[25] Knowing the free and vigilant power of others, the wise man acted prudently in the exercise of his own power. The system protected the weak from their weakness, and the strong from their own strength.

The Unionist often suggested that the Union in time would diminish geographical diversities and had an obligation to prevent their growth, and hence it was prudent to be cautious about expansion. But anti-imperialism was troubling for Calhoun, who believed in Manifest Destiny, and here lay another difference from Taylor. The latter wished to find a still point in a dangerous world, looked to his local place, and wanted to be left alone. Calhoun was more worldly; he designed his theory for a dangerous world, certainly, but one whose movements he respected, from whose volatility he wished to profit. Part of him liked process, change, and growth; he wanted only to prevent disorder.

So Calhoun tried to salvage American nationality, and James Henry Hammond was right later to speak of Calhoun's "superstitious attachment to the Union." In this, Calhoun was in a minority among Southern political theorists, who conducted a long quarrel with those who contested that the United States had been made by *"one people."* Upshur was more typical when he argued in 1840 that there had been thirteen peoples in 1776, "separate and distinct," with different histories and governments. The Declaration of Independence spoke with thirteen voices and was "simply their *joint expression* of their separate wills." As for the Constitution of 1787, though its preamble began with the phrase "We, the people of the United States," the original draft had read, "We, the people of the States of New Hampshire" etc., and a revising committee had abridged the list, not to change its meaning but to effect a greater stylistic elegance. So the United States was "a league between independent sovereignties, and not one nation composed of all of them together."[26] Merely to survey its institutions (the Senate, the House, the electoral college, even the judiciary) was to observe how deeply seated was the principle of representation of states, and how absent was any institution which treated with the American people in aggregate. Such states' rights were historical facts, as well as logical necessities. Take away the federal government, and social life would go on. Take away the state, and social order itself disappeared.

Upshur had a Federalist mistrust of democracy, but Calhoun was a Jeffersonian and did not. In this, at least, Calhoun was more typical of his political culture, because Southern politics were being democratized as rapidly as any in the United States and had in Andrew Jackson an icon and catalyst of that transformation. Southern skepticisms about democracy existed, not because Southerners lived in a world untouched by change, but because some Southerners were unabashedly making the new order and others were uneasy.

One can see in Jackson the lineaments of a Southern democratic Unionism, no less influential because Jackson's spelling was bad and his anti-intellectualism notorious. In many ways, he was an old-fashioned Commonwealthman with a vivid sense of "the hydra of corruption," especially of the "Money Power." When president he destroyed the Bank, eliminated the national debt, vetoed schemes of internal improvement, and sought to mitigate the development of entrenched bureaucratic interests by encouraging rotation in office. He spoke often of preventing "consolidation and the destruction of states' rights," and John Randolph, at least, felt him to be an ideological ally against Leviathan. Jackson did not see himself as an innovator. He once said, "My notions . . . are not those now taught in modern Schools & in fashionable high life; they were imbibed in ancient days."[27] In this, he misunderstood himself, because his was a political ideology of striking modernity.

This was so because Jackson (like Lincoln later) stood for the people's sovereignty and a perpetual Union, connected ideas formed by the experience of Andrew Jackson the soldier, who had been old enough to take up arms against the British during the Revolution. Anglophobia had been in the making of his identity, as at New Orleans it was in the creation of his fame. He never saw a reason to doubt the exceptionalism of the United States or the fact that Britain was "the common enemy of mankind, the highway robber of the world," sprung from a "*Barbarous Europe*," every one of whose governments was marked by "despotism and corruption" and presided over "chained and shackled Peasants."[28] His was an expansionist exceptionalism, and Jackson became the American imperialist par excellence, who fought in the Creek War, saved the Louisiana Purchase from the British, seized Florida from the Spanish, and, as a president and politician, brutally expelled Native Americans westward and encouraged the annexation of Texas. He hated the Spanish and Mexicans, despised the Indians, and treated the alien as he did those who challenged his honor, as people to be killed. Self-doubt about the providential mission of his country was as unknown to him as skepticism about slavery, because both were emanations of his presumption of mastery, which was exercised by kindliness if his subjects were pliant, by violence if not.

This military experience lay at the heart of his Unionism, as it did for many Westerners, whose mobility had furnished a practical experience of what Jackson called in 1809 "our common country." Calhoun was a man fixed in place, but Jackson had moved. As a general of militia in Tennessee, he did not look to South Carolina for help when the Spanish required expulsion, but to Washington, and Jackson spent most of his adult life as an employee of the federal government, and of the executive branch, at that. The only state office he ever held was as a justice on Tennessee's superior court from 1798 to 1804; he was never governor and never served in the state legislature. Though he would have despised the appellation, he was a persistent office-seeker, asking to fill several of the many jobs required for governing the American empire. He was not a natural employee, since he liked to give orders but did not like taking them. Jackson knew that empire building was a rough-and-ready business, better handled by people like himself than Harvard graduates, who cared for futilities like treaties and international law. However, his bellicose experience conflicted with Jackson the Commonwealthman, because it made him a "military chieftain," the sort of person whom that tradition abominated, and he went to some pains to counter the accusation.[29]

Soldiers, federal administrators, and large slaveholders were not nature's democrats, but Jackson had a "great reliance on the good sense & virtue of the people," a faith which grew over the years. He believed in the people's voice and wanted to extend its power far and wide. When president, he proposed democratizing the bench by making it elective, abolishing the electoral college, limiting the president to one term of four or six years, and removing disputed presidential elections from the House of Representatives. Some of this came from an instinctive egalitarianism, a sympathy for "the great working class," and a resentment of "aristocratical tendencies" and "combinations of the wealthy and professional classes." Much, too, was a shrewder instinct. He was popular with the people: they lined the streets to fete him, they composed ballads to celebrate him. It is hard to imagine Andrew Jackson as a democrat if "the good sense of the people" had not so consistently favored him, because he was usually volcanic toward those who got in his way. But the people gave him power, so he believed in them. It was an amiable reciprocity. He became a proponent of the popular will, because his own will was so strong and became the stronger because of theirs. For Jackson, therefore, the sovereignty of the people was an executive force, not a resistance to power; through him, it made things happen. Through Jackson, "the great principles of democracy" became legitimate in Southern and American usage. At its heart was the idea of majority rule conferring sovereign power. All the old doubts, insisted upon by Madison and reiterated by Calhoun, were swept aside. This made Jackson's noises about "our political fabric being regulated by checks and balances" moot, because no check was legitimate if it checked the popular will.[30] John Taylor had understood republicanism to be freedom made by the diminishment of power, but for Jackson democracy was preeminently power and will.

When responding to the crisis of Nullification, Jackson defended "a Government of laws and a Federal Union founded upon the great principle of popular representation." Jackson the Commonwealthman had been expected by many to be sympathetic to South Carolina. In fact, his response to Nullification was apoplectically nationalist. Partly the issue was personal, because Jackson vividly personalized his politics and he had had a bitter feud with Calhoun. Mostly Jackson the nationalist believed that, short of revolution, members of the Union had obligations of conformity to laws properly enacted. In reasoning about the constitution, Jackson was very reluctant to discuss "particular theories" about whether the "federal compact" was "federal or social or national." It was enough for him that it was "a compact by which power is created on the one hand and obedience exacted on the other."[31] Most of what Jackson declined to define, of course, was what Southern political thought had spent years (and would spend more) upon clarifying, and what he presumed (that the Union was a power that exacted obedience) was what many Southerners denied. In truth, Jackson's reasoning was military. You enlisted, you accepted orders, and if you did not, you were executed for mutiny. No soldier is likely to be a Madisonian.

In the long run, Jackson's views became the American standpoint, the validation for Lincoln's prosecuting the "War of the Rebellion." In the short run, for most Southern political thinkers, Jackson's was a minority standpoint, as was Calhoun's idiosyncratic doctrines of interposition. The consensus was that the Union was a provisional confederation of sovereignties. Against this, Jackson asserted in his "Farewell Address" that "[o]ur Constitution is no longer a doubtful experiment." With that, Jackson claimed that history had ceased, that perpetuity had arrived, because American democracy had been accomplished. In this way Jackson saw the United States as a nation, whereas most Southern political thought was making individual states into nations, or even the South into one (though this was little a consideration in 1832). There could be no plausible compromise between these standpoints, except what Jackson called "the strange position" of Calhoun's theory, which convinced few.[32]

In the long aftermath of the Nullification crisis, many Southerners tried to make sense of how events had modified political thought. Calhoun, for one, though he carried older concepts into the new moment, observed a difference. At the end of his life, he struggled to compose his thoughts on the American polity during his time in two works, both probably written in 1848. The *Disquisition on Government* is prolegomenon to the *Discourse on the Constitution and Government of the United States*; the former elaborates a theory to explain the empirical events described in the latter. The *Disquisition* made its case with Calhoun's usual logical force. His presumption was that, from the first, man had been social but selfish, qualities which occasioned conflict and the necessity for government, an institution coeval with man's historical experience. But government has the temptation of power, so needs controlling by means of a constitution. For Calhoun, "Power can only be resisted by power." The power of the ruled lay in the suffrage, and a homogeneous community could most effectively monitor government, because government's actions would affect people uniformly and, if adverse, evoke a powerful response. But communities were not homogeneous and usually divided into multiple interests. In contradiction to Madison's theory but in conformity with Calhoun's experience, interests did not cancel each other out but gradually coalesced. Political society resolved itself into a majority and minority, between which were "incessant struggles."[33] Since a government's revenues were necessarily collected and disbursed unequally, it followed that government became the means by which the minority was impoverished and the majority enriched, the more so as a majority sanctioned by suffrage was effectively sovereign and, hence, irresponsible.

How to stop this? By giving minorities "a concurrent voice in making and executing the laws." A wise polity paid attention to "interests as well as numbers." Hence Madison had been wrong in overestimating the fissiparous nature of interests, and certainly Jackson was wrong to trust majority will. Everyone was wrong who saw safety in a written constitution, because checks and balances could be overridden by a majority which controlled all the departments of government (executive, legislative, judicial). Safety could only lie in "negative power—the power of preventing or arresting the action of the government,—be it called by what term it may—veto, interposition, nullification, check, or balance of power." Granted such a power, compromise became mandatory. Absent such a power, the bitter dialectical "vibrations" of minority and majority "would continue until confusion, corruption, disorder, and anarchy would lead to an appeal to force;—to be followed by a revolution in the form of government."[34] The more complex a society, the more quickly this would unfold; the simpler, the more slowly.

Calhoun was a democrat who disbelieved in a benignant human nature, and he wanted the principle of concurrence in order to make the world safer for democracy. As he saw it, concurrence minimized class conflict by compelling cooperation between rich and poor. Like Taylor, Calhoun thought the human condition could be improved by a wise polity, but unlike Taylor he saw safety not in individualism but in understanding the intricacies of the communitarian instinct. With Adam Smith, Calhoun trusted to the moral efficiency of freedom. With Hobbes, however, he mistrusted how license bred violence. Men needed a sense of security in order to develop themselves wisely. Power and liberty had their "proper spheres," because power guaranteed the survival of what liberty might prosperously create.[35] However, Calhoun (and this was consistent with his idea of a segmented society) did not think that the principle of concurrence could be universally applied to all societies. Some societies needed more power and less liberty, some the reverse, whether for reasons of landscape, climate, or a population's moral condition. Here was the discreet suggestion of an American exceptionalism, though Calhoun did not press the point. Instead he ventured the Scottish theory of stages and suggested that the United States lay in the final stage of a commercial society, as did modern Britain. However, Calhoun did make clear that liberty and equality were not good companions, since liberty created inequality as it made progress.

In succession to the *Disquisition*, Calhoun's *Discourse* didactically tried to clarify the complex debates about the American polity, mostly by venturing a history of the early republic. In this, he was abjuring his customary preference for the dispassionate and abstract. No one less liked personalizing politics, but, in offering such a history, Calhoun named names. One might read the *Disquisition* and think Calhoun an Enlightenment philosophe who liked abstract patterns, but the *Discourse* was the work of a man who had lived through half of the nineteenth century and noticed the messiness of historical experience. He did not like messiness, but he observed it as a fact.

So, what was the United States? It was "a system of governments, compounded of the separate governments of the several States composing the Union, and of one common government of all its members, called the Government of the United States. The former preceded the latter, which was created by their agency." These governments shared structural similarities, the separation of powers executive, legislative, and judicial. The federal government had delegated powers, the rest being reserved to the states, and collectively "ours is a democratic, federal republic," indeed "democratic throughout." Further, the powers conferred on these governments were only delegated and hence held in a revocable trust. This was a federal polity, not national, not confederate. By "federal," Calhoun meant "a political union, in contra-distinction to a government of individuals socially united." That is, the Constitution of 1787 retained the essential form of government designed by the Articles of Confederation, that is, a union among "*free, independent* and *sovereign* States." The phrase "We, the people" meant "We, the people of the several States of the Union." The establishment of the Union had not created a government "over" the people and the states. Rather, the people remained "over" the Union, as its guardian and judge. So there was "no such community, *politically* speaking, as the people of the United States." Thereby Calhoun was at pains to repudiate not only nationalism ("a fiction . . . of recent origin") but also Madison's "perfectly absurd" idea of a polity which was partly federal, partly national. For Calhoun, the polity was "federal through-out," because the states mattered in all its political institutions. Further, Calhoun refused the most fundamental of Madisonian ideas, the divisibility of sovereignty: "Sovereignty is an entire thing; to divide, is,—to destroy it." In fact, sovereignty remained, but not in any government (state or federal) but "in the people of the several States."[36]

Equally, Calhoun refused the conception of the United States as a confederacy, that is, a government which was little more than "an assembly of diplomatists . . . [from] their several sovereignties." This was mildly inconsistent of him, because elsewhere he had insisted on continuity with the Articles of Confederation. Now, however, he claimed that 1787 had altered what had been "a league between the governments of the several States." His rationale for the distinction lay in the process of ratification, by which the sovereignty of the people had been consulted. That is, the Union had been made not by state delegates who carried the sanction of their peoples into the Philadelphia convention but by the peoples of the states afterward. This was, in essence, Taylor's idea that the people's wishes had been doubly consulted and doubly the people had created their governments. But, crucially for Calhoun, this process of ratification had not created an irresistible national government but, to the contrary, one which subsisted on the sufferance of the people's mandate. Most importantly, it had made the state governments and the federal government "equals and co-ordinates."[37]

Though Calhoun was a democrat, he resisted the presumption that the United States was "an absolute democracy," because the constitution took account of interests as well as individuals. In the Senate, small and large states were equally represented, just as in the electoral college the election of the president was not based on a numerical majority. This aspect of Calhoun's exposition should be stressed, because it is often suggested that he wished (by establishing a dual presidency) to create a principle of concurrence in the

American constitution. But, in fact, Calhoun thought concurrence was intrinsic to the *existing* structure ("the constitution and the government . . . rest, throughout, on the principle of the concurrent majority"), though he thought the principle had been weakened by the developments of the early republic and needed re-strengthening.[38] The chief aim of the *Discourse* was to narrate the history of this weakening in order to prove the case for a strengthening.

The middle passages of the *Discourse* consist of a strict-constructionist analysis of the various powers lodged in differing parts of the polity. Calhoun's conclusion was that, again contra Madison, separated powers have a natural tendency to be overcome by the coalescences of power. Here Calhoun poked a toe into the murky waters of Romantic social theory, since he saw that these political combinations, perhaps amounting to sectionalism, were partly made out of cultural materials, such as "similarity of origin, language, institutions, political principles, customs, pursuits, interests, color, and contiguity of situations." Of these, contiguity was the greatest, because closeness occasioned sympathy.[39]

Such coalescences being undesirable, but the present system tending inevitably to create them, one needed to turn to state interposition (a "great repairing, healing, and conservative power") and, in an extremity, secession, but mainly one needed to roll back the aggrandizements of the Supreme Court, which had come to embody the mistaken premise that the federal government could act as the judge of conflicts between the states and itself. This matter ran deeper than John Marshall's various decisions, but went back to Section 25 of the Judiciary Act of 1789, which illegitimately had given to the federal courts the right to hear appeals, not only on federal matters or interstate conflicts, but on issues confined to the province of a state. This section needed repeal, as it had led to the wider doctrine that the states were "inferior and subordinate."[40]

The destination of Calhoun's *Discourse* was the sentence which read: "The sectional tendency of parties has been increasing with the central tendency of the government." It was only here—over 370 pages into his disquisiting and discoursing—that Calhoun averted directly to slavery. He saw the first thirty years of the republic as a period when the status of the peculiar institution had been "adjusted to the satisfaction of both parties," but then this harmony had been deranged by the Missouri crisis and the novel possibility of antislavery forces mobilizing a centralizing federal government. Each party, striving to gain the center, had begun to cultivate the remoter fringes of the political spectrum, and so worsened the problem. Calhoun's solution was the restoration of federalism, partly to be accomplished by the repeal of Section 25 of the 1789 Judiciary Act and the Twelfth Amendment (to restore the original mechanism for the election of president and vice president). Even more drastic was his suggestion that there must be two presidents, each elected from the two sections, whose double approval would be needed for the passage of all legislation. This would be "the means of restoring harmony and concord to the country and the government"; there would be "mutual affection and brotherhood."[41]

The last words of the *Discourse* are "concord and harmony," words which occur regularly in Calhoun's political theory.[42] Though he grounded his theory upon the premise that only power can resist power, there was a curiously genteel quality in Calhoun. His disinclination to name Jackson and Clay in the history of his times, his polite skirmishings with Madison's theory, his minimizing of the bitterness of Nullification (which scarred a generation), all point to a sensibility which hated raw conflict. He was no John Randolph or Andrew Jackson, both of whom loved a good fight, who swished their riding crops and cried, "By the Eternal!" Calhoun was not the dueling sort. He preferred a world in which his will would go unchallenged, in which if he did not get his way, at least he might have a veto to prevent his opponents from prevailing. His vision was not of a world in which the will of a Southern president would persistently clash with that of a Northern president, but one in which each section would rapidly learn the futility of self-assertion and then relax into a spirit of generosity. Madison had presumed that tension was the perennial human condition. But Calhoun looked away from tearing flesh. He wanted an apolitical politics, safety, a world where nothing dangerous and unexpected would be allowed to happen, because human intelligence had divined the little secret mechanisms by which difficulties might be prevented. Though his theory started with Hobbesianism, it ended with a sentimental liberalism. This was perhaps his final impracticality, because he wanted power and safety, all at once, and wished to have a powerful will and be admired for it.

There was little that changed in the last years of the antebellum period which had not been implicit in the debates of the preceding decades, except mood. For a long time Southern thinkers calculated the value of the Union, but mostly the balance came out in favor of staying in. But it was a small step from reasoning within an unsatisfactory Union to imagining life outside it. It was the intellectual accomplishment of Southern political thought to make such an act of imagination and will possible. Cynicism about the Union grew or, what often came to the same thing, idealism about the South. There had been a thin strain of skepticism even in Calhoun, when he spoke of the futility of written constitutions and argued instead for the exercise of a power beyond appeal. In 1850 James Henry Hammond coldly asserted that, for twenty years, the Constitution had been "a dead letter" and had played no role in sustaining the Union, which had been, rather, "held together by habit—by the recollections of the past and a common reverence for the patriots and heroes of the Revolution—by the ties of political parties, of religious sects, and business intercourse."[43] By then some of these ties began to break; the Baptists and Methodists had separated, and political parties had begun to grow more sectional.

Political thought had teased out two insights, at least: that power was the only reality of politics, and that governments needed to rest upon a shared social basis, what sometimes was called "community." On the whole, the older traditions of political thought had been less impressed with belonging. There were individuals who and "interests" which made their compacts, but social identity as the underpinning of a polity was a more modern idea, which first came to the South as a vision of culture, removed from the realm of politics or political science. In the writings of men like Upshur, the conception of culture and the definition of the "people" made little connection; the "people" were just those who sanctioned the polity. They or it, "the people," did not have to be homogeneous; in fact the tradition said that diversity was why government was necessary, at all. So, on the whole, older political thought had reasoned backward from the polity. But the newer tradition required one to reason forward from the people to the state and insisted that, unless one could define the people by a catalog of social habits, economic institutions, racial characteristics, and religious customs, there was no legitimate sanction for a state. This process of reasoning had many sources, of which Romantic social theory was most important, but the tensions of the older way had helped to make this newer idea attractive. As Calhoun had often wistfully observed, things went more easily in a homogeneous world. So, considering the incessant tensions of the Union, why not opt for a political world posited on the shared culture of the South? Certainly, if power was the only reality, why not opt for real power, rather than eking out a fragile existence as a minority and dreaming up constitutional amendments which were but paper stipulations?

Beverley Tucker's *Series of Lectures on the Science of Government* (1845) is the closest thing to a systematic "study of political science" undertaken by a late-antebellum Southerner, and it is striking for its emphasis on community. To be sure, many things in Tucker were conventional, at least for a lawyer and college professor: his dislike of democracy and the mob, his intellectual snobbery and elitism, and his endorsement of the compact theory of the American constitution, in which the federal government was seen as but the creature of the states. (He dismissed the phrase "the people of the United States" as "a mere noun of multitude.") Nonetheless, Tucker was among the first Southerners to offer a Romantic theory of government, expressed by a man of modern sensibility who quoted Carlyle and debated with Tocqueville. Tucker had a richer sense of the scope of human emotions than was evident in the cooler world of Calhoun. Tucker's earliest pages, when he was introducing the problems of political science, were murmurous. He spoke of mystery and enthusiasm, quoted poetry that intimated mortality, referred to "moods" and "feverish excitement," wondered whether the progress of natural science would increase human happiness and whether knowing "the secrets of the abyss" would not tragically remove wonder from the world. He was conscious of growing old and spoke of his coming death. He observed, as a crucial insight, that though God had given to man dominion over the earth, "one thing, and one alone, rebels against him, and defies him. IT IS HIS OWN HEART."[44] Religion mattered to Tucker, who by the end of the 1820s had become an evangelical Christian, and this fact moved him outside the older tradition of Southern political thought which had been less intense about religious belief. There had been deists (Jefferson), Unitarians (Calhoun), and Episcopalians (Taylor), but few Presbyterians.

Whereas John Taylor had been individualistic, for Tucker the world had been peopled by communities and tribes from the first. Tucker saw societies as having "a sort of collective personality" and the body politic as "a sort of artificial moral person," which led him to see rights as not individual but social, "reciprocal and correlative." In that sense, Tucker was closer to the Hegelian vision, in which man and the state are dialectically bonded. The individual is responsible to the community, the community to the individual, and this reciprocity is exclusive; the community owed nothing to those individuals beyond its membership, and "the individual member is responsible to none but his own community."[45] Humanity was little, the tribe was all.

In another sense, however, Tucker was more old-fashioned than Taylor. The former believed in the old cycles of the Machiavellian imagination; societies licensed freedom, they grew prosperous but bred cupidity and flattering demagogues, they acquired mobs and disorder and sloth, they brought forth mercenaries and military despotism, then an aristocracy developed to share power, and from the quarrel of monarchy and aristocracy the idea of liberty was reborn. Tucker offered a very tepid hope that the United States would transcend all this. As a Burkean, the usefulness Tucker accorded to political theory was the slim hope that knowledge of this cycle might slow or mitigate it. History was not a linear process of improving the good and removing evil, but rather the unstable process of sacrificing the good for a greater good, also flawed. Every society must kill the thing it loves, and one might only entertain the faint hope "of checking the car of destiny in its fatal career, and postponing the evil day when the history of the liberty and happiness of Virginia shall but furnish school-boy's themes in distant lands."[46] So Tucker's *Lectures* were elegiac, filled with a sense that, one day, a New Zealander might stand upon a James River bridge and survey the ruins of Jefferson's Capitol.

In this way, Tucker was less dismissive of nature than Upshur, who had a stronger sense of mastery. Upshur said, in reversal of the ancient Arab saying, that nothing is written. But Tucker felt himself a happy prisoner of what went before, someone husbanding a heritage draining away. This was his John Randolph theme, the notion that one should nurture the past and postpone the moment when the frail experiment of Virginia and the United States (though the latter mattered less) would falter. So Tucker wrote often of reverence for fathers and filial duties. In his politics, Tucker was ultra, a secessionist decades before others, but his radicalism intended a revolution which might conserve; he could not imagine virtue in the new. Not the least reason for this was that, though he spoke of the influence of the wealthy and talented and he descanted on the value of the human will, he was (as a historicist) not very sure that the human will was efficacious and wondered whether men were not more molded by society than molding.

Such skepticism was the by-product of Tucker's Burkeanism. Our government, he said in quoting *Hamlet*, had not been made by theory but "was the creature of circumstances, which stamped their very form and pressure upon it."[47] During the Revolution, Virginians had striven no more for freedom than anyone else, and perhaps had understood popular government less than New Englanders. But Virginians had blundered upon a happy circumstance. This insight perhaps explains why Tucker's lectures, though eloquent in their praise of Virginia, were remarkable for not lavishing ritual praise on magisterial Virginians. History had happened to the Founding Fathers, but less something they had made; the Virginian and American world had formed them into giants. Here Tucker's history was strictly Tocquevillean, because social; in the latter's history of the French Revolution, Turgot and Louis XVI are little compared to the invisible workings of administrative centralization, and in Tocqueville's study of American democracy, Andrew Jackson barely rated a mention.

Hence slavery mattered as a Virginian social habit. Just as slavery had helped to make Virginian freedom, so slavery's maintenance would sustain that same freedom. On the whole, Tucker's proslavery stance was of the

Herrenvolk variety; slavery created a safe worker ant population, made color a bond of sympathy between rich and poor, constrained the tendency of poorer whites to insurrectionary envies, and schooled the wealthy in noblesse oblige and self-control. In this analysis, Tucker was coldly racist, contemptuously paternalist. But, like most Southern political theorists, he correlated the social institution of African slavery with the moral problem of human freedom. Unlike them, however, he understood slavery as provisional; it might "save us, at least for a time," but no more.[48]

Beverley Tucker was only an implicit Hegelian, and though his Christianity was important, its effect was oblique. By contrast, James Warley Miles of South Carolina was a close student of German thought and, above all, an Episcopal minister and a meditating Christian, who grounded political theory in a theodicy. In so doing, he was not untypical of mid-nineteenth-century Southern thinkers, who often reprobated the godlessness of their predecessors. For Miles, the state was in the mind of God, and had been so from the beginning. It followed that man cannot be perfected until the state was likewise. Man needed the small world of the family, as well as the "still wider sphere" of the state. Like Calhoun, Miles believed that government was intrinsic to the human condition but, unlike Calhoun, that human nature was changing, so government was molded by "man's progress." The most advanced stage was that in which the governed and the governing became identical, because they shared "the general intellect," the premises of the culture. An individual earned the right of citizenship by becoming "conscious of the true principles of self-control," and likewise "when a *Nation* becomes conscious of the true principles of government, and of social and national duty, it also possesses the *natural right* of self-government." This was a dialectical process: a people must be free to earn a free government, but that government in turn must foster the "moral and religious elements" which made the knowledge of freedom. Miles was a German idealist, so for him it was self-consciousness which mattered, the ability "to comprehend the true nature of freedom." Those who lacked such self-knowledge must necessarily be excluded from the polity. Even more, he saw the state as differing from government and as "the nation existing as a political being, developing and exercising determinate functions, according to the law of its nature or constitution." Such a state exercised moral functions and, in so doing, became sacred. Under this reasoning, liberty ceased to be freedom from the state and became, instead, "a nature . . . [with] inherent laws of its own," which was conflated with the state, a religious authority answerable to a moral critique. Since "the only safety of States, and the only permanent support of individuals, are to be found in an adherence to the principles of Religion, and an obedience to the precepts of Revelation," a judgment was pending on the American state.[49]

Miles's simpler message, that government should be constituted on the social nature of the people, spelled danger for the Union. "E pluribus unum" had been the old motto, but this he deemed to be impractical, impious, and unphilosophical. Self, history, morality, and the state were confounded. The rationale of secession lay in the obligation to abandon an immoral polity in order to establish another, truer to the idea of liberty, truer to self, indeed making a true self possible. In so contending, Miles had moved the argument far beyond the older tradition of political thinkers like John Taylor, who had presumed self to be prior to the social compact and autonomous, who had insisted that it was by the individualism of willful citizens that the state was held accountable, as a thing to be ordained, adjusted, or abolished. Upshur had abolished the idea of nature but kept that of the individual will. Calhoun then saw how individuals had begun to crowd together, as a way to use power and to resist others, also aggregating and seeking power. After this, Tucker began to speak of community as the sanction of the state, partly because he saw individuals as unpredictable and passionate, and hence in need of community. Finally, Miles argued that self, family, and the state were God's work mediated through the mind of man, and thereby greatly raised the psychic stakes for judging and creating a polity. For Taylor, the state might disappear and he, John Taylor, would still exist, might decide or not to make another state, in concert with other reasoning men. "Individuals, in forming a society, may arrange their rights in such forms as they please," he had chirpily said.[50] But, for the grimmer Miles in a later Southern world, the disappearance of the state would be a self-abolition. The world was not all an experience of freedom, but structured by meaningful constraint. Faced with the choice between a prison made by others and a home within one's own community, who would refuse to move to the latter? Who would refuse, even knowing that home was a prison, too?

POLITICAL ECONOMY WAS the modern discipline par excellence, which promised the world much, that it is to say, wealth. The world noticed these promises, or so the political economists had reason to think. To understand the discipline's function, therefore, requires looking at both intellectuals and those politicians who struggled to impose the discipline's imagined truths. As M. R. H. Garnett put it, "In free countries, the chief questions, which divide parties, depend for their resolution, on the principles of Political Economy. Nearly all the arguments which have resounded in our legislative halls, and on our hustings, for the last twenty years, for and against the Bank and the

Independent Treasury, the Protective System and Free Trade are professedly drawn from this science."[51]

The South had been unusually well schooled in the discipline because its academic study began earlier there than almost anywhere else outside of Scotland and was, on the whole, more studied than in the North. *The Wealth of Nations* was in use at William and Mary from the mid-1790s, Jefferson made political economy fundamental to the curriculum of the University of Virginia, and Thomas Cooper began teaching it at South Carolina College in 1825. The South had inherited from its founding statesmen a deep engagement with money; the tariff, the national bank, the funding of state debts, all had been vital to the revolutionary and federal enterprise, and came to be informed by readings of Adam Smith, Thomas Malthus, Jean-Baptiste Say, and David Ricardo. As Madison observed to Say in 1816, "the true principles of political economy are everywhere needed . . . more so in our young country than in some old ones."[52] But these principles sometimes preceded Smith's, were often dictated by pressing political circumstances, and often unsystematic.

Though interested in the millennial promise of such principles, the Virginian founders tended to see them as part of a broader science of man; in this, they were closer to Smith's ambition than to how the discipline later developed, when its authority rested upon its being a practical theory which had survived the intellectual shipwreck of the Enlightenment, a theory which even the critics of reason might think reasonable. And in their practice as statesmen, the Virginians had transmitted a confusing message to their heirs. The early years of the republic had been unstable, inheriting the old problems of revolution and facing the new problems of a world at war. Finance had been alternately chaotic, ordered, and then deranged. Formally, Jefferson and Madison had spoken warmly of farmers and independence, expressed suspicion of manufactures and cities, preached laissez-faire and republican frugality. But Jefferson had imposed an embargo, a Napoleonic action gravely at odds with laissez-faire, while Madison had raised tariffs and chartered a national bank. No doubt, the Virginians had pleaded exigency and sometimes deprecated themselves, while observing that life was often exigent. Political economy (all agreed) was the observation of what men did, not what they preached should be done. So, though the generation of 1820 knew the older orthodoxy, they knew that wise policy might vary from orthodoxy. And they were to experience their own instabilities, their panics and trade cycles, their depressions and booms. As Thomas Dew suggested, it was supposed to be the value of political economy that, amid this incessant flux, it offered the ability to stand back and see a pattern.

One may broadly see two tendencies in Southern economic thought. There were those who adhered to classical economics and preferred the free market: among these, one can count John Taylor, Thomas Dew, and Thomas Cooper. And there were those who saw merit in government intervention and were interested in the possibility of urban and industrial development: among these were George Tucker, Henry Clay, and Jacob Cardozo. And then there was John C. Calhoun, who in this (as in much else) effected a synthesis.

John Taylor's most economic work was *Arator*, which reached its final edition in 1818. This shows that Taylor had read his Adam Smith, who provided a stinging critique of mercantilism and government interference, as well as an analysis which favored agriculture over industry, and tended to relegate the commercial world to the realm of the parasitic. Taylor's starting point was the Virginian planter's fear of decline, occasioned by soils wearing out, crops diminishing, and people moving westward. In this context, margins had become too thin to bear the taxes of a Hamiltonian state, whose protectionist duties only created an "aristocracy of capitalists" imitative of an English model, capitalists who distributed wealth by law in violation of true republicanism. Thereby agriculturalists, "our sound yeomanry" who formed nine-tenths of the population, were made subservient to a swindling tenth.[53] Taylor did not oppose manufactures themselves, merely unfair patronage of them, and thought they could only flourish by the investment of surpluses generated by a free agriculture.

Taylor was Anglophobic and wished to improve agriculture, so it was a difficulty for him that modern English agriculture had been more productive and innovative than American. His solution was to argue that it was English oppression which had "goaded [agriculturists] into ingenuity, labour and economy," and in America there was too much land and freedom for this pattern to recur. No doubt, the United States had its own system of compulsion in chattel slavery, but this did not help, because it was "a misfortune to agriculture, incapable of removal, and only within the reach of palliation." On slavery, Taylor was unclear in *Arator*. He did not believe with Jefferson that it excited a spirit of despotism in masters, because slaves were too lowly to influence masters, whose characters were formed by relationships with peers. Yet Taylor was anxious not to "approve of slavery," while seeing no route to its ending, since he assumed that emancipation would occasion a Haitian race war. For the most part, he recommended that slavery be made to work as well as statesmanship and prudence could contrive, while being opaque on how this might be done. That slavery was an evil he said clearly, though not for the slaves, who were "docile, useful and happy, if . . . well managed" and had no capacity for liberty.[54]

Arator mostly consisted of practical advice. Keep your overseers for a long time and pay them good wages, not a share of crops; do not be absentee; put up fences; manure; build slave quarters with brick walls; provide slaves with adequate rations; prefer a four- to a three-crop rotation; drink cider. Therefore *Arator* was a book in the tradition of the *De Agri Cultura* of Cato the Censor, and that of the agricultural manuals which crowded the shelves of eighteenth-century libraries. Contrary to usual opinion, *Arator* was not a pastoral, because devoid of apostrophes to nature. Taylor's chapter on "The Pleasures of Agriculture" says nothing Coleridgean about moonlight on the Rappahannock. It was the patriarchal *arator* who mattered, not nature; he who exploited, not that which was exploited.

John Taylor's vision was moral, whatever one may think of his morality, but not macrocosmic. He did not give to stock exchanges, tariffs, rent, currency, and population the detailed consideration which he gave to enclosing pastures, and it is hard to extract from *Arator* a broad economic analysis, addressing the practical problem of American life, though easy to find pessimism. (Cato is seldom upbeat.) In this pessimism, Taylor's Anglophobia was significant. A degenerate England was a lesson in what the world, including America, tended to become. The schemers always had the advantage, because they came to control the rules by which the virtuous were forced to play, unless the latter exerted themselves in the public realm. This view was common among old-school Jeffersonians, and Jefferson himself (not always a Jeffersonian) was indecisive about whether the economic future was more to be trusted or feared. The intellectual traditions of political economy shed only inconsistent light. Adam Smith himself had been urbane and reassuring, sanguine about a world ordered on his principles. Thomas Malthus had introduced a disquieting analysis, intended to rein in the optimism of Condorcet and Godwin, if more friendly toward them than usually thought; Malthus's caution was set down more in regret than anger. For the most part, he preferred the moderate realist, who was prepared for "the constant struggle . . . calculated to rouse the natural inactivity of man, to call forth his faculties, and invigorate and improve his mind." Southerners caught this tone, though they did not always read Malthus in this way and they were as interested by the confident sophisms of the French school, by the likes of Claude-Frédéric Bastiat and Say, who saw political economy as a Baconian science, which might offer liberation from constraint. For Southerners, a complication of the English tradition was its Christian concern with luxury, poverty, and the distribution of wealth. A slaveholder might have mixed feelings about ethics, so it was often simpler to see political economy as a dispassionate science. "Men and prejudices have gone against us," someone observed in *De Bow's Review* in 1856. But "science cannot be swayed by prejudice and outcry. . . . All that is now needed for the defence of United States negro slavery and its entire exoneration, is a thorough investigation of fact . . . fact! fact! fact! . . . and Political Economy . . . will and must be our judge."[55]

Thomas Dew was the local political economist whom most thought soundest, partly because his tone was so comfortingly didactic. The South sat in the classroom of Dew's *Lectures on the Restrictive System* (1829) and was told what to think by a professor who claimed to be as "calm and unprejudiced as the stoic philosopher of old." Dew's political economy was thereby supposed to be all economical and little political, but in practice it was everywhere political, because his object was to turn Virginians into disciples of free trade and so enemies of Henry Clay. But Dew did not teach easy lessons, since his vision of the human experience was bleak, more so than Adam Smith's. For Dew, man desired happiness but was beset by anxious difficulties and was doomed to the unceasing effort of selling, buying, and working. He "resembles the waterman, who rows his boat against the running stream," a workman who cannot slacken if there is to be progress. Fortunately, man was habitually a striver, capable of understanding an enlightened self-interest, more so than governments, which were remarkable for little but "incompetency and imperfections."[56]

Unlike Taylor, Dew saw beyond Virginia to the American experience and took nationality seriously. Like Taylor, however, he saw the nation as no more than the sum of its parts, with no "corporative capacity . . . distinct from the individuals who compose it."[57] A government had no prerogatives which might oppose the interest of individuals, and was but a broker who prevented the strong from exploiting the weak, and protected the community against external enemies. So Dew's was a very limited nationalism. He did not think, for example, that an individual had to buy more expensively at home what he might buy more cheaply abroad. Dew came close to articulating a global vision of a consumer society, which might legitimately acquire goods from India, Brazil, Portugal, or Missouri. Rowing upstream, the individual might find provisions for the journey as cheaply as wherever he might. In all this, Dew was closer to the Enlightenment sense that nations were a thin buffer between the individual and the world, a bargain and not a kinship.

Dew liked change, though he knew it occasioned short-term pain. Migration was a case in point, significant because it was the anguished Virginian experience to see people leave. Many opposed such movement and argued for density of population as a remedy and a prerequisite of prosperity. But Dew believed that prosperity lay in dispersal, because "a thin population, spread over a great extent of soil, will accumulate capital more rapidly than a dense population, enclosed in narrow limits." In this sense, Dew was a more American political economist than Thomas Cooper or even George Tucker, both of whom fitted the United States into theories drawn from European experience. Instead, Dew reasoned from a portrait and history of the American economic scene, and, as a Jeffersonian, he turned his back on a Europe "torn, disjointed, and oppressed." His opposition to Clay's American system arose because he saw it as an artificial remaking of the United States in the image of Britain as it had been. Dew wanted America to be itself. Migration was the American way, as it expressed "a man's natural liberty." Still, a free market was a messy business, which only worked in the long term, and Dew partly echoed the chastened mood of Malthus, however little he thought the precise doctrine of Malthus was applicable to the American experience. But only partly, because Dew was an Episcopalian not an Anglican and sometimes optimistic. "Where, I would ask, is the nation that enjoys the freedom of America? When we walk abroad, we are as free as the air that encircles us. . . . Energy can never be wanting, where this is the case."[58] To be free to act was to act.

On the moral claims of agriculture and industry, Dew was blunt. Though he saw the professions as intellectually stimulating, he was otherwise silent about the merits of urban life and eloquent about the anomie of the factory worker trapped in "a vast machine," of which he was but "a contemptible appendage."[59] Unlike Taylor, however, Dew did gush about waving trees, darkening clouds, and sunshine. He quoted Jefferson on farmers as God's chosen people and, inversely, rejected the argument that manufacturing begat invention and human improvement. Manufacturing brought the genteel into contact with the vulgar, and thereby the former were diminished. Above all, manufacturing created great cities, which created mobs, political instability, police, espionage, and standing armies. However, this understanding did not make Dew a strict Commonwealthman, because he was relatively indifferent to the possibility and desirability of independence in a modern world. While Clay hated economic reliance on Britain, Dew saw safety in reciprocal dependencies and had little interest in plantations as isolated, patriarchal communities. With Dew, all was mixed. From any individual there spread out myriads of interconnections. This explained why governments could not assist economies: the thing was too complicated and shifting even to be grasped, let alone rationally to be influenced.

Though Dew valued his community and was rooted in eastern Virginia, he preferred a localism influenced by the exogenous. "Improvement . . . ," he said, "arises, when we associate or come into collision with those who can correct our faults." The world was constantly moving, things changed too quickly for Burkeanism to be plausible, and so theorists, alert to change and possessed of self-knowledge, were a necessity. As Dew put it, "When men rise in deliberative bodies, and thank their God they are no *political economists, no theorists,* they in a short time shew by their unwarrantable generalizations, how much they stand in need of that sound theory against which their philippics are directed." What was needed were "philosophers who sit as passengers in the ship of State, and observe with calm but scrutinizing eye, all the movements on the deck."[60]

In Dew's terms, Thomas Cooper was not the man to perfect a Southern political economy, because no one was less calm. Nonetheless, Cooper's *Lectures on the Elements of Political Economy* provided a good, if volcanically idiosyncratic, tour of the new discipline, a book widely used not only in the South. This influence arose partly because Cooper had a gift for swift précis, useful for students in need of nostrums, and, unlike Dew, was polemically enthusiastic for the beneficial consequences of these dry matters. He was reassuring about modernity and located political economy in a progressive intellectual history, in which the ancients had known little, the Middle Ages were hobbled by "monkish Christianity," and the early modern era was besotted by mercantilism and "the silly fallacy of the Balance of Trade." But then, happily, had come the new science of political economy, commenced by Sir Dudley North in 1691 and now practiced by writers like James Mill. In sketching this genealogy, Cooper was able to list the erroneous maxims of exploded orthodoxies in order to arrive at a definition of political economy as "that science which develops the sources, the distribution, the accumulation, and the consumption of national wealth."[61]

Cooper remained an English political radical in his own funny way. The attraction of this new discipline was its message of freedom, a thing he felt more deeply even than Dew, who had never been jailed for defying a government, as Cooper had. The ethic of liberty which had drawn Cooper from Manchester to Jacobin Paris and then into exile in America found a satisfactory echo in the nostrums of political economy, where political morality and financial expediency were supposed to coincide. Cooper liked political economy's hostility to "privileged orders, classes, professions and pursuits," and its preference for equality and "the unrestricted expenditure of all his honest earnings." Even more than Dew, Cooper mistrusted nationality and saw the nation as no more than a "grammatical being." The individuals who made up this being had moral obligations which were not absolute but social, arising from "our connections with other creatures" but not from the nonsensical concepts of natural rights or natural law. Cooper, after all, was a sort of utilitarian. It had been his father-in-law, Joseph Priestley, who had popularized an idea of Francis Hutcheson by speaking of "the greatest good for the greatest number."[62]

Cooper leaned to the moral superiority of agriculture over manufacturing, while believing that cities were indispensable to human improvement. Agriculture was the healthier for a commercial sector which produced consumers for agricultural products and furnished technical inventiveness. By intermittent training, Cooper was a chemist, and his experience in precipitating sulphur dioxide occasioned a vanity about science as the master of nature, and scientists as more important than poets or rhetoricians, who were but "the inventors of play things for the childhood of society." Francis Bacon's observation that "knowledge is power" was one of Cooper's favorite maxims, but some kinds of knowledge were more powerful than others. Nonetheless, Cooper knew that industry could breed unemployment, misery, and starvation, and he cautioned against those economists like Ricardo who were too sanguine. Manufacturing destroyed independence and health, occasioned wars, and made men the instruments of an industrial oligopoly. In the short run, new machinery put untrained workers out of work. But, in the long run, new machinery meant better products, increased national wealth, greater capital, more employment, and a healthier population. Little of this, however, was possible without the end of protectionism and the inauguration of laissez-faire. To prefer the American system was mere "*ignorance*."[63]

Cooper was the American editor of *The Institutes of Justinian*, he wrote frequently on the law, and his belief in free trade was rooted in legal philosophy. Laissez-faire was for him, above all, a matter of freedom and equality before the law. This mattered more deeply to Cooper than even the practical matter of wealth or its absence. In this, he was influenced by his experience as an émigré, someone whom William Pitt had driven from England, the Federalists had jailed, and the Presbyterians had made unemployed. "*Laissez nous faire*," the old maxim which French merchants had uttered to Jean-Baptiste Colbert when he had asked them what they needed from government, was for Cooper personal. He wanted to be left alone to work in his chemical laboratory, write his books, be indiscreet about the Pentateuch, and not pay a price for it. By the same token, he did not ask to be helped and his *Lectures* contain a blisteringly misogynist passage about the foolishness of charity, a vituperation of poor William Paley for lauding the instinct of pity. Rather Cooper leaned to education as the imperfect palliative and demanded, for his time, extraordinary support for it from government. It was the duty of every state, he said, to provide immediately "a complete and comprehensive system of impartial and universal education," open to all "without money and without price," who might attend lectures or neglect them, "so long as he sees his own advantage in so doing."[64]

So the Southern undergraduates who learned from Cooper had a curious guide. The *Lectures on the Elements of Political Economy* were tumultuously European in emphasis, digressive, full of heterodoxies struggling against the conventionality of its laissez-faire doctrines. There was little comfortable in Cooper. His narrative voice was confident, but his vision was of an uncertain, tense, and shifting world. His myriad of tiny facts made a pattern, but only just. For Cooper, the classroom was no dispassionate antechamber to the real world, just a place where free discussion might take place. Reading his book is like nothing so much as hearing in a tavern an opinionated old man raising his voice, above the din.

Amid such a cacophony, Southern students usually chose to hear the conventional more than the unconventional dimensions of Cooper's thought, because it was unusual for a Southern professor, at least, to do other than endorse a strict laissez-faire. George Frederick Holmes asked Francis Lieber in 1847, "Is there any instance of any scientific writer upon Political Economy laying down other doctrine than those of free trade?—or any Professor of this Branch of study in any of our colleges lecturing against it?" Yet there was debate. Henry Clay and George Tucker were to argue strongly for government activism and supervision, and from a New Englander in Baltimore there had long since come the most urgent argument for government involvement in the form of Daniel Raymond's *Elements of Political Economy* (1823). Such debate engendered what Tucker called "controversy and discord," even "the opinion that there is no certainty in Political Economy . . . [but only] a mass of conflicting theories, and dogmatical assertions, or illogical deductions from principles not fully established, or entirely without foundation." Somehow the irrefutable clarity of political economy proved hard to achieve, to the point that it might be "regarded as of little value by the greater number of intelligent individuals in this country," precisely because it was thought "impossible to construct any scheme, which shall provide, or account for, the varieties of human acts or legislation."[65]

For some, then, the injunction to laissez-faire was not enough. The most thoughtful of these was George Tucker, in publications which first culminated in his *Essays on Various Subjects of Taste, Morals, and National Policy* (1822), where one can read a defense of cities, government responsibility, and even the usefulness of national debts. Tucker was an urbane and urban man, bored by the tedium of the countryside, devoid of Taylor's sense that agriculture was intellectually invigorating, and greatly interested in progress. As a progressive, he felt obliged to push away "the gloomy and disheartening picture of the condition of man" which Malthus encouraged.[66] Tucker doubted that population would ever outrun subsistence, since exigency compelled frugality, and he saw little evidence that war was habitually occasioned by subsistence crises. Most fundamentally, Tucker believed that population growth, instead of being wildly destructive, bred its own social mores which tended to mitigate the birth rate. Hence Tucker took up a middle position between William Godwin (too visionary) and Malthus (too bleak), because Tucker was a Humean who believed that reason was the slave of the passions and that selfishness, as one of the passions, had its own useful cunning.

This cautious optimism, which thought little of human reason and much of urbane civilization, Tucker explicated in a remarkable prognostication on "the future destiny of the United States," a country whose demography might be used as a commentary on Malthusianism. As Tucker saw it, the country might be expected to reach 120 million by 1922. Such rapid expansion had dangers, which might even occasion the dismemberment of the Union, but not because there would a subsistence crisis. The problem would be the pressure of economic diversity, that this state would be free and another slave, that one might have a stake in foreign commerce and another none. But, for the most part, Tucker was sanguine. Like John Quincy Adams later, he thought the federal government might undertake "acts of splendid beneficence," internal improvements of interstate utility. He envisaged the West becoming "the Flanders of the United States . . . covered with populous cities, and . . . the seat of wealth, of luxury, and of arts more or less liberal," from which the East would import its finished goods.[67] No longer would the United States be industrial Europe's countryside, but would by its self-sufficiency occasion European economic crisis and decline. So Tucker favored density of population, because more people meant more manufactures cheaply made and dispersed, and the greater means to facilitate the liberal arts, including publishing. Great cities like London doubtless bred great vices, but Tucker was unsure that, proportionate to population, they bred more vice than the countryside. As to the relationship between material progress and happiness, Tucker was agnostic, considering that the prosperous can suffer and the poor find enjoyment.

Tucker was an apolitical man who implausibly disclaimed bias. He was a dilettante in the older sense of the word, that is, he took pleasure in reasoning out problems, sifting through statistics, and weighing logics, with a thoroughness that a later age would call professional. Among the Southern political economists, he was the one who slighted the singleness of truth, because he wanted to get complex issues right. He seldom bothered to state the obvious, so that undergraduates might remember it. (He was a professor for part of his life, but diffidently.) But the undidactic man had a way of being passive: he observed, analyzed, and folded his hands. Nonetheless, Tucker had his preferences, which made him a cautious modernizer. From the 1830s, he favored the development of manufacturing in Virginia, defended the utility of national debts, supported a managed banking system, opposed the Jacksonian onslaught on the second Bank of the United States, and was inclined to think that slavery in the long run would falter because it was less efficient than free labor. Like Hugh Legaré, Tucker understood that credit was an essential element in the successful functioning of a modern economy, though he believed, too, that paper money needed to be convertible into specie and thought a silver standard, not the traditional policy of bimetallism, most workable for the United States. As to tariffs, he had when in the House of Representatives voted against them in 1824, with the standard objection that they were discriminatory, but he saw the occasional (usually temporary) case for them and thought people exaggerated both their advantages and disadvantages. Mingling optimism and pessimism, he held implicitly to a theory of increasing returns and a rising living standard, though he came around to a qualified acceptance of Malthusianism, at least to the extent that he thought wages, when density of population came to pass in America, might tend to settle toward subsistence.

The most original feature of Tucker's political economy was his attention to the role of psychology. It seems probable that this arose because he lectured on the Scottish philosophers, especially on Thomas Brown, who moved that tradition closer to modern psychology. Crude versions of classical economics had a way of simplifying human nature into a fiction of the economic man, but Tucker saw man as more complicated. For him, economic value meant more than what accrued from labor, but was an emotion, even a pleasure, something which contributed to "endless diversities of objects, and of human tastes or opinions."[68] Likewise, value was more than utility, because men might value sensibly or stupidly, gallop after mindless fashions or disdain the wise purchase.

Tucker's urbane sense that emulating Europe might not be a disaster was to be curiously intensified by the Anglophobe who was to set the agenda of the South's views on political economy, for good or ill. It is customary to neglect Henry Clay in intellectual histories, for the good reason that he was not very intellectual. Yet discussing Clay and the American system was what Southern political economy came to do, and even his enemies, even Calhoun, understood that Clay was "a man of genius, activity and resources."[69]

Clay's protectionism was nationalist, little theoretical, and arose from his circumstances. He represented a Kentucky growing and needing connection to other markets, and he himself was an owner of or investor in slaves, mills, banks, town lots, and even a tavern. Growing up during the French revolutionary wars and making his name as an instigator of the War of 1812, Clay despised England and its power. For Clay, as for Calhoun, political economy was the continuation of war by other means. The former wanted a United States free from Europe, and he understood protectionism as independence, though his critics argued that he was merely translating mercantilism from Britain to the United States and that his faith in the role of tariffs in making prosperity was illusory. His nationalism was expansive, even hemispheric, and his first usage of the term "American system" arose from his sympathy with the revolutionary regimes of Latin America. As he put it, "Let us no longer watch the nod of any European politician; let us become real and true Americans, and place ourselves at the head of the American system." Instinctively, Clay understood what economic historians in the twentieth century came to believe, that free trade was a kind of British imperialism, because free trade was not "of perfect reciprocity." "The truth is," he observed in 1820, ". . . that we are a sort of independent colonies of England—politically free, commercially slaves." So the sinews of nationality needed strengthening with rational controls; hence, internal improvements, a national bank, and a protective tariff applied to selective products (iron, wool, cotton). That this involved discrimination between interests little bothered Clay. He thought that, though in the short run somebody might briefly suffer, in the long run sustained prosperity would help all classes and regions. Moreover, he had little fear of industry, though he assumed that agriculture needed to be dominant in any healthy economy, that "all others should bend to it."[70] Whatever grinding poverty might be like in Lancashire, American manufactures were different, being neat and comfortable, and Clay liked technology, the thrill of steamboats and spinning jennies.

This was not sophisticated, but effective. Clay barged into people's lives and changed them. On South Carolina he had the most effect, because he raised issues about which the state was passionate and conflicted. The Panic of 1819, a depression in cotton prices, and unease about slavery prompted a reappraisal which turned into a critique of the American system by the late 1820s, a process during which Calhoun turned himself into the free trade statesman par excellence. No small role in these transformations was played by technical interpreters of the discipline of political economy, by men who whispered or bellowed into the ears of politicians.

A benchmark was the *Notes on Political Economy* (1826) of Jacob Cardozo, a Charleston editor whose newspapers endorsed free trade, commerce, banking, economic diversification, and scientific agronomy. As a theoretician,

Cardozo was a quasi-sympathetic critic of Ricardo and concerned to disentangle the universal truths of political economy from the cultural specifics of Ricardo's Britain, when considering Ricardo's emphasis upon value, distribution, exchange, and taxation. For Cardozo, value was the compound of land, capital, and labor, as they fluctuated within the constraints of supply and demand. As to rent, Cardozo defined it as the interest on capital invested in land, not different from other capital investments, and thereby he became an economist who, contra Smith, denied the primacy of agriculture but instead saw it as one economic activity among many. So Cardozo's economics were expansive, reluctant to see fixed limits, and sanguine, to the point that he came to believe that, in the progress of capitalism, gradually more would accrue to the worker and less to the capitalist. Consistently he favored a strong banking system, though his views evolved from supporting the second Bank of the United States, to supporting Van Buren's subtreasury plan, then free competition among banks, and finally, in the 1850s, government regulation. In general, he wanted banks to serve the national interest and mistrusted them when cynically self-interested, though he had no Jacksonian nightmares about monsters. On the tariff, Cardozo was moderate; he saw a case for some wartime duties but opposed the American system, and never thought hostility to protectionism justified secession. Though he was a free trader, he knew that the South suffered less from protectionism than many claimed. His objection to high duties was that they depressed demand and rashly forced the pace of industrialization, while free trade would effect an easier transition, regulated by producers and consumers alike.

Cardozo's economics were attentive to changing events, because he was a journalist who wrote episodically, but always as a formidable technician. His pamphlet *The Tariff: Its True Character and Effects Practically Illustrated* (1830) was sophisticated about statistics, amid a debate which habitually produced vague and passionate waffle. Thereby he helped to create a Southern tradition of statistical thoroughness which culminated in J. D. B. De Bow, the first of American statisticians. In his numbers Cardozo expressed the optimism of a bourgeois gradualist, devoted to private property and entrepreneurship, while being opposed to unions and socialist "leveling." On balance, he was content to live in a South which he described as "in form of government . . . democratical—in internal organization . . . oligarchical." But he had faith that science would overcome the tendency of economies to deplete their resources. Above all, Cardozo realized that classical economics had been propounded by Europeans unaware of American conditions, and so a Southern political economy needed to be a reconsideration. In part, this was because often Southern wealth came from "involuntary services," but his case was American, too, and proceeded from the sense that a science which had as yet been too "detached and desultory" might be more systematically pursued in a culture where "the natural order of things" had not been distorted by Europe's "vicious social organization."[71]

So there were differing opinions about political economy even in South Carolina, and Calhoun himself, the doyen of free traders, was less orthodox than he seemed. He was the most sophisticated of Southern politicians when it came to economics, and intellectually he could run rings around Clay's simpler nostrums. Though how Calhoun arrived at such sophistication is obscure, because he was not someone who acknowledged intellectual debts and he had little contact with other Southern thinkers. He was what Matthew Arnold would later call a Philistine, a man indifferent to belles lettres, art, music, and metaphysics. He used to repudiate indignantly the suggestion that he had a gift for abstraction as an insult, and, unlike many of his contemporaries, he was a provincial man, who liked his home, mistrusted the exotic, and thought localism a law of God's nature. It is possible, in fact, that Calhoun was no better read than Clay but was more adept at synthesizing his own reasoned observations with conventional wisdoms.

In later years, Calhoun was nettled by the accusation that he had inconsistently gone from being friendly to a national bank, internal improvements, and the tariff to being hostile. For later historians, this apostasy seemed emblematic of Southern change in the early nineteenth century. The evidence suggests that Calhoun and his critics were each half-right. Calhoun insisted that his votes of the mid-1810s were explicable by the context of war, the embargo, and national debt, and in this he was right. He was then convinced that, between a restlessly imperial Europe and a militarily supine America, there needed to be an energetic federal government to fend off the former and stimulate the latter. On the other hand, Calhoun claimed that he had been a reluctant protectionist, as befitted an old-school Jeffersonian, but the evidence for this is mixed; his early words selectively support the contention, but his tone seldom did. At both moments, however, he was self-confident about himself and his culture. His famous injunction, "Let us conquer space," was not said by a man seized with doubt, though later he became convinced that the conqueror could not be the federal government.[72]

His complicated transition was compelled by political pressures. By 1828, Clay had escalated the scale of protectionism, and, under this stimulus, opinion in South Carolina started to outstrip Calhoun, who had then to shore up his base. It was typical of Calhoun that, having appraised the situation, he leapt with great abruptness into the new cause, while claiming that nothing was sudden. Nonetheless, there was some consistency. He had been a nationalist because convinced that the Union was best served by federal activism, but the late 1820s convinced him that this activism drove wedges into the Union, created inequities and resentments, special interests and victims, and so the game was not worth the candle and a different game was demanded. A new economic philosophy eventually flowed from this, but not immediately. Almost for the first time, Calhoun had to think hard about political economy, at first to find an economics which suited his political situation. Laissez-faire, apart from being intellectually respectable, suited him well, because his new politics were fearful, suspicious, wary. Better not to act, better to pull in the horns of government, better to quiet the dogs and let them sleep, and in their quietude the Union might survive. Ironically, however, first there had to be the uproar of Nullification to force the concession of quietude from Clay. For Calhoun was convinced that it was interposition (the word he preferred to nullification) which had been the political and economic saving of the Union. Important in all this (and easy to miss because a silence) was the lessening of his old concerns. It was less plausible in 1830 that an imperial Europe was a danger.

Between 1828 and the compromise tariff of 1833, Calhoun worked out most (not all) of his views of American political economy. It is important to reiterate that he had nothing, per se, against American industry, and in this his views were remarkably similar to Clay's, almost guilelessly so. However, Calhoun thought the tariff bad for the South and manufacturers, because it took purchasing power from American consumers. The economy in all its sectors did best when most free, and he could become almost lyrical (though lyricism was not his gift) about free trade, removing burdens, breaking shackles, and taking down toll gates. But he was a moderate, who knew that economies disliked sudden discontinuities.

Calhoun was an austere man who believed in hard work, and he advocated a prosperity grounded in productivity and the making of things. He was inclined to jeremiads about "the love of gain," which might "overspread the land, to the absorption of every other passion and feeling."[73] This austerity helps to explain what became, by the late 1830s, his preoccupation (the currency, banking, and credit), a problem forced on him by the Jacksonian evisceration of the American banking system. He set about studying the problem; his speeches grew more discursive, more statistical, more condescending to dull-witted colleagues. He came to know how the Bank of Amsterdam had worked in the seventeenth century, and how the Bank of England worked in his own day.

Like John Taylor, Calhoun disliked bankers, speculators, and capitalists and once explained that banking ought to be regarded as a lowly occupation, requiring only "inferior qualities."[74] Nonetheless, Calhoun was a man who saw deeply into the changing nature of economic modernity. Taylor had thought that the coming world might be waved away, but Calhoun knew better. He knew that banks, paper, and credit were of the essence of a modern economy, that there was no going back, and that specie was a small proportion of the money that drove an economy, and this must be so. The difficulty was, what should be the proper relationship between government and the currency, remembering that the Constitution mandated responsibilities upon the former for the superintendence of the latter, and remembering that Calhoun defined "currency" very broadly? The Panic of 1837, especially, forced him to ponder the question of whether the government should be depositing money in private banks, even in Nicholas Biddle's bank, and he came to the view that government and banking needed to be radically dissevered; hence his support for the subtreasury.

The tariff was a crucial issue, in part because the surpluses generated by the tariff fed the expansion of the currency and multiplied the number of banks. Calhoun became both a free trader and (to use a later jargon) a monetarist, who advised that it was necessary to reduce the fiscal scale of government, remove it from an influence on the market, and trust to supply and demand, then all would go well. He especially dreaded the surpluses generated by the tariff. Little of a tariff was needed to pay governmental expenses, but a large revenue was essential to marginalize cheap imports. What to do with this money, which had paid off the national debt and now piled up in the Treasury? Give it to the pet banks? This led to economic derangement. Spend it on an enlarged government? This created a centralized power, armed to the teeth with the power that revenue created. Distribute the surplus to the states? This created clients in state legislatures, who governed with this money. Given that Calhoun believed that, unresisted, tariffs had a natural tendency to be raised, this was a vicious spiral he was determined to break. He thought that Nullification had commenced movement in the other direction and consummated a Jeffersonian revolution which had stalled. To this belief he adhered for the rest of his career. Matters looked good in 1840, after the Compromise of 1833, the death of the Bank of the United States, and Calhoun's unholy alliance with Van Buren which had achieved the subtreasury. They looked less good when the Whigs returned to power in 1841 and Clay rose again to prosecute his old programs.

Though Calhoun's technical command of these economic problems was formidable, his venture had been to elaborate an economics that vindicated the politics he had embraced from 1828 onward. His statistics and historicizing of the American economy were suspiciously coherent, tidily Manichean.

Free trade not only was moral and favorable to constitutional liberty, but made for economic prosperity, North and South. Protection not only was immoral and destructive of constitutional liberty, but made for economic derangement, North and South. These were the economics of a partisan, but a clever one.

Late in his career, Calhoun reached beyond these considerations into intellectual territory which Thomas Dew had begun to occupy in the 1820s and Karl Marx and J. A. Hobson would refine later. Earlier in their careers, both Clay and Calhoun had shared a desire to foster economic independence. Calhoun never had time for the foreigners who put their money into American ventures. But, as Dew had insisted, free trade had little respect for the nation-state. Calhoun was among the first Americans to understand this and suggest a political economy for the coming moment. He came to believe that the precedent of Britain, which had so entranced Clay, was inapt. Britain was a small island with few natural resources and a small internal market, so it needed an export trade. For the United States, on the other hand, extracting her abundant resources and shipping them, exchanging them for "the products of the rest of the world, [form] the basis of our industry." But Calhoun discerned something deeper. He observed to the Senate in 1842 that modern civilization had reached the point where industry had grown so productive that only a little of a country's capital and labor was needed to supply its own needs. This necessitated competition in foreign markets, among "less advanced, and less civilized countries." Such trade would spread "civilization, and prosperity, far and wide over [the globe's] entire surface."[75] In one sense, this was the old message of free trade. Yet there was an imperial undertone in Calhoun's version. He believed the problem of home industry was all but solved, the industrial sector was mature, and the notion of the United States as an economic child needing protection was passé. Similarly, the developed world was growing full of mature economies, whose surpluses needed export and who needed the less developed world to keep their workers employed. In this scramble for Africa and Asia, the United States had the advantages of its great resources, but needed the freedom to trade, which only a laissez-faire policy could provide. So, he suggested, conquer Lima, Dakar, Canton with American exports or face domestic difficulty. As prognostication, this was strikingly, disquietingly prescient.

This injunction spoke to an optimistic vein in Calhoun, at odds with the dark demons of the Commonwealth tradition otherwise haunting him. In this brighter vision, the mature man must compete or die, must subjugate or fail. Calhoun as an American, a Southerner, and a slaveholder did not doubt that in the plenitude of his means and competence, he would succeed. Why should Southerners doubt their capacity to compete successfully? he asked, and knew the glad answer. All his life, he believed in the Union and tried to save it, but not because he was afraid for the South if it went its own way. "As for ourselves," he observed in 1836 when debating the abolitionist petitions, "I feel no apprehension. . . . As great as is the danger, we have nothing to fear if we are true to ourselves. We have many and great resources; a numerous, intelligent, and brave population; great and valuable staples; ample fiscal means; unity of feeling and interest, and an entire exemption from those dangers originating in a conflict between labor and capital. . . . With these impressions, I ask neither sympathy nor compassion for the slaveholding States. We can take care of ourselves." There is no reason to doubt that this optimistic political economy took root in his self-confidence as a slaveholding patriarch, in his sense of self-sufficiency, which was not individualistic, and blurred the line between self and society. He famously articulated a vision of the South as "an aggregate . . . of communities, not of individuals. Every plantation is a little community, with the master at its head, who concentrates in himself the united interests of capital and labor, of which he is the common representative."[76] This mirage was not a refusal of the world, a building of barriers, as it had been in John Taylor, who was anxious to stave off decline. In Calhoun, this aggregation of communities was the social bedrock for an engagement with the world, for the imperialism of an economy which might take Americans and Southerners far beyond the American shore, beyond the old fascination of Britain and Europe, into an American century.

TO THINK ABOUT slavery was to engage the most profound dimensions of a Southern life, to confront what it meant to be human, to consider how society should be structured and history shaped, and to wonder how a self was possible. As George Fitzhugh put it, "We did not intend to write the history of slavery, or to treat of it in all its aspects. It has been so interwoven with all the relations and history of human kind, that to do so would require a Moral Cosmos and a history of the world."[77] This scope, however, meant that the genre of the proslavery argument had a very weak center; with the possibility of touching everything, it had the discretion to omit almost anything, even slavery itself. Nonetheless, a pattern is evident. Broadly, the movement of thought from the 1820s onward was from the concrete to the abstract, the skeptical to the millennial, the disillusioned to the optimistic, the focused to the diffuse, from the idea that slavery exemplified how all fallible humans were entrapped to the conviction that some humans might be free, even happy.

There was no tidy beginning to the proslavery argument. It stretched back to antiquity, was modified by the Church Fathers, debated by the scholastics, revised by the early moderns, and warily discussed by the Founding Fathers. The eighteenth century, which abolished serfdom in most of Europe, began to end the slave trade, and started to emancipate slaves in the American North, had no shortage of occasions for meditating upon the nature of slavery. The generation of 1776 in Virginia and elsewhere had toyed with the idea of emancipation, not without hope, because theirs was a generation which had seen the world change and ancient things die, and they had reasons to believe that human decisions could be efficacious. Most famously, St. George Tucker in 1796 had published *A Dissertation on Slavery: With a Proposal for the Gradual Abolition of It, in the State of Virginia*, which was founded on the dark knowledge that America had been a "vale of death" for millions of Africans. Despite this, Tucker was blithe on what Virginians might do, considering man's capacity for reason in an "enlightened age," the "genial light of liberty," and slavery's shrinkage in the modern world. He offered neat tables to prove that a gradual scheme of emancipation might comfortably work. True, he noticed that "prejudice, usurpation, and tyranny" might interfere, but, since government was a science and science served freedom, all might be well. A little talk among gentlemen might reason it out: "From the communication of sentiment between those who lament the evil, it is possible that an effectual remedy may at length be discovered. Whenever that happens the golden age of our country will begin."[78]

Thirty years of communicating sentiment yielded not a remedy but a conviction of intractability. Six months before the death of Thomas Jefferson, Edward Brown of Charleston placed upon the title page of his *Notes on the Origin and Necessity of Slavery* lines from Shakespeare's most cynical play, *Troilus and Cressida*, wherein Ulysses argues that only hierarchy stands between man and the abyss: "Take but degree away, untune that string, / And hark! what discord follows; each thing meets / In mere oppugnancy." For Brown, modern progress had been made not by freedom but by slavery. Tucker had seen American history as made by the freedom of Europeans and the enslavement of Africans, and had thought that the American future would be the process of extending the liberality of the former to the lives of the latter. But Brown saw slavery as having made the settlement of the New World possible, indeed in having made man capable of civilization. In this, Brown was influenced by the Scottish Enlightenment's theory of the four stages in human history, which had explained how humans had advanced from hunting societies, to pastoral, to agricultural, and lastly to commercial. Slavery had been history's Malthusian schoolroom, wherein primitive man's instinct for unbridled liberty had been changed into discipline. Slavery arose not from greed but from necessity, and had been governed by the laws of supply and demand. In countries where the supply of labor had outstripped its demand, slavery had been redundant; this was so of modern Britain and France. Elsewhere, notably in newly settled lands where labor had been expensive and subsistence cheap, slavery had proved essential; it was the price paid for exploitation of the land, that is, for the establishment of civilization.

This was an economic calculus, though the analysis rested upon a vision of human nature. As Brown saw it, men are unlovely creatures, lazy and corrupt, with no natural propensity for virtue. "The true and only motive which operates on the mass of mankind," he insisted, "is the reward which is expected to follow a moral course of life; which reward, consists in the facility of obtaining subsistence, the comforts, credit and respectability, which, in civilized society, are consequent on correct conduct." So a class system was essential to an advanced culture, for gradations made ambition and distributed esteem. In Brown's Tory vision, the value of slavery lay in helping to depress the working classes, which might otherwise rise in affluence and power to challenge and overthrow their betters, who are necessary to sustain standards of culture. Slavery was "the only barrier to [a] disorganization of civilized society," because forced labor, by competition, depressed the wages of free labor and prevented "universal equality, which is but another phrase for barbarism."[79]

For the rest, Brown briskly stated themes which subsequent Southerners were to elaborate: the tone of grievance that the world misunderstood the South and was conspiring to destroy it, the claim that slaves were humanely treated by godly masters, the repudiation of Thomas Jefferson's egalitarianism and view of slavery as fostering an unrepublican and despotic psychology, the assertion that slaves lived better than British industrial workers and that free blacks degenerated, the suggestion that slavery was sanctioned by the Bible. Still, these came at the end of his pamphlet as extras to his main argument, that slavery was a problem in political economy and that thinking about slavery helped to locate Southern culture in the historical trajectory of human civilization. His driving question was, who are we? For St. George Tucker, the answer had been, we are an enlightened people who control our own destinies. For Brown, it was, we are a flawed people who are in the grip of historical necessity but nonetheless advancing the purposes of civilization. Brown's was to remain the basic answer throughout the antebellum period. It helps to explain why political economy and its bastard stepchild, sociology, were the queen disciplines of the proslavery argument, because each embodied the ethic of necessity, were thought (as Dew put it) "to be sustained by facts and reasoning as irresistible as the demonstration of the mathematician."[80]

Nonetheless, the 1820s retained a residual sense that necessity might move to subvert slavery. The colonizationists had their schemes, hopes, and money. As late as 1832, Jesse Burton Harrison could observe, "There is a serious disposition to look the evil of slavery (nothing less!) in the face, and to cast about for some method of diminishing or extirpating it." Like most Southern antislavery people, Harrison was little moved by the plight of slaves and most affected by "the injuries slavery inflicts on the whites." That is, slavery incapacitated the work ethic, prevented the growth of manufactures, was hostile to dense population growth, and discouraged white immigration. In this judgment Harrison was not very remote from Thomas Dew, who was rendering a different verdict on the 1831–32 emancipation debates in the Virginia state legislature. Dew, too, doubted the long-term prospects of slavery, but he was scathingly precise that "every plan of emancipation and deportation which we can possibly conceive, is *totally* impracticable."[81]

Thomas Dew was a thinker who half-stepped beyond the historical reasonings of Edinburgh into the sharper relativism of historicism. Like Brown, he knew that man was imperfect, trapped in a stadial history, and "the creature of circumstances." Knowledge and morality were local, and slavery specific to time and place. Like Brown, Dew believed that slavery encouraged the development of civilization, because it was linked to the invention of property and agriculture. Further, slavery mitigated the warlike instinct for vengeance and elevated the condition of woman by removing her from the degrading necessity of chattel labor. In short, slavery was part of the origins of modern society, of what others would come to call capitalism. To be sure, Dew gestured toward the moral case for slavery. He duly cited his Bible and trotted out his lawyers (Grotius, Pufendorf, Vattel), but his argument was located in the twilight zone where political economy met social ethics, where necessity was thought to create morality. In this place, Dew occupied a guardedly optimistic position. Since God was benevolent, slavery as one of his institutions advanced civilization. History mattered, since it explained what had been and what might be. Thomas Dew was a Burkean, suspicious of Enlightenment abstractions, skeptical of the notion that morality could stand outside of history and, by force of virtue, successfully change the world. For Dew, no legislature could enact bills "upon purely abstract principles, entirely independent of circumstances, without the ruin of the body politic." Circumstances were what made "every political scheme beneficial or noxious to mankind." Nothing should be "stript of every relation in all the nakedness and solitude of metaphysical abstraction."[82] Context was all.

Dew's *Review* is a description of the South's actuarial limitations. The estimated worth of Virginia's slaves was $100,000,000, which was a third of the state's wealth, so compensated emancipation was an impossibility, because there were no means to pay the bill. Similarly, it would require an annual expenditure of $27,000,000 to purchase and transport 60,000 slaves to Africa. Further, the economic effect of emancipation on slave prices, land values, immigration, emigration, and the domestic slave trade would, whether done slowly or quickly, turn Virginia into a desert. Slavery, after all, was property, and, as Dew saw it, the state rested upon and was instituted to protect property. No Virginian government that sought to end slavery could survive, nor could society itself, since even the nonslaveholder depended on slavery as an institution.

Continually Dew made the case for necessity. To the argument that slavery was "in the *abstract*" un-Christian, he responded that practical circumstances were determinant, that nothing was driven by a "rule of conscience or revealed law of God." His metaphor for the Southern position was chilling: "The physician will not order the spreading cancer to be extirpated although it will eventually cause the death of his patient, because he would thereby hasten the final issue."[83] The image is stronger than Dew's subsequent palliations, that slavery was sanctioned by the Bible, Jefferson misunderstood its psychology, self-interest required kindliness in masters, slaves sympathized with their owners, slavery was republican, fear of insurrection (even after Nat Turner) was exaggerated and white police power was supreme, and slave labor was productive and historically had produced most of American prosperity. Dew offered the best case, but it was predicated on allowing for the worst. More, he was moving toward a theory of historical irony, the idea that the bad created the good. This was a theme developed by William Harper in the 1830s and one that Fitzhugh in the 1850s would turn into a playful, grinning paradox.

Thomas Dew was a sort of bourgeois accountant, a man in a black frock-coat who lived a life of exemplary domesticity, while keeping the books for an irregular world. By contrast, William Harper of South Carolina reasoned more like an eighteenth-century gentleman. Immorality worried the priggish Dew, but Harper was relaxed about it. As he observed in 1828, the abstract question of whether slavery was natural, humane, or just was irrelevant. God himself had been silent on the matter, though he had enjoined "obedience upon bondsmen and . . . [this seemed] to make the inference inevitable, that He considered the institution as altogether a matter of political expediency."[84] Still, Harper built upon Dew, which was a pattern in the proslavery argument. It was, preeminently, a cumulative discourse in which thinker referred to thinker, in which the South was conscious of itself as an intellectual community. The obverse of this was a growing sense, absent in an earlier generation, that slavery prevented community with others beyond the South, that its writers were pleading before a tribunal whose judges did not listen.

Very few proslavery thinkers had any expectation of transcending their locality. Dew addressed himself to the makers of public policy in Virginia, Harper spoke to other South Carolinians, while others addressed Southern college students. James Henry Hammond did write letters to Thomas Clarkson, the aging English abolitionist, but it is doubtful that Hammond expected an answer. The theologians, to be sure, entered into intersectional dialogues, but perhaps only George Fitzhugh believed, almost innocently, in a wider conversation: he corresponded with antislavery periodicals, traveled to New Haven to debate Wendell Phillips, and was convinced that Dew was wrong to think that cultures did not speak to one another.

Harper was among the first to understand that the defense of slavery mandated the systematic repudiation of egalitarianism.[85] In this stark Federalist impulse, he followed Brown, anticipated Fitzhugh, and quietly modified Dew, who had tiptoed around the Declaration of Independence. For Harper, there was no logical relationship between freedom and equality, but rather society was a texture of power and dependency. Slavery was no anomaly in the human condition. Slaughtered animals, children, women, criminals, unenfranchised whites, slaves, all formed part of the pattern of exclusions and inclusions which made the world. This came close to understanding morality as power alone. Nonetheless, the proposition "man is born to subjection" was deemed a truth with its own ethics. Man had no inalienable rights, and governments habitually deprived men of liberty: that was what laws were for. Hence the ideological legacy of the American Enlightenment was but the "well-sounding, but unmeaning verbiage of natural equality and inalienable rights."[86]

Believing this, Harper could be at ease in acknowledging fault. Native Americans had been cruelly defrauded of their lands and exterminated, the African slave trade had been an evil, and slavery itself was full of abuses. With Dew, Harper agreed that slavery occasioned social progress, but he acknowledged that each historical stage had its peculiar evils, and he was unsure that there was such a thing as a trans-historical standard. Even in the best of societies, there was "petty competition," envy, hatred, malice and dissimulation, not to mention "licentiousness." This was close to Harper's central message. He was an aging cynic, who knew human frailty because he had experienced it. He was a judge, after all, before whom human depravity had been incessantly paraded. So he thought it silly to imagine that happiness was anything other than a fleeting accomplishment. He mistrusted the do-gooder and gleefully quoted Coleridge, who had said, "I have never known a trader in philanthropy who was not wrong in heart somehow or other." Harper's best case for slavery was, not that it was a positive good, but that it might create a society slightly less evil or at least not significantly worse. Since "human life is a system of evils and compensations," there was "no reason to believe that the compensations with us are fewer, or smaller in proportion to the evils, than those of any other condition of society." This made him insouciant about "the actual and alleged evils of slavery," which he was content to document: brutality, flogging, sexual abuse, cruelty, the splitting up of families, the limitation placed upon the moral, intellectual, and economic development of the slaves, the encouragement in them of petty theft, lying, and licentiousness. Further, he acknowledged that slave women were readily used to gratify "the hot passions of men."[87] In fact, he was deeply interested in the sexual dimension of slavery, to which he devoted several warm pages, which wandered into reflections upon white and black prostitutes.

There were limits to Harper's cynicism. His standard response to the evidence of Southern abuses was evidence of abuse elsewhere. Slaves were flogged, but so were English sailors. Slave women were seduced, but London was full of stews. He pulled back from the abandonment of American exceptionalism, which was what would happen if all human experience became a comity of vice. The United States and the South must be better. Southern brothels were few, South Carolina had no divorce, slaves were secure and Christian, crime was uncommon, so the South had the human vices but in a "mitigated form."[88] This was the best that life could afford, this mitigation.

Harper was deep enough into the nineteenth century to accept the comforting explanations of race, even to flirt with polygenesis. But this was a bonus, which undercut his logic, which mostly rested not upon the distinctiveness of Southern slavery but on its normality. Harper integrated the slavery around him into the trajectory of world history by defining slavery so generally that it was hard for it not to belong. Harper's definition read: "Where a man is compelled to labor at the will of another, and to give him much the greater portion of the product of his labor, there *slavery* exists; and it is immaterial by what sort of compulsion the will of the laborer is subdued." So, blows, starvation, fear, the compulsions of any society, made slaves. By this reasoning, even the legally free person was but a "masterless slave."[89] Fitzhugh was to inherit this notion of slaves without masters.

By stressing the inevitability of inequality, Harper had a tendency to derogate the value of social mobility, even for whites. He asked, "Is it not better that the character and intellect of the individual should be suited to the station which he is to occupy?"[90] This amounted to a suspicion of the modern theory of competition, and this insight, too, Fitzhugh was later to develop. Harper himself little believed in progress, and his sense of modernity was Malthusian, in that progress was seen as mostly change, in which the mix of affluence and poverty might alter but the world on balance would remain the same.

In Harper, the omnipresence of vice and pain was sensually invoked in a manner almost Sadean. More than most, Harper exemplified the tendency of the proslavery argument, like its antislavery opponent, toward a cultural pornography. Images abound of young men pawing willing slaves, of English prostitutes walking the streets, of whips on backs. But the Marquis de Sade was the spiritual ancestor of Friedrich Nietzsche, and this anticipation, too, was in Harper. He thrilled to the idea of the master, of the leader, of beating the odds. Slaveholders were a minority in the United States, but they had produced a wealth of political leadership, which even the South's enemies had been forced to acknowledge. This preeminence had emerged precisely from the inegalitarian ethic of slavery, which produced leaders whose greatness filtered down: "The whole of society receives the benefit of the exertions of a mind of extraordinary endowments." Nonetheless, Harper pulled back from superman, which Henry Hughes later would not. The final pages of Harper's 1837 oration are a confession that history is an irony, beyond prognostication and control. This was the unavoidable lesson of slavery for his generation, that there were limitations to will and fallibility in intentions. William Wilberforce and Thomas Clarkson, for example, had striven to improve the world. But had they? Even they might not know. Slavery might advance a Manifest Destiny of conquest, but it did not follow that this empire would increase the sum of human happiness. History required and taught only "labor and self-distrust."[91]

In calculating where slavery positioned the South in the modern world, deciding what to make of British society was of special importance. Political economy, often the intellectual underpinning of reasoning about slavery, had been largely a British invention, with most of its evidence and logic drawn from British social experience: just like Karl Marx in Germany or Henri Saint-Simon in France, the Southern slaveholder in thinking about modern society had to engage English life and Scottish thought. Further, the proslavery argument was a debate about American exceptionalism, a meditation on the trajectory of the American Revolution and a defense of the new republic. It had, therefore, its roots partly in books like Robert Walsh's *An Appeal from the Judgments of Great Britain Respecting the United States of America* (1819), which Dew praised, and Edward Gibbon Wakefield's *England and America: A Comparison of the Social and Political State of Both Nations* (1833), which was significant for Harper. So, though it was to become a defense of the South against the North, the proslavery argument began life as a defense of the United States against the old enemy. The urgency of this deepened as Britain, the vanquished foe of 1783, grew not weaker but the industrial Leviathan of an imperial age. Rational men could fairly question where the world's future lay, in the direction of American or British society, and rational slaveholders had to ask what role slavery might play in all this. Their dilemma was great. Prove that slavery was historically normal, and you might suggest that America belonged to an unchanging human experience and to a world with a bleak, inegalitarian future. Increasingly, this idea was felt to be diminishing, so many Southern thinkers tried to remake American slavery into evidence of America's transcendence of the human condition. Asked to choose between being American and being slaveholding, exceptionalist or not, Southerners tried to have it both ways.

It is no accident, therefore, that James Henry Hammond, in his two letters to Thomas Clarkson in 1845, betrayed a nativist temperament which grumbled about the foreigner who "naturally hates everything American" and was hated back for "infamous libels."[92] What had been a tension in Harper between acknowledging vice and claiming virtue became in Hammond a hypocrisy. Few in the South exceeded the latter in arriviste amorality. He had had a very modest upbringing and married a plain heiress coldly for money, then abused her (she left him), built a plantation empire, fitfully neglected his children (white and mulatto), scoffed privately at Christianity while issuing gubernatorial proclamations in praise of the Redeemer, and became a political pariah for sexually molesting his nieces. Despite or because of these experiences, Hammond had a shrewd mind, and he was a pitiless judge of character, including his own. This was the man who stepped forward to vindicate the probity of his culture. He did so for political reasons, at a time when his career needed help, and the action served his purpose, which was not to persuade Thomas Clarkson but to earn Hammond credit with Southern opinion.

Hammond's letters were written with a self-conscious sense that the lines of the debate had long been set and innovation was improbable. It was his amorality that created his originality. Hammond's most heartfelt insight was that morality was irrelevant. This denuding of Dew's priggishness to leave only necessity was so trenchantly expressed by Hammond, and encapsulated so important a feature of antebellum Southern thought, that the passage in which he made the case is worth extended quotation.

If you were to ask me whether I am an advocate of slavery in the abstract, I should probably answer, that I am not, according to my understanding of the question. I do not like to deal in abstractions. It seldom leads to any useful ends. There are few universal truths. I do not now remember any single moral truth universally acknowledged. . . . Justice itself is impalpable as an abstraction, and abstract liberty the merest phantasy that ever amused the imagination. This world was made for man, and man for the world as it is. We ourselves, our relations with one another and with all matter are real, not ideal. I might say that I am no more in favor of slavery in the abstract, than I am of poverty, disease, deformity, idiocy or any other inequality in the condition of the human family; that I love perfection, and think I should enjoy a Millennium such as God has promised. But what would it amount to? A pledge that I would join you to set about eradicating those apparently inevitable evils of our nature, in equalizing the condition of all mankind, consummating the perfection of our race, and introducing the Millennium? . . . [E]very attempt which has been made by fallible man to extort from the world obedience to his "abstract" notions of right and wrong, has been invariably attended with calamities, dire and extended, just in proportion to the breadth and vigor of the movement. On slavery in the abstract, then, it would not be amiss to have as little as possible to say. Let us contemplate it as it is.[93]

So, morality was God's business. Men dealt only with the world "as it is," and ideality was irrelevant. The only pertinent question was, how fared the Southern world? Rich, powerful, and successful was Hammond's answer, for cotton was king. What else did one need to know?

This conclusion affected manner. Brown, Dew, and even Harper had been earnest men who wished to establish that slavery was both necessary and moral. Hammond rehearsed their arguments as part of the game, not because he believed in morality, but because others, less astute and disillusioned than himself, did. But amorality made Hammond's rhetoric, which was satirical. With Hammond, slavery is the occasion for jokes, by which the parvenu patrician mocked those who believed in or attacked the world in which a parvenu was making his way. For Hammond understood that style was the man and, by extension, the culture.

Self-confidence or its illusion—there was little difference for Hammond —was all. Americanism was part of this. Hammond's predecessors had been closer in spirit to the eighteenth century and, with it, the anxiety of British influence. Hammond did not care for Europe, except as a place cheaply to pick up art. A trip there in 1836–37 had cured him of whatever lingering deference he might once have had, and he came to think of England as a land of detestable "humbuggery and pillage."[94] In this, Hammond outlined a theme that Fitzhugh was to develop: that the South might solve the problem of modernity, a task that required self-confidence. That problem was the pell-mell indiscipline of progress, which had burst out in the bloodiness of the French Revolution, an event whose spirit of transcendentalism was regaining confidence and renewing rash experimentalism. The South, as a conservative power, was needed as the safeguard of the world's orderly progress.

With this went the idea that the South's racial and class structure provided it with an insulation against the ideological instability of modernity. It was Hammond who first stressed that "isms" had no purchase on the Southern mind, because Southerners were uninterested in abstraction. This was to prove a powerful idea, one of the myths of Southern culture, which has lasted to the present day. In Hammond's case, it was little more than a debating trick. He made this claim in the midst of arguing that Southern religion was peculiarly amiable, uninterested in matters of class or color, devoid of a controversial literature. This was at odds with his private views. Though he did believe in God, Hammond saw God as a greater slaveholding patriarch, against whose malevolent power he was doomed to struggle. The battle was lonely, since Hammond had no sense of religious community, and pride left him alone to face this God, in a world that (like a gnostic) he saw as a hell. These personal feelings were excluded from the smiling benignity of Hammond's public portrait of Southern slaveholding culture. Not everyone could pull off this cynical hypocrisy. Some even thought Hammond was speaking the truth, that the mask was the face. And so they set about establishing the morality of slavery.

The 1840s saw an elaboration of proslavery arguments, very seldom innovations, though the tone grew more urgent as the political scene grew more unpredictable. The denominational splits of Baptists and Methodists generated controversial apologetics. Ministers were consistently the most energetic proponents of slavery, because not only did the Bible help to sanction slavery, but proslavery helped to legitimate an expansive evangelicalism once suspect for its radical tendencies. Both sides paid a price for the alliance. Proslavery put on a reforming and humane face, stepped away from Harper's calm acceptance of vice, and argued that slavery, being Christian, helped to ameliorate the human condition, slave and free. But religion became more literalist in biblical exegesis, because it was in inerrancy that the Bible was serviceable to the proslavery case.

One consequence of this conjugation was the growing stress upon slavery as a patriarchal institution, as the descendant of the social system of Abraham. "I propose to show from the Scriptures," Thornton Stringfellow had written, "that this state, condition, or relation [of slavery], did exist in the *patriarchal age*, and that the persons most extensively involved in the sin, if it be a sin, are the very persons who have been singled out by the Almighty, as the objects of his special regard."[95] An emphasis on the patriarchal strengthened a tendency to see slavery as antimodern (thus moving away from the themes of Dew), as well as the tendency (traceable in Calhoun) to see slavery as a series of small worlds presided over by a patriarchal master, around whose feet clustered wife and children, overseer and slaves.

The prominence of the religious argument for slavery had the further consequence of weakening the discreteness of the idea of slavery, by enfolding the issue of man's relationship with other men into theodicy, the justifying of God's ways. In truth, defining slavery had always been a problem. The canon provided many options: Justinian saw it as a "constitution of the law of nations, by which one man is made subject to another, contrary to nature"; Grotius as "an obligation to serve another for life, in consideration of diet, and other common necessaries"; Montesquieu, like William Blackstone, as "the establishment of a right, which gives one man such a power over another, as renders him absolute master over his life and fortune"; William Paley as "an obligation to labor for the benefit of the master, without the contract or consent of the servant"; William Whewell as an institution which converted "a person into a thing—a subject merely passive, without any of the recognized attributes of human nature."[96] From their own experience, Southerners habitually rejected or modified these definitions. They tended, rather, to claim that slavery was not contrary to nature, the master's will was never absolute, the concept of rights was elusive, the slave sometimes did consent by word and always did by deed, and the slave was not a thing but a human being. But this assertion of the slave's humanity embroiled him or her in the general problem of the human condition. If the slave had a will, he or she had a measure of freedom, and so her or his condition became important to understanding freedom; this made it unclear whether even the nonslave could be free. If slavery dissolved at the touch of definition, so did liberty.

The *Lectures on the Philosophy and Practice of Slavery* (1856) of William Smith, president of Randolph-Macon College, offered a further definition: "*the abstract principle of slavery is the general principle of submission or subjection to control by the will of another.*"[97] A willingness to use the word "abstract" without criticism was, in itself, symptomatic of Smith's times, despite Hammond's refusal of the category. The later antebellum generation was interested in the question of abstraction, by way of a reproach to an earlier generation which in its Burkeanism had been anxious to disavow Jacobin theoretical ambition. By opting for a merely local knowledge, the men of 1830 were later thought to have forfeited the South's moral place in a wider world. This place Southerners in the 1850s were concerned to reclaim.

Smith's definition had an implication: "this principle enters more or less as an essential element into every form of human government." Control was intrinsic to government and necessarily abridged freedom. Freedom was self-control, whereas slavery was control by another. Since allowing men an absolute self-control created only anarchy, it followed that slavery entered into the constitution of all societies. Governments varied this balance of freedom and slavery, from despotism to democratic republics, but the last only worked if the state controlled anarchy: "We call it, by way of eminence, a *free* government; and so it is, *relatively to other forms, a very free government! But then it is only relatively, not absolutely so.*"[98] For Smith, as for many others, this argument arose from a rejection of Locke and an Aristotelian presumption that there had been no aboriginal state of nature after which society had been contracted, but rather that man's nature had been always and intrinsically social.

A Methodist, Smith believed in original sin. Civil government was "*control by the authority of God and the people.*" Each human stood in a different relationship to self, rights, and government, because there was a continuum in which no one was absolutely free, no one absolutely enslaved, but all had differing quotients according to their capacity for self-control and self-knowledge. Slavery was throughout a system of rights and responsibilities, in which slaves and masters had agency. This being so, slave shaded into free labor: "The only difference between free and slave labor is, that the one is rendered in consequence of a contract, the other in consequence of a command." Nonetheless, slavery had a distinguishable form as a variety of the human condition, one subjection among many, one freedom among many. Hence, "Domestic slavery is one of the subordinate forms of civil government . . . an *imperium in imperio*—a government within a government."[99]

It was characteristic of those proslavery thinkers who most granted the humanity of slaves and most enfolded slavery into the metaphysical problem of human nature that they tended to be most racist. A slave which was a thing and not a human did not, after all, need a race. Without the explanatory power of racial ideology, there was little riposte to the idea that slaves might earn the right to greater civil freedom by their moral actions. This tendency was exemplified by Thomas R. R. Cobb, whose *Inquiry Into the Law of Negro Slavery in the United States of America* (1858), with a prefatory "Historical Sketch of Slavery," was the most learned survey produced by any Southerner of the multifarious forms that slavery had assumed in human history. "We recognize in the negro a man, endowed with reason, will, and accountability," he wrote, "and in order to justify his subjection we must inquire of his intellectual and moral nature."[100] This justification for "negro slavery" (not slavery "in the abstract") rested on the physiognomy of sub-Saharan Africans, duly evidenced by travel accounts, ethnologies, and learned papers before the Royal Institution of Manchester.

William Smith, too, spent time upon the racial inferiority of Africans. But Smith had another, quasi-Federalist reason for thinking that slavery was permanently beneficial to American society; it helped to stabilize a pell-mell, democratic, expansionist, and mobile society, which otherwise encouraged a weakening of self-control and so threatened social crisis. Though Smith did not wish to discourage expansion and immigration, he mistrusted the influx of so many Catholics and heathen Chinese. Since slavery excluded from the South this immigration, the South could serve to stabilize the republic: "Upon these States will devolve the duty of holding the balance of power between these great contending forces, and of preserving the ark of American liberty in the politico-religious storms that are about to sweep over the land, and shake the foundations of our confederacy."[101] In this way, slavery gave the South a moral mission to modernity. This idea of mission was indispensable to Fitzhugh, too, and had long been intrinsic to the proslavery genre, whose origins in stage theory, political economy, and moral philosophy demanded an elaboration of the South's social relationship to modernity. It was improbable that an American conjecture would do other than assert that an American society could be less than superior.

The lines of the proslavery argument had been set by the early 1850s, when they began to appear in anthologies which students might study by rote. A canon had developed. In 1852 the Charleston publishers Walker and Richard published the four-hundred-odd page *The Pro-Slavery Argument*, which contained the writings of Dew, Harper, and Hammond, as well as a summary piece by William Gilmore Simms. When *Cotton Is King, and Pro-Slavery Arguments* was published in Augusta in 1860, under the editorship of E. N. Elliott of Mississippi, it had expanded to nine hundred pages and now (while omitting Dew and Simms) added pieces by Thornton Stringfellow, Albert Taylor Bledsoe, and Samuel Cartwright; further, it acknowledged the contributions of Northerners to the argument by using essays by David Christy of Cincinnati and Charles Hodge of Princeton. However, Elliott omitted what were certainly the most original works of the 1850s, those by Henry Hughes and George Fitzhugh. This was no surprise. Both writers had been greeted with puzzlement, as eccentric and deviant, with no place in so safe a work as Elliott's *Cotton Is King*. And both were pleased to be thought idiosyncratic. Their existence pointed to the truth that the pro-slavery argument had become old enough to generate those who sported with its themes, subverted its logic, thumbed their noses at old fogies, and experimented with rhetoric.

Of the two, Henry Hughes was the more eccentric. In fact, he was one of the most original figures in Southern thought. He came from Port Gibson, Mississippi, the son of a land speculator who died with an insolvent estate. Hughes became a young lawyer in New Orleans, where he lived with his mother, kept (as we have seen) a diary, chased girls and admired men, read widely, kept a scrapbook of his faltering fame, traveled briefly to Europe, and became a Democratic politician interested in reviving the slave trade. When only twenty-five, he published his *Treatise on Sociology* (1854), whose most striking characteristic was its style, a presage of those later literary moments when the bloated discursiveness of mid-Victorian prose was stripped down. Hughes's writing is brief, epigrammatic, repetitive, neological. Few sentences have more than ten words. His tone is abruptly authoritarian; assertion is all, doubt nonexistent. The narrative is anonymous and abstract, silent about the author's identity, but also about context. The North, American society, Europe, the ancient world, Aristotle, Jefferson, the familiar historical, social, and personal referents of the proslavery argument were starkly eschewed. In Hughes there is no history, time, landscape, or individuals, only categories like "society," "system," and "regulation." This was deliberate. Hughes's diary had been painfully personal, and his other writings have the usual quotient of humanity, but the *Treatise* was designed to be otherwise. His motive is laid out in the book's prefatory epigraph, which praises perspicuity, logic, and plainness for conveying truth, while relegating the ornamental to the business of entertainment. "The thinkers rule, and must first be convinced," because they give opinion to the public.[102]

Many of the book's assertions were simple and unoriginal. There was no social contract, man was a social animal, society was intended for progress, which entailed the perfection of "health, education, enjoyment, morality, and religion." What mattered was reality, not the idea of it. Society was constituted by power, provided by physical and mental labor, of which the latter was the greater. Society is, further, intended to prevent anarchic license and furnish an ordered liberty, by means of hierarchy. Men were driven by "desire and fear," and faced the option either to compete or to cooperate; the former option created a wasteful, free-labor society, while the second made what Hughes chose to call a "warrantee" society. Like many in the 1850s, he fought shy of the word "slavery," because he found the usual definitions did not describe the society around him. Rather, he saw a system of reciprocal rights, which was what constituted "the system in the United States South." "Property in man, is absurd. Men cannot be owned. In warranteeism, what is owned is the labor-obligations, not the obligee."[103]

What was new in Hughes was his annexation of the private to the public realm. The state should be responsible for all; individuals have only such rights as are ceded by the state. In Hughes's world, it was not the state which represented individuals, but individuals who represented the state. This was a philosophic, but mostly an administrative, matter. Henry Hughes was an organization man. He had schemes, diagrams, and flow charts, and the number of his beast was seven. He thought society should be divided into and governed by a heptarchy, a term he acquired from an odd reading of "the system for civil administration of laws, completed by King Alfred," the only human being that gets a mention in the *Treatise*. "A societary organization is therefore a union of seven organs for seven ends," Hughes said.[104] These organs were economics, which provided subsistence; politics, for security; hygiene, for health; philosophy, for education; aesthetics, for enjoyment; ethics, for morality; and religion, for spirituality. Each should have its own administrative structure, each its own (what Hughes's spiritual successors were to call) mission statement, each its own regulatory authority. The scope of this welfare state, by the standards of 1854, was breathtaking, even beyond what the mid-twentieth century accomplished in Sweden.

The origin of Hughes's vision lay partly in Charles Fourier and Auguste Comte, both of whom Hughes had read in the early 1850s. From these Hughes derived the boldness to use sociology as the basis for a newly imagined political and social structure. The *Treatise* has two sections, "theoretical" and "practical," a division intended to convey Hughes's sense that intellect must first discern reality, then create the institutions to perfect the human condition. Unusually for a proslavery thinker, Hughes was convinced that perfection was possible. In this, his religion mattered, because he had a messianic and millennial streak. The final two pages of the *Treatise* offered a lush religious vision of a fulfilled Fourierite world, in which the sun shone upon "leagued plantations" and "happy warrantees" who banqueted in refectories, worshiped in chapels, studied in schools, told stories, sang in "plantation-saloons" in the cool of the evening, and rested in dormitories.[105] These pages have a biblical rhetoric little matched in Southern thought until the rhapsodies of Henry Grady, who likewise used the sonorous language of the King James Version. But such a romantic eruption was, for Hughes, the only such rhetorical moment in a work otherwise of studied, inhuman restraint.

Restraint was close to the core of Hughes's vision. He was a very troubled young man, divided between megalomania and self-contempt, worried about his health and sanity. He became interested in ways to discipline these swings between euphoria and melancholy, these impulses toward drink, sex, and gluttony, which were the usual temptations of the young lawyer in New Orleans. So he imagined a world where resolve and will would not matter, since the state would regulate and ensure all. He abolished individuality, perhaps because he could not trust his own. This new world a-coming would be orderly, kindly, cultured, prosperous, free of all conflict. Hughes's contemporary William Henry Trescot asserted that history was made by antagonism, but Hughes opted for "syntagonism." Above all, this world would be "hygienic." This clinical language of purity is most evident in his discussion of race, a topic that surfaces late in the *Treatise*. Like others, including Fitzhugh, Hughes acknowledged that race was logically inessential to slavery, but he did admit that in the South "warranteeism with the ethnical qualification is ordained and established." For Hughes, race had to do with bodies, some superior, some inferior. Men "have hygienic duties," and "hygiene is both ethnical and ethical."[106] In this was presaged the logic of racial segregation, which said that bodies must not touch.

Henry Hughes was an oddity beyond the pale of conventional Southern thought, though mostly by being so stringent. Repudiating individualism and stressing collectivity had been the tendency of Southern thought for thirty years or more. Hughes just took the next step in acknowledging the power of the collectivity and suggesting how that power might be used. George Fitzhugh, too, idiosyncratically exemplified trends and was a man half in and half out of what his world thought, with a relationship to Southern intellectuality which was complicated, since he had a strange mix of conventional ideas, startling insights, and avant-garde philosophy. This oddity partly arose from his isolation. He was a Virginian with little formal education and a lawyer whose practice was local and desultory. Fitzhugh never held political office, and he scarcely traveled until the 1850s, so neither by family, profession, nor ambition did he acquire a place in wider circles. (Anyone for whom the solitary George Frederick Holmes represented a link to the Great World is someone who was in deep trouble, socially.) In Fitzhugh unworldliness became an intellectual strength, because the most original part of Fitzhugh was that he hated what most Southerners admired, chief among them the doctrines of laissez-faire.

First, the unoriginal parts of his thought. Fitzhugh attacked the abuses of modern industrialism and the cruelty of a free market system. He refused the idea of individualism and the social contract, while rejecting natural rights theory and the Jeffersonian doctrine that the world needed as little government as possible. He mistrusted the philosophical premises of the Enlightenment and had a Burkean preference for tradition. He saw domestic slavery as another variety of subordination, in a world where power and subjection was intrinsic to social relations. He stressed the historical normality of slavery and believed that the South, because of slavery, was peculiarly free from the modern world's tendency to social crisis. He looked upon Africans as children, especially fitted for the condition of servitude. He was a Christian who regarded the Bible as a proslavery document, a dogged localist who mistrusted centralization, and a xenophobe who worried about foreigners. He favored economic diversification and was interested in technological innovation. He favored patriarchalism and had a great respect for the ancients, especially Aristotle. In short, much of his reasoning could be found abundantly in previous Southern thought. However, Fitzhugh was an original, and his originality lay in the peculiar force with which he combined these thoughts into a metanarrative. At the heart of his analysis was a refusal of imperialism.

Fitzhugh's argument was that free trade was the ideology of a rapaciously acquisitive, competitive modernity, which trapped people into an atomized individuality, where they were powerless and exploited. He dated the emergence of this system to the disintegration of feudalism and the emergence of an early modern world which found in Hobbes a shrewd, dismayed prophet, and in Adam Smith an apologist for selfishness, peddled as a system of ethics. Hence the philosophy of liberty expounded during the American Revolution was a delusion. For Fitzhugh, governments did not derive their powers from the consent of the governed; rather they "originated in force, and have been continued by force."[107] By this, Fitzhugh cut the Gordian knot of Southern thought, which had deprecated the consequences of industrial modernity but simultaneously had lauded Adam Smith and American liberty. Fitzhugh told Southerners that they could not have it both ways, that wisely to choose slavery was to refuse a debilitating liberty.

Fitzhugh had derived this critique from many sources other than the Southern intellectual tradition and partly from those whom he liked, commodiously, to call socialists. These did not include Karl Marx, of whom he seems not to have heard, but did cover many upon whom Marx was drawing. Some of these (Pierre-Joseph Proudhon, Henri Saint-Simon, Louis Blanc, and Charles Fourier) might have answered to the name of socialist, but Fitzhugh lumped them together with many others (Robert Owen, Thomas Carlyle, and Fanny Wright) who were only critics of modern society. In this, Fitzhugh was not especially idiosyncratic. In the mid-nineteenth century, "socialism" was a word that denoted little more than a repudiation of modern society and a preference for collectivism.

However, though Fitzhugh learned from the socialists, he saw them as products of free society and incapable of solving its problems. They were but continuing "the little experiment of universal liberty that has been tried for a little while in a little corner of Europe." Only slavery could afford a solution to the crisis of freedom. By "slavery," Fitzhugh meant any social system which formally recognized inequality, the necessity of authoritarian order and human interdependence, and embodied "a safe, efficient and humane community of property."[108] For Fitzhugh, slavery was about being safe and protected, about people being unequal but nice to each other.

Fitzhugh's own history as a domestic and sentimental man mattered here. For him, the family was a "holy and charmed circle" and the solution for social ills was to make the family's values general. "Man loves that nearest to him best," he wrote. "First his wife, children and parents, then his slaves, next his neighbors and fellow-countrymen." The master was a harassed but kindly man, in control yet obliging, gratefully enmeshed in a system of reciprocal obligations. He was the strongest person in a world where most were naturally weak and all, even the master, required protection. Being interdependent, humans needed what Fitzhugh liked to call "association."[109] This was a theory of gender as much as anything else, because Fitzhugh was committed to Victorian notions of domesticity and separate spheres. This alone placed him far from William Harper, for whom the family furnished no respite from the world's cares.

It is a strikingly naive vision, which gravely undercut what had long been the proslavery argument's strongest suit, its cold cynicism about the intrinsic brutality of the human condition. With Fitzhugh, Southern thought passed abruptly into the world of *Godey's Lady's Book*, and it makes sense that he admired Charles Kingsley, whose novel *Alton Locke*, about English industrial squalor, came from the same hand which was to write *The Water Babies*. Fitzhugh's sentiment was expansive, even Wordsworthian, because it extended to "dogs, horses, birds and flowers." Like Calhoun, Fitzhugh wanted power and to be loved, even to belong to a Christian "band of brothers." He invented women, children, and slaves who might dote upon his masterly kindness. Fitzhugh's was the trust of a timid man, who averted his eyes from what was unpleasant, if that ugliness intruded upon his world. Ugliness elsewhere might be fine, since it pointed a contrast and fed the comforting illusion of a "South, quiet, contented, satisfied" and a slavery "healthy, beautiful and natural."[110] In these ways, Fitzhugh noticed the tendency of the age to favor compassion, because he shared the impulse.

This impulse helps to comprehend Fitzhugh's political vision, otherwise puzzling. Fitzhugh was no reactionary but a moderate progressive who praised reformation, deprecated revolution, and kept up with the most advanced social thought. He favored democracy, had little time for agrarian utopias, wanted universal public education (as well as a modernized banking system), and encouraged modest urbanization. Large cities were a curse, but small towns "great blessings." He describes glowingly his own town of Port Royal, a "village of flowers" with pleasant cottages "surrounded with trees, flowers, ivy, and other evergreens." Further, he favored internal improvements, especially roads which connected immediate localities and trams which might allow towns to spread and acquire the suburban, and he endorsed the establishment of a "great Southern University," for the same reasons that John Quincy Adams had once wanted an American national university.[111]

What held Fitzhugh's political philosophy together was an understanding of boundaries. Class mattered here. Contrary to his reputation, Fitzhugh was a bourgeois thinker, inattentive to the plantations that surrounded the small towns he admired. The slavery he described was the intimate slavery of an urban household, presided over by a town lawyer, which was the world Fitzhugh knew. He is clear that he disliked not only the vulgar munificence of the parvenu millionaires which industrialism had thrown up but the old aristocracy, too, in Europe and Virginia. "Tide-water old fogyism retains its dogged, do-nothing spirit," he once snorted. "It hates and opposes railroads, canals, daily mails, and other modern innovations, quite as cordially as its ancestry hated and opposed the looms."[112] This was remote from the quasi-aristocratic reasonings of Abel P. Upshur and Beverley Tucker. This progressive impulse seems to have strengthened in Fitzhugh, the deeper into the 1850s he got. Writing for De Bow's Review, the great Southern periodical of modern improvement, doubtless helped. But he was reading the drift of the times, too, because this was a decade when many Southern states resumed the sponsorship of internal improvements.

True to this, Fitzhugh dismissed those who dwelled on the Cavalier origins of Virginia, though he did admit that they had helped by their military discipline to carry the young colony through its brutal inception. Instead, he was happy to observe that many Virginians had begun life as transported convicts and that, despite this, their descendants had fitted well into society. Rather, Fitzhugh favored a society of modest competences, widely dispersed, in which the state fostered public works. "We should discourage private luxury and encourage public luxury" was his motto.[113]

This instinct for the *aurea mediocritas* extended to culture and the state. "Almost the only secret of high civilization and national greatness consists in narrow and confined territorial limits," he said. A thing too small, such as a plantation alone, was overly constricted, but a thing too great (Rome, London, an empire) became a despotism. Society should keep in touch with the proportions of the family, for "Counties, States, and nations, are but collections of families," which was why Fitzhugh favored genealogical researches. The scale of the individual American state seemed about right. It ought to be perfected as an independent nationality and thereby "counteract the centralizing tendency of modern improvements in locomotion and intercommunication, which naturally rob the extremities to enrich the centres of Power and of Trade." So Fitzhugh was a proponent of states' rights, though not for the usual reasons; he was, for example, opposed to the doctrines of Nullification, contemptuous of the Kentucky and Virginia Resolutions, and doubted the cogency of "the Calhoun school." Rather, each Southern state should "condense within its boundaries all the elements of separate independent nationality" and "every institution and pursuit that pertain to high civilization."[114] It followed that power exercised by too great a society was a tyranny, but power within discrete boundaries was an aid to civilization.

Anti-imperialism was an economic doctrine, as well as a cultural protest against hegemonic metropolitanism and cosmopolitanism, a protest influenced by a Romantic sense that cultures were healthiest which arose on native grounds: "We should encourage national and even State peculiarities; for there are peculiarities and differences in the wants and situations of all people, that require provincial and national, not cosmopolitan, institutions and productions." This theme was more prominent in *Cannibals All!* (1857), a book preoccupied with the problem of language, which Fitzhugh understood to be "a thing of natural growth and development, [which] adapts itself naturally to the changes of time and circumstance."[115] For Fitzhugh, new places and times required new words, which cosmopolitan centers of culture strove to kill with standardization. Hence he was an enemy of the neoclassical, hated the age of Louis XIV, mistrusted imitation, and (like the German Romantics) admired Shakespeare for his rough inimitability.

Fitzhugh had written *Sociology for the South* (1854) without thought to language or authorship. But this first book had gained him some fame, brought him correspondents, and propelled him more into the world. Eventually, after the publication of *Cannibals All!*, he was to get a minor political job in Washington and soon became a sort of columnist for *De Bow's Review*, whose editor regarded him with mingled admiration and puzzlement. During this process, Fitzhugh began to be self-conscious about writing, language, and what having an audience might entail. In the vein of Carlyle, whose rough bluntness the Virginian admired and imitated, Fitzhugh became a playful, confessional, whimsical writer, in a way unusual in the Southern tradition. He was freely vain, admitted to ignorance, threw out extravagant generalizations, quoted a lot, and then paused to comment discursively on his own literary habits, on what sort of author he was. Fitzhugh had the reader on his mind, and often addressed him (not her) to reveal narrative strategy. He apologized when method failed him, reminisced about his career by way of explaining his style, expressed his opinions on how readers read, admitted to impetuosity, commented on his habit of using poetry for epigraphs, and guessed at how the reader might grow irritated at all this disorder. This chatty exuberance might be read as postmodern, but Fitzhugh was closer to Laurence Sterne in *Tristam Shandy* (which might come to the same thing), wherein author and reader wandered together through an unstable world of short episodic chapters and the unfolding plot was by no means the most important preoccupation of either. In this manner, *Cannibals All!* was rhetorically a more ingenious work than *Sociology for the South*, but a work that tended to admit defeat in the struggle for ideological power, because it was half-content to be playful. Fitzhugh's comedy was born of resignation, though he had a sense of humor. "There is nothing in this world that we like so much as a good, hearty laugh," he once wrote, by way of explaining why he liked Byron.[116]

Nonetheless, Fitzhugh was skeptical about the efficacy of ideas. He proposed to "build up no system, attempt to account for nothing, but simply point out what is natural and universal, and humbly try to justify the ways of God to man." Hence he had Romantic philosophy in an unusually pure form, especially by submitting a self-conscious critique of the Enlightenment, which Fitzhugh understood to have commenced with John Locke. In France in the eighteenth century, intellect had become presumptuous and "undertook to form governments on exact philosophical principles, just as men make clocks, watches or mills." This was a mistake, because there were "no truths which the human mind can comprehend and follow out, in all their ramifications, and to their whole extent." Rather, it made sense to derogate philosophes in order to praise mechanics, the makers of "the cannon and the gun, the compass, the steam engine, and the electric wire." The enemy was Mary Shelley's Victor Frankenstein, "the anatomist, who should attempt to create a man," because "[s]ocial bodies, like human bodies, are the works of God, which man may dissect, and sometimes heal, but which he cannot create."[117]

However, Fitzhugh added that "invention alone begets civilization," and by invention he meant not only the making of spinning jennies but the effect of "words, written, printed, and disseminated in books." If society, too, was an invention, intellect might usefully undertake intelligent observation, then propose moderate action. Along these lines, Fitzhugh struggled to explain what role he himself was trying to play. He hazarded: "A Moral Pathology, which feels its way in life, and adapts itself to circumstances, as they present themselves, is the nearest approach to philosophy, which it is either safe or wise to attempt. All the rest must be left to Religion, to Faith, and to Providence." But even of this he was unsure, because Fitzhugh had the modern sense that the world was growing too complex for understanding, and, with this, he flirted with the existential conclusion that means and not ends were all that one might have. Each man had his own theory, and, at best, one treated the symptoms of a diseased world; causes were beyond knowledge or control. One of the therapies was religion, that usefully irrational thing. Fitzhugh seems to have been an Episcopalian of High Church tendencies, who smiled upon Puseyism, thought ritual might delay the crisis of agnosticism, and confessed that "we must all believe what we cannot understand."[118]

This was a long way from St. George Tucker's smooth confidence in human reason. With Fitzhugh, the proslavery argument imploded into paradox. Other social thinkers, less intelligent or imaginative, did not see that the collision of freedom and order might disintegrate individualism and leave only the provisional and momentary. Hughes solved the problem by commanding a greater dose of order and erasing the free individual, but this went too far for most thoughtful Southerners, who wanted to be more than only the guardians of a happy prison camp. Most tried to muddle through and have it both ways, to define a history and sociology acquainted with morality, a morality traceable in history. This kept the anarchy of both history and morality at bay, because they understood that the past was full of vice and morality full of contradiction. Nonetheless, strikingly, Southerners contrived to be hopeful in the 1850s, which was an expansive decade. In forty years, the proslavery argument had drifted from a bleak sense of human limitation to a quasi-millennial vision. But, along the way, the slaves themselves had dropped out of the proslavery argument. By the end, it became habitual to deny that Southern social relations constituted slavery, at all. In truth, real slaves had never been central. The genre had been a way for white Southerners to articulate a theory of society, and they had always been more preoccupied with how whites related to one another in politics, economics, and society than with how whites related to African Americans. The slave was the most inexplicit figure in the discourse, a shadowy presence, significant only as a type. He or she was never given a name, was never an individual with a history or an opinion, despite the fact that all these proslavery works were written within a few yards of particular slaves, many of whose experiences and voices and bodies were used and known, however imperfectly. This silence Mary Chesnut, at least, was to remember and evoke. "People talk before them as if they were chairs and tables," she inserted in her diary in 1861 on Jefferson's birthday. "And they make no sign. Are they stolidly stupid or wiser than we are, silent and strong, biding their time?"[119]

6 · Philosophy and Faith

For most Americans, philosophy was something written by ancient Greeks and modern Europeans, whom they were forced reluctantly to read in college. Though philosophy had intellectual prestige, it occasioned anxiety, because its terms were elusive and difficult. The most accomplished intelligence could find itself reduced to dribbling idiocy, the more so as philosophy might inform you that there was no such thing as intelligence, anyway.

Over the years, Southerners surveyed the options. First, there were the Scottish realists, dominant within the collegiate curriculum until the Civil War. Among these, Thomas Reid and Dugald Stewart were most influential, though they were often criticized and used as sounding boards. Second, there were the English philosophers, who offered greater variety. Among them, Francis Bacon was most admired and understood, while John Locke was more praised than grasped, and both (at a pinch) were seen as compatible with the Scots. George Berkeley and David Hartley were a different matter, because, like David Hume, they were destabilizing, by suggesting that man's knowledge of external reality was unreliable, God unknowable, and only matter and not spirit reliable. Third, Southerners increasingly looked toward German transcendentalism and French positivism, both traditions which had themselves partly arisen out of a sense that neither Reid nor Hume could be right, if intelligibility was to be demonstrated, efficacy achieved, and morality sustained. By 1861, in fact, Southerners had run through the canon and found nowhere a body of philosophy that answered to the needs of their complicated position.

It will be useful to begin with the text with which most Southern college students began their philosophical education, the *Inquiry into the Human Mind on the Principles of Common Sense* (1764) of Thomas Reid. There Southerners found a book which offered to resolve youthful uncertainties, with a homely evocativeness which was part of Reid's attraction for several generations. As a young man, Reid himself had been attracted to Berkeley's idealism, but then had been appalled by what was partly built upon Berkeley, David Hume's radical skepticism. Reid turned on both, while being aware that Hume was not easy to refute, especially the claim that there was nowhere beyond mind from which one could look back and demonstrate the reliability of what an inward consciousness described. Boldly, Reid removed the intervening trouble, consciousness and ideas, and contended that humans knew the world directly. True to this, the *Inquiry* was arranged into sections which examined the human senses (smell, touch, sight), because these were the faculties that connected the inward and the outward world, and these made immediacy possible. That is, Reid abolished metaphysics and substituted physiology or faculty psychology, and thereby he claimed that the mind could safely trust what the body gave it to know.

Reid was intervening in a complicated debate, begun in Scotland by Francis Hutcheson and implicating Locke and René Descartes, a controversy in which Reid's plain Aberdonian unworldliness was not always an advantage, certainly not in Europe, but even in a Scotland which had long been European as well as provincial, because of its adaptation of the civil law, old alliance with France, and connection to Dutch medicine. Hume was a European man of letters, who gave Edinburgh a standing in the world of the Enlightenment by his diffident glamour and sharp intellectuality, and Reid needed help before he could be regarded as a serious philosophical rival to such a man. For a while, Reid had only rottweiler advocates, who did him more harm than good, until help came from Dugald Stewart, who urbanely invented the idea of a Scottish philosophy (with Reid at its center) in works of sweeping cogency, which came to bridge the worlds of Adam Smith and Victor Cousin. Most accessibly, Stewart contributed supplements to the *Encyclopedia Britannica* in the editions of 1815 and 1821, which together formed his *Dissertation Exhibiting a General View of the Progress of Metaphysical, Ethical, and Political Philosophy, Since the Revival of Letters in Europe*. So, from the 1790s onward, when the French Revolution suggested the baleful consequences of skepticism and the urgency of self-evident truths, Stewart carried Reid forth in a struggle against the "universal deluge," whose stakes were now more than philosophical, more even than the old struggle between the Kirk and dissent.[1] Together, Reid and Stewart fashioned a renewed history of philosophy, which used Hume respectfully as a straw man in the serious game of elevating Baconian realism and derogating idealism, and insisted that Christian morality and religion be used as the standard by which one should discriminate among metaphysicians. On the other hand, Reid and Stewart offered a moderate philosophy, as hostile to Calvinists as to atheists, and this assisted their widespread acceptance, because they had made themselves the middle ground.

Common sense philosophy had lodged itself in the American mind, almost as quickly as in the Scottish. Editions of almost all the Scottish writings appeared in the colonies, then in the United States, with great rapidity and with an influence almost beyond their immediate impact in Britain. With Scottish books came migrant Scottish teachers, then (reversing the flow) many American students found their way to Scottish universities, though these personal exchanges tended to become less common from the 1820s onward. A not untypical instance was Robert Henry, born in Charleston in 1792 of a Scottish father and German mother. Henry studied at the University of Edinburgh between 1811 and 1814 and there studied moral philosophy with Thomas Brown, Dugald Stewart's successor, before returning in 1816 to a professorship at South Carolina College. His lectures on metaphysics, given in 1825, survive in a student's careful transcription and give an insight into how Scottish philosophy was taught in the South. Henry broadly accepted how the Scottish realists had expounded metaphysical issues, but not un-critically. Like them, he stressed the activity of the mind, described and categorized mental faculties, presumed a demonstrable connection between the internal and the external, and worried about moral and religious implica-tions. However, he was troubled by Reid's insistence that the link between mind and matter was unmediated and instant.

Others in the South were delivering critical disquisitions on Scottish realism. Henry Junius Nott, also at South Carolina College, was using John Abercrombie's *Inquiries Concerning the Intellectual Powers, and the Investiga-tion of Truth* (1820), but with "copious explanations and corrections." George Tucker at the University of Virginia, though he expounded the Edinburgh succession of Reid, Stewart, and Thomas Brown, did so only loosely. Like Henry, Tucker ran over faculty psychology, but he alerted his auditors to the differences between the various Scots and was impatient when their distinc-tions between mental faculties grew too minute. And Tucker coupled discus-sion of the Scottish realists with a consideration of Hobbes, Locke, Condillac, Hume, and Destutt de Tracy, and thereby was expansively drawn to the history of philosophy, a topic that had little interested Henry. In particular, the variations between French and British philosophy were a significant issue for Tucker. In this, he was being faithful to Thomas Brown, who was influ-enced by the physicality of the French school and saw the philosophy of mind as a "physical enquiry," and for this later came to be regarded as a founder of the British school of psychology.[2]

While Henry saw metaphysics as a theodicy, Tucker saw it as a discipline whose purpose was to train young men for society and its intellectual life. Likewise, Tucker was impatient with logic, which had been a preoccupation of Henry's. The former was happier with aesthetics and explored a different kind of physicality from Brown's, by arguing that "physical beauty does exist" and by dwelling sensually on "the clearness and smoothness" of marble in an elegant Grecian building and "the brilliancy of the eyes, the coral of the lips, the transparent polish of the skin" of "female loveliness."[3]

In 1828 Hugh Legaré had agreed with Francis Jeffrey by arguing that it was impossible to make new discoveries "in 'the subjects of our consciousness' (to use Dugald Stewart's phrase for what is vulgarly called, the mind)" and that this fact distinguished philosophy from natural science.[4] In this dispute, Tucker took Stewart's side against Legaré and thought that empiricism had brought progress, even in the philosophy of mind. As evidence of this faith, Tucker undertook a little empirical research himself. In 1836 he went to New York to question the Siamese twins Chang and Eng, since he calculated that here was an unusual opportunity to observe two minds, with a single body and shared experiences.

The instances of Henry and Tucker do not diminish the centrality of Scottish realism to philosophical awareness in the South, but they do suggest that, in some hands, there was leeway in using a tradition, more fractured than Stewart liked to suggest. No doubt, in many colleges the texts were more doggedly expounded. However, whether the Scots were endorsed or criticized, it is tolerably clear than many were discouraged and puzzled by "the incomprehensible jargon of the metaphysicians" and reluctant to get lost in "the mazes of their deceitful labyrinths." What was common sense to Thomas Reid was impenetrable to others, and not infrequently Southerners questioned "the vagaries of learned men" and asked whether there was a point to philosophy.[5]

Robert Henry taught in the same college as Thomas Cooper, though they personified different philosophical schools. Cooper stood for a truculent materialism which "the *Scotch doctors*," as he used dismissively to call them, had been at pains to repudiate. Materialism was a doctrine as ancient as Democritus, but in the eighteenth century it had received a fresh impulse in England from David Hartley's *Observations on Man* (1749) and Cooper's father-in-law, Joseph Priestley. Cooper himself had defended materialism as early as 1787, when he was a member of the Literary and Philosophical Society of Manchester. His argument then had been that there was no evidence for immateriality of mind or anything else, including the soul, that implausible phantasm willed upon the Western imagination as "a spawn of the Oriental or Gnostic and Platonic christians." For Cooper, an idea was "*a motion in the brain, perceived*" pure and simple, with no intermediate processes, and so was but a corporeal thing.[6] None of this need vitiate Christianity or the possibility of an afterlife. One did not need a soul in order to be resurrected, because God could transform dead bodies as easily as living souls.

Cooper studied medicine as a young man and became a chemist, and these materialist disciplines informed his standpoint, which saw mind as matter and claimed physiology and chemistry could explain thought. Understandably, he was drawn to those French philosophers who mingled metaphysics, psychology, and physiology. Pierre Jean Georges Cabanis, Destutt de Tracy, and François Joseph Victor Broussais were among Cooper's guides, and in 1831 he published a translation of Broussais's *On Irritation and Insanity*, subtitled *A Work, Wherein the Relations of the Physical with the Moral Conditions of Man, Are Established on the Basis of Physiological Medicine*. This new work served, however, mostly to update the materialist case which Cooper made during all his life. "No man is qualified to write on metaphysics and the phenomena of intellect, who is not well versed in physiology," was his reiterated opinion. In the early 1820s, unsurprisingly, Cooper was hostile to the Scots for being (by his lights) badly versed in physiology. "I am aware," he sniffed, "of the 'faculties of the mind,' the numberless brood of the Scotch metaphysicians. I cannot and will not condescend to reply to the dreadful nonsense on this subject assumed as true by Dr. Reid and Dr. Beattie, or to the shallow sophisms of Dr. Gregory, or the prolix pages of inanity of Dr. Dugald Stewart, or the ignorant hardihood of assertion of Dr Barclay in this late enquiry." Alone among these, Cooper gave some exemption to Thomas Brown among "his superficial and dogmatic predecessors," for having better views on cause and effect. However, Brown, though "a clear sighted and able metaphysician," was nonetheless "of the Scotch school; whose characteristic is, a dreadful ignorance of all physiological facts."[7]

It had been the contention of the Scots that the premises of materialism destroyed the possibility of morality. Cooper replied that morality was social, not innate. The discernment of right from wrong was learned in the home, school, college, and adult life. Hence the doctrine of the association of ideas, articulated by Locke, was a vital component in the formation of morality, not "the supposed moral sense . . . one of the numerous ontological reveries of the Scotch school of metaphysics." It was, therefore, with curiosity that Cooper monitored the work of Franz Joseph Gall and Johann Caspar Spurzheim, the pioneers of phrenology, because they struck at the heart of these matters. On the whole, Cooper recognized Gall's work for what it was, pioneering work on the brain's physiology. Cooper's long 1828 review of Gall's *Sur les fonctions du cerveau* (1825) was a respectful explication, conceding that much in Gall was new, especially the evidence that the brain was "not one organ" but many, the suggestion that "the divisions of the faculties of the mind usually adopted by metaphysicians . . . are merely abstract terms," and the stress on nature as more important than nurture. Though he had some sympathy with the idea that environment was formative, Cooper nonetheless thought that education could only modify and not create character, and then mostly because experiences changed physiognomy.[8] More ominously, Gall had claimed that brains grew more complex as one proceeded upward from brute creation and this differentiation applied not only as between species, but as between sexes, nations, and individuals. Arguably, Cooper's assent to this line of reasoning helped to underpin his racist writing, which was to be influential on racial theorists like Josiah Nott.

Oddly, the person who was formed by the twin influences of Robert Henry's Scottish realism and Thomas Cooper's materialism was James Henley Thornwell, the Calvinist. As an adolescent, Thornwell had come across Stewart's *Elements*, whole pages of which he had learned by heart. At South Carolina College from 1828, he fell under the influence of both Cooper and Henry, at a time when his religious vocation was as yet unclear and he fancied becoming a man of letters, who might read Jonathan Swift as well as David Hume. Eventually, Thornwell turned against Cooper's infidelity, but the materialism expounded by the old man retained a fierce fascination.

To understand Thornwell's philosophy, it is well to remember that he was a Calvinist because greatly emotional and anxious to find a system of repression. As he was say in 1839, "A truly good man does not eradicate the emotions of the heart—he is not a cold and ice-bound stoic—he feels, he wavers not, he weeps, but stands his ground, he denies himself." This is why Thornwell was insistently lyrical and so liked passionate metaphors, even amid a discourse of stern rigor informed by a contempt for the "flimsy, superficial, trashy," as well as by a dislike for the "cold, barren, and lifeless." With middle age, an awful tenseness of responsibility descended on him, in part because he became persuaded that philosophy was foundational, not only for liberal education in colleges, but because men of mind changed history. This had been so once with Francis Bacon, and in modern times there was still the need for "a class . . . of moral philosophers," among whom Thornwell hoped to be numbered.[9]

Yet Thornwell was a strange Baconian and a stranger Calvinist. In the warfare of science and religion, it had become customary to believe that matter was easy to prove but spirit and God required faith. Thornwell did not find this logic satisfactory. To resolve the dichotomy, he did not go for the option most preferred, which was to make matter and God coequally real. For Thornwell, even matter required faith.

To learn anything, though, Thornwell thought logic indispensable, and, in the ancient dispute between Aristotle and Plato, he stood with the former. Still, he did not overestimate the usages of logic. As he once explained, the eighteenth century had confused logic with metaphysics, when instead logic only supplied "the *instrument* by which we reason, and not the *principles* on which we reason." After all, logic (and the syllogism) were necessarily tauto-logical, so they could not by themselves generate anything new. In this, however, logic worked like other forms of knowledge, even scientific induc-tion itself, because "we cannot form a general principle without induction— nor can we form a syllogism without a general principle," as Aristotle and the schoolmen had known.[10]

On induction, Thornwell was unorthodox. George Campbell in the eigh-teenth century had restated the conventional view that general truths arose from the collation of particularities, that theory rested on facts, and it is familiarly said that it was Sir David Brewster in 1855 who first argued that hypothesis, not fact, was the driving force of scientific progress, and that no one in the United States before Chauncey Wright in the 1860s understood this. However, this had been Thornwell's position, too, before the Civil War, and he probably learned it from Thomas Brown. As Thornwell had put it: "It is indeed very questionable whether induction, without the aid of hypothesis and analogy, ever could lead to the discovery of a new truth."[11]

It had been Francis Bacon who had instigated the modern commitment to the orthodox techniques of induction, so it is unsurprising that Thornwell was not a Baconian for this reason. Rather, he valued Bacon in part for having made possible Descartes, "the father of the true science of the mind," because the philosopher had kept constantly before him the distinction between mind and matter, and had insisted that consciousness afforded the "only certain knowledge of our spiritual nature," however slippery was that knowl-edge. Like Brown, Thornwell believed that investigating the mind involved the same methodology deployed in "all the departments of physical science," because the mind was "certainly a physical entity or natural substance." However, since the mind was used to study the mind, its investigators were disadvantaged and their conclusions refractory. Nonetheless, Thornwell did hazard that recent investigations tended to see the mind as so many discon-nected compounds, its constitution being riddled with "minute and imper-ceptible chasms." Because of this, the proposition that mind was a unity was illusory. "Our thoughts are countless," he said, "[and] the connections among them and the complex or apparently compound results to which these con-nections give rise must be equally numberless."[12]

To argue that knowledge was an invention, the imposition of illusory order upon the disorderly, was Humean. Thornwell did concede that man's limited power to interpret facts consisted only "in understanding the estab-lished order of sequences in nature so as to know with a good degree of certainty what consequents will follow what antecedent." Man dealt only in probabilities, and the premise of cause and effect was only a linguistic convenience. "Mr Hume has unanswerably proved," Thornwell said, ". . . that . . . what we call the power of one event to produce another amounts to nothing more than the statement of our firm conviction that the one will infallibly succeed the other in the order of time." A belief in cause was "an instinctive principle of our nature," not a deduction from hard evidence.[13]

So Hume had been logical to doubt "a great first cause," a God. But, as Thornwell saw it, Hume had mistakenly confounded antecedence with power. Whatever the difficulties humans faced in connecting cause and effect, God did not face them, because God had the power to force connections. For men, however, on their feebler plane a true knowledge of physical reality was impossible. Thornwell's view of this was unusually thoroughgoing, because his sense of the disconnections of nature was so heightened. Many supposed, he said, that "the laws of nature are efficient causes established and ordained by God which bring about, by their imparted efficacy, all the changes which unceasingly take place." This was wrong. "Without his special and constant interposition, the wheels of nature would stand still and all succession be everlastingly arrested." God tended not only to the planets but to "every particle and atom," by way of "sustaining, supporting, and directing the manifold movements of universal being."[14] That is, so disconnected was nature that God's will was needed at every point to hold it together. Man had been given a mind which provided a useful illusion of pattern, while all around him God labored unceasingly to turn chaos into cause and effect, or at least to persuade man that chaos was cause and effect. This was a very dark vision of the human predicament, deployed to celebrate a very energetic vision of the godly predicament.

Thornwell confronted Berkeley and Hume directly, because he did not underestimate the bracing gravity of their challenge, which had jettisoned many "antiquated opinions" and created many new insights, some mistaken, some not. In them, "skepticism had assumed a form which put faith upon the defensive," and they needed answering. Of the various respondents to Hume, Thornwell found the Scottish realists inadequate, for inventing "a peculiar and separate faculty of the mind of which they have given us very contradictory descriptions but which the majority of them agree in calling Common Sense." Not only was this "incapable of being proved," but it leaned toward that gnosticism which overestimated human powers. If God gave common sense to men, then men might think their discernments godly.[15]

Thornwell had other objections to the Scots. Reid had wrongly confounded sense and intelligence, the Scots had revived "the exploded dogma of Des

Cartes in regard to the existence of innate ideas," and they did not see that truth was but another word for faith. This was so, because evidence did not determine belief. As Thornwell put it, "every step in demonstration is nothing but a succession of intuitive perceptions." Hence, however humbling to human reason it might be, "all our intellectual acquirements are ultimately resolvable into faith." In this, Isaac Newton and a child were both forced into being trusting and both were "possibly . . . totally ignorant of the real constitution of substances" in the material world. Like Robert Henry, for Thornwell "the evidence of the existence of mind was much more conclusive than the evidence of the existence of matter, and of the two, the ideal hypothesis of Berkeley does much less violence to our nature than the scheme of materialism."[16]

In his criticism of Scottish realism, Thornwell rejected its emphasis upon faculties, and in this he agreed with Cooper. For Thornwell, the mind was "one and indivisible" and consciousness rapidly ephemeral. Still, there were patterns. There were no faculties, but there were, as Brown had put it, "states of the mind." It was customary to make a division between will and understanding, or between intellectual and active powers (this had been Reid's distinction), but Thornwell found this unsatisfactory, because too static. Though he leaned toward Brown's division of "external affections" (that is, things to do with the physical senses and material experience) and "internal affections," Thornwell was restless when Brown tried to make a Procrustean system out of what was fluid: "The egregious blunders of Hartly should have taught Dr Brown that the minute analysis which would destroy the diversities of our intellectual faculties and refer them all to the operation of a single principle is likely to be only a childish play in ringing the changes on mere words."[17]

So Thornwell's skepticisms ran deep. "Our conceptions," he insisted, "cannot with propriety be said to be either true or false. . . . [They] may be real or imaginary. . . . [T]hey may be the creatures of our fancy or the objects of perception, but the apprehension of them does not involve any judgment except the momentary belief which accompanies."[18] At one point, Thornwell was uncomfortable even with Hume, for leaning too close toward the association of ideas and speaking too loosely of an attraction between them. Thornwell, instead, retreated to Brown's weaker hypothesis that ideas might tend to suggest others.

That Thornwell could be more skeptical than Hume seems odd, but it was not. Even Hume had worried about the implications of his own radicalism and in later years had politely withdrawn from metaphysics to the safer ground of historical writing and political thought, there to talk urbanely as though the fabric of existence was reliably real. Thornwell had less reason to be concerned. He could push skepticism to its limit, because he rested content in the knowledge that he had a coup de théâtre. Yahweh stood in the wings, ready to hold together nature, mind, man, and morality, when the actors forgot their lines or could not remember if they were performing Sophocles or Thomas Otway. That is, believing in the principles of Calvinism made it possible for Thornwell to be Humean. Nonetheless, one should not underestimate the peculiarity of Thornwell's beliefs. Even most Calvinists arrived at their beliefs by a different route and doubted neither God nor reality. Thornwell, to the contrary, came to God because he doubted the reality of both matter and mind, and secular philosophy could prove no logical order in existence. Nothing was left but God, if there was to be order, at all, outside the mind. For Thornwell, faith did not flow from a real man to an indemonstrable God made real by faith. Rather, faith flowed from a real God to man and matter otherwise unreal, disordered, swift, and shadowy. When Thornwell was writing as a theologian, this outflowing from God was to be called grace.

Hence it was easy enough for Thornwell, being so radical, to dismiss as unmeaning an issue (the problem of the will) that had bedeviled American philosophy since at least Jonathan Edwards and interested other Southern intellectuals. The contention that man had a will capable of choosing between right and wrong, and that therefore man had a capacity to discharge or deny his moral responsibilities in God's order, was an issue that ran deep in the old dispute between Calvinism and Arminianism. With too much necessity and too little free will, a moral man became but an automaton, unworthy of praise because merely forced into virtue. With too much free will and too little necessity, God's predestinations were deranged by human whim. But what was will? A faculty of the mind? If so, where did it stand in relationship to understanding or judgment or other faculties so painstakingly described by the Scotch doctors? For Thornwell, these categories were too static. It was implausible that evidence reached the mind and its faculties leisurely took their turn in making their discriminations. No, Thornwell said, everything was mobile, instantaneous, and compounded: "We regard man as inherently a being of motion, and, therefore, we variously denominate that principle or being as soul, spirit, or will. We, therefore, do not consider man as indebted to his mind, or to his reasons, for his motion, (and under motion we include conduct and practices,) but as being moved to action by the resistless hand of nature. He moves because it is the good pleasure of God, his creator, that he shall have power to move." Therefore man had no free agency, which was not to say that Thornwell denied morality or rationality, only that he thought "moral truth and reason [lay] outside of man," who moved spontaneously and, so moving, might move in ways that conformed to the moral order defined by God, or might not.[19]

Others in the South were more traditional in their deliberations on this matter. Someone writing in the *Southern Quarterly Review* in 1847, it is true, after having rehearsed the various definitions of the will given by philosophers from Locke to Cousin, made fun of the will and mocked Jonathan Edwards for his confusing terminology. But this satire was too much for Daniel Whitaker, the periodical's editor, who did not often reprove his own contributors but who instantly tacked on a fierce denunciation of this essay and stood in amazement that anyone could doubt the fact that "the human will [was] a fundamental part of the mental constitution." For, good American that he was, Whitaker saw in necessity an undemocratic thing, since it contradicted freedom: "We are the advocates of moral as well as civil liberty, and the age, including all the metaphysicians, should come up to the defence of this great doctrine, and maintain it as a sensible creed, and an essential element in any sound system of metaphysics, as well as morals and religion."[20]

By Whitaker's lights, Albert Taylor Bledsoe—restlessly itinerant Methodist, mathematician, and Arminian—was doing his best to come up. His blustering *Examination of President Edwards' Inquiry into the Freedom of the Will* (1845) was an anxious defense of human freedom and religious morality. For Bledsoe, Edwards was muddled, tautological, and, while asserting freedom for the will, made it too dependent upon the authority of a "strongest motive" to justify the assertion. Bledsoe's own position was that man was free to choose, it was just that God already knew what man would freely choose. Further, Bledsoe believed that more must be allowed to the will than a responding to motive, that something extra must happen in the mind explicable by the pressure of the external world. To plead that the will was formed by circumstances was to deny freedom. Rather, God had made "a being that acts freely, without labouring under any necessity, either natural or moral, in its accountable and moral agency." It was in a "tri-unity of the sensibility, the intelligence, and the will, that the glory of man's nature, as a free and accountable being, consisted."[21]

Bledsoe little troubled himself with philosophical skepticism. He wrote as though matter and mind were real, if a mystery, but he had a few propositions similar to Thornwell's. First, Bledsoe stressed spontaneity in human action and thought. Second, he concluded that the mind did not really know whether it was free or not, but only inferred freedom. Third, like Thornwell and against Reid, Bledsoe admitted that men were not conscious of their existence, but only of their consciousness asserting existence. Still, very unlike Thornwell but conforming to Whitaker's demand for optimism, Bledsoe did euphorically claim the probability of progress under the auspices of a Baconian modernity which had transcended "the philosophy of antiquity." No one, he said, should imagine "that the great problem of the intellectual system of the universe is not within the reach of the human faculties."[22]

It will have become evident that, for slaveholders in a modern world, the question of consciousness, freedom, and will was unusually pertinent. As individual masters, they were often taught to believe that their will was binding, that to command was to be obeyed. As citizens of the slaveholding South, they were as often told that they were the creatures of necessity, trapped by historical circumstances, their will irrelevant. It is little surprise, therefore, that when they considered the abstract questions of consciousness, reality, and freedom, they did not speak with one voice but veered between Bledsoe's optimism in human freedom, Henry's moderate sense that circumstances constricted a freedom that was real but limited, and Thornwell's bleak sense that man was trapped in a universe disordered but for God's grace. Hegel in the *Phenomenology* had argued that a master, who was only a master, could not be finally free, because his sense of self-consciousness was mediated through another, his slave, whose reality he believed to be "unessential." Only the slave could achieve true knowledge of self, because only through risk and fear, denied to the master by his complacency but inherent for the slave, could that knowledge come. As Hegel put it, "In the master, the bondsman feels self-existence to be something external, an objective fact; in fear self-existence comes to be felt explicitly as his own proper being, and he attains the consciousness that he himself exists in his own right and on his own account."[23]

If it is asked whether the philosophical Southerner believed that there was an objectivity beyond self, let alone within it, the answer is unclear. The Scottish realists commanded the Southerner to believe that bodies and minds could be trusted, and, if the accounts of antebellum American philosophy outside the South are reliable, most Americans gladly followed the command. Philosophical Southerners were troubled, however; their belief in the reality of the world was an effort, and for them the Scotch doctors had not settled the matter. Little occurred more often than their assertion that it was "easier to maintain the non-existence of matter than the non-existence of mind." Even for Bledsoe, mind was a mystery. For Thornwell, mind was a mystery that moved blindly and only blundered into morality by chance, and this was not a bad description, not of slavery as it was defended, but of slavery as it was experienced.

DISSATISFACTION WITH SCOTTISH realism led to a search for other options. One might expect that utilitarianism would have had its adherents, but Jeremy Bentham found very few sympathizers. Hugh Legaré's 1831 essay on "Jeremy Bentham and the Utilitarians," for example, was typical in being dismissive. In Legaré's view, Bentham had been right when unoriginal, wrong when distinctive, and often incoherent. Nothing in the doctrine of utility was new, it being little more than warmed over Epicureanism. Mathematical calculations about social behavior based upon logarithms of self-love misunderstood not only human nature but even expediency, which necessarily embraced the rational and irrational. Bentham had morality backward: "True philosophy . . . is studious to inculcate not that whatever is expedient is right—but that whatever is right is expedient." For Legaré, both pleasure and pain were intrinsic to human nature, as well as poetry, "the imagination and the heart."[24]

It was habitual to make fun of Bentham's prose. Thomas Cooper, the nearest thing to a utilitarian that Southern culture had, though he sympathized with Bentham's assault upon the common law, religious skepticism, and wish to simplify the law, nonetheless despaired at "the obscure, involuted, Benthamee dialect" and often "found only common-place notions arranged with pompous, needless accuracy." To this objection was added the widespread belief that utilitarianism was the philosophy for a commercial age inexcusably turning away from liberal education toward "exclusive professional attainments." And, of course, no one who thought that morality had to be Christian could be patient with Bentham, especially when he contended that selfishness was creative. These objections taken together explain the resistance to utilitarianism in the South, where it was hard to find agnostic, commercially minded, unpoetical proponents of rationalist expediency who were indifferent to mangled prose.[25]

Southerners knew there were philosophical options beyond Britain. Philosophy was an international discourse with national emphases, in which Germans were aware of Scots, the French were influenced by Germans, and Americans were conscious of these interpenetrations. Victor Cousin strove to reconcile the valid insights of all these traditions into a happy eclecticism, especially in trying to make common sense lie down with transcendentalism. Few were persuaded, and most presumed it was necessary to choose. Of the various alternatives, the French offered the more relaxing option, because they turned philosophy away from the problem of mind toward principles of social action. The Germans pushed deeper into the mind, though in troubling ways. In these matters, chronologically the Germans preceded the French and significantly predicated their philosophy, so one must begin with the Southern reaction to Kantian and post-Kantian German philosophy, or else one cannot understand why some Southerners turned to Paris.

In the 1820s, Kant was little more than a name in the South or anywhere in the United States. In 1828 Legaré was typical in speaking of the "cloudy transcendentalism of the German school" and in acquiring his scant knowledge through the medium of Coleridge's *Biographia Literaria*, though unusual in hinting cannily that Kant was the wave of the philosophical future. Likewise, Robert Henry, though he read German and tried to study Kant, thought of him as Dugald Stewart did, dismissively. "As to Kant's successors," Thornwell was later to recall, "we do not believe that Dr. Henry could ever be induced to read a line of their writings." In 1829 Stephen Elliott knew enough to discern that Henry Dwight's views of German "schools of philosophy" were "defective," but he was skittish about venturing more: "We are willing at present to leave the philosophy of Fichte, Schelling and Kant, to a future day, and to more profound and more thoroughly initiate adepts."[26] These adepts eventually appeared, even though German philosophy reached the South in unsystematic ways.

One way lay through James Marsh, who usually lived in and influenced New England culture but who between 1823 and 1826 taught at Hampden-Sydney College, where Jesse Burton Harrison was an undergraduate. It is tolerably clear that Marsh encouraged in Harrison a sense of the importance of Coleridge (Washington Allston's friend) and, beyond him, of the Germans, which was one reason Harrison went to study in Germany. While in Berlin in 1830, Harrison came to know something of Hegel's as yet unpublished lectures on the philosophy of history, through either attending them or hearing them discussed. In Harrison's 1832 essay for Legaré and the *Southern Review* on "English Civilization" is a sentence that reads, "The philosophical mind of Hegel has divided the past history of civilization into four Missions, the Oriental, the Greek, the Roman, and the Teutonic." Harrison was the first American to mention Hegel's name in print, appropriately so in an essay that repudiated British empiricism and claimed Baconianism was not enough, in part with arguments and quotations from Coleridge, "*plus Allemand que les Allemands.*" Some of Harrison's objections were aesthetic, some social. The English too little valued "the ideal" and were too Burkean, so they privileged inherited prejudice over abstract truth. Instead of being influenced by Stewart's disregard for the Germans, Harrison was influenced by Friedrich von Schlegel's contempt for Scottish philosophy, which was (as Harrison paraphrased Schlegel) "a paltry, mechanical art, rather than a science." However, Harrison was clearer on what was wrong with the British school than he was on what was right with the Germans, except in indicating that they were right not to turn away from the pursuit of, in Coleridge's words, "the science of ultimate truths" and in agreeing that there was a domain of reason which empiricism could not comprehend.[27]

During the 1830s, knowledge of German philosophy grew. Francis Lieber brought some command of the subject, and later he was to put a bust of Kant in his Columbia lecture room. The Prussian's *Manual of Political Ethics* (1838) contained several flattering and a few critical references to Kant, and the book's subject matter, the ethical relationship between the individual and the state, lay squarely within the preoccupations of the German philosophical tradition. To be sure, Lieber more commonly referred to Hobbes, Harrington, Locke, and Hume (as a political thinker) than to Fichte, Schelling, and Hegel. Nonetheless, Lieber was willing to argue that there needed to be a middle ground between English utilitarianism and German idealism, if there was to be an "instauration of philosophy," and he encouraged an awareness (if not an advocacy) of German philosophy.[28] It was no accident that Thornwell, who uncomfortably shared a campus with Lieber, and James Warley Miles, who studied with Lieber, sharpened their enquiries into German philosophy during the 1840s and 1850s, at the moment that George Frederick Holmes did likewise. Of these three, the spectrum from the least to the most Germanic ran from Holmes to Thornwell to Miles, and one is inclined to put Lieber somewhere after Holmes, but before even the later Thornwell.

By the mid-1840s, references to German philosophy had become commonplace. Then Southerners had access to many English translations, scholarly histories, and epitomes. In 1847 a discussion of American literature, even a book review of writers as homespun as Rufus Griswold and Alexander Beaufort Meek, was thought to require a disquisition on Kant and Hegel, Jacobi and Fichte, if with the intention of protecting the mind of "the young student . . . against the dangerous reasonings and conclusions, with which this philosophy abounds." Most undergraduates were little tempted. As one put it, "I [have] adopted a sure expedient for not getting my brains utterly bewildered when reading the incomprehensible jargon of the metaphysicians— and that [is] to get quietly down on my hands and knees and crawl along through all the mazes of their deceitful labyrinths, touching sure Mother Earth all the while. As long as one gropes thus, there is something to hold on by, but let him try to walk on his two feet only, and some will-o'-the-wisps, the Hegels and Schellings and Kants, the Berkeleys and Bolingbrokes and Humes, will infallibly lead him into mires and gins and pitfalls."[29]

A new interest in German philosophy came from three sources. First, theologians were concerned with the higher criticism of the Bible, which posed a pantheist and agnostic challenge to Revelation, and turning back this challenge mandated an engagement with the Germans, who were brought to life by the refutation. Second, Coleridge had been succeeded by Thomas Carlyle, whose *Sartor Resartus* influentially offered an eccentric tour through the issues of German transcendentalism. Third, New England developed an indigenous American version of transcendentalism, and many Southerners kept a wary, even sometimes sympathetic, eye on intellectual developments to the North.

Thornwell and Miles represented the two poles of those who seriously engaged German philosophy, the former polemically negative, the latter elegantly appreciative. More Southerners agreed with Thornwell than Miles, though seldom with the former's subtle rigor. Typical was an essay in the *Southern Presbyterian Review* for 1850 which enumerated "objections to the German Transcendental Philosophy." These shortcomings were very numerous, including the encouragement of religious skepticism, pantheism, and vaunting pride. The reviewer quoted from Fichte, as though the quotation itself showed the quintessential folly of German metaphysics: "There is absolutely nothing permanent, either without me, or within me, but only an unceasing change. I know absolutely nothing of any existence, not even my own. . . . *Images* there are. . . . I am myself one of these images; nay, I am not even so much, but only a confused image of images."[30] This was a problem because the philosophy of the Scotch doctors had been static. Mental faculties were elements in human nature, and they did not change over time. A sense of the formative power of historical flux, however, was intrinsic to German philosophy, though even the Germans tried to find a consoling still point. Most Southerners preferred to look elsewhere for their still points, even if a Calvinist God could prove as hard to fix as a Hegelian Absolute. Still, not everyone found "unceasing change" repellent, and a few came to the view that "movement is the great law of the universe."[31]

George Frederick Holmes, for one, accepted that change was ineluctable. As a young man impatient with metaphysics and psychology, he had been uninterested in either Hume or Reid and had felt that such old ideas had worn out. Instead, Holmes was drawn to historicism, precisely because he saw himself as living through a period of change, when societies were being transformed, church and state assaulted, science challenged, and literature renewed. In time, Holmes came to incline toward those active on the side of the future, especially to Jules Michelet and Auguste Comte, and he concluded that the Germans were too conservative socially, however radical their epistemologies. Holmes was drawn to synthesis, to bringing together what was otherwise fragmentary into organic wholes. By itself, this instinct did not foreclose the German philosophical tradition, for who was more committed to the love and pursuit of the Absolute than the Germans? For this reason, Holmes gave them a try, and, during the early and mid-1840s, he looked at Johann von Herder, Friedrich von Schlegel, and German classical scholarship, but found them wanting. They seemed too aware of the elements of synthesis, too insistent on the dialectic, too mobile. Holmes wanted something cleaner, freer of doubt. But between "the timid range of Scotch empiricism" and "the arrogant and blighting pretensions of German transcendentalists," where was one to look?[32] To evade disbelieving in empiricism (which could sanction mysticisms indifferent to evidence) and evade dismissing the human capacity for error (which could lead to an overconfident positivism), where was one to turn?

On the whole, to France, though not to Victor Cousin and eclecticism, which Holmes dismissed as an "*olla podrida* (which is not Philosophy)" and thought worthwhile only for its encouragement of the history of philosophy and incitement to read original texts. Nonetheless, as Holmes saw it, "the History of Philosophy is not Philosophy itself." In particular, Holmes was anxious to find a body of philosophy not too metaphysical and capable of reconciling science and religion. He did not presume this reconciliation would be easy, because he was conscious that his times had changed both sides of the equation. Nor did he presume that traditional religion would necessarily survive such a reconsideration. Holmes always wrote with a sense that, if he could not honestly demonstrate the cogency of Christianity, he would forego it, but that he had a duty to "strain every nerve to establish that reconciliation between religion and philosophy which has been asserted to be impossible."[33]

This duty explained Holmes's passionate interest in Auguste Comte. Rightly Holmes saw the earlier Comte, the author of the *Cours de philosophie positive* (1830–42), as a scientific systematizer, a maker of patterns, a classifier of the hierarchies of human knowledge, all roles with which Holmes was sympathetic. At first, Holmes regarded Comte as the preeminent philosopher of the age, a thinker of immense range and capacity for synthesis, who might help to change that "universal spirit of resistance to all authority," which was leading to "anarchy, political, social, and religious." Synthesis and system were necessary, because of "the universal distemperature of the times, which threatens to convert the human family into a pandemonium upon earth" and disordered intellect itself.[34]

Although Holmes thus honored Comte, the former criticized the details of positivism so extensively that it can be hard to see why he honored Comte, who was in no doubt that Holmes was "an adversary." That Holmes was taken aback by this accusation and saw criticism as mere suggestiveness is evidence of his unworldly inability to see that many medium-sized criticisms had a way of adding up to repudiation. Holmes, for example, though he was impressed with Comte's attempt to describe how the theological, metaphysical, and positivist systems had evolved historically to form a new science of sociology, was unsure that one system died utterly when another was born, but suspected that much survived. Likewise, though Holmes was attracted to Comte because the latter promised synthesis, Holmes could not eradicate a skeptical sense that the synthesis arose not because there was order in the world but because men needed it; it came "from the almost hopeless incapacity of the human mind to contemplate in their coexistence and interdependence the complex multiplicity of natural phenomena, whence men are driven to seek for a delusive simplicity by a necessary exclusion of those data which refuse to be systematized." Moreover, while Comte was passionately antitheist, Holmes was insistent that man needed religion. While Comte relegated metaphysics and logic to the intellectual childhood of man and thought that they might be pertinent only at moments of intellectual crisis and transition, Holmes believed that metaphysics, being indispensable to theology, was persistently relevant to human needs. While Comte thought that metaphysics had been stagnant since ancient times, Holmes saw modest progress. While Comte put his faith in mathematics as the queen science with the greatest access to "absolute, eternal, infinite, and immutable truth," Holmes saw no reason why mathematics escaped that familiar problem, the inability of the mind "to go out of itself."[35]

What Holmes did admire in Comte were "wider, and healthier views of science," his arrangement of the human and natural sciences (especially his elaboration of sociology or "social physics"), "the application of the historical method to the philosophy of society," and "criticism of the speculative and practical errors of the times."[36] Being convinced of the necessity for an *instauratio nova* for intellect to meet the crisis of the times, Holmes had looked over the candidates for the new Bacon and found them all wanting. Comte, too, narrowly missed being Bacon, but he seemed the best candidate. Less formally and less philosophically, Holmes was drawn to Comte by a sort of aesthetic pleasure. Symmetry, compactness, boldness, ambition, insouciance, these qualities in Comte had an almost sensual attraction for Holmes, the myopic, awkward, isolated, discursive rusticant in western Virginia. Comte was what Holmes was not, as well as possessing a purification of qualities Holmes possessed in lesser measure: learning, ponderous strength, sincerity, simplicity, a subtle mind of critical power.

Soon after developing these views in the early 1850s, Holmes abandoned Comte. In the *Systéme de politique positive* (1851–54), the latter elaborated a humanist replacement for Christianity, which should have a new calendar, a pantheon of intellectual saints, and rituals of social sacraments. For this "revolting travesty of the Christian faith" Holmes thought only ridicule and contempt appropriate.[37] This gnostic debacle had turned Comte's narrow miss of being the new Bacon into a grotesque pretension. Holmes's revulsion was, no doubt, assisted by a correspondence with Comte, which showed the old man to be prickly, vain, and condescending.

Thus disappointed, Holmes turned in two directions for a solution to the crisis of his times: Aristotle and Roman Catholicism. To Thornwell he said in 1856, "The more I study Aristotle, the less necessity do I discover for any other philosophy than modernized and Christianized Peripateticism. Aristotle is still, as in the Thirteenth Century, 'il maestro di che chi sanno.'" Thereby, with Fitzhugh, Holmes became one of the first intellectual Southerners to take this step, not because they had a deep belief in God, but because Catholicism offered a refuge from a disorientating modernity. For Holmes, as for Allen Tate in the 1930s, Protestantism was too gnostic, introspective, and individualistic. Both wanted a structure that was communal and traditional. Nonetheless, Holmes's turn to Rome was a backhanded compliment to Comte, who had suggested in a letter that "in the middle of the nineteenth century, the only mode of renovating society—of regenerating the sentiments, of removing the anarchy of the intellect—which [I] can discover, is the revival of a spiritual despotism more crushing, more exclusive, and more arbitrary, than anything the world has yet seen." Comte's own proposed priesthood was, as Holmes thought, but "an expanded and thinly disguised resuscitation of the Roman hierarchy."[38] Why bother with imitations? If one had a taste for system, why not Thomas Aquinas, whom Holmes began to study just after Comte had failed him? As we shall see, James Henley Thornwell knew why not, or thought he knew.

THE SOUTHERN RELIGIOUS scene was complex, with as many faiths as there were peoples, as many theologies as there were individuals. Native Americans had a myriad of religions, some Christian, some not. Black religion was fractured between varieties of Protestantism, Roman Catholicism, Islam, and various beliefs brought from Africa or invented in America. The Jews were divided between Sephardic, Ashkenazim, and Reformed. The Shakers had two communities in Kentucky, and the Moravians controlled Salem, North Carolina. The Roman Catholics were in theory unified, but in practice the French Catholics, the Irish Catholics, and the German Catholics treated one another with suspicion. White Protestants were dizzyingly denominational and growing more so. To the older sects which had migrated from Reformation Europe (Anglicans, Presbyterians, Lutherans) had been added those invented subsequently (Quakers, Methodists, Baptists) and those born of recent schism (Unitarians, the Church of Christ, Cumberland Presbyterians, Republican Methodists, Hardshell Baptists, African Methodist Episcopalians, Landmark Baptists, Stoneites, Primitive Baptists).

Then there were those who experimented with beliefs which the orthodox found heretic. All Christians granted a spirit world, but many skeptics of Christianity began to think that ghostly forms inhabited a realm beyond that described by the Bible and John Milton. James Henry Hammond and William Gilmore Simms both took up Spiritualism, and the latter went to a medium in New York to interrogate the dead with questions which he and his friend had drafted. Hammond, in particular, was dismissive of Christianity as resting "on fear of the Devil & hatred of all who differ from us" and ridiculed "the Divine pretensions of the Bible," while seeing some value in its disciplining of the masses.[39] In addition, there was the New Church, which had been born in Sweden in a Calvinist culture and was, in many ways, Protestantism suddenly grown optimistic and imaginative. It had an especial appeal for restless Presbyterians, so it is not surprising that the South had its share of Swedenborgians.

This religious diversity is too extensive to narrate here, but a look at four traditions (Jewish, Roman Catholic, Episcopalian, Presbyterian) will indicate a range, however inadequately. These, in turn, are narrowed to four intellectuals (Isaac Harby, John England, James Warley Miles, and James Henley Thornwell). In fact, the range will seem still narrower, because these all inhabited South Carolina. This restriction is deliberate. Religious diversity was a local thing; each Southern space echoed with different voices, with broken conversations about God, with insistent hostilities and the occasional ecumenical gesture.

In 1820 Charleston had the largest group of Jews in North America. The community was an old one, complicated and enriched by ethnicity. There had been two synagogues in the mid-eighteenth century, one for the Portuguese, another for the Germans. This schism had healed by 1794, when a new and united synagogue was built. Tensions remained, however, and these revolved around the divisions of the Old World, as they interacted with the difficulties and promises of assimilation to the American, English-speaking world. What was to happen in Cincinnati and New York later in the century happened first in Charleston. In 1824 the first American congregation of reformed Judaism, the Reformed Society of Israelites, was established there. The reformers mostly wished to change the liturgy (more brevity, the use of English, having sermons) and to encourage missionary endeavor among lapsed Jews. They were conscious of the precedent of Moses Mendelssohn, the German Jewish philosophe who had translated the Torah into High German, urged Jews to leave the ghetto, and counseled the seizure of "the magnificent opportunity of entering the world of western culture."[40]

Curiously, conservatives and reformers alike presumed the benignity of Southern culture, and there were some grounds for this trust. There was no ghetto in Charleston and no civil disabilities in South Carolina, at all. By 1787, in the United States as a whole, only New York and Virginia had granted full emancipation, but by 1800 in the South, Virginia had been joined by Georgia, South Carolina, and Delaware. In 1826, after a campaign lasting eight years, Maryland (which had long permitted Jews to vote) permitted them to hold political office, serve on juries, and join the militia as officers. (Atheists were less favored.) The new states to the west all gave Jews full civil rights by 1840, usually in their first constitutions. By then, only North Carolina did not grant civil equality, and it would not do so until 1868, though efforts were made in the 1850s. In practice, however, Jews could be elected to office, because almost no one cared to enforce the exclusion. In this, the Jewish case in North Carolina was similar to that of Roman Catholics, who had gained legal equality only in 1835 but had served before then, by a nod and a wink.

Anti-Semitism was scarcely unknown—as Jesse Burton Harrison put it, "a Jew is *toutes choses egales* a filthy brute"—and mostly functioned as a variety of ethnic prejudice.[41] It was relatively absent from Southern racist theory, and Josiah Nott, for one, followed Gobineau, whom he helped to introduce to American culture, in a respect for Jewish culture. There seems to have been a working distinction (familiar in other cultures) that, while Jews in general might be suspect, particular Jews were acceptable. Significantly, aggressive expressions of anti-Semitism were most often elicited in Europe, where travelers encountered large numbers of Jews wearing traditional clothing and speaking Yiddish. In the South, Jews were few and unintimidating, they dressed like everyone else, they conformed to local customs and civic beliefs. They might slip into synagogues on a Saturday, but the synagogues looked remarkably like Episcopalian churches, and thereby Jews posed a modest challenge to Southern toleration.

Because of this, antebellum Southern Jews seldom complained of discrimination, and their contentment may have been sincere. In 1815 Rachel Mordecai of Warrenton, North Carolina, sat down with nervous temerity to write a letter to Maria Edgeworth, the Irish novelist. In 1812 Edgeworth had published *The Absentee*, which Rachel had disliked, because therein a Jewish character had been portrayed so as to confirm the prejudice that Jews were "by nature mean, avaricious, and unprincipled." Perhaps, Mordecai ventured, in some parts of the world, the combination of oppression and scorn created such men, but "in this happy country, where religious distinctions are scarcely known . . . we find the Jews form a respectable part of the community." Mordecai herself lived in a small American village, and "all her juvenile friendships and attachments have been formed with those of persuasions different from her own; yet each has looked upon the variations of the other as things of course—differences which take place in every society."[42] Edgeworth was impressed by this and promised reform, whereupon a remarkable correspondence ensued. In all this, Mordecai had a sense of ease in Southern society and displayed a sense of community with the Enlightened spirit of the improving Miss Edgeworth. A similar spirit can be found in the writings of Isaac Harby, the gadfly of letters who struggled to reform the Old World tenacities of Charleston's synagogue.

Mordecai's father, Jacob, thought that Harby was too little a Jew to have earned the right to reform Judaism. There is something to the criticism. Harby was an assimilated American before he was a Jewish reformer, a man whose informal education had been secular. He was the very model of a young Charlestonian philosophe, and, if his surviving library is a guide, his reading had been eclectic: classics like Aeschylus and Horace; poets and dramatists like Tasso, Milton, and Wordsworth; philosophers like Berkeley, Stewart, and Bentham; philosophes like Rollin, Lavater, and Voltaire. By contrast, he owned few books of Jewish provenance and most of his knowledge of ancient Judaism came from Gentile sources.

Harby's views were typical of the liberal Enlightenment, as it began to wander into the more emotional landscapes of Romanticism; that is, he spoke the language of reason with passionate urgency. He mistrusted priests and superstition, believed in science and progress, had faith in the New World, felt that there was value in vernacular languages, desired toleration, and trusted the natural. "If we slight the language of the heart, and oppose to its dictates the cold and backward exertions of reason," he wrote in 1806, "we will soon [lose] sight of truth & nature, and be ruled by arbitrary decisions, and methodical frailty. *Where we begin to reason, we cease to feel, is an observation of Rousseau, which is as firmly grounded in truth, as its belief leads to virtue and happiness.*"[43] His most famous effort, the "Discourse before the Reformed Society of Israelites" in 1825, bears the marks of all of these beliefs.

Language was crucial to Harby, because he believed that Judaism could only flourish by a coupling of the antiquity of Hebrew with the modernity of English, at least for Jews in an English-speaking culture. Words narrated meaning, and meaning needed to be clear. Time had darkened the faith, so reason must bring light. In the spirit of Voltaire, Harby especially reprobated the rabbis who had shut themselves away from the light and spread darkness, the "men, who nursed and fed in the lap of idleness like the monks of the middle ages, converted into mystery and absurdity what God intended his people should plainly read and rationally understand, and practically follow." (From this indictment, Harby exempted only Maimonides, who worked with his own vernacular, Arabic.) From this "Egyptian darkness" had emerged Jewish bringers of light like Baruch Spinoza, Moses Mendelssohn, and Isaac D'Israeli. In the Zion that was the United States, rabbis might enjoy the light of reason. A biblical land of "flocks and herds, of waters and fruitfulness, of plenty and of exceeding excellence" was not now to be found beside a Dead Sea but in that "portion of God's beautiful creation, more favoured by nature," America. So Harby talked of Charleston as *"home,"* praised Gentiles, blamed Jews, wanted to use English as the means of enlightenment, desired to mingle and remain.[44]

In the South, mingling and assimilation often meant the ownership of slaves. Slavery was a bond, connecting ancient Israel and modern America. Christian thinkers ransacked Harby's "sacred record" for usable evidence and Southern Jews welcomed this proof of their relevance. Reform or Orthodox made no difference. Shoeless Bill Simmons, a slave who delivered newspapers in battered evening clothes, slipped into the synagogue on Yom Kippur and claimed to be a Rechabite, but he could not be a member, since this was forbidden to "people of color" by the constitution of Beth Elohim.[45] In 1830, 83 percent of Jewish households in Charleston had slaves, which was barely below the average for everyone else. The case was little different for the Jewish communities of Richmond and New Orleans. Slavery was part of the meaning of belonging, part of the content of *home.*

Curiously, the opportunity to belong came more readily to the Jew than the Roman Catholic. John England, bishop of Charleston, moved with less ease in a Southern world than did Isaac Harby. Anti-Catholicism ran deeper, was more habitual than even anti-Semitism, and mattered to far more people, since anti-Catholicism was in the marrow of the cultural tradition that Britain had bequeathed to the United States and its South. The bishop was familiar with such hostility, because he had experienced the same thing in the Ireland in which he had been born, where Catholics had been civilly disabled. And he came to know it in the New World, too, where they were citizens only barely tolerated.

He was a *wunderkind*, bishop in 1820 at only thirty-four and a bold choice when Rome went looking for an incumbent for the newly created, impecunious, and faction-ridden diocese of Charleston, whose scope was the states of North Carolina, South Carolina, and Georgia. The larger American church was in a very great minority and in 1800 had but fifty priests, its hierarchy being divided between those of "native" birth, those connected to the worlds of Canada and Louisiana, whose priests came from France, and those newly arriving from Ireland. So John England, guardian of an ancient and vast tradition, came to Charleston as an odd intruder into a wealthy Protestant world, wherein he had few priests, no nuns, no seminary, no parish schools, and no organs of publicity. Gradually he pieced together the foundations of a Roman Catholic establishment, partly with subventions from Catholic charities in Europe, partly from his own efforts, for England was young, eloquent, and headstrong ("a turbulent fellow . . . who carries his manner with a high hand," as one Charlestonian observed).[46] By the time of his death in 1842, England had more than bankrupted the diocese by his initiatives. As a publicist, however, he had been preeminent. He wrote well and often in his own journal, the *United States Catholic Miscellany*, which from 1822 issued weekly from Charleston and made itself the country's leading Catholic publication. It was to last until the Civil War and arguably was the most stable periodical in the South.

From John England's standpoint, the difference between North and South was not crucial. The Methodist, the Presbyterian, the Bostonian, and the Charlestonian concurred in abominating the Papist. There was the same depressing round of vilification and self-congratulatory reasoning everywhere he looked. The difference between Italy and the United States, however, was all his world. This was so physically, as well as ideologically, because he constantly traveled back and forth. The Vatican did not concern itself with the niceties of the Mason-Dixon line, which it showed abundantly when in 1833 Gregory XIV made England his apostolic delegate extraordinary to Haiti, with little regard to the resonance of the word "Haiti" to England's Charlestonian parishioners and neighbors.

The Catholic Church had been dealing with the issue of slavery since St. Peter had come to Rome and had been developing policies in the New World since Columbus. From the standpoint of the Vatican, the arguments between William Lloyd Garrison and Thomas Dew, let alone the disputes between Frederick Douglass and Thomas Smyth, were but squabbles among heretics, which scarcely impinged upon the majesty of dogma. It was more important to John England to stand in a right relationship to his church than to his neighbors, though he tried to please both. In 1840, for example, the pope issued an apostolic letter on slavery, which some read as a condemnation and so an embarrassment to Catholics in slaveholding states. The apostolic letter had, in fact, condemned not slavery but the slave trade, so it was easy enough for England to show that, in this, the pope's letter did no more than the Constitution of the United States. The Vatican, in South America and elsewhere, numbered many slaveholders among the faithful and, as England patiently explained, a papal edict condemning slavery would have necessitated the withdrawal of communion from these, which was not something that the Vatican or the archbishop of Baltimore or the bishops of Charleston, Mobile, New Orleans, Bardstown, Nashville, and St. Louis had any interest in doing. Equally, it was easy though laborious for England, like his Protestant contemporaries, to demonstrate that slavery had been a biblical institution, entailed by God upon man for his sins. To add to this scriptural evidence, he had to hand a battery of Church Fathers, popes, councils, canon lawyers, Catholic historians, saints, and bishops, who had spoken and legislated upon the subject. Abraham, Christ, Paul, Augustine, Gregory the Great, Thomas Aquinas, all were brought in evidence to prove that slavery and natural law, slavery and God's dispensation, had been compatible since the Fall, and to argue that Christianity had worked to ameliorate the institution. Such ancient precedent was useful, partly because it deflected attention away from the present. But John England could not evade everything contemporary with his erudition. He had to say a few words about modern circumstances, albeit evasively: "I have been asked by many, a question which I may as well answer at once, viz.: Whether I am friendly to the existence or continuation of slavery? I am not—but I also see the impossibility of now abolishing it here. When it can and ought to be abolished, is a question for the legislature and not for me."[47] This, too, had ancient precedent. Render unto Caesar the things that were Caesar's.

John England was an indefatigable controversialist, even within his own church. Many of his contacts with the culture beyond his flock were adversarial, though he seems to have made some connection to Southern intellectual culture. He published an essay in the *Southern Review* in 1828 and another later on Vergil in the *Southern Literary Journal*, and delivered two addresses to the Literary and Philosophical Society of South Carolina, of which he was a member, as well as sundry orations to various Southern institutions. Still, he was surrounded by hostility, and this seems to have told on the bishop, as did the strain of traveling to Haiti, Ireland, France, Austria, and Rome, then back to Charleston. He grew inattentive to diocesan matters, more isolated when in the city, older faster than his years. The incessant pressure of controversy, of justification and explanation, engendered bitterness and alienation.

The bishop was a theologian, and this did not help him, because religious people in the South were suspicious of theologians. In this, they did not differ from other Americans and Europeans. Many in eighteenth-century England had been doubtful about the value of teaching theology to undergraduates, because too much thought and learning might confuse that simpler belief which vicars needed to be effective pastors in their country parishes. Some denominations in the South, especially the Baptists, had long been anti-intellectual and had spoken against "the learned gentry of the day, who swarm out of the theological institutions like locusts, and are ready to devour the land."[48] Revivalism had been inattentive to the life of the mind, but, rather, had massaged the emotions of fear and hope, anxiety and catharsis. Yet even the simplest backcountry preacher had been the prisoner of some defunct theologian, whether it was Augustine, Calvin, or Wesley. And revivalism was never as important to Southern religion as many thought, though it had jarred complacencies, briefly challenged conservatisms, and drawn fascinated voyeurs like Frances Trollope, who saw it as sexual theater and democratic frenzy. Revivalism was to dwindle (save as a formalized ritual) as the nineteenth century went on, cities grew, churches were built, schools were founded, bank accounts were opened, and property was acquired.

When once-marginal preachers became well-paid men whose views mattered on public issues, intellectual sophistication (in uneasy alliance with emotional force) came to seem more desirable. Sites of learning and discourse proliferated. Periodicals grew legion: the *Virginia Evangelical and Literary Magazine* (1818), the *Protestant Episcopal Pulpit* (1835), the *Southern Baptist Preacher* (1839), the *Quarterly Review* of the Methodist Episcopal Church, South (1846), the *Southern Presbyterian Review* (1847), these were just a few among many, growing to be more. Seminaries and church-sponsored colleges were founded: for Episcopalians, the University of the South at Sewanee (1857); for Presbyterians, the Columbia Theological Seminary (1828); for Methodists, Randolph-Macon (1830); for Baptists, the Furman Institution (1826); these and many, many more. Further, state institutions like South Carolina College came increasingly under religious influence, though cautiously, for denominations had to be balanced against one another.

Among those who administered and taught in these institutions there was ambivalence about theology. Jefferson had banned divinity from the University of Virginia, because he regarded the sects as wrangling and ambitious, but this exclusion was accepted even by the pious. In 1853 Thornwell presumed that sectarianism had to be shut away from public education and that it was wise to "leave creeds and confessions to the fireside and church, the home and the pulpit." Rather, colleges should have "godly teachers," the "spirit of religion," not its dogma.[49]

Nonetheless, theology was a Southern preoccupation, even an export trade. At Princeton, Virginia's Archibald Alexander was from 1812 to his death in 1851 the leading figure in the nation's dominant Presbyterian seminary. Within the South itself, works of theology found ready publication and a market, though the intellectual sophistication of such texts tended to be in inverse proportion to the popularity of a theologian's denomination. In numbers of adherents, from high to low, the sequence ran Baptists, Methodists, Presbyterians, and Episcopalians. From most to least complex in dogma, it ran Presbyterian, Episcopalian, Methodist, and Baptist. So, an intellectual history will best be served by a look at the Presbyterians and Episcopalians. James Henley Thornwell was the former's most sophisticated thinker, as well its most influential churchman: in the South almost everyone agreed on this at the time, and posterity has not changed this opinion. Among the Episcopalians, preeminence is less clear, but James Warley Miles, though insignificant in the ecclesiastical hierarchy, was their most advanced thinker.

There is no record of Thornwell's opinion of Miles, though it is unlikely to have been flattering. Like most people, Miles regarded Thornwell with a mix of admiration, fear, and mistrust. Their differences were profound, wider than the distinction between Calvinist and theological liberal. Thornwell was polemical and sectarian, while Miles aspired to a gentle ecumenism. Thornwell did not like to stray too far from his theological and philosophical interests, while Miles was a theologian, essayist, philologist, social theorist, literary critic, and poet. Thornwell was a patriarch and a career man, bent on rising, while Miles drifted from job to bankruptcy and back again, and was a lonely and depressed bachelor who wrote overwrought letters to married ladies and languished in a Pre-Raphaelite gloom. Thornwell was a pedagogue who wanted to mold minds and be admired for it, while Miles recoiled from influence. In his own way, however, Miles was the bolder spirit, if the weaker temperament. It is hard to imagine Thornwell going as a missionary to the Near East or spending two years in Berlin to clarify mind and spirit, as Miles did.

James Warley Miles felt himself to be inadequate, expected little but the worst, and elicited kindness. Sometimes he drifted close to madness, especially in his darkest days during the early 1850s. Often he dwelled on being alone, poor, dependent, and weak. In Charleston, he called himself "a sort of tolerated shadow . . . a stranger and foreigner," to whom "the city and its doings have . . . a sort of mythical vagueness." He had the usual Romantic theory about the value of this deprivation and the sense that being persecuted evidenced virtue. Like his near-contemporary William Henry Trescot, Miles thought struggle and antagonism necessary: "Progress can only be achieved through contest and successive conquest of error and opposition." He even flirted with Comtean vanities in the late 1850s, when he prophesied that most current orthodoxies would "in a future age, be exhumed from libraries as literary fossil remains," while independent thinkers would "no longer, as now, be isolated, but will as a class constitute a ruling power in the world."[50]

Why this Keatsian melancholy, the mood he called "The Dark Hour"? He had physical difficulties: his eyes could be bad, he slept badly, and he worked late. No doubt he had unrealistic hopes and standards, even a slight touch of paranoia. He disliked the rote of the weekly sermon because he wanted inspiration, which did not come on schedule. He had Platonic hopes for friendship, so he found the ordinary fallibilities and hypocrisies of society unsatisfying, even repulsive. But there seems to have been a deeper wound, to which he could not or would not give a name. He wrote of "the secret chambers of my soul, [where] there is a darkness . . . into which I dread to look."[51]

When young, Miles was influenced by the Oxford Movement, though in 1843 he renounced this impulse toward Rome. Formally, he objected to John Henry Newman and his ilk because their views conflicted with "the doctrine of justification . . . in the experimental apprehension of which, the sinner can alone find true peace and the spirit of adoption."[52] As an Episcopalian, however, he belonged to a church which, by its origins in an established Church of England, preferred to blur the finer points of doctrine. Miles's experience in Constantinople strengthened this ecumenicalism, because there he had to deal with a bewildering range of Christian sects—Monophysite, Greek Orthodox, Armenian, Syrian, Chaldean, and many others. In the Near East, belief came to seem an anthropological problem of communication, and, partly because of this experience, language became Miles's passion. He knew most of the western European languages and some of the Near Eastern, including Turkish and Arabic. Among the Asian, Chinese he knew little, but his command of Sanskrit and Persian was more accomplished. Miles was an heir of the revolution wrought by Sir William Jones, Friedrich von Schlegel, Franz Bopp, and those who had taken philology into new realms by expanding its range beyond Latin and Greek into the South Asian languages, and thereby invented the idea of the Indo-European.

As Miles saw it, language was "the expression of connected thought, [which] implies an internal and organic unity springing from mental laws involving, by implication, the very structure of language itself." Eighteenth-century philology had been conflicted on whether language (and so reasoning) had been given by God to man from the first or subsequently invented by humans themselves. Miles took the latter, historicist position. Any commonalities discernible among the world's many languages were there not because once, in the Garden of Eden, God had transmitted a single language to all mankind and then, long after the Fall, this aboriginal language had splintered. For Miles, this fact had been demonstrated in "the immortal work of Wilhelm von Humboldt." To be sure, it was possible and even desirable to group languages by cataloging their "*psychological, grammatical, and ethnical* characteristics," and one great value of philology was that it assisted historical understanding. By studying words, "We may follow the organic growth of languages, and the filiation of tongues; and thus, not only discover the Laws or Forms of the Language-faculty, but also the progress of Nations in periods when historical records fail us, but where the extant fragments of a language, like fossil remains, enable the scientific Philologist to re-construct the character, relations, and migrations, of a people."[53]

Further, Miles believed that "the character and spirit of a Nation are expressed more distinctly in its Language, than in any other of its productions; for the Language is the immediate product and embodiment of the Intellectual Life of the Nation: it is, in fact, the objective side of the Nation's essential Being." Like animals and vegetables, men and their languages developed organically as "a living process, a continuous Becoming." When a society died, its language died with it. In so arguing, Miles was doubtful that languages begat other languages, as Schlegel had thought Sanskrit had begotten Greek. Rather, languages arose each in its own place and "they cannot be explained by derivation from one another. . . . [T]hey rest back in those unfathomable depths of diversities of characteristics which define each People to be what it is, and which constitute the impassable boundaries of its development and peculiarities." Upon this reasoning, national languages were trapped in their own world, interacted little with other worlds, and had "their peculiar modes of envisaging the Universe." Cultures were like scholars, that is, poor, struggling, unassisted, and solitary.[54]

This sense of the incommensurability of cultures affected Miles's understanding of slavery. For a cleric, he was unusually tempted by the idea of polygenesis, partly because his theological liberalism allowed him to take lightly the Mosaic account. As he saw it, the Bible sanctioned slavery for whites, too, even as "the whole spirit of Christianity tends to bring about the abolition of *white* slavery, by elevating the white man and fitting him for freedom." Hence the Bible was "a foundation of sand" for any proslavery argument because it said nothing about enslaving Africans. Rather, Miles rested his case for slavery upon "the Negro [being] a totally different man from the white man," given in bondage by Providence and nature's law. In Miles's only full-dress discussion of slavery, an 1861 pamphlet titled *The Relation Between the Races at the South*, he declined to call the Southern institution slavery, at all, but insistently called it "(so called) African slavery," because he defined slavery as "the compulsory subjection, through conquest or superior force, of a race equally endowed with the subjecting people."[55]

Miles's standing as a theologian rested squarely on a single brief work, the *Philosophic Theology; or, Ultimate Grounds of All Religious Belief Based in Reason* (1849), which John Russell published and the great German theologian Johann Neander translated into German. The book began life at St. Michael's in Charleston, where Miles gave some lectures in the summer of 1849, and was quickly written and haphazardly formed. Its first part consisted of letters exchanged between "a sceptic and his friend," and the second took up "sundry points" of theology in no particular order (the idea of God, the role of reason, miracles, the character of Christ, the psychology of religion, faith, and the Scriptures). As will become apparent, it was a work at odds with Thornwell's theology, not least in its different appraisal of recent German philosophy and theology. John Morell's *Historical and Critical View of the Speculative Philosophy of Europe in the Nineteenth Century*, which was Thornwell's whipping boy, was Miles's guide. The distinction between reason and understanding, which Thornwell refused, Miles took as an axiom. Christ, whom Thornwell slighted, was central to Miles, to whom God was less important. The Higher Criticism, which Thornwell regarded as an impiety, was formative for Miles as a philologist and theologian. Above all, the *Philosophic Theology* was a trusting book; it found kindness in God's order, not putrefaction.

Miles began by discussing atheism, which he understood as a psychological, not an intellectual, condition. An atheist was someone who looked for God, failed to find him, and became frustrated and, finally, nihilistic. Like most in his era, Miles could not imagine someone indifferent to the idea of God. An atheist was only a failed theist, repulsed by the spectacle of religious dissent. True to this view, Miles's skeptic was not very skeptical, indeed was willing to believe at the slightest prodding. Nonetheless, Miles did presume that any thinking man must have felt the depression occasioned by doubt and that being religious involved having transcended that doubt. Perhaps alone among Southern theologians in his time, Miles understood that widespread atheism was a historical possibility, perhaps even a probability, and grasped that the coming struggle would be more profound than that with the deist skepticism of the eighteenth century. This prospect alone made denominationalism supererogatory: "The true and all-absorbing danger is really in the ominous contest which is drawing near . . . [which] will render utterly insignificant all disputes between different christian communities . . . in the vast contest for any revelation whatever." In a society like that of the South, where Christianity was so ebulliently expansive, his was an odd pessimism, more prescient of what was to happen in European culture than of what was to happen in the United States. But he was often pessimistic, an impulse which, in its more benign form, could occasion a calm sense of resignation. Though Miles argued, for example, that the finite could not grasp the infinite, he argued as well that this limitation should not occasion anger or mysticism, but only resting "placidly and contentedly before a barrier." Knowing what was limited ought to be enough. So Miles was bemused at those who imagined the afterlife, because "death is as veiled a mystery to us as it was to the ancient pagan."[56]

But *how* do we know? Miles was uncomplicated: "We possess a direct intuition of the existence of the objective universe." Man has understanding, a logical faculty which "by reflection forms conceptions, distinguishes and compares relations, generalizes, classifies, judges and reasons." That is, the understanding offered "the *forms* of thinking" and acted upon what the senses furnished of knowledge of the external world. By contrast, reason was what the mind furnished from within itself: its qualities included "perception of the beautiful, of moral truth, of the absolute goodness, the effort to grasp the real, the highest unity, beneath all the diversity of phenomena, the instinctive effort to solve the problems of the universe, of existence, of God, of immortality, the conceptions of eternity, of the infinite, of ultimate, universal, necessary truths." This was Hegelian, but also drew upon Friedrich Schleiermacher, because Miles understood religion to be an emotional and psychological fact, a "sensibility implanted in our nature" by God. This was why atheism or pantheism were unsatisfying; they denied "the religious wants and instincts of humanity, which can never cease feeling after a Personal God." This God revealed himself in history, preeminently in the Gospels with their account of Christ's life, death, and resurrection. In this belief, Miles was influenced by Andrews Norton's *Evidences of the Genuineness of the Gospels* (1837–44), a cautious exposition of the Higher Criticism, which stopped short of David Strauss but did argue that the Scriptures were answerable to historical evidence external to the texts. Miles himself was less interested in the Old Testament (a "jewish history . . . half fabulous") but most in the New, even if it did embody "imperfect memoranda of Christ." Miles was content to argue, for example, that Christ nowhere sanctioned the Penta-teuch as divinely inspired and to explain, during the Civil War, that the first chapters of Genesis were a compilation from three distinct sources. Rather, the value of the Bible lay in "the immortal visions of men whose spiritual intuitions were awakened to see moral and religious ideas," not in "myths and false notions, and narrow national prejudices, and human follies . . . all that venerable rubbish." From God, Miles wanted love and merciful clarity, not the "dark traps of enigmatical oracles." So denominational and theologi-cal wranglings were beside the point; they were just a sad record of man's meddling understanding overweening his reason.[57]

Being a scholar of language, Miles the theologian believed that Revelation was a linguistic phenomenon, known through eyewitnesses whose testi-monies were expressed in words, which may or may not have been reliable. For Revelation to be of transhistorical significance, it had to appeal to what was constant in human nature, to be able to go beyond that first century in a corner of the Mediterranean to "*our* state of development, *our* intellec-tual, moral, and religious wants." So, though Miles took history seriously, like most theologians he wanted to transcend it, because God lived beyond history. Moreover, by believing in Revelation, Miles believed that Chris-tianity marked a providential discontinuity and could not be understood as merely an organic historical development from what antedated Christ. For all his being influenced by Romanticism, Miles had an older faith in the "universal wants of a common nature." The means and purpose of the ap-peal to this nature lay in Christ, whose wonder was so great as to survive even Strauss's deconstructions of the historical evidence, which Miles found "hyper-sceptical and fanciful."[58]

Being more interested in grace than in what required grace, that is, sin, Miles showed no interest in Adam and the Calvinist doctrine of federal representation. However, he was entranced by "*reconciliation through a Per-sonal Redeemer*." In this sense, Miles came close to the modern evangelical sensibility, because he was confident that an ecstatic knowledge and accep-tance of Christ would be healing. Unlike those evangelicals, he was conscious that the religious instinct could legitimately take many forms: "In the ancient science of Etruscan Augury, in the dark oracle of degraded Obiism, humanity has exhibited its indomitable and irrepressible want of guidance from God.—Through the manifestations of Vishnoo, and the endless incarnation of the Dalai Lama, there gleams the imperative demand of humanity for union with divinity."[59]

True to these standpoints, Miles as a metaphysician claimed that man was self-aware, was conscious of external reality, presumed causation, and necessarily conceived of the infinite and God. Man had reason and moral freedom, by which he distinguished between right and wrong. This was a rationalist position, even if Miles did hold that the religious instinct arose from despair at "the barriers of this dark and narrow earthly circle," against which man beat "like an imprisoned bird." It was reason which apprehended God, not a mystical faith that abandoned rationality as hopeless. Knowing God arose from "a fundamental and original law of the intellect." Further, Miles believed that Christianity's rootedness in man's reason meant that the Christian acquired a purified and amplified reason. Nonetheless, since God was apprehended by reason, but reason (unlike the understanding) did not come directly into contact with the external world, it followed that men believed in God but had no concrete experience of him. God did not appear shining and real in the world—each person would see him differently, anyway—but was a voice heard within and felt as an intuition. This multiplicity of voices might threaten chaos, if each man's intuition made God, but Miles had faith that "the entire range of nature demonstrates that the idea of life involves that of a complex law, necessarily involving unity in complexity." There were individuals, but they were subsets of the generality of mankind, which was organically evolving as an organized form of life: "Human nature is not a mere aggregate of individual men, it has a certain objective validity as a universal humanity, of which each individual partakes."[60]

These arguments were a radical way of arriving at some orthodox conclusions, because Miles conventionally mistrusted both "a mighty pantheism of nature" and "a vast subjective idealism," though he came closer to the latter than he imagined. Rather, he thought that religion mediated between "the fleeting, the changing, the weak, the erring, the human" and "the fixed, the absolute, the eternal, the true, the divine," or tried to.[61] Man alone could not manage such a mediation, because he was trapped in self, in the toils of the understanding. But Revelation and Christ could achieve it by offering a helping hand to the imprisoned bird, beating against the bars of its cage.

These propositions lay at the heart of the *Philosophic Theology*, the second half of which was more episodic. There Miles reiterated the possibility of the Incarnation and defended the reality of miracles by using and abridging John Stuart Mill's refutation of David Hume in the *System of Logic* and by arguing that a miracle was not a suspension of known experience (and so incredible), but only a new experience subject to the usual rules of experience. He meditated on the distinction between consciousness and personality, before gliding into a defense of the Trinity ("plurality in the Divine Essence"), without the idea of which one must "land in [either] the material pantheism of Comte, or the immaterial pantheism of Hegel," a dilemma which Schelling's later writings had moved to recognize and resolve with trinitarianism. He offered an ecstatic reading of Christ's character, if a reading informed by a Higher Criticism which helped to distinguish among the disparate historical evidence offered by the differing Gospels. He considered the philosophy of the ancient Greeks, warmly expounded Plato, and spoke of Heraclitus with a shudder. In the Greeks he found anticipations of Christianity and modern philosophy, but he still concluded that they had offered but intelligent conjectures, necessarily sterile because unconfirmed by Revelation. He elaborated on the nature of reason, as a refuge from the controversialism engendered by the understanding, and repeated his dislike of polemical dogmatism wrapping itself in the vain claim of divine inspiration. He reimagined the bleak dilemma of the skeptic and insisted upon the moral pertinence and consistency of the Bible, against which minute historical enquiries were, however pedantically accurate, "paltry." Lastly, Miles showed himself untroubled by any possible conflict between geology and the Mosaic account of Creation, because he saw the Bible not as a reliable guide to history or science but as the "spiritual nourishment of the soul."[62]

In short, few theologians were further in standpoint from Thornwell, who was busy in Columbia in reexamining the starker logics of Calvinism, than Miles. Yet their differences became paradoxical. Curiously, Miles's theological liberalism eventuated not in agnosticism, as most would have predicted, but in a Christocentric evangelicalism, with which many Southerners came to be comfortable. Even avowing orthodoxy, Thornwell was in many ways more radical than Miles and would have been more mistrusted, if orthodox Southerners had but noticed the subtle nuances of the Presbyterian's theology.

JAMES HENLEY THORNWELL was an overseer's son, whose father died when the son was eight. We do not know the details, the "stern necessities," but there was poverty. When young he was short, thin, sallow, with skin like parchment. He prospered because he was taken up by two local men who gave their patronage to the gifted, "poor, dirty-looking, malarial-looking boy" and provided him with an education.[63] In later years he would refer only lightly to all this. He liked to stress his transcendence of this beginning by having the best, in cigars, in clothes, in horses, and he used to sport a natty beaver hat. The scars were not self-evident. Clerical friends found him amiable, even bantering, though he had a street-fighter side. Many feared him for relentless logic, sarcasm, and a streak of intellectual brutality.

In his own way, he was rooted. Born on a plantation in the Marlboro District of South Carolina, he went to the state college and remained to become a professor and the president. He held ministries in Charleston and

Columbia, and at his death in 1862 he held a chair at the Columbia Theological Seminary. But he studied, too, at the Andover Seminary and the Harvard Divinity School, if briefly and nervously, and twice made long trips to Europe, while within the United States the business of the church carried him often hither and yon. And he nearly left South Carolina in 1845, when he accepted a ministry in Baltimore; he was retained by the college insisting on a year's notice and managing, by pressure and wiliness, to keep him. In truth, he was restless; in the twenty-seven years between his first adult job and his death, he held seven positions and dallied with more. It was soothing to be asked to come or stay. So his rootedness had limits. Though he felt no discomfort with his state's social relations and defended them, he was not given to talking about its landscape, people, or places, because he was very abstract, fearfully so to others.

So he was a parvenu, who accepted the world which had invited him in but remade it subtly in his own image. He took little for granted; he watched and certified. He wished to belong, but on his own terms, to be orthodox, but in his own way, which grew more distinctive the older he got and the more assured he became.

He was a Presbyterian by intellectual conviction, not by inheritance. His poor and illiterate mother had been a Baptist, William Henry Robbins (his first patron) was a Unitarian who became an Episcopalian, and General James Gillespie (his second patron) was known for his "unbelief." Thornwell betrayed few immortal longings when young and studied law before going to college. Though he was to announce in 1829 that he wished to forswear Mammon and was "determined to adopt theology as a profession," his undergraduate career was not noticeable for religiosity. He read philosophy, belonged to the debating society, admired Thomas Cooper, read worldly periodicals like the *Southern Review* and the *North American Review*, to which he aspired to contribute. Many thought he would go into law or politics, which was what the alumni of South Carolina College mostly did. His contemporary J. Marion Sims later observed that Thornwell "was no more religious than I was when he was in college" and claimed that the latter became converted to get a girl, who was "a rigid member of the Presbyterian Church." Though he failed in the wooing, as its memento he retained a conviction of the rightness of the Westminster Confession of Faith, the text which the young woman had thought an aid to courtship.[64]

Later in life, Thornwell hazarded that he had succeeded in only one thing, persuading others to duplicate his own personal history of conversion. Like many a convert, he believed more intensely than the ordinary believer and was insistently concerned that faith and reality fit together, as though he were poised to disbelieve if the logic of faith faltered. Unlike many of his Christian contemporaries, for Thornwell "the cheerless darkness of Atheism" was not unimaginable, because he knew how to provide proofs of the non-existence of God and "set aside the Jehovah of the Bible."[65] So Thornwell never had ease or smiling Episcopalian comfort, but was drawn to what marked Calvinism, anxiety and the iron will. Mind had to be satisfied, before faith could be licensed.

It took him a while to hit his stride. His early writings, from the late 1830s to the mid-1840s, were often sermons, pastoral efforts sometimes published. They were exhortatory, close to the Scriptures, and expository of Presbyterian doctrine, and they show a man anxious to distance himself from the philosophical reading of his youth by showing mastery of a different language. He was then drawn to what to believe, not how to believe, the latter being the theme of his mature theology. His later writings—they change in the late 1840s—were to be more deeply engaged by the problems of modern philosophy, which he now understood not only from the English and Scottish tradition (Locke, Hume, Reid), but from the French and German (Cousin, Kant, Schleiermacher). His later thought was still determined to sustain Calvinism, but a lot had rubbed off in his engagement with modernity, such that by the end he was deeply unusual as a Calvinist, even heterodox.

Thornwell was an Old School Presbyterian, instrumental in keeping the New School marginal. In the 1840s the Baptists and the Methodists had split south from north, conservative from liberal, but an orthodox hegemony had been maintained among the Presbyterians, a process in which Southerners had been prominent. Presbyterian theology was a world in which, unusually, a Southern thinker might feel in medias res, not remote from the rest of the American world. For an Old School proponent, Presbyterian doctrines had been stable since at least the seventeenth century, though Jonathan Edwards had introduced nuances during the early eighteenth for the American branch. The old words were still in use. Thornwell used Calvin's *Institutes* as his textbook at the Columbia Theological Seminary in the late 1850s. Thornwell's writings and teaching grapple with Augustine, Aquinas, Francis Turretin (whose *Institutio Theologicae Elencticae* of 1679–85 was the text at Princeton), and Bernard de Moor and Gisbert Voetius of the Dutch School, these and many others. The problem of man's relationship to God was an old one and thought to be little affected by historical events. The thinkers who had subtly meditated on these matters could be seen as removed from time, as survivors who talked to one another, and always vulnerable to refutation. They were not significant or minor because they lived in one century rather than another, one place rather than another. All stood equal in the face of God, all flawed, all hopeful, most doomed.

It would be well to start with what was conventional in Thornwell: his adherence to the federalist school of theology, his attitude toward science, his separatism, and his intolerance.

As was the norm in the Calvinist tradition, Thornwell's was a God-centered Christianity in which Christ was marginal. He was thus far from the twentieth-century tradition of Southern evangelicalism, whose every second word was to become "Jesus." Most of what mattered—the Sublapsarian doctrines of the Creation, the Fall, election, redemption, vocation, and imputation—had occurred long before the second Revelation, though Christ was the messenger of the doctrine of grace, even if the Presbyterians drastically constrained the scope of God's grace. In this theology, God was all-powerful, personal, the maker of heaven and earth, unintelligible to man except in fragments licensed by God to man's feeble capacities. The universe was not "a vast clock of complicated machinery," as William Paley and the Supralapsarians believed, but a living, continuing creation of God's inscrutable will, active not only in the beginning but now and always. God made nature ex nihilo, but made it a thing separate from himself. Thornwell's language about God was often ecstatic, almost sensually masochistic, and centered more on God's power and will than on his love. Thornwell spoke glowingly of God's omnipotence, of the fact that God "simply *wills*" and things happened. This thrilling spectacle, this occasion for man's servitude, gave Thornwell satisfaction. So he bubbled that "the Bible is without a rival when it speaks in the language of command."[66]

Predestination, for example, was (he admitted) a thing hard to fathom, given that someone was predestined for redemption by God not because of any human action but because God willed it, not arbitrarily but for reasons known only to God: "He chooses one and passes by another, not because one is better or worse than another, but because such is His sovereign will." It was God's otherness that was his majesty and wonder, so one could not know his mind, and this was a reason to refuse the doctrine of salvation by works (impiously urged by the Roman Catholics), a doctrine which made providence the plaything of man's choosing and, as Turretin had argued, made God dependent on man's will. It was hard but true that "God has no purpose of salvation for all": if anything, it was the truer for Thornwell, because hard.[67]

The federal principle contended that God had never had a direct contact with men but had "dealt with men collectively through a common representative." So, "the Covenant of Works was entered into with Adam as the federal head of his race, and the Covenant of Grace was entered into with Christ as the federal head of His seed." Adam was created as a man, not infantile or barbarian or naively natural, but in the image of God with reason and will. He had a natural ability for holiness, as well as a potential to fall, because God had implanted a defect in man from the beginning. Theologians varied in their opinions as to the nature of this defect, but Thornwell took the hard line. For him, it was implausible that the Fall had happened through inadvertence, confusion, or weakness. Rather, it was "a falling away from God; a deliberate renunciation of the claims of the Creator; a revolt from God to the creature, which involved a complete inversion of the moral destiny of man."[68] The problem lay in man's will, which was free, had chosen sin, and so had defied God. Adam's transgression was voluntary and deliberate. This path once chosen, the will had become corrupted.

On sin Thornwell was chillingly unforgiving: "If a man had obeyed for years and then in an evil hour had been tempted into an act of disloyalty, that one act would have changed his whole relations to the lawgiver and have effaced the entire merits of his past life." Sin weighed man down even at the moment of grace, Christ's sacrifice, that "terrible tragedy enacted before the eyes of all creatures to display the holiness of God and illustrate the transcendent enormity of sin." The knowledge of sin was the awful obligation even of the elect, because sin broke the link between God and man, made the sinner "an alien and an outcast . . . for ever estranged from good." Sin was not, as Augustine had argued, an absence of holiness or a weakening of rectitude but a real force in man "interwoven in the very texture of his soul" and connected to the perverting power of Satan, with whom "our nature is in such intimate alliance." (Thornwell gave Miltonic credence to the reality of the Devil.) At the heart of sin was self-love, and its consequences were "all those afflictions and sufferings of the present life which terminate in the dissolution of the body," such as fatigue, pain, disease, aging, eventually death, and (for many) the final punishment of hell.[69] Thornwell's words for what man's will to sin had made were relentless: they included malignity, putrefaction, carnality, corruption, depravity, disease, deformity, and loathsomeness.

This was conventional Presbyterian doctrine, though Thornwell felt the thrill of depravity with especial eagerness. Here and there, he was unorthodox. He was conscious, for example, that the federal principle was troublingly imperfect, mostly because, as a consequence of Adam's sin, each man was born with instincts of depravity, without ever having acted in ways that earned the instincts; depravity made man first, before man in turn deepened depravity. These instincts manifested themselves immediately in children, who "as soon as they begin to act . . . begin to show that self-will and self-affirmation are as natural as thought and reflection." (Thornwell had no truck with Victorian sentiment about childish innocence.) This was a problem for a theology that was interested in man's free will and capacity for holiness. To resolve the conundrum, Thornwell fell back on Wordsworthian mysticisms about preexistence and an organic unity transcending time: "I cannot escape from the doctrine, however mysterious, of a generic unity in man as the true basis of the representative economy in the covenant of works. The human race is not an aggregate of separate and independent atoms, but constitutes an organic whole, with a common life springing from a common ground. There is an unity in the whole species; there is a point in which all the individuals meet, and through which they are all modified and conditioned."[70] As we shall see, this mysticism helped to form Thornwell's social thought.

Calvinism was a supremely intellectual doctrine, not only in its complexity, but in its respect for man's intellect. To be sure, it stressed that man's mind was insignificant in the face of God's mind. Still, man's mind was much, perhaps the best of him. Man's passions—"hunger and thirst, the appetite of sex and the desire of repose"—in themselves meant little, until given meaning by the mind. It was the thinking man of will and understanding who had the best chance of transcending sin. Certainly, Thornwell mistrusted those emotions which had not first been licensed by mind, hence his dislike of the cruder manipulations of contemporary evangelists, the weeping and ecstasy elicited by Baptists like Basil Manly, who counted success by the number of damp handkerchiefs in a congregation. Rather, Thornwell thought, one should be equidistant between "the extreme of a dead and spiritless formality" and that of "the extravagant follies of a rabid enthusiasm." He spoke scathingly of "these days of morbid excitement and reckless enthusiasm," of "a counterfeit spirit," of "measures . . . adopted and encouraged and defended which manifest more of the cunning and dexterity of worldly-minded policy than the honest simplicity of an unsophisticated Christian."[71] When seeking conversion, one needed simplicity, decorum, and sobriety.

This respect for human intelligence made Calvinists into natural allies of Francis Bacon, especially since Baconianism acknowledged the claims of Revelation. For Thornwell, as for his American times, Baconianism was an orthodoxy, an inductive philosophy which had "discovered design, the operations of intelligence and will, and penetrated beyond nature to nature's God, as the author and finisher of all." The scientist described nature but did not seek to control it (or so Thornwell oddly thought), and empiricism made man an interpreter of reality not its legislator. Still, Thornwell detected odd moments of weakness even in Bacon. He disagreed with the claim that morality was only supernatural in origin and was troubled that Bacon bore an oblique responsibility for encouraging "the prevailing tendency of some modern speculations to aspire at universal truths," which was a blasphemy.[72]

Nonetheless, if science was Baconian, all was going well, because thereby science became a doxology, a singing of hymns to God. When science became Darwinian, the gulf became harder to bridge, as it did for Thornwell's successor at the Columbia Theological Seminary, James Woodrow, who flirted with Darwinism and ended up in the mid-1880s expelled from his professorship for this dissidence. But there were problems even in Thornwell's day, since geology was calling into question the Mosaic chronology, but he papered over these cracks with remarkable insouciance. Considering that he took the challenge of modern philosophy with seriousness, he turned aside that of modern science with a blithe spirit. He believed that geology (in the catastrophist version of Cuvier) showed the interventions of God in the discontinuous violence with which transformation had occurred. Geologists might be quarreling with Moses, but not geology with religion. As Thornwell mysteriously put it, "It is a war of theories, of speculation and conjecture, against the historical fidelity of a record supported by evidence in comparison with which they dwindle into the merest figments of the brain." This was feeble, but Thornwell had a slim excuse. Unlike Thomas Cooper in Thornwell's undergraduate days, the younger geologists of the South were in the 1840s and early 1850s making reassuring noises. Richard Trapier Brumby was arguing that nothing in Genesis contradicted the findings of modern science, even if the world did seem to be older than it was conventional to assume. Many pious people in many places, American and European, had been working out escape routes, usually involving the reinterpretation of the six days of creation to mean geological epochs. So confident was Thornwell that in 1859 he sanctioned the creation at the Columbia Theological Seminary of the Perkins Professorship of Natural Science in Connexion with Revelation, whose purpose was "to evince the harmony of science with the records of our faith and to refute the objections of Infidel Naturalists."[73] This was the chair from which James Woodrow was later to be expelled.

In his views on separatism, Thornwell was likewise orthodox. The church was godly, she spoke in the language of Canaan not that of Caesar, she was different, not least because "the ties which bind men together in other societies are only mediately from God and immediately from man; she is immediately from God and mediately from man." So in 1859 Thornwell was resolute that the church should take no position on African colonization. As he observed in 1860 when apologetically delivering himself of his political philosophy, "I have never introduced secular politics into the instructions of the pulpit. It has been a point of conscience with me to know no party in the State."[74] This separatism gave him a fierce protectiveness about the inner workings of the church, even when dealing with other Presbyterians. Being "immediately from God" could create priggishness, the sin of vanity, of which he was often accused by his peers.

Separatism did breed an intolerance which it would be too polite to call anti-ecumenical. Even by the standards of his denomination's rote hostility to the Roman Catholics, Thornwell was relentlessly inimical, startlingly condescending, so much so that the postbellum editors of his Collected Writings had to edit out from his anti-Catholic writings his "very strong language" and "considerable asperity." To be sure, some of Thornwell's objections were technical disputes of dogma. Presbyterians understood baptism to be a sign, the Catholics a physical regeneration. Presbyterians affirmed that justification was by grace "without any reference to personal obedience or inherent righteousness," but the Catholics thought grace might be earned by works. There were disagreements over governance, the Roman hierarchy as it stood opposed to the Presbyterian system of ministers and elders, about which Thornwell was very fastidious, to the annoyance even of other Presbyterians who saw things differently. In the Protestant way, Thornwell stressed the individual's direct connection to God and saw no need for the intercession of the Roman church between the believer and God. And, likewise, Thornwell had the standard objections to Catholic idolatry, the cult of relics, the worship of saints and the Virgin Mary, "grotesque images" of God as an old man and the Holy Spirit as a dove, all the "centaurs, gorgons, mermaids, with all manner of impossible things" that crowded the worshipper's eye when participating in the "disgusting fetishism" implied in the doctrine of transubstantiation.[75]

But things ran deeper than this. To speak of "the slime of the Papacy" might be regarded as a conventional pleasantry. To say that "the creed of Rome cannot be a saving one" was mild, though to assert that such a creed "robs God of His glory and the Saviour of His honour; gives us ashes for bread, a scorpion for an egg, and death for life" was not. More was at stake, however, when Thornwell argued that Catholic belief made psychological casualties and enslaved men to tyranny, and that scholasticism was the godparent of modern skepticism. Worst, Thornwell argued that Catholicism was literally the instrument of Satan. So it rang hollow when he ventured the dry courtesy of conceding that Papists were Christians and not "in the same category" with

Mohammedans, pagans, Jews, infidels, and Turks. Nonetheless, they were heretic Christians, like the Pelagians, Arians, Universalists, and Socinians.[76]

Intolerance ran very deep. Thornwell was unimpressed with the idea (favored by Miles) that God might be found in many ways. Still less did he respect the Enlightenment conjecture that heathenism was the religion of mankind's childhood. This was a fundamental error, because "heathenism is a crime . . . so enormous and aggravated that the marvel is how a God of infinite justice and purity could endure it for a single day." Possessing their "countless rabble of gods," heathens were "the spawn of a whorish fancy by a corrupt heart," men of brutal lusts and Bacchanalian revels, whose ways were "unnatural and monstrous."[77]

Strangely, this contempt was partly born of Thornwell's weak historical sense and high regard for human intelligence. Like Catholics, heathens were, after all, "men like [our]selves, moral, religious." As such, they faced the same choices as Thornwell, but they chose wrongly, even as he, in the 1830s, had chosen rightly. Further, Thornwell's intolerance was born of a fierce respect for the value of tension. Christian doctrine was "the product of many and protracted controversies, and all the creeds of Christendom . . . are at once a confession of the truth and a protest against error." Even heresy nurtured truth, because it forced self-awareness. Thornwell's own truths needed the grist of polemical violence, which included him assaulting other Presbyterians, unappreciative of this service. Naturally, this brutality constrained Thornwell's standing in the world, and tolerant gentlemen frowned at the wrangling overseer's son. To be sure, those within the circle of the devout were dazzled by their champion, and admirers spotted his anonymous articles by their "usual amount of bellicose pugnacity," the mark of "an unrivalled logician and peerless intellectual gladiator." But those less committed to the cause saw something crabbed and narrow, something "hardshell." As Lieber put it, Thornwell was "a man, of whom Mr Breckinridge once printed, that since Calvin there had been no man like him. I hope so."[78]

He being so committed to mind, the nature of consciousness was important to Thornwell's theology. For a minister, this had awkward implications. When he gave his inaugural address to the Columbia Theological Seminary in 1857, he had to promise to be good: "I shall not indulge a licentious liberty of speculation, nor teach for doctrines the commandments of men." He had spent most of his adult life in a secular college, so they must have been a little worried about him, the man whose library was so suspiciously full of the texts of modern philosophy. But even in the same address, Thornwell showed why they were right to worry, why he was not a safe man, because he explained why philosophy was needful: "[It] is a fundamental want of the human soul and cannot be dispensed with. Reflect man must and will, and religion has no sanctity to protect it from the torch of a searching inquiry into its principles." No doubt his years at South Carolina College did help to explain this willingness to strip religion of untouchability. Being president of South Carolina College had pushed him more into the public realm. In the 1840s he had helped to found the *Southern Presbyterian Review*, but in 1856 he assumed the editorship of the *Southern Quarterly Review*, whose founding editor in 1842 had been insistent that the periodical would "sustain and advocate the claims of *no* party in Religion, of none whatever." Thornwell saw matters more diffidently: "Religion and philosophy touch at every point; and we agree with Suarez that no man can be an accomplished theologian who is not, at the same time, an accomplished metaphysician, and that no man can be an accomplished metaphysician without imbibing principles which should lead him to religion." This was delicate work, because metaphysics was slippery, seductive in its complexity, and unexpected in its implications.[79]

John Calvin had instigated a creed that wished to step over the bankrupt realism of the Scholastics and, in trying to get back to the Primitive Church, often reached toward humanist flexibilities about the grounds of knowledge. From Petrus Ramus onward, Calvinists had shadowed modern philosophy in order to pick up the useful, reject the heretic, and understand how things were going as a test of their own intellectual coherence. In his turn, Thornwell was attracted by recent philosophy, especially its focus on the nature and limits of humans' ability to comprehend external reality. For Thornwell, the point of religion was that, though consciousness could not prove reality, religion offered a structure of faith that made the working hypothesis of reality compelling. Nonetheless, the problem of knowing God and the problem of knowing anything were identical: "the knowledge of God is . . . not different in kind from the knowledge of any other being."[80]

So mind could not grasp "things as they are in themselves, but things as they appear," and could not grasp transcendent reality. It followed that man understood God in human terms: "Our own consciousness is the storehouse from which [concepts of God] are drawn. We can conceive no intelligence but the human; we can think no power but that which is suggested by the energy of our own wills; we can have no moral intuitions but those which are given by our own consciences. Man, therefore, sits for the picture that he sketches of God." This was to flirt with annihilating reality and, with it, the God who had made reality, yet Thornwell did believe there was such a thing as reality: "It is not . . . a sham, a dream, *a mere shine*. . . . [A] phenomenal or a relative is none the less a real knowledge; it is the knowledge of real existence as that existence is manifested to us."[81]

In his belief in mind having a structure, Thornwell split the difference between John Locke's sensationalism and Thomas Reid's doctrine of direct apprehension, and thereby he went with a modified version of Sir William Hamilton's melding of German and Scottish philosophy. This may not be surprising, since Hamilton's intellectual career mirrored the influences that bore upon a mid-nineteenth-century Southerner with philosophical interests. Hamilton had imbibed Scottish realism by studying at Glasgow and Edinburgh; at Oxford he had a classical education, especially in Aristotle; he had then traveled in Germany, where he had studied Kant, Fichte, and Schelling; he was an inheritor and critic of Thomas Brown's Humean revision of the psychology of common sense. With a learning which many contemporaries admired and others regarded as random antiquarianism, Hamilton had stood at the confluence of turbid philosophical streams (the Scottish and German) and had struggled to quiet them into an orderly flow. It was the verdict of posterity that, in this, he had failed. Nonetheless, Hamilton was influential upon many, especially for his contention that human nature demanded a connection between cause and effect as well as a sense of unity, because otherwise "we are lost in the multitude of the objects presented to our observation, and it is only by assorting them in classes that we can reduce the infinity of nature to the finitude of mind." That is, universality was not found but made by the mind. Further, like Thomas Brown, Hamilton believed that "the form of all our knowledge is determined by human limitations and that paramount among these limitations is an inability to think about things except relationally."[82] Nothing was known by itself, only as it related to other things; hence the significance of analogy.

Thornwell's high regard for Hamilton was not uncommon in the 1850s, when John Stuart Mill felt the Scot worth an elaborate critique. Hamilton's long review of Victor Cousin in the *Edinburgh Review* of 1829 had been regarded as the most professional of introductions to British intellectual circles of the issues raised by Kant and his successors; even Victor Cousin had thought so. Samuel Tyler of Baltimore, perhaps the most prominent American Baconian and Thornwell's correspondent, in 1855 praised Hamilton and many more, including George Frederick Holmes, believed or hoped that Hamilton had found a way to reconcile faith and reason.

In theological circles, though, Hamilton was a controversial figure. The Princeton theologians, notably Charles Hodge, were for some years his enthusiast, but, when the implications of Hamilton's thought were teased out in the Bampton Lectures on *The Limits of Religious Thought* (1858), given by Hamilton's disciple the English theologian Henry Mansel, Princetonians changed their minds. They charged that, in denying that reason could apprehend the absolute, Mansel had removed reason from religion and thrown man back upon irrationality for any conviction of the truth of God. Significantly, Thornwell did not endorse this criticism, because, as was his wont, he found an odd comfort in the thought that inadequacy of mind occasioned the necessity of faith.

With some caviling, Thornwell thought Hamilton a rival to Aristotle, a match for Leibniz, and an equal to Bacon. To be sure, as Thornwell put it, "[Victor] Cousin was wrong in maintaining that the relations of the finite and infinite are eternal, necessary and fully intelligible; Sir William wrong in maintaining that they are wholly and completely unknown. Cousin arrogated too much, Sir William too little, to intelligence." Nonetheless, with Hamiltonian logic, Thornwell argued that "the conditions of consciousness are such that we can never directly apprehend aught but the phenomenal and relative." Hence "the infinite is never apprehended in itself; it is only known in the manifestations of it contained in the finite. . . . We know *that* it is, but we know not *what* it is."[83] What saved the idea of God was human belief, and the intelligibility of God was man's protest against the idea of the imperfect, which history forced on him.

That "the relative necessarily implies the absolute" was fundamental to Thornwell, and the proposition denoted an edging away from the starker relativism of Hamilton and Mansel, just as the word "implies" suggested the tentativeness of this intellectual move. For Thornwell, religion arose not from any confidence in the reality of God but from doubt about the sufficiency of reason and knowledge. Hence Thornwell could affirm "that our relative analogical knowledge of God is . . . amply adequate for all the purposes of religion," even though it did "not satisfy the needs of speculation." Because philosophy offered few assurances, God was necessary. Both ignorance of God and absolute knowledge (which would make men "the equals of God") would make worship supererogatory. It was "our dependence, marking us out as finite beings, which renders us creatures of religion." There had to be something real upon which dependence could fasten itself, because religion was more than "an indefinite feeling of emptiness and want." There had to be the external thing, "something known; something perceived as beautiful; something acknowledged as supreme." Nonetheless, it was a leap, if not into the dark then into the gloom, as well as an act of will, something that "must" be done.[84] No word occurred more often in Thornwell's writings than "must," and it signaled both the authoritarianism of a moralist and a sharp awareness that meaning could be made only by effort.

This awareness of how limited was human knowledge lay at the heart of Thornwell's dissent from modern German philosophy, which he regarded as pantheist and arrogant, though insightful. He had the usual objections to German obscurity of expression, but his Germans were worthy opponents, who unusually inspired in him a sense of humility. He was aware that too many dismissed the Germans without bothering to understand them. For his own part, Thornwell found himself "brought in contact with men of the highest order of mind, the severest powers of logic and the utmost coolness of judgment. They do not *rave*, but *reason*. They do not *dream*, but *think*; and that, too, with a rigour of abstraction, an intensity of attention, and a nicety of discrimination, which he is obliged to respect."[85]

Still, they were wrong. If Hamilton underestimated the competence of reason, the Germans overestimated it: "They seem to think that . . . omniscience . . . may become the attainment of man, as it is the prerogative of God, and that, in the very structure of the mind, the seeds are deposited from which may be developed the true system of the universe." In truth, they were wrong partly because they carried to a logical conclusion those philosophical premises which Thornwell himself had granted but refused to apply. John Morell, for example, had "plunged into the depths of consciousness and fetched from its secret recesses the materials for proving that, in the very nature of the case, every system of doctrine not only *is*, but *must* be, human in its form and texture." Such narcissism nourished the illusion of pending omnipotence. While Stewart, Reid, and Brown had been the Newtons of mind, modest "inductive psychologists" who contented themselves with picking up pebbles on the seashore, Fichte, Schelling, and Hegel were "bold and rampant ontologists, unfolding the grounds of universal Being from the principles of pure reason." The former had restricted themselves to the phenomenal and relative; the latter had essayed the absolute and infinite. Rather, instead of seeking the ideal, the Germans ought to have contented themselves with the representative: "To affirm that the representative does not truly mirror the original is to invalidate the only conceivable process by which we can pass from the ideal to the actual" and thereby "lay the foundations of universal skepticism."[86] The terror here was that, consciousness being so mutable, man would be left only with the transient and could never imagine anything synthetic. Thornwell wanted nothing of the world of self that Virginia Woolf was to describe, though he knew of its possibility.

In refuting the Germans, Thornwell often found himself driven toward a firmer theory of reality than he was wont to express when refuting the Scots. Partly, this was because he read some Germans who were not transcendentalist, or only mildly so. His late writings and lectures draw upon German theologians and critics who were themselves critical of the Kantian and Hegelian tradition or were trying to find a way to reconcile it to older theological traditions. Chief among these was Ernst Wilhelm Hengstenberg, who had been long known in the South: his most influential work, the *Christology of the Old Testament*, had been translated by Reuel Keith of Virginia in 1836, and (from the opposing camp) Miles knew enough to damn Hengstenberg as "the selfish, narrow minded tool of despotism." From these theologians, however, Thornwell took a strengthened sense that the mind had shapes that could represent external reality, however obliquely: "The operations of the understanding . . . are *representative*, and hence it deals with realities through their symbols." This insight grounded Thornwell's dissent from Kant, for whom, as Thornwell read him, conceptions were "purely the products of the mind, and corresponded to nothing beyond the domain of consciousness." Thereby Kant had not seen that "every intellectual act is *cognitive*, and every act of the understanding *representative*."[87]

This desire to demonstrate the ability of the mind to represent reality could wander into a disinclination on Thornwell's part to allow that the mind had leeway and imaginative freedom, because he worried that freedom could lead to error. This belief helps to explain Thornwell's hostility to Coleridge, who celebrated fancy and the imagination. Instead, Thornwell was troubled by "the irregular influence of imagination," which ought to be "a handmaid to the understanding, vivifying its conceptions and imparting a glow of life and beauty to the knowledge of nature," but nothing more.[88]

So he felt the Germans had slid into pantheism, "the prevailing tendency of modern philosophy," whose error was to overlook the nature of Creation. In the pantheist worlds described by Spinoza and Hegel, God was seen as infusing himself into all things, including man, and so man became godlike. Pantheism, too, by blurring man into wider realities, put him out of focus. Thornwell wanted something firmer: "We are not a sham—we are a something; and, as being a something, can do something."[89] Action was at stake. Reality made it possible for man to act morally, to worship God, to be in the world.

Thornwell was hesitant about individualism. He did not think individuals had sharp outlines, because they were social creatures, too. This premise of sociability emerged from Thornwell's conception of mind, because "one of the most mysterious attributes of mind [is] the power by which it can impart to others the knowledge of what passes within itself." This lay at the foundation of society: "If each soul existed only as an individual, and there was no medium by which its thoughts and feelings and affections could be communicated to other souls, there might be contiguity in space, but there could be no such moral unions among men as those which are presented in the Family, the Church and the State. Intense individualism would be the law of all human life." And this could not be, because such a radical individualism would vitiate the theology of federal representation. God had "constituted our species a race connected by unity of blood, and not a collection of individuals belonging to the same class, simply because they possess the same logical properties. He made Adam the root, because He designed to make him the head; the father, because He designed to make him the representative of all mankind. . . . We are one by birth, because we were destined to be one by covenant."[90]

This impulse brought Thornwell ominously back to Romantic organicism and so pantheism. He could write of "the organic unity of life" and fashion sentences of Hegelian resonance. So, "[t]he world presents an aspect of mutability, a successive influence of cause and effect, a constant interchange of action and reaction." But he hesitated and lurched away from the fence. He claimed, too, that seeing the universe "as a living organism" was a disfiguring belief which had marred even the "masterly" Cosmos of Alexander von Humboldt. Still, organicism did help to explain culture. Humanity was "not an aggregate of separate and independent atoms, but . . . an organic whole, with a common life springing from a common ground." There was unity, "a point in which all the individuals meet, and through which they are all modified and conditioned." This dialectic was asymmetrical. Society had the upper hand: it "exerts even a more powerful influence upon the individual than the individual upon society, and every community impresses its own peculiar type upon the individuals who are born into it." This explained national character and why "the Englishman is easily distinguished from the Frenchman, the Chinese from the European, and the Negro from all."[91]

Thornwell took the social so seriously that it informed his idea of God. Just as man was individual but connected to those around him, so God was personal but connected, not only to himself in the mystery of the Trinity. "I confess that, to my mind, absolute solitude of Being is wholly incompatible with the actual exercise of moral qualities," Thornwell argued. "Society is the element of virtue, and hence I turn with delight to those representations of the Scriptures in which it is implied that God is necessarily social as well as holy—that such is the nature of His essence that while absolutely one it exists eternally in the threefold distinction of Persons." This belief in sociability explains why Thornwell was interested in the ethics of Ciceronian humanism, puzzlingly so for so stern a Presbyterian. He thought well of "a delicate refinement of manners . . . that gracefulness of character which Cicero so warmly commends in his Offices." In general, Thornwell's savage disregard for pagans did not apply to the Greeks and Romans. The ancients (Aristotle, Cicero, the Stoics) knew that "all virtue is a species of truth." Likewise,

"Aristotle, among the ancients, was unquestionably in advance of every age which preceded the introduction of Christianity, and is still in advance of many who call themselves Christians, in his clear and steady perception of the indissoluble connection betwixt the cogitative and practical departments of man's nature in reference to duty."[92]

An element in this regard for Aristotle lay in a respect for logic, which had long been cultivated at South Carolina College. Thornwell once boasted that he had the largest collection of works of logic in the country, and, consistent with this, for Thornwell, little could be true that was illogical and unity was a preoccupation. He spoke of "the unity of a higher energy," of "the mysterious unity in our race," of how holiness gave unity to disparate virtues, of "a higher unity in which all these laws are ultimately grounded." Above all, he stressed that "truth is one, and the end of philosophy is the intuition of unity."[93] Here, again, he was nicely poised in Hamiltonian fashion. The world we experienced was contingent, but we made a unity of it.

Compellingly, there was a fear of alienation. Christianity was the means by which man had been offered the chance of ending isolation and marginality. Here Thornwell's position as a parvenu, as someone who as a child had lived at the edges of society, seems richly to have inflected his theology. When discussing the arbitrary doctrines of election and reprobation, he observed how cruel were human inequities: "Some are born to affluence, honour and distinction, while others by the sweat of their brow can hardly procure a scanty subsistence for themselves and their families." He was often offended by "arrogant pretensions" and pompous claims. Above all, what this sensitivity meant was that Thornwell had a special stake in the doctrine of federal representation. He understood the doctrine to mean that, when the bargain created by Adam had been superseded by that offered by Christ, man had passed from being a servant to being a son of God. The purpose of God's order was "to adopt the servant into the family and make him an heir," as long as the servant had proved himself worthy, as Adam had not. By Christ, man had been given a second chance, he could cross the porch without cap in hand, enter the parlor, sit by the fire, be loved even while subject to paternal discipline. So God "has always proposed a fundamental change in [man's] attitude toward Him, and that change has consisted in the adoption of sons—in the substitution of filial for legal ties."[94]

Such language had many layers, because Thornwell had been, in his own life, many of these things. He was the overseer's child, he was taken into the households of General Gillespie and William Henry Robbins, he became himself a father and a master of servants. In his theology, however, Thornwell was anxious to insist that, while man became a son to God, man never became himself a master. It was the burden of Thornwell's objection to modern philosophy that it imagined the possibility of such mastery. It was, further, a theme of Thornwell's theology that the modern propensity to reduce religion to psychology be resisted, and hence that his own experience not be made the explanation for his faith. Thornwell skittered away from the private, even though he knew that "all truth must be individually apprehended" and "private judgment is always and on all subjects the last appeal." He knew that there were "crises in the history of each of us," that there were agonies as each debated which way duty lay, as each experienced a crisis of inner conflict, as each made decisions and faced the irrevocability of choices made.[95]

Nonetheless, "To us, we frankly confess, it is amazing that the essence of mind *as* mind should consist in something that is not common to all minds." He shrank from "the idiosyncrasies and oddities of individuals." He did so because he thought idiosyncrasy led to the notion that men make reality, not the notion that reality makes man. With a shudder he quoted Fichte, who asserted, "There is absolutely nothing permanent, either without me or within me, but only an unceasing change. I know absolutely nothing of any existence, not even my own," except images, dreams. He especially shuddered when he related Madame de Staël's anecdote of Fichte beginning a lecture with the words, "We shall proceed to make God."[96] This was nihilism, entrapment in a self.

Thornwell inconsistently skittered away from the historical. When refuting the Roman Catholics, he was happy enough to scour the records of early Christianity for evidence useful to anti-Papist polemics. Here and there, he talked about the events of the Reformation, though as events producing godly texts, not as events putting meaning into those texts. This resistance to history was not untypical of the Calvinist Protestant, who rejected the Catholic insistence that religious truth was a tradition transmitted from God to man through apostles, saints, popes, and councils. Rather, "conformity with the Scriptures, and not ecclesiastical genealogy, is the true touchstone of a sound church-state."[97] Further, Thornwell had an aversion to the concrete and tactile. He spoke of sin or punishment, but he did not relate the history of a sinner or describe a prison; there are no Fagins or Newgates in his narratives.

Thornwell was very little a political thinker. In his youth, he wrote a few newspaper articles during the Nullification crisis in defense of Unionism, but, from then until the late 1840s, he preoccupied himself with godly things. To be sure, the business of his church resonated with political philosophy, because Presbyterians flattered themselves that the American constitution was but their principles of governance applied to public life. Thornwell himself spoke of the Presbyterian system as using the representative principle to avoid the perils of democracy, monarchy, and oligarchy, and he insisted that majoritarianism should be subject to the moral judgment of representatives. As for the secular political world, he thought that electors should be divided into small units, whose representatives should serve the interests of both their community and the state, and legislatures should be bicameral. In general, Thornwell was a conservative Whig and, for a while in the 1850s, a Know-Nothing, unsurprisingly so for so fierce an anti-Catholic. Though he did boast of American constitutionality and was a bullish proponent of Manifest Destiny, he was too bleak to be a Jacksonian. "The future will always be blacker than the present—the night ahead more appalling than aught behind," he once announced. "Those ingenious theories which undertake, from principles of human nature, to explain the history of man's progress from barbarism to refinement, are nothing better than speculative romances," he said in 1853. So he was irritated by perfectionist reformers and, as a Presbyterian, stood firmly against the organization of voluntary societies, "aiming at the promotion of universal good," and against those prone to "organizing the girls of a township into a pin-cushion club."[98] Naturally, this hostility encompassed abolitionists.

Thornwell's writings on slavery were few: a discussion of the religious instruction of slaves in 1847, a sermon in 1850 at the dedication of the Zion Church in Charleston (built for a black congregation), a report to the Synod of South Carolina in 1851, and some remarks occasioned by the secession crisis.

The first of these writings was an endorsement of the merit of giving religious instruction to slaves, and of the plan to create not separate churches but annexes to existing congregations where this instruction might be safely conducted by whites; it was, in addition, an insistence that this experiment need not be feared but would tend "to elevate and improve the intellectual and moral character of the negro," because "we want this people made better, more intelligent, industrious, tractable, trusty, better men, better servants, better Christians." To those who were concerned that Christianity might intimate revolutionary doctrines, Thornwell replied that "[d]omestic Servitude is an institution not inconsistent with Christianity," and the Christian religion itself taught no egalitarian doctrines. While the Bible gave slaveholders privileges, it also gave duties, and the institution would not survive without these duties being discharged. For, if the religious felt that slaves were being quarantined from the Bible, Christians might begin to feel alienated from slavery. Rather, the problem was that slaves were ignorant and superstitious.

Thornwell was troubled by this as a prudent slaveholder, who worried that ignorance was "so much explosive material exposed to the incendiary's touch." It troubled him as a theologian, too, because the slaves knew only heresy. Fortunately, the slave was a dependent. According to Thornwell, whites made black religion: "Our will regulates, to a great extent, the character and amount of their religious privileges."[99] Hence, there was a duty to give religious instruction.

The Anson Street Church, founded as an annex to the Second Presbyterian Church in Charleston, was the embodiment of this middling vision for a "partial separation" for black Christians At its dedication, Thornwell delivered a testier sermon to an audience exclusively white. He started with a sustained complaint about the South's isolation and "the ban of the publick opinion of the civilized world" upon Southerners, and he spoke against those who in the "insane fury of philanthropy" sought to incite servile insurrection. This urgency of tone is explicable by the fact that the sermon was given in the midst of the separate secession crisis of 1850, it was less than two months after the death of Calhoun, five weeks after Thornwell's own eulogy to the senator, and only a few days before the Nashville Convention was to meet. This crisis had deeply troubled Thornwell and even caused him to lose sleep; he had said in his Calhoun eulogy that "[n]ever in the annals of our confederation has there been a more critical period than this."[100]

This political prolegomenon in the Anson Street Church sermon belies a more ambivalent text, which, in fact, went on to suggest that Southerners had overreacted to the world's pressure. Thornwell conceded the value of that pressure, because it had forced Southerners to think hard about society and government, and they thereby had usefully come to understand that they were "eminently conservative in [their] influence upon the spirit of the age." Like Fitzhugh later, Thornwell felt that the world's ideological disorder (socialism, unchecked democracy, absolutism) would abate and all would turn back to the principles sustained by the South. In that sense, slavery was a dimension of a larger struggle, that of "the relations of man to society—of States to the individual, and of the individual to States." Here Thornwell waxed Gothic, with the European events of 1848 on his mind. On one side were atheists and socialists who saw society as a machine, on the other the Christian "friends of order and regulated freedom" who saw society as the ordinance of a God who had made a world full of puzzling irregularity. But man could "never make that straight which God hath made crooked."[101]

This was Thornwell's usual blistering partisanship. For all that, he felt restrained and argued that the Southern response to external pressure had been remarkably moderate in refusing the intellectual option of polygenist infidelity or opting for bloody repression. Southerners had not insisted that their "safety depended upon the depression and still lower degradation of the black race." Thornwell was adamant that blacks were "of one blood with ourselves" and made in God's image, and that he was "not ashamed to call him our brother." That is, "there will be no bondage in Heaven" and slavery needed to comport with Christianity, or else Southerners as Christians would have to "labour for its destruction."[102]

But did it comport?

On this, Thornwell was uneasy. He quoted William Ellery Channing: "The very idea of a slave is that he belongs to another, that he is bound to live and labour for another, to be another's instrument, and to make another's will his habitual law, however adverse to his own." Thornwell conceded that, if this was the meaning of slavery, the slave ceased to be a person and slavery would be wrong. But this was not so, because slavery was "a form of civil society, of which persons are the only elements, and not a relation of man to things." Slaves were moral agents under God's law, not blindly passive instruments of the master's will, and the master was likewise a moral agent. Further, masters did not buy souls and did not even buy men as property, but only bought labor. As an employer, a master was not a despot but answerable to the rule of law. So—here Thornwell's argument grew strained—slavery was not even involuntary servitude, because the slave needed to consent to it. God's law enjoined upon the servant "hearty consent" and "cheerfulness."[103] After all, all men were God's slaves and slaves to sin, and only God could offer liberation. Both masters and slaves waited for and hoped for this freedom, but neither had the right or the ability to hasten God's will. Acting true to God's law, both masters and slaves might achieve dignity and rectitude, but both might fail. Given the tenets of Calvinism, almost all would fail.

In granting humanity to the slave, Thornwell left himself with a problem, which he took to be "the whole moral difficulty of slavery." Did slavery place "a limitation upon the moral freedom of the slave"? Did slavery "preclude him from discharging his *whole* duty as a man; and, therefore, [was] . . . the relation . . . not ultimately destructive of the full complement of human rights"? The answer seems to have been, yes, though Thornwell gave it obliquely. Slavery had begun with man's Fall and would cease only with the millennium, when man's transgression would be purged: "Slavery is a part of the curse which sin has introduced into the world; and stands in the same general relations to Christianity as poverty, sickness, disease or death."[104] It was an impiety in abolitionism to wish to change this state of affairs, to make by man's will a moral perfection that only God could make.

This was clear Calvinist doctrine. Thornwell's other arguments in 1850 were more slippery, as though he were conscious that Calvinism might discomfit his white listeners, not necessarily Calvinist. The overseer's son could plausibly argue that "the distinctions of ranks in society . . . is an evil; but in our fallen world, an absolute equality would be an absolute stagnation of all enterprise and industry." The minister was on more dubious ground in asserting what later times would call situational ethics: "Good and evil . . . are relative terms, and what may be good for one man may be an evil to another—or what is good at one time, may be hurtful to the same individual at another." Governments and social arrangements varied. The "free citizen of England and America" could not endure slavery, but the African could, just as Asians endured despotism. This was weak for a Calvinist, and it did not answer Thornwell's most troubling question, which was whether slavery prevented the exercise of "the offices of piety or virtue." After some havering, he ruled that it did not, that slavery was "no abridgment of moral freedom," because the slave had his own moral duties to perform, however different those duties might be from those of the master: "The question with God is—not *what* he has done, but *how*—man looketh at the outward circumstances, but God looketh at the heart." The words were clear, but the body language of the prose was uncertain. More positive were his concluding arguments that duties justly discharged were the guarantors of social order and human progress, that all had a differing but important stake in the stability of the commonwealth. It was the obligation of the state to police the benevolent administration of slavery, so that in turn the slave (feeling this justice) would feel impelled to discharge his own duties faithfully. Slaves ought to be afforded education, "the right of the family," access to religion. This would, better than repression, afford protection against "insurrection, anarchy, and blood shed."[105]

So this was a mixed effort. He was clear on the issue of social conservatism and the proposition that slavery stabilized the American order, and as clear that the slave was a Christian and moral agent who merited justice from masters. He was more obtuse, however, on the problem of whether slavery impeded the moral freedom of the slave. His final words said no. His meandering argument hinted yes.

It may be significant, then, that Thornwell's 1851 report on slavery to the South Carolina Synod avoided the question of the slave's moral freedom and was a more conventional piece, asserting that the Bible sanctioned slavery, abolitionists had decided against the institution and then sought vainly in the Scriptures for their contrary sanction, the South asked only to be left alone, and slavery should be judged "upon considerations of policy and prudence" and ought only to be opposed as inexpedient, not sinful. Its most original note was to import into the proslavery argument Thornwell's recent quarrel with John Morell and the modern spirit of "rationalism," though doing this was only giving a philosophical name to his familiar quarrel with "visionary theories of human nature and society."[106] Nonetheless, one cannot be surprised that in 1861 Thornwell countenanced gradual emancipation, because his commitment to slavery had been contingent and too committed to the just behavior of the masters and the wise legislation of the state to offer a blanket approval of the working institution.

To be sure, Thornwell was a racist, not in the formal sense of believing in the scientific doctrines of race, but in casually presuming that blacks were inferior. At least in Palmer's unreliable account, he seems to have been an easy master on the plantation near Lancaster, which he acquired upon his marriage, as well as in his household in Columbia. South Carolina College itself owned slaves, who were his charge when president; during his tenure, he was troubled by the necessity to prevent undergraduates from abusing the college's slaves, as they commonly did.

As one might expect, Thornwell on slavery was guided by his theological presumptions, which gave him mixed signals. As he saw it, man was God's servant, who might hope to become God's adopted son. Insofar as Thornwell admitted slaves to the circle of Christian humanity, this was their situation, too. But slavery to God was what men (black and white) had, and adoption was what a man might get, if God's mysterious predestinations worked in his favor. If adoption did not come, as it probably would not, one had to buckle down to life's duties, which might include being a slave or a master. So Thornwell necessarily wavered between the proslavery argument and the desire to purify slavery, which could easily slip into a willingness to end it. For it was not that, in principle, he objected to freedom for slaves, it was that he was afraid to surrender the idea of man's slavery to God upon a spurious promise of liberation. William Lloyd Garrison, too, was God's slave. If Thornwell was not first God's servant, he could not become God's son. On the whole, it was prudent to play it safe. But it was hard not to be disquieted, knowing that, around the corner from a study filled with books of Aristotelian logic, a student was beating a Christian slave.

Epilogue · Cool Brains

On the eve of the Civil War, intellectuals in the South had reasoned and felt their way toward some propositions: that mind helped to form reality, but dialectically; that blending mind and emotion was of the essence of life; that society and government organically emerged from the interaction of individuals and the community; that freedom was insecure and mastery incomplete, but necessary; that God was real but difficult to comprehend; that the world moved and, to survive, Southerners needed to move with it; that much depended on keeping your nerve and the adequacy of will. The 1850s was to see a younger generation who knew these premises, which their elders had struggled to clarify, almost as an instinct. Those who had gone before had hoped that the choice between power and morality was escapable. Those in the 1850s knew that survival required choosing, which must rest not on republican individualism but on identification with something beyond self. A state, a religion, a race, the Union, and the South, these were among the candidates as sites of belonging. But what happened if the choice was made and survival failed, anyway? As it did, as the Civil War brutally showed that it must.

Four younger writers, two women and two men, laid out the options: Augusta Jane Evans, James Johnston Pettigrew, William Henry Trescot, and Mary Chesnut. Evans said, go for God and duty. Pettigrew urged, try the South and the warmth of belonging. Trescot argued, cold power is the only reality. Writing in the 1850s, these three faced the future. Since the passing of John Randolph's generation, which had pined for the old order of the eighteenth century, this forward-looking had become the Southern way. During the Civil War, Chesnut would come to live urgently in a present which raced catastrophically by her. After 1865, she had only the past to inhabit and realized that there had never been a choice, the world had never made sense, and strength of will could not ensure efficacy.

Not only the timing of Augusta Jane Evans's *Beulah* (1859) argues for its summing up the antebellum South's intellectual and moral experience. This was not the less so because, in this book at least, Evans was uninterested in contemporary political controversy and ignored slavery, and, though she made a little of landscape and Southern bowers, she did so unobtrusively. One can read *Beulah* without having a sharp sense that it was written by a Southerner about the South, and doubtless many have over the years, though it was the novel that answered Henry Timrod's contemporary request for a work that would by a "thousand nameless touches" express an author's grounding in a culture. In *Beulah*, a sky is blue and cloudless, a "negro waiter" opens a door, a harbor glitters, China trees border the pavements, moonlight passes through honeysuckle to silver a piazza floor, someone goes up the river to a plantation, someone else is "going off to the North," a couple disappear to "fashionable watering-places on the Gulf." Explicitness about place is rare, however, and Mobile and Alabama are never specified. Evans's slaves speak with only a bare hint of dialect, are called only maids or coachmen, and are nameless, not Pompey or Dilsy. As an urban novel, *Beulah* knows nothing of slave cabins and cotton gins, and in it the problems of race and social order put no pressure on events. Rather, class matters, because *Beulah*'s characters are preoccupied with status, of who calls upon whom, of how wealth sneers at frugality. A young woman is adopted into a wealthy family, and her sister is told brutally not to call, because "when you remember the circumstances, you ought not to expect to associate with her as you used to do."[1]

In one sense, *Beulah* was but a variant on Charlotte Brontë's *Jane Eyre*. In it, an ugly but intelligent orphan girl finds her way into the care of a guardian with a troubled past, their relationship grows closer, she draws back, he travels to the Orient to ease his Byronic melancholies and returns, and they marry. But *Beulah* was also *Middlemarch* before its time, as a meditation on the intellectual problem of modern knowledge, because *Beulah* was pre-eminently a novel of ideas, a work of such high intellectual and abstract seriousness that it is hard to find a peer in antebellum American literature. In a well-ordered world, Europeans were licensed to think about philosophical problems more than Americans, Northerners more than Southerners, essayists more than novelists, and men more than women. A Southern female writer of fiction was not supposed to hazard these matters, at all, and it is no surprise that Evans had difficulty in finding a publisher and unexpected that she found so many readers, because *Beulah* was quickly popular, despite its cool, spare, and assured style and a voice at odds with the turbulent emotions which its plot narrated.

As one of the most sophisticated and cosmopolitan explorations of the problem of knowledge in Southern intellectual life before the Civil War, *Beulah* both summed up older debates and pushed the discussion into new realms. Evans had an assured command of Southern cultural practices. In her book, young men go to study at Heidelberg, married couples take themselves off to Paris and Florence, men wander the Near East, homes have large libraries, publishing is a hit-and-miss confusion, intelligent minds grapple with atheism and metaphysics. At the same time, travel could narrow the mind and young men back from Germany might lose intellectual ambition, marry brainless belles, and drink themselves into oblivion. Like William Gilmore Simms, Evans had the disdain of the petit bourgeois intellectual for the fripperies of fashionable society, but unlike him she did not feel threatened by its existence, or imagine that her intellect was illegitimate because not praised or understood by such people. *Beulah* is a self-confident book, though it is a mystery where this confidence came from.

The novel's heroine, Beulah Benton, is emotionally clumsy but intellectually sophisticated, which was the obverse of the heroines found in the works of Caroline Lee Hentz, writing elsewhere in Alabama. Both the heroine and the hero of *Beulah* are flawed, since "proud, gifted and miserable" Guy Hartwell has a "repellently cold and grave" face and a "calm, frigid smile," in which the reader is invited to discern "a volume of hieroglyphics" and a charm beyond the physical.[2] Even more unusually, Beulah's leitmotif is independence, moral and social, the old masculine dream of John Taylor. She does not rush toward a rich man with a warm heart but a feeble mind, as women were supposed to do and as Eulalia had in Hentz's *The Planter's Northern Bride*. Rather, Beulah stays single, chooses to be a teacher despite the world's sneers, makes her own money, reads, thinks, and sets the tone of her intellectual society. The novel and its men wait upon her, as she reasons out the complicated issues that she explores in Emerson, Coleridge, Carlyle, Feuerbach, Cousin, Goethe, and many others, including Thomas Brown, Victor Cousin, even Hegel at second hand.

At first, Beulah is doubtful, lonely, and awkward; "she leaned over the vast whirring lottery wheel of life, and saw a blank come up, with her name stamped upon it." She has lurid dreams, in which she drifts on a sea strewn with wrecks and floating corpses, and she is sucked drowning into the deep. She reads Edgar Allan Poe and is drawn to his phantasmagoria; "his unique imagery filled her mind with wondering delight, she shrank appalled from the mutilated fragments which he presented to her as truths, on the point of his glittering scalpel of logic." Poe "coolly informed her that she was her own God," and Beulah is "shocked, and yet admiring." (Such admiration is unusual in Southern literature, which usually saw atheism as a rumor drifting in from dissolute places.) In *Beulah*, Guy Hartwell never accepts religion but coldly speaks to Beulah of life as a "dead sea of nothing." Evans donates the same conviction to Beulah's friend Cornelia, who is allowed to die, having debated the merits of God and godlessness, and preferred the latter. Cornelia calmly sees herself as the "doomed prisoner of Poe's *The Pit and Pendulum*. "I wish I could help you, Cornelia. It must be terrible, indeed, to stand on the brink of the grave and have no belief in anything," Beulah says, and adds, "I have no truth to offer you; I have yet discovered nothing for myself."[3]

Beulah wants to believe that "chance does not roam, like a destroying angel" through the cosmos, but she needs proof. This is not quick work; it would not come from a rapid conversion in a pew at a revival meeting, nor flow from easy exhortations about Christian faith from the pulpit. A description of a church service is used to explain, not why Christianity was right, but why one might be an atheist, because revolted by fashionable people with their "slanderous chit-chat" and smugly hypocritical ministers. Rather, an extended course of reading, meditation, and debate is at the heart of the novel, and the excitement of ideas matter, even if it threatens to encourage a pride which destroys. So, Beulah "grasped books of every description with the eagerness of a famishing nature." Emerson, Carlyle, Goethe worked on her "like the waves of the clear, sunny sea." Eagerly, "she plunged into the gulf of German speculation" and confronted, through *Sartor Resartus*, "a howling chaos" and stood "wailing in some starless desert." In Emerson, she contemplated pantheism, but she found his works Pyrrhonist, "dim and contradictory," confused and fragmentary. In Beulah's debates with Cornelia, the fundamental question is asked, "How do I know that all truth is not merely subjective?" In her other exchanges with Hartwell, he gives the modern answer: "I stand on the everlasting basis of all skepticism, 'there is no criterion of truth!' All must be but subjectively, relatively true."[4]

Eventually, a preacher explains to Beulah "that human reason was utterly inadequate to discover to man his destiny" and only the Bible furnished true wisdom. At this point, Beulah refuses the argument, but she does listen because the minister is intellectually impressive and shows a command of the philosophical issues. No old-time religion would convince her. Beulah wants to be Christian, but the religion has to prove itself to her. She is passionate to resist the cold conclusion that "death is annihilation" and helped in this resistance because the metaphysicians were divided, spiteful, and rancorous, and their historians little better. So, "[s]ick of systems, she began to search her own soul. . . . She constituted her own reason the sole judge; and then, dubious of the verdict, arraigned reason itself." Her problem was the modern one: "On every side she saw the footprints of skepticism; in history, essays, novels, poems, and reviews." In her time, "Old Faiths had crumbled away; she stood in a dreary waste, strewn with the wreck of creeds and systems; a silent desolation!" But, "[a] belief in something she must have; it was an absolute necessity of the soul."[5]

So Beulah inhabits the world of Matthew Arnold's *Dover Beach*, or at least of Tennyson's *In Memoriam*. Her atheists warn her to avoid their path. Hartwell cautions Beulah not to read too deeply in his library and, on her deathbed, Cornelia says: "Beulah, do not follow me to the end! Take my word for it, all is dark and grim." There is nothing glad about Beulah's atheists: one dies and the other wanders miserably in the Orient. Beulah is never given the test of knowing cheerful atheists, so the unsurprising conclusion of the book, when Beulah becomes a Christian, is rigged. Still, in a curious way, the atheists are given the casting vote in favor of the Christian way, if Whiggishly, since they see it as the option for ordinary people, not themselves. It is a contradiction that Beulah, so touted for her strength and independence, is deemed too weak to stand the alienation occasioned by skepticism. This is not a gendered accusation, because Cornelia, too, is a woman and has the grim strength not to believe. Immediately before Cornelia's death, Beulah feels "that atheism, grim and murderous, stood at the entrance to her soul," and "her courage forsook her." She questions the idea of individualism itself, the business of thinking for oneself and being alone with one's beliefs. "How far was 'individualism' allowable?" she asks. It was Feuerbach's question, but his answer that "religion is merely the consciousness which a man has of his own, not limited, but infinite nature; it is an early form of self-knowledge" is not sufficient for Beulah.[6] She rejects it as she had rejected Emerson, and for the same reason. In Emerson, self was offered as a rich thing, which opened out into the world; in *Beulah*, self is a lonely thing, which cuts off and kills hope. Cornelia dies, regretting not her unbelief, only the loneliness it had occasioned.

This fear of the solitary self is at the heart of the novel. So seriously did Evans take ideas and so clearly did she enact them that one can fail to notice that she grounded philosophy upon psychology, in the manner of the Scottish realists. What we are as humans determines what we need and can know. "Faith in some creed is an absolute necessity of human nature," Beulah explains at the end of the novel, and "faith is based on mental conviction." On this point, modern philosophy, as in Sir William Hamilton, and Christianity concurred. Humans are too finite to grasp the world, their understanding is necessarily incomplete and fragmentary, and any attempt to transcend these human limitations is, finally, too exhausting and futile. More seriously for Evans, it was too proud. Still, at the moment she described her heroine accepting Christianity, the phrasing was very careful: "Her proud intellect was humbled, and falling on her knees, for the first time in many months, a sobbing prayer went up to the throne of the living God; while the vast clockwork of stars looked in on a pale brow and lips, where heavy dews of moisture glistened." God was living, but the stars had not ceased to be clockwork. Beulah is a Christian because it makes her happier: "Her face reflected the change which a calm reliance on God had wrought in her feelings. The restless, anxious expression had given place to quiet."[7]

Yet the narrative shows that, the conclusion notwithstanding, Evans was unsure. Sometimes she suggested plainly that God acted in the world and had agency. Beulah tells Hartwell that she has prayed "that God would melt your hard, bitter heart, and give you a knowledge of the truth of the Christian religion." Elsewhere, however, she seems to argue not that religion is true, just that it works and for her. So *Beulah* flirts with being an existential book, one of the first in American thought, and even comes close to anticipating William James on the varieties of religious experience. Finally, though, Beulah's choice is orthodox, if a choice achieved so laboriously can be orthodox. Beulah explains to Hartwell that she respects natural science and expects that, in due course, there would be a reconciliation between science and religion: "I believe that every scientific fact will ultimately prove another ramp, planted along the path that leads to a knowledge of Jehovah!" Like many an intellectual converted, she calls her religion and the universe a "mystery," because it is the human inability to explain the universe coherently which has necessitated her religious conversion.[8] So it is not understanding she seeks, but its absence. Mind licenses emotion, and emotion in turn gives comfort to mind.

In *Beulah*, tension mattered, and one might reasonably conjecture that, even after embracing marriage and Christianity, Beulah Benton would have found it hard to pray and love with an easy, laughing trust. James Johnston Pettigrew, perhaps as a man freer to move through the world, offered a different vision, devoid of tension and exuberant about self and society. His *Notes on Spain and the Spaniards* is a remarkable book, if little read, since it was published in Charleston in an edition of only three hundred copies and in the summer of 1861, when minds were distracted. The book was occasioned by two trips. After academic studies in Germany, Pettigrew had spent the winter of 1851–52 in Spain, and, in the summer of 1859, he had returned there after a too-tardy attempt to aid the Sardinian army in its war with Austria. In between these visits, he had passed from being a young North Carolinian to a Charleston lawyer and politician. These experiences influenced his book as a meditation on culture and individuality. In offering Spain as a suggestive model, Pettigrew was dissenting from older traditions of Southern thought, but he was in tune with younger writers like Paul Hamilton Hayne who were drawn to the sensuality that southern places like Spain were supposed to embody, as opposed to "the cheerless regions of the

North."[9] Boston against Charleston, Berlin against Córdoba, were pitted in Pettigrew's imagination.

The book's voice was intimate and implied that particularities made a culture. Inns, customs, food, architecture, painting, women (especially women) were smilingly described. For Pettigrew, incidents mattered. A woman vomits from seasickness on his voyage from Genoa to Marseilles, an Aragonese guide wears hempen sandals, a boy comes "with a tambourine, leading two blind old guitar-players" to be followed by "a lady with a mantilla and fan, gliding along from vespers." Pettigrew mixed disillusioned realism and glad romanticism, nowhere more so than in his long, thoughtful, and wary description of a bullfight in Seville. Along the way, to frame particularities, the peninsula's history was unobtrusively narrated, its literature appraised, and its contemporary politics discussed. Pettigrew clearly wished to make Spain relevant to American debates. He wrote, for example, of northern Europe as "a civilization which reduces men to machines, which sacrifices half that is stalwart and individual in humanity to the false glitter of centralization, and to the luxurious enjoyments of a manufacturing, money age." This was a reproach to the France of Louis Philippe and Napoleon III, as described by Honoré de Balzac, and to the United States of Henry Clay and Lowell, Massachusetts. Further, praising how the Spanish take pride in their localities, Pettigrew in Burkean mode disagreed with those modern philosophers who construed this God-given instinct as a barbarian relic and preferred cosmopolitan empathy. He singled out Aragon for its contractual theory of government and cited its famous coronation oath: "We, who are as good as you, and together more than you, make you our King and Lord, upon condition that you respect our privileges and liberties; and if not, not." He went on to argue that "Aragon and the United States are the only countries in the world that have ever embodied the true conception of a free Government, viz: a machine which shall preserve order and protect the nation, while guarantying the rights of the minority against the power of the mere majority."[10] Thus John C. Calhoun became Aragonese.

In language that George Santayana might later have used, Pettigrew praised Spanish religion. He traveled to Zaragoza's cathedral and bent down before the Virgin Mary to enjoy "a pure, placid emotion," despite believing little. As he saw it, Protestants overly condescended to Catholicism. "Every revealed system must rest for its foundation upon either reason or faith," he observed. Reason being exhaustingly complicated, beyond the capacity of the ordinary person, the worldliness of Protestantism made it "better fitted for the affairs of this world" and better for the strong who "need no assistance." Protestantism offered little consolation "for the broken in spirit, for those who, disappointed in their hopes, and crushed beneath an unrelenting fate, would fain turn from the world and forget its pleasures and sorrows alike."[11] That is, though Pettigrew did not yet know it, Protestantism might be inapt for the South that would survive beyond surrender at Appomattox courthouse.

Spain and the Spaniards was, in part, a defense of the Goths against the nineteenth-century fashion for eulogizing the Anglo-Saxons. Pettigrew was insistent that, in the Middle Ages, the Goths and the Catholic Church had preserved civilization by adopting the civil and canon law and by resisting the pretensions of the Papacy. Nor was Pettigrew slow to admit to an admiration for Arab and Jewish contributions to Spanish culture. From the Goths, Spain got "fierce courage, valor, the sentiment of personal honor, the duel, the judgment of God, fidelity to his chieftain." While from the Arabs, there came valor, too, as well as "poetry, grace, elegant horsemanship, skill in weapons, gallantry, fidelity to plighted word, and mercy to the conquered." Out of this fusion came chivalry, "which spread gradually over Europe, and contained the first germs of civilization."[12] To Pettigrew, as a soldier, soon to be a Confederate general, who devoted many pages of his book to the Spanish army, the interconnection of civilization with the military was important.

Pettigrew was at great pains to repudiate Anglo-American condemnation of Spain, even to the extent of saying kind words for Spain's grandees, by arguing that its modern aristocracy differed from its medieval. It was proud, to be sure, but so were the poor and the middling classes. The dons took satisfaction in birth but not in money and were even unostentatious, and they were so numerous that the aristocracy lacked cohesion and, without this, had forfeited any automatic right to power. Like all elites, it consisted mostly of drones, if noble drones. Lower down the social scale, the peasantry was uncorrupted, a people "worthy of admiration," with "manly but uneducated virtues." Hence all of Spain's classes were conservative, and, for them, resisting the vulgarity of a money-making modernity was a dogma. To be sure, such virtues could be vices, too. Nobility could become excessive pride and jealousy, a contempt for trade become laziness, religious cohesion become inquisitorial intolerance, and a Stoic ability to withstand pain become a "want of appreciation of human suffering." As Pettigrew saw it, the growth of compassion, so evident elsewhere in European and American culture, was absent from Spaniards, who were indifferent to the goring of the bull or the matador. This premodern pitilessness Pettigrew deprecated, but he was less enthusiastic about aspects of modernity other than compassion, like "atheism, deism, and philosophistic religion, so prevalent in the *soi-disant* enlightened countries."[13] He rendered the opinion that John Crowe Ransom was to reiterate nearly seventy years later, that a God without thunder made a pale religion, scarcely deserving of the name.

Like many German-educated Southerners, especially those who valued the American revolutionary tradition, Pettigrew liked abusing the English, as well as praising the Germans for valuing "freedom of the intellect and the inquiring spirit." Less usual was that he was nettled by the cult of the Anglo-Saxon and was dubious about the inheritance of the English language, which he saw as "fit for serpents only." He acknowledged trial by jury as a gift, but not English law "in substance," not the English class system, and not their worship of money.[14] So Pettigrew cautioned his countrymen to beware perfidious Albion and embrace her natural enemies, among them the Spanish. The price of this friendship, however, must be the abandonment of acquisitive designs upon Cuba. Patience was a better strategy; since the colonial age was passing and Cuba, too, would be detached from Spain and the United States need only wait. Or, if American patience was too limited, it would be better to negotiate for Cuba in exchange for material aid to Spain in its two great ambitions, the expulsion of the British from Gibraltar and the reunion of Spain with Portugal.

This assault upon the English was a familiar aspect of the cause of the Mediterranean South, which recoiled from fogs, sleet, and cold hearths. In the final sentences of his book, Pettigrew listed the things he liked about Spain: the "flowery vales of Andalusia and the tawny mountains of Aragon," prayer in a cathedral, promenades by moonlight, "prancing horses and pawing bulls," fandangos and olés, guitars and "wild, plaintive melodies," oranges and pomegranates, marble courts and fountains, the bravery and elegance of the men, and the Spanish language itself. "But far above all these do I adore its women—the immortal, the ever-beautiful!"[15] So, one should mistrust the mind and look to the body, and this would be the salvation of Southern culture, to be less English and more Mediterranean, more dashing and less calculating. This opinion was popular enough when the Civil War began, though it was hard put to survive the Civil War.

Evans and Pettigrew's suggestions were not so different, because faith and sensuality both required a willingness of the heart. William Henry Trescot was more engaged by the intellect. In him, pieties dissolved, weaknesses were despised, and morality itself disappeared in the face of historical necessity. As Mary Chesnut was to observe, "Mr. Petigru said of that brilliant Trescot, 'He is a man without indignation.' He and I laugh at everything."[16]

Hugh Blair Grigsby was born in Norfolk in 1806, Trescot in Charleston in 1822. The former was a postrevolutionary man who looked back; the latter was an antebellum man who looked forward. Trescot's education was more local than was usual: Charleston academies, the College of Charleston, and legal apprenticeship. He belonged to his locality and was a man with many friends, rising men who shared jokes, cigars, and women. He married richly in 1848, an alliance which brought him a Beaufort cotton plantation and $10,000 a year. He had wit, ability, leisure, sometimes rural boredom, and a platform for worldly forays. He liked to travel and especially enjoyed his brief time in 1853 as secretary to the American legation in London, where he knocked around with Thackeray, met Macaulay, interviewed Prince Albert, and flitted over to the continent. Scrambling for public office held no attractions for him, and, as an aspirant mandarin, he argued for the necessity of a qualified civil service. However, apart from his stay in London, before 1861 he was only to hold office once, as assistant secretary of state under James Buchanan from June 1860 until his state's secession in December, though briefly he ran the foreign policy of the United States and conducted a shuttle diplomacy between Buchanan and South Carolina.

In the 1850s, Trescot published two histories—*The Diplomacy of the Revolution: An Historical Study* (1852) and *The Diplomatic History of the Administrations of Washington and Adams, 1789–1801* (1857)—works important enough to be admired by Macaulay and earn Trescot a posthumous accolade as "the father of the writing of diplomatic history in the United States." That he was one of the first historians to use the archives of the Department of State is less important than his analytical standpoint, which in turn is less important than his tone. Grigsby had seen history as the refuge of those disappointed of power, but Trescot saw it as a means to power and wanted to learn from the past so as to use it in molding the future. He felt that diplomacy, at crucial moments in history, offered an intoxicating mix, because it reflected and directed the nation, was representative but required "in its sphere as thorough a concentration of power into individual hands as is compatible with national safety."[17] Diplomats sat at the interstices of history, where nations collided, and worked out new systems of power.

As Trescot explained, "The leading fact of modern history is—to borrow a philosophical phrase almost generalized into common use—its progress by antagonism . . . the contest of opposing parties." By "modern" Trescot meant two things, the disparate order of vernacular nations which succeeded the Roman Empire, and more restrictedly the international system after the Peace of Westphalia which had created the balance of power, necessary because of the failure of empire. Modern progress arose from this "constant conflict of equal nations." Selfishness drove and restrained history, because nations checked one another. The system was conservative, even as it changed, and Trescot would readily have assented to the sentiment, famously to be pronounced in Giuseppe di Lampedusa's great novel about Sicily and that other revolution of 1860, the creation of Italy: "If we want things to stay as they are, things will have to change."[18]

Trescot's vision of Realpolitik was revisionist, because he was arguing that the United States had been born in this system of nationalist antagonism, was governed by its laws, and would only flourish by recognizing its course and position within the system. Nothing could have been further from traditional interpretations of the American founding and Manifest Destiny. On this, Trescot was blunt: "It is the mistaken pride of present opinion that we stand apart from the world, intrusted by God's Providence with our peculiar and separate mission; that our wisdom is the summary of the world's experience, and our future independent of the world's control." Of the opinion of almost all his countrymen, Trescot was dismissive. "We are an essential and insepa-rable portion of that Christendom whose deliberations are common because their interests are one; and . . . our progress can neither be safe nor wise un-less we realize, not only our value in, but our connexion with that world."[19] Thus both of Trescot's volumes were designed to show, not how in its birth the United States had broken free from European history, but how it had assumed its place in a system of antagonistic interdependence.

Vital to this analysis was historicism. A nation earned its place by having a distinctive social reality, and it is obvious from Trescot's essay "The Position and Course of the South" (1850) that he believed the South to be a nation and that he wrote his diplomatic histories, not only or not even to inform any future American diplomacy, but to learn how a diplomatist could contribute to creating nations. The legitimacy of a government depended upon its sympathy with "the social institutions of a nation"; slavery had made the South socially distinct; this had led to sectional antagonism; hence, "in such a political crisis the only safety of the South is the establishment of a political centre within itself; in simpler words, the formation of an independent nation." Loose empires and confederations might serve a purpose, as witness Russia and Austria, but "where the administration is . . . the representative of conflicting interests, the decided strength of any one great interest must, of necessity, explode the machine, or re-adjust its arrangements."[20] Just as the British Empire had exploded in 1776, so would the United States, and for the same reason, its lack of social homogeneity.

Trescot's historicism had none of Herder's cheerful populism, no benign belief that a world could be made where peoples would respect one another, dwell in their own linguistic and moral worlds, sing different folk songs, read different literatures, and occasionally get on the ferry from Folkestone to

Boulogne for an amiable shopping expedition. To the contrary, Trescot believed that history, being driven by antagonism, was necessarily scarred by war. In 1850, he replied to those who argued that secession would bring civil and servile war that it was probably so: "It is a truth of history, untouched by an exception, that no nation has ever yet matured its political growth without the stern and scarring experience of civil war." Unlike David Ramsay, who saw polite unanimities in the American Revolution, Trescot saw ugly division in 1776 and refused to acknowledge that the United States had advanced the world's morality. "The independence of the United States," he wrote in 1852, ". . . introduced into history a new power, not a new principle," an assertion that would have been unintelligible to Grigsby, so proud of the Virginia Declaration of Rights.[21]

Such cool impertinence could occasion a neglect of an aspect of Trescot's historicism. He saw the past as instructive, but different. Patterns repeated themselves, but new conditions mandated fresh analysis and action. Most of his contemporaries, when they wrote of the American Revolution, saw it as a living heritage, even when they thought themselves unequal to it. For Trescot, only the lessons of the Revolution were alive, and even they were undistinctive. The phrasing is startling for an American of his day, but he wrote of going back to the time of Revolution and the early republic as visiting "our old days and . . . ancient rulers." He spoke of the difficulty for someone living in the late 1850s of imagining the situation in 1783, with its different conditions and men. Like a good historicist, Trescot tried to puzzle out the differences, though (such confusion was typical of historicists) he believed that, though history changed, nations were continuous. As he put it, "Although temporary necessities may compel a nation to occupy unusual positions, there is an individual character stamped on the policy of each nation, which can be traced through its whole career; that Providence seems to have trusted certain interests to each large combination of political society, in obedience to which it should govern its political life, and its fidelity to which is the measure of its general prosperity."[22]

This was as true of the sections of the United States as of nations, because those sections were but nations which had not ascertained their positions and fixed their place in the system of international life. The Pinckneys in the 1780s had thought the stream of the South's history was intermingled with that of Massachusetts and acted accordingly. Trescot saw differently and thought new action necessary. The Union, he said in 1850, had done useful things, "fertilized a wilderness," begun a commerce, spread Anglo-Saxon law and language, grown in population, given birth to thirty-three states: "It has given to history sublime names, which the world will not willingly let die—

heroic actions which will light the eyes of a far-coming enthusiasm. It has achieved its destiny. Let us achieve ours."[23]

As a diplomatist, Trescot was in the tradition of Machiavelli and Metternich, and had the intellectual pride of the realist. He said to his readers, I have looked coolly upon reality (selfishness, carnage, the interests of labor and capital) and seen where prudence resides. Put away your dreams, look steadily on yourself, and you will have, if not happiness, then at least a chance of survival. Obviously, there was no radical epistemology in this advice: no realist is Humean. Steadiness of gaze is not born of wondering whether there is a gaze to be steadied. So Trescot's tone was not that of early historicism, certainly not Herder, not even Ranke, and very far from George Bancroft. The trusting quality of that early historicism, the sense that one could find times and societies both reliable and emotionally adequate, was almost—not quite—gone from Trescot. Mitchell King had said to the historian, know thyself. Trescot had followed the advice and concluded, this was not much, this history and this self, but it was all there was.

It was no accident that when in 1876 Henry Adams, as editor of the *North American Review*, wanted to find a Southerner to give a dispassionate account of "The Southern Question," he turned to Trescot. There were similarities between the two men, the one having written a *Diplomatic History of the Administrations of Washington and Adams*, the other going to write a *History of the United States in the Administrations of Jefferson and Madison*; the one having scoured the manuscripts of the State Department, the other about to do so; the one a disaffected and impoverished remnant of a destroyed social order, the other a disaffected and affluent remnant of an alienated social order; the one having been bored with Beaufort, the other with Quincy. Adams judged Trescot well enough in 1876 to expect from him writing on the condition of the South that would be different from that of most other Southerners, who "seemed possessed with the literary theories of fifty years ago, and let their feelings get the better of them." Rather, Adams wanted science: "We are nothing if not scientific. We analyze like chemists; we dissect like surgeons; we construct like architects; we never lose our temper; we are never ornate; we are always practical." We "respect the calmness of intellectual power." By "we" Adams claimed to mean the Northern reading public, though it was easy to know that he meant himself and, as significantly, that he expected this of Trescot, too.[24]

Writing during his most scientific phase as a historian, Adams was famously to use the image of history as a Heraclitean river. Jefferson and Madison, he observed, "appear like mere grass-hoppers, kicking and gesticulating, on the middle of the Mississippi River. . . . This I take to be the result that students of history generally reach in regard to modern times. The element of individuality is the free-will dogma of the science, if it is a science. My own conclusion is that history is simply social development along the lines of weakest resistance, and that in most cases the line of weakest resistance is found as unconsciously by society as by water." Trescot had used the same image in 1852, though with a variance. For Adams, history was the river. For Trescot, "system alone as it founds itself on the nature of things" was the river, for only such a system, "if there is a spirit in the people correspondent to it, commands fortune." The stream might pass through an "ever varying series of events," flood, endure drought, pass through rapids, be briefly diverted, "but its general course flows uniform with itself, conforms to the nature of the country it passes through, and maintains the general direction which its issue bears to the source." But the distinction between Adams's and Trescot's images was more apparent than real. The latter's "system" was intellect, but intellect could only be efficacious if it conformed to the landscape: the reward of commanding fortune was not changing the landscape but surviving to the sea.[25]

The nuances of difference between Adams and Trescot lay in varying experiences. Though Trescot was never as powerful politically as he wished, he aspired to power more than Adams and had more power. Consequently, Trescot had more pride in power, more interest in its capacities, and was more entranced by the moments of detachment when the maker of treaties analyzed and settled the fate of nations. Trescot saw himself on the boat with Jefferson and Madison; Adams saw himself on the river bank. In both places, however, as historians they put faith in analysis and detachment, in gathering documents and constructing narratives, and, in both places, they were unsure of efficacy. Out of this doubt came, for Adams, the radical skepticism of *Mont-Saint-Michel and Chartres* and *The Education of Henry Adams*. Out of it, for Trescot, had come armed revolution, a different sort of art.

There had been pride in Evans, Pettigrew, and Trescot. They had said that one could decide upon love and faith, on sensuality and community, on power and nationhood, and the world would respond to the will. Of course, it did not. Their generation had resolved to act, but the splendid moment of resolution yielded to many more moments of irresolution, death, and defeat. There had been, as Trescot was to admit in 1870, a "terrible mistake." Pettigrew himself did not survive the war. In July 1863, not long after the battle of Gettysburg, in which he had commanded a brigade, he was standing in a garden in Pennsylvania when a troop of the Sixth Michigan Cavalry charged down. He tried to mount his horse, but it shied and he fell. He saw a Union corporal shooting several of his men, he advanced to kill the assailant, but his pistol misfired, and he was himself shot in the stomach. Since his brigade was in retreat, he could not be left to recuperate but was carried for eighteen miles in a jostling litter until they reached Berkeley County in what had been Virginia. Trescot was to observe that Pettigrew's death and life showed that the dogma of the will had been a vanity: "We are always working either better or worse than we can know; and whether by victory or defeat, we are always achieving or sacrificing ends that we never purposed."[26]

Yet the will had seemed to hold history together. If it failed, or if it proved only to occasion irony and instability, what was left? Mary Chesnut worked her way toward an answer, as she spent the years of the war and its aftermath in meditating upon the fate of her culture. She had been born the daughter of a parvenu who became a rich planter and politician, she studied at Madame Talvande's school in Charleston, and she married prosperously to the son of a "lordly" planter. The marriage was not a success; she was childless; there was between them a grievance, unnamed but formative. As a U.S. senator, however, James Chesnut gave her an assured place in society and access to the political world she loved knowing. She was a member of Trescot's conversable generation. Most of its other members would come to appear in her writings: William Porcher Miles, Henry Timrod, Paul Hamilton Hayne, Varina Howell Davis, Susan Petigru King, James Johnston Pettigrew, L. Q. C. Lamar, and Trescot himself. Like her, these were skeptical people, putting up with their privileged lot with a half-smile, very interested in the salon and scandal (some of which they occasioned), fashionable, witty, analytical, acting more from necessity than hope, a little sad. They were conscious of themselves as a generation, at odds with if polite toward their elders. Above all, they were clever. This became Mary Chesnut's favorite adjective. "Agreeable men, clever and cultivated men, seem to spring up from the sands of the sea," she was to write. The word meant force of mind, touched with irresponsibility and wit. Cleverness was usually associated with being a man. For a woman like Mary Chesnut, there was a price for being clever and showing it. "Another personal defeat," she was to write about an incident in 1862. A child called Kate came to her and said, "'Oh, Cousin Mary, why don't you cultivate heart? They say at Kirkwood that you had better let your brains alone awhile and cultivate heart.'"[27]

She came omnivorously to read the books that her culture had abundantly furnished. She was accomplished in modern languages, in French and German, though she knew the classics only in translation. She was only unusual in being "intensely English" in her cultural tastes, and she read the customary English authors, old and very new, as well as Jane Austen, then seldom read. Russian literature was largely unknown to her, the Germans featured a little more (Goethe, Schiller, Richter), and she was drawn to contemporary French literature (Balzac, Sand, Dumas, Mérimée, Sue) although Baudelaire, Rimbaud, and Flaubert made no impression on her. Balzac became important because she wanted to write a Southern *comédie humaine*, swarming with vignettes of character and sensitive to social nuances. She had a taste, too, for older French authors like Montaigne, Molière, and, above all, Pascal. She aspired to the epigrammatic, which might comprehend life's hurly-burly, and she was to scatter sentences like "In a revolution shy men are run over. No one stops to pick them up" and "Jealousy of the past is most women's hell."[28]

In this reading, she preferred narratives of social interaction with a cynical edge. This taste disdained what most women wrote and liked, the literary domestic novel, which was too much the occasion for "piety and pie-making" and too little candid. Rather she preferred Thackeray, who of all the Victorian writers was least committed to the principles of realism and understood that, whatever fiction did, it did not mimic real life. Thackeray had begun his career by writing parodies, was someone who debated genre and style, and understood relativism. As he observed in *Pendennis*: "Ah sir—a distinct universe walks about under your hat and under mine. All things in Nature are different to each: the woman we look at has not the same features, the dish we eat from has not the same taste to the one and the other. You and I are but a pair of infinite isolations, with some fellow-islands a little more or less near to us."[29]

Mary Chesnut was sociable, but she did not belong. She was a childless wife who came to be skeptical about God, so the choice imagined by Augusta Evans was not open to her. She was a woman, so she could not play Trescot's game of public power, only observe it, and she could not be a soldier like Pettigrew, whose sensuality made her skittish. Still, she shared a sense that one started with alienation. What she came to lose was any belief that the will could transcend alienation. In so doing, she moved beyond realism, almost to the brink of the literary modernism of the twentieth century, and advanced the process which created modernism, that is, stripping Romanticism of the consolatory hope that human intelligence could make efficacious moral patterns out of the world's disorder and hazarding the contrary conjecture that the human condition was meaningless and only fleetingly intelligible in art.

At the beginning of the Civil War, she began to keep a diary. How consistently she kept it is unclear because she was later to destroy many manuscripts. What remains are her entries from 18 February to 8 December 1861, and from late January or early February 1865 to 26 June of the same year. That there were other volumes is evident, since she used them as the basis for the vastly expanded narrative of the war, cast in the form of a diary, written in the 1870s and 1880s. Only the passages from 1861 and 1865, in both versions, survive to indicate how she reappraised her understanding between 1865 and 1880, and the evidence of how she began to see differently during the war is elusive, if compelling.

The two versions of the diary point to the essential moral. The earlier version began where her generation had begun, with the idea of the will. Her first words were: "I do not allow myself vain regrets or sad forebodings. This southern Confederacy must be supported now by calm deliberation—& cool brains. We have risked all, & we must play our best for the stake is life or death." The later version ends, "And—and the weight that hangs upon our eyelids—is of lead."[30] Clarity had given way to blindness, which was the true state of anyone trying to understand the human condition.

It seems likely that what became a philosophical stance started as a personal grievance. She entered 1861 discontented with the betrayals inherent in human relationships. Her unhappy marriage and problematical relationship to the self-satisfied matrons around her were part of her alienation. One early entry reads: "Talked all night—*exhausted*. & nervous & miserable today—raked up & dilated & harrowed up the bitterness of twenty long years—all to no purpose. This bitter world." She squirmed when her mother-in-law boasted to "me a childless wretch" of having twenty-seven grandchildren, and reflected, "God help me—no good have I done—to myself or any one else—with the [power] I boast so of—the power to make myself loved. Where are my friends. I am allowed to have none."[31]

She was troubled by the propensity of Southern men, including her father-in-law, to form liaisons with slave women, and she complained, like an abolitionist, that the South was a sort of brothel and slavery a "*monstrous system.*" She understood society, more generally, as consisting of many tangled and bitter interrelationships, and she retained a sense (as any cynic must) that there was a moral order to be betrayed. She did go to church regularly, though she was alert to religion's hypocrisy and felt awkward around the pious. Chesnut noted of a Catholic lady called Munro who began a religious discussion in 1865 with her, that she "seemed to find me a worldling—& my christian doctrines *utterly* crude & undigested. I ran away as she had so much the best of the argument—knowing I was right, but failing for want of practice in talking on that subject."[32] There were moments when she lost hold of belief altogether.

The part of her that in 1861 could say that "the ways of this world are never to be divined" and that "no body understands the under current of unseen motives" furnished the insight that structured her postwar literary efforts.[33] God and the South, cool brains and calm deliberation, had not worked. What she came to realize, what perhaps no one else in her culture realized as fully, was that failure required a new technique of narration. A discordant and unintelligible world mandated a literary form that suggested, not life's order, but its disorder. It was not that Mary Chesnut became Dadaist. Her revised diaries retained chronology; day followed day, year followed year, the bombardment of Fort Sumter preceded the battle of Gettysburg. Time was not an illusion she wished to shed, because time showed how men, especially her men, had failed. Time explained her own self, too, because she was the product of history's damage.

She wished to show how the world had occasioned such damage and thereby to pull "ostrich heads out of the sand." She was anxious to be candid: old Colonel Chesnut's mulatto children, Buck Preston's cruel and innocent flirtations, sexually frustrated soldiers grabbing at their nurses, the murder of an old woman by slaves, the beating of a pregnant slave by a mistress, a man gleefully fishing out a tumbled oyster from between a startled woman's breasts, the incessant human folly of society. Few were spared, because Chesnut was habitually skeptical about the pieties of her culture. She laughed at honor, made fun of the rituals of courtship, condemned beauty for its ruthless hard-heartedness, amused herself at the feebleness of conventional oratory, and savaged Southern integrity. Nor did she spare herself, a character in her own narrative, someone mocked as "the Explainer General," full of foible and weakness, shown "spinning [her] own entrails," taking her opium, exercising her "power to hide trouble." Though Chesnut policed these self-revelations and toyed with omitting herself and being merely "objective," she confessed all but the most intimate secrets.[34] She made it possible, for example, for the reader to understand the pain of her childlessness, though not its cause.

The thing that distinguished the original diary from the narrative journal was its use of voices. Chesnut offered snatches of conversation and solitary voices, commenting on events, often incoherently. These voices embodied her quasi-modernist leanings, par excellence, because they were intentionally fragmentary. It was often unclear who was speaking, voices were not always answered, the profound and trivial lay next to one another unreconciled, contemporary voices sat next to literary quotations, Medea was adjacent to someone called Albert, and subject matters changed abruptly.

Chesnut's narrative journal everywhere speaks that she understood what would become Virginia Woolf's complaint, that the three-decker novel had failed to show what it meant to be human: out of evasion had sprung "those sleek, smooth novels, those portentous and ridiculous biographies, that milk and watery criticism, those poems melodiously celebrating the innocence of roses and sheep which pass so plausibly for literature at the present time."[35] This could pass for a description of the Southern literature that came Mary Chesnut's way in 1880, and she realized the necessity for a change more than Augusta Jane Evans, whose novels held to traditional forms. Narrative did not break down for Chesnut because she was incapable of coherence. Her narrative journal is full of stories, vignettes, and anecdotes as coherently fashioned as any Victorian novelist could have wished. The tale of the "Witherspoon Murder Case," the old lady murdered in her bed by slaves, is a chillingly effective allegory which has stuck in the minds of generations of readers. The old patriarch, James Chesnut, is a character whom his daughter-in-law described and invented with stiletto care, to stand as the "last of the lordly planters who ruled this Southern world."[36]

Chesnut's voices were artful, their incoherences intended. Why? Because, finally, she had concluded that the world had not added up to a smooth story with an ordered moral. Rather, it was "full of strange vicissitudes, and in nothing more remarkable than the way people are reconciled, ignore the past, and start afresh in life, here to incur more disagreements and set to bickering again." Chesnut disbelieved for the reasons classically adduced to explain the onset of modernism. She had no faith in the old gods of Christianity, the new ones of science, the justice of her society, the goodness of human beings, and the probability of happiness for them. She did not even trust herself. But she knew that these skepticisms did not disavow the vitality of life—"so excited and confused—worthy of me"—but made it more urgent and necessary to be portrayed.[37] Life and art might persist, even when power and philosophy failed.

The fate of Mary Chesnut and her manuscripts shows what happened to antebellum understandings when transmitted to later generations. She herself went to live in genteel impoverishment in Camden, South Carolina, which even during the war she knew would be her fate, if the Confederacy should lose. In her journal, few moments are more chilling than that when, at the end of things in 1865, she has her husband express the sentence and doom, "Camden for life." The wealth from slaves gone and the land yielding little income, they lived on odd legacies and her selling of eggs and butter. Her father-in-law's will specified that the land transmitted to James Chesnut could not pass to her, and so, when her husband died in 1885, she came to an annual income smaller than the amount she had been used to spending in 1859 upon a cape of Alençon lace. Such shabby gentility—she would wear her husband's old trousers when gardening, and a relative described her, when wearing "an old western mackintosh and a funny old hat," as looking like "an old market woman"—partly impelled her interest in writing, because she entertained hopes of making money from it.[38] Over the years she fiddled with three novels and did a little translating from the French, but her last years were preoccupied with the million words of her narrative journal. Little found its way into print, and, upon her death in 1886, the manuscripts passed into the hands of Isabella Martin, a Methodist schoolteacher in Camden, whom Chesnut had liked and from whom she had extracted a promise to try to publish them. Martin was not worldly about publishers and the manuscripts were in confusion, so little happened for nearly twenty years, until Myrta Lockett Avary came along. She was a Virginian, a journalist, and latterly a New Yorker, who had published in 1903 *A Virginia Girl in the Civil War*. She knew the firm of Appleton's and about marketing Civil War memoirs, and she took on the project of seeing Mary Chesnut into print. The manuscript was briskly butchered down to a manageable size, and an in-house editor at Appleton's manufactured chapters, furnished footnotes, re-wrote passages, and assisted Avary in making sure that the journal said nothing inconvenient to the sentimental legends of the Old South and Confederacy which had been selling books so agreeably for the last twenty-five years. The *Saturday Evening Post*, which serialized some of it, decided to call it *A Diary from Dixie*, though Chesnut herself disliked the term and the song. The book was a success, though its readers were never told that they were reading a postbellum revision of a war diary, and they were not to be illuminated further when a novelist called Ben Ames Williams revised the book further in the late 1940s, added extra material from the manuscripts, altered punctuation, moved passages around, added his own prose, and ensured that Mary Chesnut was left in possession of no thoughts and no rhetoric that might confuse a reader of *Gone With the Wind* or draw an aficionado of *To the Lighthouse*.

At least, Mary Chesnut survived the war. Others did not make it through, being old like William Grayson, or ill like James Henry Hammond, or victim to the war's violence and disease, like Henry Hughes. A few of advanced years lasted a while, in varying degrees of impoverishment or bitterness. Louisa McCord took herself off to Canada as a political exile, then returned to live with her daughter in Charleston, before dying in 1879. Simms resumed writing, but his market was gone and in 1869, the penultimate year of his life, he traveled to New York in the summer (as he had always done) to deal with publishers, but the venture was fruitless and he had to borrow the money to get back home. George Fitzhugh showed flexibility in working as a court agent for the Freedmen's Bureau in Richmond, wrote a few articles on Reconstruction policy, and published articles in *Lippincott's Magazine* in Philadelphia, but he had little money, and, after his wife's death in 1877, he went to live briefly with his son in Frankfort, Kentucky, and then in 1880 permanently with his daughter in Texas; he died in 1881. Charles Gayarré, in stark poverty and overwhelming resentment, hung on for decades, until ancient and virtually blind he died in 1895. Others, younger than these, were often crippled by the experience of the war. Sidney Lanier, the Georgian poet and musician who contracted tuberculosis in a Federal prison, became an elegiac symbol and furnished the quintessential quotation for those Victorian Southerners for whom death had acquired exquisite charms. "Perhaps you know," he told Bayard Taylor in 1875, "that with us of the younger generation in the South since the War, pretty much the whole of life has been merely not-dying."[39]

Elegy is seductive, but would be mistaken. Many others adapted, even flourished. Josiah Nott moved to New York in 1868, set up a successful practice, and became president of the New York Obstetrical Society. Though it took him a decade and more to clear his debts, Trescot ended up as a senior diplomat for the State Department, a special emissary used to handle tricky problems such as the Halifax Fisheries dispute and American rights in the Isthmus of Panama. Just like Beulah Benton, Augusta Evans married a rich widower and continued to have a very successful career. Her novel *St. Elmo* became a best seller third only to *Uncle Tom's Cabin* and *Ben-Hur*, became a play and, in 1923, a film. Judah P. Benjamin, though in political exile, became a Queen's Counsel in London, where he raked in guineas by the bagful, became so grand that he declined to appear in any cases not before the House of Lords or the Judicial Committee of the Privy Council, and died in resplendence in his Parisian mansion.

Elegy is inapt for another reason. The intellectuals of the antebellum South had helped to invent, administer, and advance an imperial regime of ruthless ambition, which had conquered an empire, enslaved millions, and seldom hesitated to shed others' blood for the sake of its own comfort. They had been intelligent, learned, creative, even self-aware, but they had gambled to sustain their own power, which, they had carefully explained to themselves and the world, needed to be exercised at someone else's expense. For playing the game of power and losing, they do not invite pity. For replaying the game in 1875 and 1900 with equal brutality, still less do they invite sympathy.

Still, they do need to be understood, which latterly they were not. This was partly their own fault. In painful retrospect, some reinvented their earlier experience. Paul Hamilton Hayne, who ended up isolated in rural

Georgia and scraped a living as a writer, reimagined Charleston as a vanished idyll, partly to fend off those Northern (and some New Southern) critics who dismissed "the whole department of Southern *ante-bellum* literature [as] a desert of antiquated rubbish, with nothing of permanent beauty or power."[40] Others did not bother to defend or understand the minds of the defeated order, but found it safer to change the subject. They minimized slavery, admired manners, praised valor, and stressed whiteness. The old instinct of survival now advised that it would be prudent to read Emerson and let Fitzhugh go, considering the intellectual power of Harvard College and the materialist promises of the United States Steel Corporation. The old, ill-organized texts drifted away. The novels went out of print, the periodicals sat on neglectful shelves, the manuscripts were stuffed into armoires or went into archives, to be visited by scholars who cared for little but fathoming Pickett's charge. It was simpler for Southerners and Northerners alike to believe that the Old South had defied the American way out of ignorance, or guilt, or stupidity, or romantic innocence. There was little to be done in 1910, even in 1960, with the insight that the Old South had chosen its own way with clarity of mind, had even understood things about the intractability of the human condition, and had been consistent with the later trajectory of the American republic, which usefully flattered itself that aristocracy, illiberal-ism, and rapacity had died in 1865 and could be killed.

Notes

ABBREVIATIONS

ADAH
Alabama Department of Archives and History, Montgomery, Alabama

DBR
De Bow's Review

DU
Manuscript and Special Collections Department, William R. Perkins Library,
Duke University, Durham, North Carolina

FL
Francis Lieber

GF
George Fitzhugh

GFH
George Frederick Holmes

HEH
Henry E. Huntington Library, San Marino, California

JHT
James Henley Thornwell

JWM
James Warley Miles

SCHS
South Carolina Historical Society, Charleston, South Carolina

SCL
South Caroliniana Library, University of South Carolina, Columbia, South Carolina

SHC
Southern Historical Collection, Wilson Library,
University of North Carolina, Chapel Hill, North Carolina

SLM
Southern Literary Messenger

SQR

Southern Quarterly Review

SR

Southern Review

UA

Hoole Special Collections Library, University of Alabama, Tuscaloosa, Alabama

VHS

Virginia Historical Society, Richmond, Virginia

WGS

William Gilmore Simms

INTRODUCTION

1. Thomas R. Dew, *Lectures on the Restrictive System Delivered to the Senior Political Class of William and Mary College* (1829; New York: Augustus M. Kelley, 1969), 187.

2. Ronald Hingley, ed., *The Oxford Chekhov*, vol. 3, *Uncle Vanya, Three Sisters, The Cherry Orchard, The Wood-Demon* (London: Oxford University Press, 1964), 182–83.

3. Caroline Gilman, *Recollections of a Southern Matron* (New York: Harper and Brothers, 1838), 134.

4. Stephen Elliott, "Views of Nature," *SR* 2 (November 1828): 416.

5. Michael O'Brien, ed., *An Evening When Alone: Four Journals of Single Women in the South, 1827–1867* (Charlottesville: University Press of Virginia, 1993), 102.

6. Francis W. Pickens to Albert J. Pickett, 30 September 1847, Pickett Papers, ADAH; O'Brien, *Evening When Alone*, 129.

7. GFH, "Philosophy and Faith," *Methodist Quarterly Review* 3 (April 1851): 185–218.

8. C. Vann Woodward and Elisabeth Muhlenfeld, eds., *The Private Mary Chesnut: The Unpublished Civil War Diaries* (New York: Oxford University Press, 1984), 3.

9. Edgar Allan Poe, "The Narrative of Arthur Gordon Pym of Nantucket," in *Poetry and Tales*, ed. Patrick F. Quinn (New York: Library of America, 1984), 1179.

CHAPTER ONE

1. William Elliott to William Plumer, n.d. [1847], Beverley Scafidel, ed., "The Letters of William Elliott" (Ph.D. diss., University of South Carolina, 1978), 500; Basil Manly Jr. to Basil Manly, 24 February 1845, Manly Family Papers, UA.

2. John Melish, *Travels in the United States of America, in the Years 1806 & 1807, & 1809, 1810, & 1811* (Philadelphia: John Melish, 1815), 284.

3. Lucian Minor, "Letters from New England," *SLM* 1 (November 1834): 87; Minor, "Letters from New England," *SLM* 1 (January 1835): 218–19; Minor, "Letters from New England," *SLM* 1 (April 1835): 425.

4. Alice B. Neal, "Marrying a Planter: A New Chapter of Romance and Reality," *Godey's Lady's Book* 52 (January–June 1856): 327–28, quoted in Susan-Mary Grant, *North Over South: Northern Nationalism and American Identity in the Antebellum Era* (Lawrence: Univer-

sity Press of Kansas, 2000), 41; A. W. Plumstead and William Henry Gilman, eds., *The Journals and Miscellaneous Notebooks of Ralph Waldo Emerson*, vol. 11, *1848–1851* (Cambridge, Mass.: Belknap Press of Harvard University Press, 1975), 233; *Albany Evening Journal*, 20 April 1849, quoted in Grant, *North Over South*, 52; Thoreau, quoted in Howard Russell Floan, *The South in Northern Eyes, 1831–1861* (Austin: University of Texas Press, 1958), 69; uncited Parker quotation in Henry Steele Commager, *Theodore Parker: Yankee Crusader*, 2d ed. (Boston: Beacon Press, 1947), 197.

5. Francis L. Hawks to David L. Swain, 3 January 1860, David L. Swain Papers, SHC; "A Letter on Slavery" (1848), in Theodore Parker, *The Slave Power*, ed. James K. Hosmer (Boston: American Unitarian Association, 1916), 77; Cornelius C. Felton to Hugh Blair Grigsby, 17 April 1861, Grigsby Papers, VHS.

6. Robert Young Hayne to Warren Davis, 25 September 1827, Hayne Papers, SCL; "Prospectus of the *Southern Review*," [24 September 1827], in Linda Rhea, *Hugh Swinton Legaré: A Charleston Intellectual* (Chapel Hill: University of North Carolina Press, 1934), 236–38.

7. Thomas Cooper to Trustees of South Carolina College, 30 November 1831, Thomas Cooper Papers, SCL; Basil Manly to Basil Manly Jr., 10 March 1845, Manly Family Papers, UA.

8. Edward W. Johnston to Langdon Cheves Jr., 16 February 1836, Langdon Cheves Papers, SCHS.

9. William Campbell Preston to FL, 6 March 1859, FL Papers, SCL.

10. Susan Petigru King, *Gerald Gray's Wife and Lily: A Novel* (1855; Durham, N.C.: Duke University Press, 1993), 24.

11. Charles Dickens to John Forster, 24 February, 13 March 1842, in Madeline House, Graham Storey, and Kathleen Tillotson, eds., *The Letters of Charles Dickens*, vol. 3, *1842–1843* (Oxford: Clarendon Press, 1974), 88, 126, 90.

12. "Thackeray's English Humorists," *SLM* 19 (July 1853): 437.

13. Gordon Norton Ray, *Thackeray: The Age of Wisdom, 1847–1863* (New York: McGraw-Hill, 1958), 216–17.

14. William S. McFeely, *Frederick Douglass* (New York: W. W. Norton, 1991), 127–28, 133; Thomas Smyth, *Autobiographical Notes, Letters and Reflections*, ed. Louisa Cheves Stoney (Charleston, S.C.: Walker, Evans and Cogswell, 1914), 362; R. Davidson and Torrens to Thomas Smyth, 16 July 1846, Smyth-Stoney-Adger Collection, SCHS, quoted verbatim in Smyth, *Autobiographical Notes*, 371–72.

15. James Robertson to Thomas Smyth, 6 July 1846, Smyth-Stoney-Adger Collection, SCHS; Smyth to Davison and Torrens, 17 July 1846, in Smyth, *Autobiographical Notes*, 373–75.

16. George S. Hillard to FL, 7 December 1842, FL Papers, HEH.

17. FL to George S. Hillard, [23 June 1851], FL Papers, HEH.

18. FL, "Letter on Races," clipping from the Boston *Daily Journal*, 6 June 1851, pasted in notebook, FL Papers, HEH; see also FL to George S. Hillard, April 1850, ibid.

19. FL to George S. Hillard, 1 May 1856, FL Papers, HEH.

20. FL, manuscript headed "Chapter: Of the Love of Country and the Obligation of sacrificing one's self or one's interest to the Common Weal," ca. 1835–51, FL Papers, HEH.

21. Basil Manly to James L. Reynolds, 17 July 1838, Manly Family Papers, UA; Michael

Tuomey to James Henry Hammond, 13 September 1845, James Henry Hammond Papers, Library of Congress, in Lewis S. Dean, ed., *The Papers of Michael Tuomey* (Spartanburg, S.C.: Reprint Company, 2001), 73.

22. William Henry Trescot, *Memorial of the Life of Johnston Pettigrew, Brig. Gen. of the Confederate States Army* (Charleston, S.C.: John Russell, 1870), 22–23.

23. Augustin Louis Taveau to his sister, [March 1853], Taveau Papers, DU.

24. "Spirit of the Sub-Treasury" (1837), in Mary Swinton Legaré, ed., *Writings of Hugh Swinton Legaré*, 2 vols. (Charleston, S.C.: Burges and James, 1845–46), 1:304.

25. James Henry Hammond to Francis W. Pickens, 6 September 1836, Hammond MSS, DU; John Young Bassett to Isaphoena Bassett, 13 March, 27 March 1836, Bassett Papers, ADAH.

26. Robert Massengill Porter, "Journal, 24 April 1845–3 June 1846," Miscellaneous Collection, Tennessee State Library and Archives, Nashville.

27. John Blair Hoge to Moses Hoge, 25 July 1815, Hoge Family Papers, Presbyterian Historical Society, Montreat, N.C.

28. Entry for 12 September 1829, Jesse Burton Harrison, "European Diary, 1829–30," Francis B. Harrison Papers, Special Collections Department, Alderman Library, University of Virginia, Charlottesville.

29. Stephen Elliott, "Education in Germany," *SR* 4 (August 1829): 87, 117.

30. Jesse Burton Harrison, "The Prospects of Letters and Taste in Virginia" (1827), in Fairfax Harrison, ed., *Aris Sonis Focisque, Being a Memoir of an American Family, the Harrisons of Skimino* (n.p.: privately printed, 1910), 294; John T. Krumpelmann, *Southern Scholars in Goethe's Germany* (Chapel Hill: University of North Carolina Press, 1965), 52, 55–56, 58–59.

31. Hugh Swinton Legaré to Thomas Caute Reynolds, 6 February 1841, in Legaré, *Writings*, 1:236; George Henry Calvert, "Göttingen in 1824," *Putnam's Monthly Magazine* 8 (December 1856): 607.

32. Basil L. Gildersleeve, "Formative Influences," *Forum* 10 (February 1891): 614–15; Henry Adams, *The Education of Henry Adams: An Autobiography* (Boston: Houghton Mifflin, 1918), 71.

33. GFH, "Critical Notices—Anthon's Greek Prosody," *SQR* 6 (July 1844): 248.

34. John Taylor, *Tyranny Unmasked*, ed. F. Thornton Miller (1822; Indianapolis, Ind.: Liberty Fund, 1992), 191.

35. William B. Crawford Journal, Gorgas Family Papers, UA.

36. William Campbell Preston to Washington Irving, 16 March 1818, Preston Family Papers, VHS.

37. Edward L. Tucker, *Richard Henry Wilde: His Life and Selected Poems* (Athens: University of Georgia Press, 1966), 43.

38. Richard Henry Wilde, *Hesperia: A Poem*, ed. William Cumming Wilde (Boston: Ticknor and Fields, 1867), 66, 24, 73, 72.

39. Nathalia Wright, "The Letters of Richard Henry Wilde to Hiram Powers," *Georgia Historical Quarterly* 46 (December 1962): 430–31.

40. Paul Hamilton Hayne to Richard Stoddard, 23 July 1855, Hayne Papers, DU; Brantz Mayer, "Italy," *SQR* 10 (July 1846): 99.

41. Henry Junius Nott, "A Year in Spain," *SR* 8 (November 1831): 154.

42. J. D. B. De Bow, "Literature of Spain," *DBR* 9 (July 1850): 66.

43. Edwin DeLeon, "The 'Prometheus Unbound' of Shelley," *SLM* 8 (March 1842): 196.

44. John B. Adger, *My Life and Times, 1810–1899* (Richmond, Va.: Presbyterian Committee of Publication, 1899), 100.

45. Clifton Jackson Phillips, *Protestant America and the Pagan World: The First Half Century of the American Board of Commissioners for Foreign Missions, 1810–1860* (Cambridge, Mass.: Harvard University Press, 1969), 160–61.

46. J. Leighton Wilson, *Western Africa: Its History, Condition, and Prospects* (New York: Harper and Brothers, 1856), 379–80.

47. Augustine Lamberth McDonagh to John McDonagh, 8 March 1844; Pascal Woodson to Isaac R. Wade, 21 February 1853, in Bell I. Wiley, ed., *Slaves No More: Letters from Liberia, 1833–1869* (Lexington: University Press of Kentucky, 1980), 132, 165.

48. Jonathan Spence, *God's Chinese Son: The Chinese Heavenly Kingdom of Hong Xiuquan* (New York: W. W. Norton, 1996), xxvi.

49. Ibid., 286–88.

50. Brantz Mayer, *Mexico, Aztec, Spanish and Republican: A Historical, Geographical, Political, Statistical and Social Account of That Country from the Period of the Invasion by the Spaniards to the Present Time*, 2 vols. in 1 (1851; Hartford: S. Drake, 1853), 2:40, 155, 160.

51. Douglas R. Egerton, *Gabriel's Rebellion: The Virginia Slave Conspiracies of 1800 and 1802* (Chapel Hill: University of North Carolina Press, 1993), 47.

52. "Autobiography of George Tucker, 1775–1861," *Bermuda Historical Quarterly* 18, no. 3 and 4 (Autumn/Winter 1961): 94.

53. Joel R. Poinsett, *Notes on Mexico, Made in the Autumn of 1822: Accompanied by an Historical Sketch of the Revolution* (Philadelphia: Carey and Lea, 1824), 220.

CHAPTER TWO

1. Stephen Elliott, "Views of Nature," *SR* 2 (November 1828): 413.

2. Stephen Elliott, "Classification of Plants," *SR* 4 (November 1829): 471; Elliott, "Views of Nature," 416.

3. Elliott, "Views of Nature," 429–31.

4. Tocqueville to Gobineau, 20 December 1853, in Alexis de Tocqueville, *Selected Letters on Politics and Society*, ed. Roger Boesche (Berkeley: University of California Press, 1985), 303.

5. Johann Friedrich Blumenbach, *The Anthropological Treatises of Johann Friedrich Blumenbach*, ed. Thomas Bendyshe (London: Longman, Green, Longman, Roberts, and Green, 1865), 162.

6. Ibid., 100, 151, 99, 155.

7. Ibid., 209, 264.

8. Thomas Smith Grimké, "Origin of Rhyme," *SR* 2 (August 1828): 68, 37, 66; Grimké, "Origin of Rhyme," *SR* 3 (February 1829): 157, 191; Thomas Cooper, "Higgins' Celtic Druids," *SR* 3 (February 1829): 208.

9. Josiah C. Nott, "The Mulatto a Hybrid—Probable Extermination of the Two Races If the Whites and Blacks Are Allowed to Intermarry," *American Journal of Medical Sciences*, n.s., 6 (July 1843): 254.

10. Paul Broca, *On the Phenomena of Hybridity in the Genus Homo*, ed. Charles Carter Blake (London: Longman, Green, Longman, and Roberts, 1864), 32.

11. Blumenbach, *Blumenbach Treatises*, 98–99.

12. *Proceedings and Debates of the Virginia State Convention, of 1829–30* (Richmond, Va.: Samuel Shepherd, 1830), 227.

13. Sarah Grimké, *Letters on the Equality of the Sexes and Other Essays*, ed. Elizabeth Ann Bartlett (1838; New Haven, Conn.: Yale University Press, 1988), 33.

14. Ibid., 64, 67, 99; Margaret Fuller Ossoli, *Woman in the Nineteenth Century and Kindred Papers Relating to the Sphere, Condition and Duties of Woman*, ed. Arthur B. Fuller (1845; Boston: John P. Jewett, 1855), 37.

15. Grimké, *Equality of the Sexes*, 100, 78.

16. Richard C. Lounsbury, ed., *Louisa S. McCord: Political and Social Essays* (Charlottesville: University Press of Virginia, 1995), 115–16.

17. See, for example, Lounsbury, *McCord: PSE*, 77, 114, 115,

18. Ibid., 73, 108, 131, 119, 406.

19. Ibid., 109, 110, 108, 119, 149; Louisa S. McCord to William Porcher Miles, 12 June 1848, in Richard C. Lounsbury, ed., *Louisa S. McCord: Poems, Drama, Biography, Letters* (Charlottesville: University Press of Virginia, 1996), 275.

20. Dexter Clapp to Henry W. Bellows, 12 January 1844, Henry W. Bellows Papers, DU; Louisa S. McCord to Henry C. Carey, 18 January 1854, in Lounsbury, *McCord: PDBL*, 297.

21. Louisa S. McCord to Langdon Cheves Jr., 18 February, 25, 28 January, 5 February 1856, in Lounsbury, *McCord: PDBL*, 312, 304, 308, 333.

22. Louisa S. McCord to William Porcher Miles, 12 June 1848; Louisa S. McCord to Langdon Cheves Jr., 7 March, 1 February 1856, in Lounsbury, *McCord: PDBL*, 274, 318, 309.

23. Charles E. A. Gayarré, *Essai historique sur la Louisiane*, 2 vols. (New Orleans: B. Levy, 1830), 1:iii.

24. Charles E. A. Gayarré, *History of Louisiana: The Spanish Domination* (New York: Redfield, 1854), 627.

25. Ibid., 627, 525–26.

26. Charles E. A. Gayarré, *History of Louisiana: The American Domination* (New York: William J. Widdleton, 1866), 2; John W. Monette, *History of the Discovery and Settlement of the Valley of the Mississippi*, 2 vols. in 1 (1846; New York: Arno Press and New York Times, 1971), 2:449–50.

27. Gayarré, *American Domination*, 379–80.

28. Ibid., 632.

29. William Wirt, *The Letters of the British Spy* (1803; Chapel Hill: University of North Carolina Press, 1970), 101–2.

30. George Tucker, *The Valley of the Shenandoah; or, Memoirs of the Graysons*, 2 vols. in 1 (1824; Chapel Hill: University of North Carolina Press, 1970), 1:49, 55, 2:23.

31. John Pendleton Kennedy, *Swallow Barn; or, A Sojourn in Virginia: An American Tale*, 2 vols. (Philadelphia: Carey and Lea, 1832), 2:185, 1:75–76, 180, 181, 2:2.

32. Ibid., 2:275, 276, 1:74, 2:278.

33. Henry Augustine Washington, "The Social System of Virginia," *SLM* 14 (February 1848): 71.

34. Frank J. Klingberg and Frank W. Klingberg, eds., *The Correspondence between Henry Stephens Randall and Hugh Blair Grigsby, 1856–1861* (Berkeley: University of California Press, 1952), 76, 17.

35. Washington, "Social System of Virginia," 77; Robert L. Meriwether et al., eds., *The*

Papers of John C. Calhoun, 28 vols. (Columbia: University of South Carolina Press, 1959–2003), 14:206.

36. Abel P. Upshur, *A Brief Enquiry Into the True Nature and Character of the Federal Government; Being a Review of Judge Story's Commentaries on the Constitution of the United States* (1840; Philadelphia: John Campbell, 1863), 97.

37. "Mr. Rives' Address," *Virginia Historical Register* 1 (January 1848): 2, 6, 7; Hugh Swinton Legaré, "The American System," *SR* 6 (August 1830): 211; William Henry Trescot, *Oration Delivered before the South-Carolina Historical Society, Thursday, May 19, 1859* (Charleston, S.C.: James and Williams, 1859), 9, 10.

38. Hugh Blair Grigsby, *The Virginia Convention of 1776* (Richmond, Va.: J. W. Randolph, 1855), 195; Beverley Tucker to James Henry Hammond, 15 March 1836, Nathaniel Beverley Tucker MSS, DU.

39. GFH, "Critical Notices—a Day on Cooper River," *SQR* 3 (January 1843): 258.

40. James C. Bonner, *Milledgeville: Georgia's Antebellum Capital* (1978; Macon, Ga.: Mercer University Press, 1985), 131.

41. C. H. Wiley, *The North-Carolina Reader* (Philadelphia: Lippincott, Grambo, 1851), 19.

42. Ibid., 9, 11, 12.

43. Ibid., 84.

44. Ibid., 86, 89; "Second Annual Message," 6 December 1830, in James D. Richardson, *A Compilation of the Messages and Papers of the Presidents, 1789–1897*, 10 vols. (Washington, D.C.: U.S. Government Printing Office, 1896–99), 2:513.

45. John Randolph to Francis Scott Key, 2 March 1814, quoted in Hugh A. Garland, *The Life of John Randolph of Roanoke*, 2 vols. (New York: D. Appleton, 1850), 2:33; Oscar Lieber to Matilda Lieber, 16 July 1851, FL Papers, SCL.

46. Basil Manly to J. L. Reynolds, 2 April 1834, Manly Family Papers, UA; Wiley, *North-Carolina Reader*, 30.

47. Basil Lanneau Gildersleeve, "Formative Influences," in *Soldier and Scholar: Basil Lanneau Gildersleeve and the Civil War*, ed. Ward W. Briggs Jr. (Charlottesville: University Press of Virginia, 1998), 35; Edward W. Johnston, "American Literature," *SR* 7 (August 1831): 443–44.

48. John Pendleton Kennedy to Alexander Randall, 9 April 1849, Kennedy Papers, George Peabody Library, Baltimore; R. B. Brashear to J. D. B. De Bow, 8 February 1856, J. D. B. De Bow MSS, DU; entry for 23 September 1831, Moses Ashley Curtis Diary, Curtis Papers, SHC.

49. Thomas C. Reynolds to James Johnston Pettigrew, 9 October 1858, Pettigrew Family Papers, North Carolina State Archives, Raleigh.

50. "The Black Race in North America: Why Was Their Introduction Permitted?," *SLM* 21 (November 1855): 683.

51. FL to "Dear Sir," 26 July 1862, FL Papers, SCL, quoted in Michael Sugrue, "South Carolina College: The Education of an Antebellum Elite" (Ph.D. diss., Columbia University, 1992), 298–99.

52. GF, "Ancient Families of Virginia, Maryland, Etc," *DBR* 26 (May 1859): 490.

53. Caroline Gilman to Mrs. Harriet Fay, 4 March 1821, Caroline Gilman MSS, SCHS.

54. "Spirit of the Sub-Treasury" (1837), in Mary Swinton Legaré, ed., *Writings of Hugh Swinton Legaré*, 2 vols. (Charleston, S.C.: Burges and James, 1845–46), 1:301.

55. "Caloya; or, The Loves of the Driver," in WGS, *The Wigwam and the Cabin* (New York: Wiley and Putnam, 1846), 410.

56. Daniel R. Hundley, *Social Relations in Our Southern States* (New York: Henry B. Price, 1860), 77.

57. Thomas R. Dew, *Lectures on the Restrictive System Delivered to the Senior Political Class of William and Mary College* (1829; New York: Augustus M. Kelley, 1969), 146; JHT to Nancy Thornwell, 29 May 1851, Anderson and Thornwell Family Papers, SHC; Samuel Gaillard Stoney, ed., "The Memoirs of Frederick Augustus Porcher: Chapter I: A Rural Homestead," *South Carolina Historical and Genealogical Magazine* 44 (April 1943): 80.

58. FL, *The Character of the Gentleman: An Address to the Students of Miami University, Ohio* (Cincinnati: J. A. James, 1846); William J. Grayson, "The Character of the Gentleman," *SQR* n.s. 7 (January 1853): 59.

59. Hundley, *Social Relations*, 251; Hugh Blair Grigsby to David L. Swain, 20 August 1857, David L. Swain Papers, SHC.

60. Entry for 22 November 1828, Hugh Blair Grigsby Diary, Grigsby Papers, VHS; "Critical Notices—Presbyterian Review," *SQR* 12 (October 1847): 535.

61. John Pendleton Kennedy to Washington Irving, 22 September 1853, Kennedy Papers, George Peabody Library, Baltimore; FL to Trustees of William and Mary, 29 January 1847, GFH MSS, DU.

62. Edward W. Johnston to Richard K. Crallé, 30 April 1841, Crallé Papers, Strom Thurmond Institute, Clemson University, Clemson, S.C.; M. J. Williams to JHT, 22 April 1854, JHT Papers, SCL.

63. Mary Ellen Hedrick to Mrs. Rankin, 8 April 1853, Benjamin S. Hedrick Papers, SHC.

CHAPTER THREE

1. Adrien Rouquette, *La Thébaïde en Amerique, ou apologie de la vie solitaire et contemplative* (New Orleans: Imprimerie Meridier, 1852); undated entry, ca. early 1838, in Louisa Penelope Davis Preston Diary, Mrs. William Campbell Preston Papers, SCL; Hugh Blair Grigsby, *Discourse on the Life and Character of the Hon. Littleton Waller Tazewell* (Norfolk, Va.: J. D. Ghiselin, Jun., 1860), 91; George S. Bryan to John Pendleton Kennedy, December 1860, Kennedy Papers, Enoch Pratt Free Library, Baltimore, quoted in William Henry Pease and Jane H. Pease, *James Louis Petigru: Southern Conservative, Southern Dissenter* (Athens: University of Georgia Press, 1995), 156.

2. David James McCord, "Memoranda of Table-Talk of Judge Cooper," in *Cyclopedia of American Literature*, 2 vols., ed. Evert A. Duyckinck and George L. Duyckinck (New York: Charles Scribner, 1856), 2:332–33; Paul Hamilton Hayne, *Ante-Bellum Charleston* (1885; Columbia, S.C.: Southern Studies Program, University of South Carolina, 1978), 20.

3. WGS, *Woodcraft; or, Hawks about the Dovecote: A Story of the South at the Close of the Revolution* (New York: Redfield, 1854), 65.

4. Hugh Blair, "Lecture XXXIII: Pronunciation or Delivery," in *Lectures on Rhetoric and Belles Lettres*, 14th American ed. (1783; New York: James and John Harper, 1826), 334.

5. Richard C. Lounsbury, ed., *Louisa S. McCord: Political and Social Essays* (Charlottesville: University Press of Virginia, 1995), 260, 261; James Waddell Alexander, "English Language in America," *SLM* 2 (January 1836): 111; WGS, *Views and Reviews in American*

Literature, History and Fiction: First Series, ed. C. Hugh Holman (1846; Cambridge: Belknap Press of Harvard University Press, 1962), 12.

6. David Rachels, ed., *Augustus Baldwin Longstreet's Georgia Scenes Completed: A Scholarly Text* (Athens: University of Georgia Press, 1998), 3–4.

7. Minutes of the Petersburg Franklin Society, 1821–24, DU.

8. Donna T. Andrews, *London Debating Societies, 1776–1799* (London: London Record Society, 1994), vii–xii.

9. Entry for 17 October 1845, Franklin Debating Society Minutes, John Esten Cooke MSS, DU.

10. Samuel Gaillard Stoney, ed., "The Memoirs of Frederick Adolphus Porcher: Chapter XIII—Continued: The Conversation Club," *South Carolina Historical and Genealogical Magazine* 47 (October 1946): 214.

11. Ibid., 220–21, 214.

12. Henry Junius Nott, "French Novels," *SR* 7 (August 1831): 346.

13. Rachel Mordecai to Samuel Mordecai, 24 April 1814, 26 September 1816, Mordecai Family Papers, SHC.

14. Louisa S. McCord to Langdon Cheves Jr., 4 April 1858, in Richard C. Lounsbury, ed., *Louisa S. McCord: Poems, Drama, Biography, Letters* (Charlottesville: University Press of Virginia, 1996), 340.

15. Samuel Gilman to Dorothea Dix, 26 June 1851, Dix Papers, Houghton Library, Harvard University, Cambridge, Mass.

16. FL to George S. Hillard, March 1853, FL Papers, HEH.

17. Entry for 2 April [1836], JHT Journal, JHT Papers, Presbyterian Historical Society, Montreat, N.C.

18. Entry for 7 March 1852, in Virginia Ingraham Burr, ed., *The Secret Eye: The Journal of Ella Gertrude Clanton Thomas, 1848–1889* (Chapel Hill: University of North Carolina Press, 1990), 100.

19. Entries for 9 January, 30 April 1848, in Stephen Berry, ed., *Princes of Cotton: Four Diaries of Young Men in the South, 1848–1860* (Athens: University of Georgia Press, 2007), 214, 219.

20. Entry for 1 December 1846, George D. Alexander Journal, Mississippi Department of Archives and History, Jackson.

21. Entry for 3 January 1857, in William Kauffman Scarborough, ed., *The Diary of Edmund Ruffin*, 3 vols. (Baton Rouge: Louisiana State University Press, 1972–89), 1:30.

22. Entries for 15 July 1857, 1 March 1858, 18 June 1865, in ibid., 1:89, 162, 3:946.

23. FL to Samuel A. Allibone, 30 November 1855, FL Papers, HEH.

24. Roger Philip McCutcheon, "Books and Booksellers in New Orleans, 1730–1830," *Louisiana Historical Quarterly* 20 (July 1937): 609; C. H. Cantrell, "The Reading Habits of Antebellum Southerners" (Ph.D. diss., University of Illinois, 1960), 283.

25. Madeleine B. Stern, "John Russell: 'Lord John' of Charleston," *North Carolina Historical Review* 26 (July 1949): 285.

26. *Catalogue of the Private Library of the Late Mr. A. A. Smets, Savannah, Ga.* (New York: Bradstreet Press, 1868).

27. Entry for 17 April 1851, in Donation Book of the Savannah Library Society, 1813–51, Savannah Library Society Papers, Georgia Historical Society, Savannah.

28. FL, *Manual of Political Ethics*, 2 vols. (Boston: Charles C. Little and James Brown, 1838–39), 2:471.

29. Thomas R. Dew, *A Digest of the Laws, Customs, Manners, and Institutions of the Ancient and Modern Nations* (New York: D. Appleton, 1853), 148.

30. Paul Hamilton Hayne to Margaret J. Preston, 10 May 1873, in Rayburn S. Moore, ed., *A Man of Letters in the Nineteenth-Century South: Selected Letters of Paul Hamilton Hayne* (Baton Rouge: Louisiana State University Press, 1982), 113.

31. D. Macaulay to Albert James Pickett, 11 July 1847, Pickett Papers, ADAH.

32. GFH to WGS, 19 February 1844, Prioleau Papers, SCHS.

33. Walter Scott to Mr. Gifford, 25 October 1808, in H. J. C. Grierson, ed., *The Letters of Sir Walter Scott*, 12 vols. (London: Constable, 1932–37), 2:104.

34. Quoted in Jay B. Hubbell, *The South in American Literature, 1607–1900* (Durham, N.C.: Duke University Press, 1954), 367.

35. Advertisement in first number, following the table of contents, quoted in John O. Hayden, *The Romantic Reviewers, 1802–1824* (Chicago: University of Chicago Press, 1968), 11.

36. WGS, "Writings of Cornelius Mathews," *SQR* 6 (October 1844): 310.

37. Caroline Lee Hentz to J. Tomlin, 1 June 1843, C. E. French Collection, Massachusetts Historical Society, Boston; "Dickens' American Notes," *SQR* 3 (January 1843): 172.

38. WGS, "International Copyright Law," *SLM* 10 (March 1844): 137, 140.

39. WGS to Thomas Caute Reynolds, 26 January 1844, in Mary C. Simms Oliphant, ed., *The Letters of William Gilmore Simms*, 6 vols. (Columbia: University of South Carolina Press, 1952–82), 1:398.

40. WGS, "International Copyright Law," *SLM* 10 (August 1844): 454, 456.

41. WGS, "International Copyright Law," *SLM* 10 (June 1844): 344, 345.

42. "Critical Notices—School Books," *SQR* 1 (January 1842): 265; "Southern School-Books," *DBR* 13 (September 1852): 259, 260.

43. Patrick F. Quinn, ed., *Edgar Allan Poe: Poetry and Tales* (New York: Library of America, 1984), 338, 400, 433, 494, 560.

CHAPTER FOUR

1. JHT to W. H. Robbins, 14 November 1830, in Benjamin Morgan Palmer, *The Life and Letters of James Henley Thornwell, D.D., LL.D* (Richmond, Va.: Whittet and Shepperson, 1875), 73.

2. GFH, "History of Literature," *SQR* 2 (October 1842): 514.

3. Edward Gibbon, *The History of the Decline and Fall of the Roman Empire*, 7 vols., ed. J. B. Bury (London: Methuen, 1909), 1:84, 4:181.

4. Mitchell King, *A Discourse on the Qualifications and Duties of an Historian* (Savannah, Ga.: n.p., 1843), 7.

5. James Boswell, *Life of Johnson*, ed. R. W. Chapman (Oxford: Oxford University Press, 1970), 304.

6. GFH, "Niebuhr," *Methodist Quarterly Review* 7 (October 1855): 547.

7. Robert Henry, "Niebuhr's Roman History," *SR* 1 (May 1828): 320.

8. Thomas R. Dew, *A Digest of the Laws, Customs, Manners, and Institutions of the Ancient and Modern Nations* (New York: D. Appleton, 1853), 14.

9. Ibid., 207.

10. Ibid., 211, 268.

11. Ibid., 326.

12. Ibid., 408.

13. Ibid., 564.

14. Ibid., 522.

15. William Brown Hodgson et al. to Ambrose Baber, 11 December 1844, Baber-Blackshear Collection, Hargrett Rare Book and Manuscripts Library, University of Georgia, Athens.

16. Leslie W. Dunlap, *American Historical Societies, 1790–1860* (1944; Philadelphia: Porcupine Press, 1974), 163.

17. Albert James Pickett, *History of Alabama and Incidentally of Georgia and Mississippi from the Earliest Period* (1851; Spartanburg, S.C.: Reprint Company, 1988), 10; Jared Sparks to Albert James Pickett, 29 November, and William Bacon Stevens to Albert James Pickett, 24 April 1847, Pickett Papers, ADAH.

18. Charles Campbell to John M. Daniel, 1 October 1846, Charles Campbell Papers, Special Collections Department, Earl Gregg Swem Library, College of William and Mary, Williamsburg, Virginia.

19. Hugh Blair Grigsby, *The Virginia Convention of 1776* (Richmond, Va.: J. W. Randolph, 1855), 195–96.

20. Hugh Blair Grigsby, *The Virginia Convention of 1829–30: A Discourse Delivered before the Virginia Historical Society* (Richmond, Va.: Macfarland and Fergusson, 1854), 13.

21. Ibid., 36.

22. Grigsby, *Virginia Convention of 1776*, 147, 37, 66, 162.

23. Ibid., 195.

24. GF, "Johnson, Boswell, Goldsmith, Etc," *DBR* 28 (April 1860): 414; John Pendleton Kennedy, *Memoirs of the Life of William Wirt, Attorney-General of the United States*, 2 vols. (Philadelphia: Lea and Blanchard, 1849), 1:5.

25. David Ramsay, *The Life of George Washington, Commander in Chief of the Armies of the United States, Throughout the War Which Established Their Independence; and First President of the United States* (New York: Hopkins and Seymour, 1807), 339.

26. William Wirt, *The Life and Character of Patrick Henry* (Philadelphia: James Webster, 1817), 6, 54.

27. Ibid., 406.

28. Kennedy, *William Wirt*, 2:163.

29. Ibid., 1:105.

30. Hugh A. Garland, *The Life of John Randolph of Roanoke*, 2 vols. (New York: D. Appleton, 1850), 2:375.

31. Ibid., 1:8–10.

32. Ibid., 254.

33. Ibid., 2:363.

34. *Proceedings and Debates of the Virginia State Convention, of 1829–30* (Richmond, Va.: Samuel Shepherd, 1830), 833; George W. Williams, ed., *Incidents in My Life: The Autobiography of the Rev. Paul Trapier, S.T.D., with Some of His Letters* (Charleston, S.C.: Dalcho Historical Society, 1954), x.

35. Charles T. Davis and Henry Louis Gates Jr., eds., *The Slave's Narrative* (New York: Oxford University Press, 1985), 319–27.

36. Ibid., xxx; Michael Meyer, ed., *Frederick Douglass: The Narrative and Selected Writings* (New York: Modern Library, 1984), 18; Gilbert Osofsky, ed., *Puttin' on Ole Massa: The Slave Narratives of Henry Bibb, William Wells Brown, and Solomon Northrup* (New York: Harper and Row, 1969), 214; Harriet A. Jacobs, *Incidents in the Life of a Slave Girl Written by Herself*, ed. Jean Fagin Yellin (Cambridge, Mass.: Harvard University Press, 1987), 34; John W. Blassingame, ed., *Slave Testimony: Two Centuries of Letters, Speeches, Interviews, and Auto-biographies* (Baton Rouge: Louisiana State University Press, 1977), 689.

37. Osofsky, *Puttin' on Ole Massa*, 198.

38. Henry Home, Lord Kames, *Elements of Criticism*, 2d ed. (1763; New York: E. J. Huntington and Mason Brothers, 1854), 23, 468, 96.

39. Ibid., 466.

40. Hugh Blair, *Lectures on Rhetoric and Belles Lettres*, 14th American ed. (1783; New York: James and John Harper, 1826), 13.

41. Ibid., 14, 22, 24.

42. Ibid., 65.

43. Ibid., 486.

44. Augustus William Schlegel, *A Course of Lectures on Dramatic Art and Literature*, trans. John Black (London: Henry G. Bohn, 1846), 22, 27.

45. Ibid., 213, 342.

46. Thomas Smith Grimké, "Origin of Rhyme," *SR* 2 (August 1828): 34, 37, 53.

47. Charles Campbell to John M. Daniel, 27 September 1847, Charles Campbell Papers.

48. Robert Young Hayne to Edward Everett, 4 August 1829, Edward Everett Papers, Massachusetts Historical Society, Boston.

49. "Address to the Patrons of the Review, and to the People of the South," *SQR* 11 (April 1847): iii–iv.

50. WGS to John R. Thompson, 10 May 1851, in Mary C. Simms Oliphant, ed., *The Letters of William Gilmore Simms*, 6 vols. (Columbia: University of South Carolina Press, 1952–82), 3:119; Archibald Roane, "American Literature—Northern and Southern," *DBR* 24 (February 1858): 176–77.

51. Edd Winfield Parks, ed., *The Essays of Henry Timrod* (Athens: University of Georgia Press, 1942), 87, 88, 90.

52. Hugh Swinton Legaré, "Crafts' Fugitive Writings," *SR* 1 (May 1828): 514; Legaré, "Classical Learning," *SR* 1 (February 1828): 21–22.

53. Washington Allston, *Lectures on Art, and Poems*, ed. Richard Henry Dana Jr. (New York: Baker and Scribner, 1850), 201, 217.

54. Ibid., 363.

55. Patrick F. Quinn, ed., *Edgar Allan Poe: Poetry and Tales* (New York: Library of America, 1984), 79, 56.

56. Richard C. Lounsbury, ed., *Louisa S. McCord: Poems, Drama, Biography, Letters* (Charlottesville: University Press of Virginia, 1996), 47, 97.

57. Alexander Beaufort Meek, *Songs and Poems of the South* (New York: S. H. Goetzel, 1857), v, 5, 243.

58. James Everett Kibler Jr., ed., *Selected Poems of William Gilmore Simms* (Athens:

University of Georgia Press, 1990), 197, 102; WGS to Theophilus Hunter Hill, 22 November 1864, in Oliphant, *Simms Letters*, 6:236–37, 239.

59. James Everett Kibler Jr., *The Poetry of William Gilmore Simms: An Introduction and Bibliography* (Columbia, S.C.: Southern Studies Program, 1979), 91.

60. Henry Timrod, *Poems of Henry Timrod* (Richmond, Va.: B. F. Johnson, 1901), 17.

61. William J. Grayson, "What Is Poetry?" (1857), in Parks, *Essays of Henry Timrod*, 151.

62. William J. Grayson, *The Hireling and the Slave, Chicora, and Other Poems* (Charleston, S.C.: McCarter, 1856), 97, 123; William J. Grayson, *The Country* (Charleston, S.C.: Russell and Jones, 1858), 13.

63. Grayson, "What Is Poetry?," 141, 145, 146.

64. Henry Timrod, "What Is Poetry?" (1857), in Parks, *Essays of Timrod*, 79; Richard J. Calhoun, ed., *Witness to Sorrow: The Antebellum Autobiography of William J. Grayson* (Columbia: University of South Carolina Press, 1990), 165.

65. Grayson, *Hireling and the Slave*, xiv–xv.

66. Joan R. Sherman, ed., *The Black Bard of North Carolina: George Moses Horton and His Poetry* (Chapel Hill: University of North Carolina Press, 1997), 56–57.

67. Entry for 1 July 1842, in Minutes of the Demosthenian Debating Society, SCL; Cranmore Wallace to Moses Ashley Curtis, 16 July 1849, Curtis Papers, SHC.

68. Albert James Pickett to Charles E. A. Gayarré, 25 November 1852, Gayarré Papers, Hill Memorial Library, Louisiana State University, Baton Rouge.

69. GFH, "Bulwer's Zanoni," *SQR* 2 (July 1842): 179.

70. John Izard Middleton, "The Confessional: A Tale," in Edward Middleton Papers, SHC.

71. Washington Allston, *Monaldi: A Tale* (Boston: Charles C. Little and James Brown, 1841), 269.

72. Quinn, *Poe: Poetry and Tales*, 267.

73. Johnson Jones Hooper, *Adventures of Captain Simon Suggs, Late of the Tallapoosa Volunteers* (1845; Chapel Hill: University of North Carolina Press, 1969), 8; Joseph M. Field, "The Death of Mike Fink" (1847), in Hennig Cohen and William B. Dillingham, eds., *Humor of the Old Southwest*, 2d ed. (1964; Athens: University of Georgia Press, 1975), 101.

74. Hooper, *Simon Suggs*, 95.

75. Caroline Gilman, *Recollections of a Southern Matron* (New York: Harper and Brothers, 1838), 201, 9.

76. Ibid., 29.

77. Ibid., 180.

78. Nathaniel Beverley Tucker, *The Partisan Leader, a Tale of the Future* (1836; Chapel Hill: University of North Carolina Press, 1971), 14.

79. Caroline Lee Hentz, *The Planter's Northern Bride* (1854; Chapel Hill: University of North Carolina Press, 1970), 41, 27, 404.

80. William Alexander Caruthers, *The Knights of the Golden Horse-Shoe: A Traditionary Tale of the Cocked Hat Gentry in the Old Dominion* (1845; Chapel Hill: University of North Carolina Press, 1970), 39.

81. Ibid., 20.

82. Ibid., 86.

CHAPTER FIVE

1. *Proceedings and Debates of the Virginia State Convention, of 1829–30* (Richmond, Va.: Samuel Shepherd, 1830), 237; "Coit's [the Reverend J. C. Coit] Eulogy," in J. P. Thomas, ed., *The Carolina Tribute to Calhoun* (Columbia, S.C.: Richard L. Bryan, 1857), 155.

2. Quoted in GF, "Popular Institutions," *DBR* 28 (May 1860): 528; the original is in the essay on "Parliaments" in the *Latter-Day Pamphlets*.

3. Nathaniel Beverley Tucker, *A Series of Lectures on the Science of Government, Intended to Prepare the Student for the Study of the Constitution of the United States* (Philadelphia: Carey and Hart, 1845), 24; John C. Calhoun, *A Disquisition on Government and a Discourse on the Constitution and Government of the United States*, ed. Richard K. Crallé (Columbia, S.C.: A. S. Johnston, 1851), 188.

4. John Taylor, *An Inquiry into the Principles and Policy of the Government of the United States*, ed. Loren Baritz (1814; Indianapolis: Bobbs-Merrill, 1969), 168, 63, 373.

5. Ibid., 375, 57, 148.

6. Ibid., 129.

7. Ibid., 375, 365, 292; Thomas Cooper, *A Tract on the Proposed Alteration of the Tariff, Submitted to the Consideration of the Members from South Carolina, in the Ensuing Congress of 1823–4* (Charleston, S.C.; Philadelphia: Joseph R. A. Skerrett, 1824), 6.

8. Taylor, *Inquiry*, 477; John Randolph, quoted in John M. Grammer, *Pastoral and Politics in the Old South* (Baton Rouge: Louisiana State University Press, 1996), 24.

9. John C. Calhoun to Joseph G. Swift, 24 August 1823, in Robert L. Meriwether et al., eds., *The Papers of John C. Calhoun*, 28 vols. (Columbia: University of South Carolina Press, 1959–2003), 8:243.

10. Benjamin Perley Poore, *The Federal and State Constitutions, Colonial Charters, and Other Organic Laws of the United States* (Washington, D.C.: U.S. Government Printing Office, 1877), 2:1908–9.

11. *Virginia Convention*, 46.

12. *Richmond Enquirer*, 28 January 1826, quoted in Claude H. Hall, *Abel Parker Upshur, Conservative Virginian, 1790–1844* (Madison: State Historical Society of Wisconsin, 1964), 40; *Virginia Convention*, 79.

13. *Virginia Convention*, 319.

14. Ibid., 55, 54, 59, 476, 103.

15. Ibid., 454, 425, 426.

16. James Madison to Lafayette, 1 February 1830, quoted in Drew R. McCoy, *The Last of the Fathers: James Madison and the Republican Legacy* (Cambridge: Cambridge University Press, 1989), 251; *Virginia Convention*, 698, 149.

17. *Virginia Convention*, 240, 119.

18. Ibid., 677, 590.

19. Hugh Swinton Legaré, "The American System," *SR* 6 (August 1830): 208.

20. Thomas Cooper, *Consolidation: An Account of Parties in the United States from the Convention of 1787 to the Present Period*, 2d ed. (Columbia, S.C.: Times and Gazette Office, 1830), 31, 6, 9.

21. Thomas Cooper, *Two Essays: 1. On the Foundations of Civil Government; 2. On the Constitution of the United States* (Columbia, S.C.: D. and J. M. Faust, 1826), 9.

22. Robert J. Turnbull, "The Tribunal of Dernier Resort," *SR* 6 (November 1830): 421–513.

23. Thomas Cooper, ed., *The Statutes at Large of South Carolina: Volume One* (Columbia, S.C.: A. S. Johnston, 1836), 201, 221.

24. Meriwether et al., *Calhoun Papers*, 11:422, 416.

25. Ibid., 417, 426.

26. "Hammond's Oration," in Thomas, *Carolina Tribute*, 302; Abel P. Upshur, *A Brief Enquiry Into the True Nature and Character of the Federal Government; Being a Review of Judge Story's Commentaries on the Constitution of the United States* (1840; Philadelphia: John Campbell, 1863), 10, 15, 41, 55.

27. John Spencer Bassett, ed., *Correspondence of Andrew Jackson*, 7 vols. (Washington, D.C.: Carnegie Institution of Washington, 1926–35), 5:53; Harold D. Moser et al., eds., *The Papers of Andrew Jackson*, 7 vols. to date (Knoxville: University of Tennessee Press, 1980–2007), 5:409–10, 4:157.

28. Moser et al., *Jackson Papers*, 3:204, 386, 5:133.

29. Bassett, *Jackson Correspondence*, 3:278.

30. Moser et al., *Jackson Papers*, 5:288; Bassett, *Jackson Correspondence*, 6:84, 5:193, 4:272, 3:294.

31. James D. Richardson, *A Compilation of the Messages and Papers of the Presidents, 1789–1897*, 10 vols. (Washington, D.C.: U.S. Government Printing Office, 1896–99), 2:631, 622.

32. Ibid., 3:293, 2:641.

33. Calhoun, *Disquisition and Discourse*, 12, 16.

34. Ibid., 25, 28, 35, 42.

35. Ibid., 53.

36. Ibid., 111, 112, 113, 116, 162, 140, 142, 150, 146, 147.

37. Ibid., 163, 165, 168.

38. Ibid., 169, 185.

39. Ibid., 232.

40. Ibid., 295, 325.

41. Ibid., 371, 372, 395.

42. Ibid., 406.

43. "Hammond's Oration," in Thomas, *Carolina Tribute*, 317–18.

44. Nathaniel Beverly Tucker, *Science of Government*, 5, 385, 7, 8, 10.

45. Ibid., 36, 67, 37, 39.

46. Ibid., 49.

47. Ibid., 255.

48. Ibid., 161.

49. JWM, *The Discourse on the Occasion of the Funeral of the Hon. John C. Calhoun* (Charleston, S.C.: John Russell, 1850), 12–16, 18, 20, 39.

50. Taylor, *Inquiry*, 354–55.

51. M. R. H. Garnett, "The Distribution of Wealth," *SQR* 11 (January 1847): 1.

52. James Madison to Jean-Baptiste Say, 4 May 1816, quoted in Richard K. Matthews, *If Men Were Angels: James Madison and the Heartless Empire of Reason* (Lawrence: University Press of Kansas, 1995), 86.

53. John Taylor, *Arator: Being a Series of Agricultural Essays, Practical and Political: In Sixty Four Numbers* (1818; Indianapolis: Liberty Classics, 1977), 103, 80.

54. Ibid., 111, 115, 124, 182.

55. Appendix to the 1806 second edition of the *Essay on the Principle of Population*, 230,

quoted in Donald Winch, *Riches and Poverty: An Intellectual History of Political Economy in Britain, 1750–1834* (Cambridge: Cambridge University Press, 1996), 295–96; "Slavery and Political Economy," *DBR* 21 (November 1856): 444–45.

56. Thomas R. Dew, *Lectures on the Restrictive System Delivered to the Senior Political Class of William and Mary College* (1829; New York: Augustus M. Kelley, 1969), 75, 4, 8.

57. Ibid., 9.

58. Ibid., 45, 185, 46, 121.

59. Ibid., 144.

60. Ibid., 146, 194, 195.

61. Thomas Cooper, *Lectures on the Elements of Political Economy*, 2d ed. (1830; New York: Augustus M. Kelley, 1971), 8, 9, 22.

62. Ibid., 27–29, 22.

63. Ibid., 212, 325, 229.

64. Ibid., 327.

65. GFH to FL, 14 April 1847, FL Papers, HEH; George Tucker, "The Theory of Profits," *Hunt's Merchants' Magazine and Commercial Review* 2 (1840): 89–100, quoted in Tipton R. Snavely, *George Tucker as Political Economist* (Charlottesville: University Press of Virginia, 1964), 39; "Raymond's Political Economy," *SR* 5 (February 1830): 27; Charles John Morris Gwinn, "Progress of Political Economy," *SQR* 14 (July 1848): 1–2, 22.

66. George Tucker, *Essays on Various Subjects of Taste, Morals, and National Policy* (Georgetown, D.C.: Joseph Milligan, 1822), 307.

67. Ibid., 16, 20.

68. George Tucker, *The Laws of Wages, Profits, and Rent, Investigated* (Philadelphia: Carey and Hart, 1837), 2.

69. Meriwether et al., *Calhoun Papers*, 10:429.

70. *Annals of Congress*, 16th Cong., 1st sess., pp. 1719–31, quoted in Robert V. Remini, *Henry Clay: Statesman for the Union* (New York: W. W. Norton, 1991), 174; Calvin Colton, ed., *The Works of Henry Clay*, 6 vols. (New York: A. S. Barnes and Burr, 1857), 5:221, 263.

71. Charleston *Evening News*, 1 October 1845, quoted in Melvin M. Lehman, *Jacob N. Cardozo: Economic Thought in the Antebellum South* (New York: Columbia University Press, 1966), 215; Jacob N. Cardozo, "Political Economy—Rent," *SR* 1 (February 1828): 193, 195; Jacob N. Cardozo, *Notes on Political Economy* (1826; Clifton, N.J.: Augustus M. Kelley, 1972), iii.

72. Meriwether et al., *Calhoun Papers*, 1:401.

73. Ibid., 13:275.

74. Ibid., 603.

75. Ibid., 16:368–69.

76. Ibid., 13:108–9, 14:84.

77. GF, *Sociology for the South; or, The Failure of Free Society* (Richmond, Va.: A. Morris, 1854), 221.

78. St. George Tucker, *A Dissertation on Slavery: With a Proposal for the Gradual Abolition of It, in the State of Virginia* (1796; New York: Negro Universities Press, 1970), 7, 64, 104; St. George Tucker, *View of the Constitution of the United States, with Selected Writings*, ed. Clyde N. Wilson (Indianapolis: Liberty Fund, 1999), 10.

79. Edward Brown, *Notes on the Origin and Necessity of Slavery* (Charleston, S.C.: A. E. Miller, 1826), 24, 30, 31.

80. Thomas R. Dew, *Review of the Debate in the Virginia Legislature of 1831 and 1832* (Richmond, Va.: T. W. White, 1832), 8.

81. "The Slavery Question in Virginia" (1832), in Fairfax Harrison, ed., *Aris Sonis Focisque, Being a Memoir of an American Family, the Harrisons of Skimino* (n.p.: privately printed, 1910), 337, 342; Dew, *Review of the Debate*, 8.

82. Dew, *Review of the Debate*, 9, 46.

83. Ibid., 106.

84. William Harper, "Colonization Society," *SR* 1 (February 1828): 233.

85. The original publication is William Harper, *Memoir on Slavery: Read before the Society for the Advancement of Learning, of South Carolina, at Its Annual Meeting at Columbia, 1837* (Charleston, S.C.: J. S. Burges, 1838), but I cite hereafter its re-publication as William Harper, "Slavery in the Light of Social Ethics," in *Cotton Is King, and Pro-Slavery Arguments*, ed. E. N. Elliott (Augusta, Ga.: Pritchard, Abbott and Loomis, 1860), 549–626.

86. Harper, "Slavery," 555, 558.

87. Ibid., 565, 566, 622, 571, 580.

88. Ibid., 588.

89. Ibid., 590.

90. Ibid., 589.

91. Ibid., 577, 626.

92. James Henry Hammond, "Two Letters on the Subject of Slavery in the United States, Addressed to Thomas Clarkson, Esq.," in *Selections from the Letters and Speeches of the Hon. James Henry Hammond*, ed. Clyde N. Wilson (1866; Columbia, S.C.: Southern Studies Program, University of South Carolina, 1978), 188, 190.

93. Ibid., 119–21.

94. Hammond European Diary, 24 August 1836, James Henry Hammond Papers, SCL, quoted in Drew Gilpin Faust, *James Henry Hammond and the Old South: A Design for Mastery* (Baton Rouge: Louisiana State University Press, 1982), 191.

95. Thornton Stringfellow, "The Bible Argument; or, Slavery in the Light of Divine Revelation," in Elliott, *Cotton Is King*, 463.

96. St. George Tucker, *Dissertation on Slavery*, 14–15; Dew, *Review of the Debate*, 19; GF, *Cannibals All!; or, Slaves Without Masters* (Richmond, Va.: A. Morris, 1857), 120; William A. Smith, *Lectures on the Philosophy and Practice of Slavery* (1856; New York: Negro Universities Press, 1969), 146.

97. Smith, *Philosophy and Practice of Slavery*, 40.

98. Ibid., 47, 55–56.

99. Ibid., 109, 150, 154.

100. Thomas R. R. Cobb, *An Inquiry Into the Law of Negro Slavery in the United States of America: To Which Is Prefixed, an Historical Sketch of Slavery: Vol. I* (Philadelphia: T. and J. W. Johnston, 1858), 21.

101. Smith, *Philosophy and Practice of Slavery*, 273.

102. Henry Hughes, *Treatise on Sociology, Theoretical and Practical* (Philadelphia: Lippincott, Grambo, 1854), iii.

103. Ibid., 47, 55, 166, 167.

104. Ibid., 267, 48.

105. Ibid., 291–92.

106. Ibid., 284, 238, 239.

107. GF, *Cannibals*, 353.

108. GF, *Sociology*, 70–71, 48.

109. Ibid., 106, 45; GF, *Cannibals*, 55.

110. GF, *Cannibals*, 301; GF, *Sociology*, 26, 81.

111. GF, *Sociology*, 139; GF, "The Valleys of Virginia—the Rappahanock," *DBR* 26 (March 1859): 276; GF, "The Valleys of Virginia—the Rappahanock," *DBR* 26 (June 1859): 615.

112. GF, "Valleys of Virginia" (March 1859), 275.

113. GF, "Oliver Goldsmith and Doctor Johnson," *DBR* 28 (May 1860): 511.

114. GF, *Sociology*, 202, 203, 139; GF, "Old Churches, Ministers, and Families of Virginia," *DBR* 26 (February 1859): 124; GF, "Small Nations," *DBR* 29 (November 1860): 568.

115. GF, *Cannibals*, 89, 90.

116. GF, "Milton, Byron, and Southey," *DBR* 29 (October 1860): 438.

117. GF, *Sociology*, 11, 175, 159; GF, "The Old Dominion—Valley of the Rappahanock," *DBR* 26 (April 1859): 385; GF, *Cannibals*, 35.

118. GF, *Sociology*, 20; GF, "Milton and Macaulay," *DBR* 28 (June 1860): 678; GF, *Cannibals*, 82; GF, "Bayard Taylor's Travels in Greece and Russia," *DBR* 27 (December 1859): 653.

119. C. Vann Woodward, ed., *Mary Chesnut's Civil War* (New Haven, Conn.: Yale University Press, 1981), 48.

CHAPTER SIX

1. Thomas Reid, *An Inquiry into the Human Mind*, ed. Timothy Duggan (1764; Chicago: University of Chicago Press, 1970), 18.

2. Henry Junius Nott to George McDuffie, undated, Henry Junius Nott Papers, SCL; "Of the Objects of Physical Inquiry," in Thomas Brown, *Lectures on the Philosophy of the Mind*, 4 vols. (1830; Edinburgh: Adam and Charles Black, 1851), 1:156–88.

3. George Tucker, *Essays on Various Subjects of Taste, Morals, and National Policy* (Georgetown, D.C.: Joseph Milligan, 1822), 207, 205.

4. Hugh Swinton Legaré, "Classical Learning," *SR* 1 (February 1828): 29.

5. Charles Woodward Hutson to Mother, undated, Charles W. Hutson Papers, SCL; "Deliramenta Philosophorum; or, The Vagaries of Learned Men," *SLM* 7 (April 1841): 289–98.

6. Thomas Cooper, *Tracts, Ethical, Theological and Political* (Warrington: W. Eyres, 1789), 301, 222, 210.

7. F. J. V. Broussais, *On Irritation and Insanity: A Work, Wherein the Relations of the Physical with the Moral Conditions of Man, Are Established on the Basis of Physiological Medicine*, trans. Thomas Cooper (Columbia, S.C.: S. J. M'Morris, 1831), 342–43.

8. Broussais, *Irritation and Insanity*, 401; Thomas Cooper, "Gall on the Functions of the Brain," *SR* 1 (February 1828): 137, 142.

9. JHT, "Address Delivered to the Euphradian and Clariosophic Societies of the South Carolina College, December 3d 1839" (this and JHT's other philosophical lectures, cited below, are in JHT Papers, SCL).

10. "Lecture First" and "Logic."

11. "Lecture—Syllogism."

12. "Lecture First" and "Part of Lecture iv—Materialism."

13. "Lecture Second."

14. Ibid.

15. "Lecture Third."

16. "Lecture Third" and "Lecture Fifth."

17. "Lecture Fifth" and "Lecture Eighth."

18. "Lecture Eighth."

19. JHT, "The Test of Truth," *SQR*, n.s., 12 (October 1855): 486, 489.

20. Daniel K. Whitaker, "The Will—Note by the Editor," *SQR* 11 (January 1847): 66, 67–68.

21. Albert Taylor Bledsoe, *An Examination of President Edwards' Inquiry into the Freedom of the Will* (Philadelphia: H. Hooker, 1845), 15, 220.

22. Ibid., 234.

23. Georg Wilhelm Friedrich Hegel, *The Phenomenology of Mind*, trans. J. B. Baillie (New York: Harper and Row, 1967), 239.

24. Hugh Swinton Legaré, "Jeremy Bentham and the Utilitarians," *SR* 7 (August 1831): 294, 296.

25. Thomas Cooper, "Bentham's Judicial Evidence," *SR* 5 (May 1830): 381–82; "American Literature," *SQR* 11 (January 1847): 124.

26. Legaré, "Classical Learning," 29; JHT, "Memoir of Dr. Henry," *SQR* 2, n.s., 1 (April 1856): 205; Stephen Elliott, "Education in Germany," *SR* 4 (August 1829): 122.

27. Jesse Burton Harrison, "English Civilization," *SR* 8 (February 1832): 463, 484, 472, 480, 479.

28. FL, "Restauratio tertia: Organum novum," dated "Columbia, S.C., March 1, 1838," FL Papers, HEH.

29. "American Literature," 166–67; Charles Woodward Hutson to Mother, "Wednesday in Apr. 1860," Charles W. Hutson Papers, SCL.

30. "Objections to the German Transcendental Philosophy," *Southern Presbyterian Review* 4 (January 1851): 342.

31. JWM, *God in History: A Discourse Delivered before the Graduating Class of the College of Charleston* (Charleston, S.C.: Evans and Cogswell, 1863), 20.

32. GFH, "Sir William Hamilton's Discussions," *SQR*, n.s., 8 (October 1853): 296.

33. GFH, "Morell's Philosophy of the Nineteenth Century," *SLM* 16 (July 1850): 385; GFH, "Philosophy and Faith," *Methodist Quarterly Review* 3 (April 1851): 187.

34. GFH, "Faith and Science—Comte's Positive Philosophy," *Methodist Quarterly Review* 4 (January 1852): 21, 23.

35. Auguste Comte to GFH, 18 September 1852, MS vol. 1808, quoted in Neal C. Gillespie, *The Collapse of Orthodoxy: The Intellectual Ordeal of George Frederick Holmes* (Charlottesville: University Press of Virginia, 1972), 142; GFH, "Faith and Science," 33; GFH, "Faith and Science—Comte's Positive Philosophy [Second Paper]," *Methodist Quarterly Review* 4 (April 1852): 189.

36. GFH, "Faith and Science [Second Paper]," 196, 195.

37. GFH, "The Bacon of the Nineteenth Century [Second Paper]," *Methodist Quarterly Review* 5 (October 1853): 504.

38. GFH to JHT, 16 September 1856, JHT Papers, Presbyterian Historical Society, Montreat, N.C.; GFH, "The Positive Religion; or, Religion of Humanity," *Methodist Quarterly Review* 6 (July 1854): 357–58.

39. James Henry Hammond to William Brown Hodgson, 2 April 1850, James Henry Hammond MSS, DU; Carol Bleser, ed., *Secret and Sacred: The Diaries of James Henry Hammond, a Southern Slaveholder* (New York: Oxford University Press, 1988), 262.

40. "The Life and Opinions of Moses Hess," in Isaiah Berlin, *Against the Current: Essays in the History of Ideas*, ed. Henry Hardy (1979; Harmondsworth: Penguin, 1982), 244.

41. Entry for 1 May 1830, in Jesse Burton Harrison, "European Diary, 1829–30," Francis B. Harrison Papers, Special Collections Department, Alderman Library, University of Virginia, Charlottesville.

42. Edgar E. MacDonald, ed., *The Education of the Heart: The Correspondence of Rachel Mordecai Lazarus and Maria Edgeworth* (Chapel Hill: University of North Carolina Press, 1977), 6.

43. Gary Phillip Zola, *Isaac Harby of Charleston, 1788–1828: Jewish Reformer and Intellectual* (Tuscaloosa: University of Alabama Press, 1994), 24.

44. Isaac Harby, "Discourse before the Reformed Society of Israelites," in *A Selection from the Miscellaneous Writings of the Late Isaac Harby, Esq.*, ed. Henry L. Pinckney and Abraham Moise (Charleston, S.C.: James S. Burges, 1829), 77, 78, 84, 59.

45. Ibid., 66; James William Hagy, *This Happy Land: The Jews of Colonial and Antebellum Charleston* (Tuscaloosa: University of Alabama Press, 1993), 101, 91; Zola, *Isaac Harby*, 221 n. 78.

46. Jasper Adams to the Rev. Sewall Harding, 8 November 1828, SCL, reproduced in *The University South Caroliniana Society: Sixty-Fourth Annual Meeting* (Columbia, S.C.: South Caroliniana Library, 2000), 29.

47. Ignatius Aloysius Reynolds, ed., *The Works of the Right Rev. John England, First Bishop of Charleston*, 5 vols. (Baltimore: John Murphy, 1849), 3:191.

48. "Brother" Scott of Cow Marsh, Delaware, quoted in Bertram Wyatt-Brown, "The Antimission Movement in the Jacksonian South: A Study in Regional Folk Culture," *Journal of Southern History* 36 (November 1970): 519, itself quoting Richard B. Cook, *The Early and Later Delaware Baptists* (Philadelphia: American Baptist Publication Society, 1880), 93.

49. JHT, *Letter to His Excellency Governor Manning on Public Instruction in South Carolina* (Columbia, S.C.: R. W. Gibbes, 1853), 23, 22.

50. JWM to J. D. B. De Bow, 25 March 1854, J. D. B. De Bow MSS, DU; JWM, "The Aggressive Nature of Christianity," *Russell's Magazine* 3 (June 1857): 194; JWM, "On Independent Thinking," *Russell's Magazine* 2 (May 1858): 106.

51. JWM to Anna Rebecca Young, [ca. 1856], beginning "I am glad that," JWM Papers, DU; JWM to Robert Newton Gourdin, 10 August 1854, Gourdin Papers, DU.

52. JWM, *Farewell Sermon, Preached by the Rev. James W. Miles (Missionary of the Prot. Epis. Church to Mesopotamia)* (Charleston, S.C.: B. B. Hussey, 1843), 11.

53. JWM, "Lieber, Nordheimer, and Donaldson, on the Philosophy of Language," *SQR* 20 (October 1851): 392, 393, 394; JWM, *The Student of Philology* (Charleston, S.C.: John Russell, 1853), 30, 28–29.

54. JWM, *Student of Philology*, 18, 25, 27, 28.

55. JWM to Anna Rebecca Young, undated, 23 and 24 July 1864, JWM Papers, DU; JWM, *The Relation between the Races at the South* (Charleston, S.C.: Evans and Cogswell, 1861), 5, 8.

56. JWM, *Philosophic Theology; or, Ultimate Grounds of All Religious Belief Based in Reason* (Charleston, S.C.: John Russell, 1849), 220, 8; JWM, "Marcus Aurelius," *SQR*, n.s., 6 (October 1852): 410.

57. JWM, *Philosophic Theology*, 11, 12, 15, 16, 30, 31, 33; JWM to Anna Rebecca Young, 28 June 1864, JWM Papers, DU, discussed in Ralph Luker, *A Southern Tradition in Theology and Social Criticism, 1830–1930: The Religious Liberalism and Social Conservatism of James Warley Miles, William Porcher DuBose and Edgar Gardner Murphy* (Lewiston, N.Y.: Edwin Mellen Press, 1984), 140–41.

58. JWM, *Philosophic Theology*, 55, 88, 122.

59. Ibid., 60, 89–90.

60. Ibid., 80, 82, 105, 177.

61. Ibid., 125.

62. Ibid., 134, 201, 205.

63. Benjamin Morgan Palmer, *The Life and Letters of James Henley Thornwell, D.D., LL.D* (Richmond, Va.: Whittet and Shepperson, 1875), 13; J. Marion Sims, *The Story of My Life* (New York: D. Appleton, 1865), 107.

64. JHT to General James Gillespie, 4 March 1837, JHT Papers, SCL; Palmer, *Life of Thornwell*, 47; Sims, *Story of My Life*, 107–8.

65. John B. Adger et al., eds., *The Collected Writings of James Henley Thornwell*, 4 vols. (1871–75; Edinburgh: Banner of Truth Trust, 1974), 2:106, 1:458.

66. Ibid., 2:22, 192, 460.

67. Ibid., 25, 161.

68. Ibid., 2:320, 1:243.

69. Ibid., 1:255–56, 305, 80, 296, 2:80, 249.

70. Ibid., 1:313, 349.

71. Ibid., 2:478, 357, 405, 481.

72. Ibid., 1:502, 3:217.

73. Ibid., 3:71; Ernest Trice Thompson, *Presbyterians in the South*, vol. 1, *1607–1861* (Richmond, Va.: John Knox Press, 1963), 504.

74. Adger et al., *Thornwell Writings*, 2:45, 4:511.

75. Ibid., 3:281, 348, 373, 375.

76. Ibid., 2:46, 3:361, 330.

77. Ibid., 1:99–101.

78. Ibid., 99, 482; R. Stuart to JHT, 5 June 1856, JHT Papers, SCL; FL to George S. Hillard, 1 December 1855, in Thomas Sergeant Perry, ed., *The Life and Letters of Francis Lieber* (Boston: James R. Osgood, 1882), 285; FL to George S. Hillard, 25 December 1851, FL Papers, HEH.

79. Adger et al., *Thornwell Writings*, 1:575, 582, 3:228; Daniel K. Whitaker, "The Newspaper and Periodical Press," *SQR* 1 (January 1842): 64.

80. Adger et al., *Thornwell Writings*, 1:107.

81. Ibid., 107, 112, 129.

82. Ibid., 129; William Hamilton, *Lectures on Metaphysics and Logic*, ed. Henry Mansel and John Veitch, 2 vols. (Boston: Gould and Lincoln, 1859), 1:47, quoted in Richard Olson, *Scottish Philosophy and British Physics, 1750–1880: A Study in the Foundations of the Victorian Scientific Style* (Princeton, N.J.: Princeton University Press, 1975), 133; Olson, *Scottish Philosophy and British Physics*, 137.

83. Adger et al., *Thornwell Writings*, 1:469, 123.

84. Ibid., 123, 129, 135, 39–40.

85. Ibid., 3:98.

86. Ibid., 11, 24, 85, 113.

87. JWM to Anna Rebecca Young, [ca. Oct.–Nov. 1858], beginning "Many thanks, my dear Friend," JWM Papers, DU; Adger et al., *Thornwell Writings*, 3:119, 120.

88. Adger et al., *Thornwell Writings*, 1:88, 87.

89. Ibid., 207, 387.

90. Ibid., 186, 270–71.

91. Ibid., 1:44, 218, 349, 3:267.

92. Ibid., 2:234, 607, 492, 481–82.

93. Ibid., 51, 64, 468, 504.

94. Ibid., 2:147, 3:417, 1:266, 486.

95. Ibid., 3:136, 2:297.

96. Ibid., 3:87, 150, 1:502.

97. Ibid., 3:295.

98. Ibid., 1:414–15, 47; JHT, *Letter to His Excellency Governor Manning on Public Instruction in South Carolina* (Columbia, S.C.: R. W. Gibbes, 1853), 19.

99. JHT, "The Religious Instruction of the Black Population," *Southern Presbyterian Review* 1 (December 1847): 103, 104, 112, 119.

100. JHT, "Slavery and the Religious Instruction of the Coloured Population," *Southern Presbyterian Review* 4 (July 1850): 107–9; J. P. Thomas, ed., *The Carolina Tribute to Calhoun* (Columbia, S.C.: Richard L. Bryan, 1857), 108.

101. JHT, "Slavery and the Religious Instruction," 111, 114.

102. Ibid., 111–12, 126, 116.

103. Ibid., 116–17, 118, 123.

104. Ibid., 126, 127.

105. Ibid., 128, 129, 131, 138, 140.

106. Adger et al., *Thornwell Writings*, 3:387, 393.

EPILOGUE

1. Edd Winfield Parks, ed., *The Essays of Henry Timrod* (Athens: University of Georgia Press, 1942), 88; Augusta Jane Evans, *Beulah* (1859; Baton Rouge: Louisiana State University Press, 1992), 25, 145, 342, 32.

2. Evans, *Beulah*, 50.

3. Ibid., 28, 121, 127, 231, 309.

4. Ibid., 128, 231, 209–11, 230, 232, 263.

5. Ibid., 255, 264, 288–89.

6. Ibid., 311, 312, 313.

7. Ibid., 360, 371, 379.

8. Ibid., 412, 419.

9. James Johnston Pettigrew, *Notes on Spain and the Spaniards, in the Summer of 1850, with a Glance at Sardinia* (Charleston, S.C.: Evans and Cogswell, 1861), 18.

10. Ibid., 68, 51, 79–80.

11. Ibid., 77–78.

12. Ibid., 330.

13. Ibid., 388, 394, 403.

14. Ibid., 415–16.

15. Ibid., 430.

16. C. Vann Woodward, ed., *Mary Chesnut's Civil War* (New Haven, Conn.: Yale University Press, 1981), 36.

17. Samuel Flagg Bemis and Grace Gardner Griffin, eds., *Guide to the Diplomatic History of the United States, 1775–1921* (Washington, D.C.: U.S. Government Printing Office, 1935), 306; William Henry Trescot, *The Diplomacy of the Revolution: An Historical Study* (New York: D. Appleton, 1852), 2.

18. Trescot, *Diplomacy of the Revolution*, 5, 6; Giuseppe di Lampedusa, *The Leopard* (New York: Pantheon, 1960), 40.

19. Trescot, *Diplomacy of the Revolution*, 8–9.

20. William Henry Trescot, *The Position and Course of the South* (Charleston, S.C.: Walker and James, 1850), 7.

21. Ibid., 16; Trescot, *Diplomacy of the Revolution*, 148.

22. William Henry Trescot, *The Diplomatic History of the Administrations of Washington and Adams, 1789–1801* (Boston: Little, Brown, 1857), v; Trescot, *Diplomacy of the Revolution*, 156–57.

23. Trescot, *Position and Course*, 20.

24. J. C. Levenson et al., *The Letters of Henry Adams*, 6 vols. (Cambridge, Mass.: Belknap Press of Harvard University Press, 1982–88), 2:286.

25. Ibid., 2:491; Trescot, *Diplomacy of the Revolution*, 158–59.

26. William Henry Trescot, *Memorial of the Life of J. Johnston Pettigrew, Brig. Gen. of the Confederate States Army* (Charleston, S.C.: John Russell, 1870), 64, 3.

27. Woodward, *Chesnut's Civil War*, 815, 358, 393.

28. Elisabeth Muhlenfeld, ed., *Two Novels by Mary Chesnut* (Charlottesville: University Press of Virginia, 2002), 191; Woodward, *Chesnut's Civil War*, 271, 449.

29. Woodward, *Chesnut's Civil War*, 65; William Makepeace Thackeray, *The History of Pendennis: His Fortunes and Misfortunes, His Friends and His Greatest Enemy* (1848–50; London: Thomas Nelson, 1901), 176.

30. C. Vann Woodward and Elisabeth Muhlenfeld, eds., *The Private Mary Chesnut: The Unpublished Civil War Diaries* (New York: Oxford University Press, 1984), 3; Woodward, *Chesnut's Civil War*, 836.

31. Woodward and Muhlenfeld, *Private Mary Chesnut*, 44.

32. Ibid., 42, 231–32.

33. Ibid., 45.

34. Woodward, *Chesnut's Civil War*, 762, 172, 23.

35. Virginia Woolf, "Character in Fiction" (1924), in Virginia Woolf, *The Essays of Virginia Woolf*, vol. 3, *1919–1924*, ed. Andrew McNeillie (San Diego, Calif.: Harcourt Brace Jovanovich, 1988), 436.

36. Woodward, *Chesnut's Civil War*, 815.

37. Ibid., 29, 216.

38. Ibid., 792; Elisabeth Muhlenfeld, *Mary Boykin Chesnut: A Biography* (Baton Rouge: Louisiana State University Press, 1981), 221.

39. Charles R. Anderson and Aubrey H. Starke, eds., *Sidney Lanier, Letters, 1874–1877* (Baltimore: Johns Hopkins University Press, 1945), 230.

40. Paul Hamilton Hayne, *Ante-Bellum Charleston* (1885; Columbia, S.C.: Southern Studies Program, University of South Carolina, 1978), 4.

Index

Abercrombie, John, 261

Abolitionism (and abolitionists), 10, 19–21, 24, 29, 65–68, 70, 101, 111, 136, 164, 187, 235, 240, 309, 311–12, 331

Abstract (and abstraction), 4, 102, 151, 160, 196–98, 210, 231, 235, 238–39, 244–46, 248–49, 263, 270, 272, 293, 304, 316

Acadia, 41

Acton, John Emerich Edward Dalberg-Acton, first baron, 140

Adam, 60, 66, 290, 296, 306–7

Adams, Henry, 154–55, 327–28

Adams, John, 137, 193, 324

Adams, John Quincy, 36, 201, 227, 254

Addison, Joseph, 119, 184

Adger, John Bailey, 16, 43

Adulthood, 31, 64, 72, 111, 112, 136, 167–68, 183, 200, 263

Aeschylus, 280

Aesthetics, 9, 35, 41, 80, 145, 154, 173, 250, 261, 272, 276

Africa (and Africans), 2–3, 8, 9, 16, 27, 30, 43–46, 50–52, 59, 61–62, 72, 79, 106, 163–65, 178–79, 187–88, 198, 203, 217, 234, 236, 239–40, 248, 252, 257, 277–78, 288, 298, 312

African Methodist Episcopal Church, 72, 278

Agassiz, Louis, 60

Aghwati, Ibn al-Din al-, 44

Agnosticism, 9, 145, 257, 271, 274, 292

Agora, 147

Agrarianism, 12, 77, 151, 195, 254

Agriculture, 82, 92, 102, 120, 124, 220–21, 223, 225–26, 229–30, 236, 238

Alabama (and Alabamians), 5, 10, 14, 24, 30, 34, 61–62, 86, 93–94, 128, 152–53, 176, 316–17

Albany, N.Y., 21

Albemarle region, N.C., 86

Albert, 332

Albert, Prince, 324

Alberti, Count Mariano, 40

Alexander, Archibald, 285

Alexander the Great, 113

Alfred the Great, 250

Algonquian language, 72

Alibert, Jean Louis, 57

Alienation, 5, 76, 83, 85, 97, 109, 177, 284, 307, 309, 319, 327, 330–31

Allegory, 167, 173, 176, 189, 333

Allston, Washington, 33, 139, 173–75, 183, 272

Alps (and Alpine), 39, 173, 175

Amateurism, 132, 134

American Colonization Society, 45

American Philosophical Society, 102

American Revolution, 3, 21, 31, 55, 73, 79, 85, 90, 142, 143, 151, 152, 155, 159, 165, 182, 192, 242, 252, 326

American System (of Henry Clay), 223–30

Amphictyonic, Council, 196

Amsterdam, Bank of, 232

Anatolia, 43

Ancestors (and ancestry), 21, 30, 32, 36, 58, 74, 78, 87, 90, 94, 95, 155, 158, 162, 242, 254

Andalusia, 74, 323

Andes, 48

Andover Theological Seminary, 293

Anglicanism. See Episcopalianism

Anglophilia, 33, 76, 79, 156

Anglophobia, 76, 135, 206, 220, 221, 228

Anglophone, 99

Anglo-Saxons, 21, 58–60, 71, 79, 150, 322–23, 326

Anonymity (literary), 131–33, 249, 300

Anson Street Church (Charleston, S.C.), 310

Anthropological Society of London, 16, 60

Anthropological Society of Paris, 16, 61

Anthropology, 16, 55, 58, 60–61, 145, 146, 152, 286

Antiquarianism, 49, 90, 122, 152, 302

Antiquity (and the ancient world), 2, 7, 15, 31, 33, 36–40, 42, 44, 58, 78, 80, 84, 87, 105, 141–42, 145–49, 151, 157, 166, 168–70, 181, 192, 199, 203, 224, 236, 249, 252, 259, 262, 264, 270, 276, 280–83, 289–90, 292, 306–7, 335. *See also* Classical

Anti-Semitism, 279, 281

Antislavery, 6, 37, 62, 66–67, 76, 114, 138, 163–64, 185, 201, 203, 212, 238, 240, 242

Antonines, 148

Antwerp, 33

Appalachians, 187, 189

Appleton, D. (publishers), 334

Appomattox, Va., 21, 322

Aquinas, Thomas, 277, 283, 294

Arabic language, 16, 43–44, 281, 286

Arabs, 43, 58, 216, 322

Aragon, 321, 323

Archaeology, 36, 152

Architecture, 20, 84, 165, 193, 321, 327

Archives, 40, 83, 152–53, 324, 336

Arctic, 121

Arden, Forest of, 177

Arians, 300

Ariosto, Ludovico, 80

Aristocracy, 5, 21, 77, 79, 90, 137, 147–50, 183–84, 189, 192–93, 195, 207, 215, 220, 254, 322, 336

Aristotle (and Aristotelianism), 15, 38, 167, 169, 247, 249, 252, 264–65, 277, 302–3, 306–7, 313

Arkansas, 10, 14, 82, 128, 176

Arkansas Magazine, 82

Armada, Spanish, 42

Armenia (and Armenians), 43, 286

Arminianism, 268, 269

Arnold, Matthew, 231, 319

Arnold, Thomas, 148

Ashantis, 45

Ashburton, Alexander Baring, first baron, 76

Ashkenazic Jews, 278

Ashley River, 177

Asia (and Asians), 30, 44, 46–47, 51–52, 59, 106, 146, 234, 286, 312

Astor House (N.Y.), 20

Astronomy, 121

Atheism (and atheists), 186, 260, 288–89, 279, 294, 310, 317–19, 322

Athenaeum Club (London), 110

Athens (and Athenians), 38, 87, 100, 147–48

Atlantic Ocean, 31, 39, 52, 87, 139

Atreus, House of, 8

Attica, 42, 147

Augusta, Ga., 40, 248

Augustan literature, 14, 100, 167, 178–79, 181

Augustine of Hippo, 157, 283–84, 294, 296

Auschwitz, 95

Austen, Jane, 329

Australia, 2

Austria, 283, 320, 325

Autobiography, 6, 51, 65, 68, 141, 151, 157, 162–66, 179, 180. *See also* Memoirs

Avary, Myrta Lockett, 334

Aztecs, 49

Babel, Tower of, 99

Bachman, John, 108

Backcountry, 86, 284

Bacon, Francis (and Baconianism), 153–54, 221, 225, 259–60, 264–65, 270, 272, 276–77, 297–98, 302–3

Baldwin, James, 10

Ball, Charles, 164

Ballads, 59, 100, 132, 180, 207

130–31, 141, 144, 149, 151, 163, 179, 181–82, 184–85, 191–92, 199, 221, 236, 239, 244, 256, 262, 265, 278, 284, 287, 289, 294, 315; nineteenth, 1–2, 5–6, 8–9, 11–12, 16, 24, 31, 45, 55, 58–59, 67, 74, 76, 80, 84, 86, 94, 104–6, 111, 123, 130, 133, 141, 166, 178–79, 185, 196, 210, 217, 231, 241, 252, 277, 284, 288, 302, 322; twentieth, 8–9, 47, 62, 87, 191, 229, 250, 295, 330; twenty-first, 9

Cervantes Saavedra, Miguel de, 117

Chaldeans, 286

Chalmers, Thomas, 26

Chang (Siamese twin), 262

Channing, William Ellery, 311

Charles II, 81

Charleston, S.C. (and Charlestonians), 1, 10, 24–26, 38, 43, 48, 53, 57, 65–67, 72, 87–88, 102–4, 107, 111, 117–23, 126, 128–29, 131, 137–40, 171, 175–76, 185–86, 229, 236, 248, 261, 278–85, 288, 292, 309–10, 320–21, 323–24, 329, 334, 336

Charleston, College of, 324

Charleston Conversation Club, 102–4

Charleston Mercury, 126

Charlottesville, Va., 37, 123

Chartres, 328

Chaucer, Geoffrey, 181

Chekhov, Anton, 2

Chemistry, 120, 136, 153, 225, 263, 327

Cherokees, 72

Chesapeake Bay, 13, 50, 189

Chesnut, James, 333

Chesnut, James, Jr., 329, 333

Chesnut, Mary, 7, 11, 98, 108, 146, 258, 315, 323, 329–34

Chester, 33

Chesterfield, Philip Dormer Stanhope, fourth earl of, 106

Chestnut Street (Philadelphia), 20

Cheves, Langdon, 70–71

Cheves, Langdon, Jr., 107

Cheves, Robert Hayne, 71

Chicago, Ill., 94

Childhood, 12, 51, 62, 66, 158–59, 161, 165,

177, 186, 198, 225, 234, 267, 276, 297, 300, 307, 329

Childlessness, 64–65, 329–32

Chile, 31, 48

China (and the Chinese), 46–47, 56, 90, 148, 248, 286, 306, 316

Chivalry, 74, 78, 79, 90, 146, 149, 178, 322

Christ, Jesus, 26, 46, 69, 278, 283, 288–92, 295–96, 307

Christendom, 300, 325

Christianity, 43, 47, 55, 143–44, 146, 148–49, 169, 175–76, 179, 186, 217, 224, 243, 262, 275, 277–78, 283, 287, 289–92, 295, 307–9, 311, 318–20, 333

Christy, David, 248

Chronology, 49, 60–61, 85, 144, 148, 272, 298, 332

Cicero, Marcus Tullius (and Ciceronian), 38, 99, 105, 113, 116, 133, 306

Cid, El (Diaz Ruy, Count of Bivar), 42

Cincinnati, Ohio, 93, 248, 279

Circulating libraries, 117, 122

Circulation, 125, 127–28

Cities, 12, 21, 33–35, 41, 43, 46–49, 73, 79, 81, 83–84, 87–88, 92, 116, 121–23, 138, 149, 154–55, 183, 185, 219, 223, 225–27, 254, 284, 286

Citizens (and citizenship), 57, 82–84, 122, 131, 135, 147–49, 158, 194–95, 217–18, 270, 282, 312

Civilization, 27, 30, 49–50, 78–80, 92, 148, 167–68, 169, 184, 227, 234, 236–38, 254–56, 272, 310, 321–22

Claiborne, William C. C., 74–75

Clapp, Dexter, 70

Clapp, John Milton, 126

Clarendon, Edward Hyde, earl of, 141, 150

Clarkson, Thomas, 105, 111, 240, 242–43

Class (social), 5, 13, 21, 53, 62, 79, 83, 85, 88–96, 99–100, 148, 150–51, 153, 156, 179, 184, 200, 203, 207, 210, 224, 229, 237, 245, 254, 264, 316, 322–23

Classical (and classicist), 6, 23, 35, 80–81, 100, 119–20, 125–26, 131, 141, 152, 168–69, 171–72, 220, 228, 230, 275, 280, 302, 329. *See also* Antiquity

Clavigero, Francisco, 49–50

Clay, Henry, 7, 11, 36, 84, 134, 195, 204, 213, 220, 222–23, 226, 228–29, 231–34, 321

Climate, 32–33, 48, 55–56, 58, 85, 149, 176, 203, 210

Clubs, 5, 13, 64, 76, 83, 88, 98, 102–4, 110–11, 117, 132, 173, 309

Coalter, John C., 199

Cobb, Thomas R. R., 152, 247

Colbert, Jean-Baptiste, 225

Coleridge, Samuel Taylor, 36, 96, 100, 132, 168, 170, 173–74, 180–81, 221, 241, 272–74, 305, 317

Colleges, 3, 13, 19–20, 22–23, 25–30, 33, 42–43, 63, 82, 87–88, 93–94, 96, 99, 101, 117, 122–23, 146–47, 152, 157, 166, 205, 207, 211, 214, 219, 226, 240, 246, 259, 261–64, 272, 284–85, 292–93, 300–301, 307, 313, 324, 336

Colonialism (and colonists), 2, 16, 32, 40, 45, 48–50, 59, 62, 73–74, 76–79, 81, 89, 91, 104, 128, 142, 156, 173, 184–85, 196, 229, 238, 254, 261, 298, 323

Columbia, S.C., 23, 27–28, 42, 70, 109, 119, 123–24, 129, 273, 284, 292–94, 298, 300, 313

Columbia Theological Seminary, 284, 294, 298, 300

Columbus, Christopher, 42, 282

Combe, George, 57

Commerce, 12, 23, 28, 41, 51, 92, 104, 122, 125–26, 136, 149, 155, 173, 178, 180, 210, 220, 225, 227, 229, 236, 271, 326

Common law, 75, 271

Common sense philosophy, 6, 32, 37, 95, 178, 262, 266, 271

Commonwealth, English (and its tradition), 84, 128, 148, 187, 192, 195, 202, 206–8, 223, 234, 312

Community (and communities), 8, 15, 29, 32, 34, 65–67, 72, 86–87, 101, 104–5, 111, 118, 122, 154, 173, 181, 185, 188, 194, 197, 200, 204, 209–11, 214–15, 218, 222–23, 235, 240, 245, 253, 278, 280–81, 289, 306, 309, 315, 328

Compacts (political), 85, 135, 194, 197–98, 201, 208, 214, 218

Compromise of 1833, 201, 233

Comte, Auguste, 250, 275–77, 286, 291

Concord, Mass., 15

Condillac, Étienne de, 261

Condorcet, Antoine-Nicolas de, 221

Confederacies, 82, 201, 208, 211, 248, 310, 325

Confederate States of America, 7, 9, 47, 115, 166, 322, 331, 333–34

Confederation, Articles of, 211

Confessional, 112, 132, 157, 161, 163–64, 182–83, 255, 285

Confucianism, 46, 53

Congregationalism, 25

Congress, U.S. (and congressmen), 40, 75, 86, 117, 194, 200

Conquest, 2–3, 49–50, 57, 59, 75, 149, 177, 180, 189, 231, 234, 242, 286, 288, 322, 335

Conservatism, 14, 23, 60, 68–69, 119, 145, 147, 150, 155, 162, 180, 191, 197–200, 202, 204, 212, 245, 275, 279, 284, 309–10, 312, 322, 324

Constant, Benjamin, 147–48

Constantinople, 27, 43, 286

Constitutions (and constitutionality), 1, 6, 45, 49, 81, 90, 97, 101, 146, 150, 154–55, 191–92, 194–97, 198, 201–4, 205, 208–9, 211–14, 217, 233–34, 246–47, 265, 267, 269, 279, 281, 283, 308–9

Conversation, 5, 11, 14–15, 27, 29, 31, 43, 63–64, 97–99, 102–5, 110, 173, 240, 278, 329, 332

Cooke, John R., 198–99

Cooper, James Fenimore, 37, 134, 137

Cooper River, 171

Cooper, Thomas, 7, 22–23, 29, 58, 97, 119, 126, 132, 194, 202–4, 219–20, 223–26, 262–64, 267, 271, 293, 298

Copyright, 134–36

Córdoba, 42, 321

Corruption, 50, 147, 206, 209, 296

Cortes, Hernando, 42

Cosmopolitanism, 2, 19, 27, 32, 43, 61, 83–

Falconer, William, 62

Falconet family, 31

Family (and the familial), 13, 27, 31–32,
51–52, 62, 65, 80, 83, 90–91, 97, 105,
107, 110, 157, 160–61, 164–65, 177, 183,
185, 187, 217–18, 241, 244, 251, 253, 255,
276, 305, 307, 312, 316

Farms (and farmers), 12, 21, 82, 87, 89,
116, 182, 219, 223

Fathers (and fatherhood), 13, 20, 41, 45–
46, 67–68, 70–71, 73, 77, 91, 102, 157–
59, 161, 164, 183, 185, 188–89, 192, 195,
216, 225, 236, 261–62, 265, 280, 283,
292, 306–7, 324, 331, 333

Faulkner, William, 7, 87, 98, 171, 182

Federal government, 83, 104, 148, 195,
202, 204, 206–7, 210–12, 214, 227,
231–32

Federalism (as a political structure), 82,
84, 200, 204, 208, 211–12, 219

Federalist (as a political persuasion), 91,
130, 143, 184, 203, 206, 225, 240, 248

Federalist Papers, 203

Federal theology, 290, 295–96, 306–7

Felton, Cornelius, 22

Female (and feminine), 13, 20, 56, 63–67,
69, 83, 98, 102, 110, 116, 122, 147, 185,
189, 262, 316

Ferdinand II of Aragon, 42, 102

Ferguson, Adam, 141, 170

Feudalism, 33, 74, 77–78, 146, 252. See also
Medievalism

Feuerbach, Ludwig, 317, 319

Fichte, Johann Gottlieb, 272–74, 302, 304,
308

Fielding, Henry, 182, 185

Filmer, Robert, 197

Fitzhugh, George, 7, 90, 108, 115, 140, 157,
235, 239–42, 245, 248, 251–57, 277, 310,
334, 336

Flanders, 227

Flaubert, Gustave, 330

Florence, 37, 40–41, 71, 141, 143, 192, 317

Florida, 10, 14, 25, 41, 74, 152, 187, 206

Folk culture, 77, 79, 93, 186, 325

Folkestone, 325

Foreigners (and the foreign), 2, 16, 19, 24,
27, 29–30, 44, 47, 60, 63–64, 72, 80–
81, 85, 93, 106, 109, 120–21, 125, 129,
134–35, 172, 204, 227, 234, 243, 252,
286, 324

Fort Moultrie, S.C., 140

Fort Sumter, S.C., 114, 332

Founding Fathers, 41, 91, 158, 192, 216, 236

Fourier, Charles, 113, 250, 252

Fourth of July, 74, 124, 173

France (and the French), 16, 27, 33–34, 39,
52, 57, 73–75, 98, 120, 134, 138–39, 142,
162, 182, 187, 189, 221, 225, 237, 242,
256, 259–61, 263, 271–72, 275, 278,
282–83, 294, 306, 321

Frankfort, Ky., 84, 335

Franks, 59

Fraser, Charles, 88, 118

Frederick William IV, 110

Freedom, 21, 39, 67, 70, 74, 110, 114, 131,
133, 148, 151, 156, 164, 175, 177, 179, 181,
188, 193–94, 197, 203, 208, 210, 215–18,
220, 223–25, 234, 236, 240, 246–47,
253, 257, 269–70, 288, 291, 305, 310–
13, 315, 323

French language, 6, 31, 38, 72–73, 74, 80–
81, 99, 120–21, 126, 138–39, 169, 329–
30, 334

French Revolution, 31, 35, 37, 50, 55, 73,
92, 97–98, 145–46, 150–51, 192–93,
202, 216, 229, 245, 260

Friends (and friendship), 5, 23, 26–28, 31,
37, 46, 71, 82, 110, 112, 121, 126, 138,
160, 170, 173, 182, 185, 272, 278, 280,
286, 288, 292, 310, 317, 323–24, 331

Frisian language, 33

Fugitive slaves, 67, 111, 163–64

Fuller, Margaret, 67–68

Furman Institution, 284

Gaelic language, 72

Gales, Joseph, 117

Gall, Franz Joseph, 57, 263–64

Garden, Alexander, 57

Garland, Hugh, 158, 161–62

Garnett, M. R. H., 218

Garrett, Thomas Miles, 113

Garrison, William Lloyd, 186, 282, 313

Gay, John: *Beggar's Opera*, 179

Gayarré, Charles Étienne, 34, 73–75, 114, 138, 182, 335

Gayle, John, 111

Gayle, Sarah, 111

Gender, 15, 65, 68–70, 88, 94, 253, 319

Genealogy, 31, 58, 90, 224, 255, 308

Generations, 3, 7–8, 10, 12, 22, 31, 70, 74, 76, 85, 97, 106, 118, 132, 136, 139, 150, 157, 168, 171, 175, 213, 219, 236, 240, 242, 246–47, 259, 315, 328–29, 331, 333, 335

Genesis, book of, 66, 290, 298

Geneva, 39

Genoa, 321

Genre, 4, 6, 23, 65, 105–6, 108, 119–20, 131, 133, 137, 157–58, 162–63, 167–69, 182–84, 191, 203, 235, 248, 257, 330

Gentiles, 280–81

Gentility, 91–92, 93, 96, 101, 122, 132, 148, 184, 213, 223, 333

Gentlemen (and gentlemanly), 21–22, 35, 74, 78, 89, 92–94, 96, 99, 101–2, 117, 121–22, 126–27, 132, 152–54, 173, 181, 236, 239, 300

Gentry, 77, 89, 284

Geoffrey of Monmouth, 58

Geography, 44, 49, 119–20, 128, 144, 153, 195, 205

Geology, 24, 30, 57, 61, 82, 86, 126, 146, 152, 292, 298

George III, 3

Georgetown, D.C., 137

Georgia (and Georgians), 10, 14, 29, 43, 53, 57–58, 63, 82, 84, 100, 122, 124, 128, 133, 142, 144, 152–53, 279, 282, 335–36

Georgia (in the Caucasus), 56, 58

Georgia Botanic Journal and College Sentinel, 62

Georgia Female College, 63

Georgia Historical Society, 122, 144, 152–53

German Friendly Society, 72

German language, 36, 38, 72, 80–81, 121, 139, 279, 288, 329

Germany (and Germans), 6, 23, 27, 30–31, 34–39, 48, 58, 72, 77, 80–81, 99, 121, 123, 131, 134, 138–39, 142, 162, 166, 168–70, 172, 217, 242, 255, 259, 261, 271–75, 278–79, 288, 294, 302–5, 317–18, 320, 323, 329

Gettysburg, battle of, 21, 328, 332

Gibbes, Robert Wilson, 51

Gibbon, Edward, 39, 141–45, 148

Gibraltar, 323

Gielgud, John, 109

Gildersleeve, Basil, 38–39, 80, 87

Giles, William Branch, 200

Gillespie, James, 293, 307

Gilman, Caroline Howard, 4, 11, 91, 127, 137, 139, 163, 185–88

Gilman, Samuel, 108, 186

Girls (and girlhood), 34, 63, 102, 126, 164–65, 249, 293, 309, 316, 334

Glasgow, 25, 139, 302

Gliddon, George, 60

Gnosticism, 245, 262, 266, 277

Gobineau, Joseph-Arthur, comte de, 55, 61, 279

God, 3, 6–7, 9, 12, 23, 25, 34, 41, 45–46, 48, 51, 53, 56, 60, 62, 66–69, 83, 86, 112, 114, 136, 143, 163, 165, 215, 217–18, 223–24, 231, 238–39, 244–47, 256, 259, 262, 264, 266, 268–70, 274, 277–78, 281, 283, 287–91, 294–301, 303–8, 310–13, 315, 317, 319–23, 325, 330–32

Godey's Lady's Book, 117, 253

Godolphin (horse), 95

Godwin, William, 221, 227

Goethe, Johann Wolfgang, 15, 36–39, 81, 169, 317–18, 330

Goldsmith, Oliver, 142, 185

Gospels, 44, 46, 289, 292

Goths (and Gothic), 6, 59, 78, 84, 176, 182–85, 193, 310, 322

Göttingen, 2, 15, 35–38, 55–56

Gracchus, Caius, 175

Grady, Henry, 176, 250

Graham's Magazine, 117, 127–28

Grammar, 45, 99–100, 168, 224, 287

Grayson, William J., 93, 118, 165, 176, 178–81, 334

Grebo language, 45
Greece and Greeks (ancient), 15, 36, 38, 44, 141, 146–49, 151, 169, 259, 272, 292, 306
Greece and Greeks (modern), 27, 42, 134
Greek language, 38, 80, 121, 162, 286–87
Greek Orthodox Church, 286,
Greek Revival, 84
Gregory, John, 263
Gregory XIV, 282
Gregory the Great, 283
Grigsby, Hugh Blair, 7, 11, 22, 79, 83, 95, 97, 108, 114, 119, 154–57, 323–24, 326
Grimké, Angelina, 65–69
Grimké, Sarah, 10, 65–69
Grimké, Thomas Smith, 58, 80, 170–71
Grimm, Jakob, 177
Grimm, Wilhelm, 177
Griswold, Rufus W., 273
Grotius, Hugo, 238, 246
Guesclin, Bertrand du, 152, 175
Guiana, 83
Guizot, François, 78, 145, 148–50
Gulf of Mexico, 51, 316

Haiti, 50–51, 220, 282–83
Hakka, 46
Halifax Fisheries dispute, 335
Hallam, Henry, 142, 150–51
Hamilton, Alexander (and Hamiltonianism), 192, 194–95, 220
Hamilton, Sir William, 302–5, 307, 317
Hammond, James Henry, 83, 105, 205, 214, 240, 243–46, 248, 278, 334
Hampden-Sydney College, 36, 272
Hanoverian dynasty, 187
Harby, Isaac, 7, 278, 280–81
Hardeman, Ann, 113
Hardshell Baptists, 278
Harper, William, 7, 139, 239–45, 248, 253
Harper and Calvo (publishers), 137
Harper Brothers (publishers), 137
Harrington, James, 89, 192, 273
Harrison, Jesse Burton, 35–38, 238, 272–73, 279
Hartley, David, 259, 262

Harvard College, 19, 22, 35, 37, 123, 207, 293, 336
Havana, 42
Hawks, Francis L., 21, 47
Hawthorne, Nathaniel, 115, 137
Hayne, Paul Hamilton, 41, 98, 109, 118, 137, 178, 320, 329, 335
Hayne, Robert Young, 22
Heathens, 248, 300
Hebrew Harmonic Society, 72
Hebrew language, 72, 281
Heeren, Arnold H. L., 36, 148
Hegel, Georg Wilhelm Friedrich (and Hegelianism), 11, 16, 37, 215, 217, 270, 272–74, 289, 291, 304–6, 317
Heidelberg, 31, 38, 316
Hellas, 147
Hengstenberg, Ernst Wilhelm, 305
Henry, Patrick, 77, 107, 156, 158–60
Henry, Robert, 81, 146, 261–62, 264, 267, 270, 272
Hentz, Caroline Lee, 133, 137, 187–88, 317
Hentz, Nicholas, 187
Heraclitus, 292, 327
Herder, Johann Gottfried, 143, 145–46, 193, 275, 325, 327
Hermann, Karl Friedrich, 38
Herodotus, 141, 146
Herrenvolk democracy, 217
Hewat, Alexander, 142
Heyne, Christian Gottlob, 142
Hibernian Society, 72
Hierarchy, 17, 42–43, 45, 56, 59, 87, 96, 156, 188, 202, 236, 249, 275, 277, 282, 285, 299
Higher Criticism, 288–89, 292
Highland Clearances, 178
Highlands, Scottish, 32, 184, 187
Hillard, George, 110
Hillsborough, N.C., 181
Hindus, 47
Historicism, 7, 15, 49, 53, 74, 143–45, 170, 196, 199, 216, 233, 238, 274, 287, 325–27
Hobbes, Thomas (and Hobbesian), 166, 197–98, 204, 210, 213, 252, 261, 273
Hobson, J. A., 234

Hodge, Charles, 248, 302
Hodgson, William Brown, 16, 43–44
Hogarth, William, 179
Hoge, John Blair, 34
Holbrook, John Edwards, 118
Holcombe, William Henry, 114
Holmes, George Frederick, 6–7, 38, 80–81, 83–84, 96, 111, 127, 132, 145, 226, 251, 273–77, 302
Homer, 39, 131
Homosexuality, 13, 112
Hong Xiuquan, 46–47
Honor (and the honorable), 16, 25, 60, 75, 93, 157, 161, 182, 189, 206, 299, 307, 322, 332
Hooper, Johnson Jones, 184
Horace (Quintus Horatius Flaccus), 280
Horton, George Moses, 181
Hottentots, 59
Households, 8, 13, 27, 65–66, 69–70, 78, 98, 101, 105, 185–87, 254, 281, 307, 313
Hudson River, 10, 20, 201
Hughes, Henry, 7, 11, 113, 242, 248–51, 257, 334
Huguenots, 5, 72
Humanism, 149, 277, 301, 306
Humboldt, Alexander von, 17, 48, 306
Humboldt, Wilhelm von, 36–37, 287
Hume, David (and Humean), 3, 15, 32, 141–42, 145–46, 150, 166, 171, 196, 227, 259–61, 264–68, 273–74, 291, 294, 302, 327
Hundley, Daniel, 92, 94–95
Hungary, 39
Hunter, John, 57
Huntsville, Ala., 34
Husbands, 63–65, 67, 107, 110–12, 159, 164, 175, 187, 333
Hutcheson, Francis, 225, 260
Hutchinson, Thomas, 142

Idealism (as a philosophical position), 213, 217, 259–60, 273, 291
Immigration (and immigrants), 4, 30–31, 71, 76, 103, 202, 238–39, 248
India, 47, 222

Indians (Native Americans), 64, 177, 179, 189, 206
Individualism, 6, 30, 79, 135, 149, 193–95, 210, 218, 251, 257, 305–6, 315, 319
Indo-European, 58, 286
Industrialism, 33, 92, 117, 135, 178, 180, 188, 220, 223, 225, 227, 229–30, 232, 234, 237, 243, 251–54, 312
Inequality, 179, 198, 210, 242–44, 253
Ingraham, Joseph Holt, 106
Inquisition, Holy, 42
Interposition (political doctrine of), 208–9, 212, 232. See also Nullification
Ionians, 147
Ireland (and the Irish), 5, 25, 30, 32, 72, 77, 99, 117, 120, 278, 280, 282–83
Irish Jasper Greens, 72
Iroquoian language, 72
Irving, Washington, 78, 96, 132, 134, 139, 185
Isabella I of Castile, 42, 102
Islam, 44, 103, 277, 300
Israel, 281
Istanbul. See Constantinople
Italy (and Italians), 31, 33, 38–42, 58, 71, 80, 121, 141, 147–49, 152, 176, 183, 282, 325
Izard family, 31

Jackson, Andrew, 1, 6, 11, 86, 191, 197, 206–9, 213, 216
Jacksonianism, 90, 94, 102, 130–31, 135, 148, 155, 187, 195, 228, 230, 232, 309
Jacobean, 183, 195
Jacobi, Friedrich Heinrich, 273
Jacobin, 28, 92, 224, 247
Jacobite, 187, 189
Jacobs, Harriet, 23, 164–65
Jamaica, 50
James, Allen, 101
James, Henry, 10, 31–32, 41
James, William, 15, 320
James Island Library Society, 122
James River, 78, 216
Jamestown, Va., 81
Jamison, David Flavel, 152

Mansel, Henry, 302–3
Manufacturing (and manufacturers), 92, 219–20, 223, 225, 227–29, 232, 238, 321
Manuscripts, 8, 28, 40, 44, 53, 104, 113, 116, 119, 138, 153–54, 163, 173, 327, 330, 333–34, 336
Marion, Francis, 81
Marlboro District, S.C., 292
Marriage, 13, 63, 64–67, 70, 82, 107, 111–12, 114, 130, 154, 162, 185–87, 243, 285, 313, 316–17, 320, 324, 329, 331, 335
Marseilles, 321
Marsh, James, 36, 272
Marshall, John, 142, 155, 158, 191, 195, 197, 203, 212
Marston Moor, battle of, 76
Martin, Isabella, 334
Martineau, Harriet, 67
Marx, Karl (and Marxism), 15, 92, 234, 242, 252
Mary, Virgin, 299, 321
Maryland (and Marylanders), 10, 13, 26, 35–36, 47, 49, 77, 81–82, 128–29, 152–53, 160, 279
Maryland Historical Society, 153
Maryland Medical Recorder, 82
Mason, George, 156
Massachusetts, 3, 19, 45, 48, 76, 82, 152, 174, 187, 203, 321, 326
Materialism, 262–64, 267, 336
Mathematics, 29, 96, 121, 238, 269, 271, 276
Mayer, Brantz, 41, 46, 49–50, 139
Mayhew, Henry, 188
McCall, Hugh, 142
McCay, Charles, 29
McCord, Charlotte, 109
McCord, David James, 70, 86, 97, 109
McCord, Louisa Susanna Cheves, 7, 11, 65, 68–70, 98–99, 107–9, 138, 175, 178, 334
McIntosh, Maria, 137
Mecklenberg Declaration of Independence, 86
Medea, 332
Medicine, 12–13, 22, 33–34, 57, 82, 117, 121–22, 126, 260, 263
Medievalism (and the medieval), 44, 87,

89, 105, 119, 121, 141–42, 148–50, 157, 164, 170, 224, 322. *See also* Feudalism
Mediterranean Sea, 35, 42, 44, 290, 323
Meek, Alexander Beaufort, 176–77, 273
Melancholy, 40–41, 161, 174, 182, 201, 251, 286, 316
Melanchthon, Philipp, 147
Melchizedek, 47
Melish, John, 20
Memoirs, 36, 66, 88, 103, 118, 157, 162–63, 334. *See also* Autobiography
Mendelssohn, Moses, 279, 281
Mercantilism, 220, 224, 229
Merchants, 3, 12, 31, 35, 43, 83, 91, 93, 103, 119, 179, 225
Mérimée, Prosper, 330
Metaphysics (and metaphysicians), 6, 145, 167, 181–82, 231, 238, 247, 260–63, 265, 267, 269, 273–76, 290, 301, 317–18
Methodists, 63, 72, 91, 214, 245, 247, 269, 278, 282, 284–85, 294, 334
Metternich, Prince Klemens Lothar Wenzel, 327
Mexico (and Mexicans), 14, 21, 47–52, 74, 206
Mézeray, François de, 142
Michaelis, Johann David, 142
Michelangelo Buonarotti, 174
Michelet, Jules, 145, 275
Middleton, John Izard, 31, 139, 152, 182
Middleton family, 31
Midwest, 13, 123, 138
Mignot, Louis Rémy, 17, 48
Migration (and migrants), 13, 16, 25, 30, 46–47, 51–52, 73, 77, 84, 86–87, 179, 189, 261, 222–23, 278, 287
Milan, 39
Miles, James Warley, 7, 16, 43, 80, 111, 118, 217–18, 273–74, 278, 285–92, 300, 305
Miles, William Porcher, 329
Mill, James, 224
Mill, John Stuart, 291, 302
Millar, John, 151, 170
Milledgeville, Ga., 84
Millennialism, 69, 113, 179, 219, 235, 244, 250, 257, 311

Positivism, 259, 275–76

Postcolonialism, 1–3, 16, 52, 57, 140, 189

Postmodernism, 14, 89, 181, 256

Postrevolutionary, 156, 323

Potomac River, 19, 201

Poughkeepsie, N.Y., 134

Poverty, 8, 13, 33, 89, 136, 188, 221, 229, 242, 244, 292, 311, 335

Powers, Hiram, 41

Powhatans, 72

Predestination, 268, 295, 313

Pre-Raphaelite Brotherhood, 178, 285

Presbyterianism (and Presbyterians), 25–26, 29, 32, 39, 43, 91, 144, 215, 225, 274, 278, 282, 284–85, 292–95, 296, 299–301, 306, 308–10

Prescott, William Hickling, 49

Preston, Buck, 332

Preston, Louisa, 97

Preston, William Campbell, 23, 29, 32, 39, 109

Priestley, Joseph, 225, 262

Primogeniture, 90, 156–57

Princeton, 19, 25, 38, 43, 248, 285, 294, 302

Print culture, 5, 8, 12, 15, 64–65, 81, 103–8, 110–11, 113, 115–18, 120, 123–24, 127–28, 131, 135, 137, 146, 149, 173, 256, 272, 300, 334, 336

Progress, idea of, 21, 27, 30, 35, 41–42, 54, 60, 82, 89, 92, 143–44, 147, 150, 179, 184, 197, 199, 210, 215, 217, 222, 226–27, 230, 236, 240, 242, 245, 249, 253–54, 260, 262, 265, 270, 276, 280, 286–87, 309, 312, 324–25

Prometheus, 43

Proslavery arguments, 6, 8, 25, 44, 61–62, 66, 111, 113, 138–39, 178, 203, 216, 235–58, 288, 313

Prosser, Gabriel, 50

Protectionism, economic, 134–35, 201, 203, 219, 225, 228–31

Protestantism, 34, 43, 46, 48, 91, 149–50, 183, 277–78, 282–84, 299, 308, 321–22

Proudhon, Pierre-Joseph, 252

Providence, 3, 179, 257, 288, 325–26

Prussia (and Prussian), 3, 10, 27, 90, 145, 273

Pseudonymity (literary), 131, 133, 164

Psychology, 95, 228, 237, 239, 260–61, 263, 274, 287–89, 299, 302, 304, 308, 319

Publishers (and publishing), 5, 22, 24, 29, 75, 103, 105, 116–18, 120, 124–28, 130, 134–39, 152–53, 227, 248, 316–17, 334

Pufendorf, Samuel, 238

Puritans, 112, 150

Puseyism, 257

Pyrrhonism, 318

Qing Dynasty, 46

Quakers, 66, 278

Quarterlies, 42, 61, 87, 125–30, 132–33, 136, 171, 269, 284, 301

Queensberry Rules, 204

Quincy, Mass., 327

Race, concept of, 5, 27–28, 36, 41–42, 44–45, 48, 50, 53–62, 55–57, 59, 61, 66, 70, 75, 88, 94, 103, 139, 141, 143–44, 146–49, 151, 164, 180, 188, 200, 203, 214, 217, 220, 241, 244–45, 247–48, 251, 264, 279, 288, 296–97, 306–7, 311, 313, 315–16

Railroads, 14, 91, 116, 138, 157, 254

Raleigh, N.C., 117, 181

Raleigh, Walter, 85

Ramsay, David, 137, 139, 142, 152, 158–61, 326

Ramsey, J. G. M., 86

Ramus, Petrus, 301

Randall, Henry, 160

Randolph, J. W., 118

Randolph, John, 7, 86, 97, 155, 158, 161–63, 195, 198, 206, 213, 216, 315

Randolph-Macon College, 246, 284

Ranke, Leopold von, 40, 145, 327

Ransom, John Crowe, 322

Rapin (Paul de Rapin de Thoyras), 142

Rappahannock River, 221

Raymond, Daniel, 226

Readers, 8, 11, 15, 35, 57, 62, 85, 88, 100,

115–16, 119–21, 124, 128–32, 135–36,
138, 142, 145, 151, 156, 158–62, 164,
166–68, 174–75, 184–85, 186, 195, 226,
256, 316–17, 327, 333–34
Realism (literary), 4, 7, 99, 165, 321, 330
Realism (philosophical), 221, 259–62, 264,
266–67, 270–71, 301–2, 319
Rechabites, 281
Reconstruction, 191, 334
Reformation, Protestant, 14, 141, 146, 149,
170, 278, 308
Reid, Thomas, 259–63, 266–67, 270, 274,
294, 302, 304
Rembrandt van Rijn, 174
Renaissance, Italian, 39, 105, 141, 149
Renan, Ernst, 16, 60
Republicanism, 39, 80, 131, 141, 147–49,
150, 157, 191–92, 199, 203, 208, 219–
20, 239, 247, 315
Republican Methodists, 278
Revivalism, 284
Revolution, 1, 31, 34, 41–42, 49, 76–77,
106, 143, 145, 150–51, 156, 170, 173,
191–92, 208–9, 216, 219, 229, 233, 254,
286, 309, 323, 325, 328, 330. *See also*
American Revolution; French Revolu-
tion
Reynolds, Joshua, 2, 38, 80, 89
Rhetoric, 63, 99, 112, 119, 121, 140, 165–
66, 225, 244, 249–50, 256, 334
Rhine River, 33–35, 183
Ricardo, David, 219, 225, 230
Richardson, Samuel, 182
Richmond, Va., 24, 62, 84, 88, 118, 126,
137, 152, 197, 281, 334
Richter, Jean Paul, 330
Rights, 27, 40, 64, 67–69, 75, 77, 81, 135,
156, 162, 191, 196–98, 201–2, 205–6,
215, 218, 224, 240, 246–47, 250–51,
255, 279, 311, 321, 326, 335
Rimbaud, Arthur, 330
Ringgold, Cadwalader, 47
Rio de Janeiro, 52
Ritschl, Friedrich Wilhelm, 38
Ritter, Heinrich, 38
Rivers, William James, 80

Rives, William Cabell, 82–83
Roane, Archibald, 171
Robbins, William Henry, 293, 307
Roberts, Issachar Jacobs, 46–47
Robertson, James, 26
Robertson, William, 32, 141, 148
Robespierre, François-Maximilien-Joseph,
97
Rollin, Charles, 142, 280
Roman Catholics (and Catholicism), 7, 32,
34, 39, 42, 48–49, 81, 91, 97, 116, 125,
150, 183, 248, 277–83, 295, 299–300,
308–9, 321–22, 331
Romance, 6, 25, 32, 35, 49, 73–74, 88, 120,
134, 162, 169, 182, 309
Romanticism (and Romantic), 3–7, 14–17,
21, 32, 35–36, 39–42, 58–59, 70, 83,
113, 132, 135, 139, 144, 147, 149, 156, 166,
168–72, 177, 180–83, 212, 214–15, 250,
255–56, 280, 286, 290, 306, 321, 330,
336
Rome, ancient (and Romans), 2, 31, 33,
38–39, 44, 87, 141, 143, 146, 148, 169,
192, 254, 272, 282, 306, 324
Rome, modern (and Romans), 2, 31, 37,
182–83, 254, 277, 282, 286, 299
Roncesvalles, battle of, 42
Rose Bud, 127
Rosetta Stone, 53
Rossetti, Dante Gabriele, 41
Roundheads. *See* Cromwell, Oliver
Rouquette, Adrienne, 139
Rousseau, Jean Jacques, 162, 280
Ruffin, Edmund, 11–12, 104, 114–15
Ruffin, Elizabeth, 5, 112–13
Ruins, 35, 40–41, 157, 201, 216, 238
Russell, John, 117–18, 125, 288
Russell's Magazine, 118, 125
Russia (and Russians), 31, 39, 56, 117, 325,
329

Sade, Donatien-Alphonse-François, comte,
242
Sahara Desert, 4, 248
Saint-Domingue. *See* Haiti
St. Louis, Mo., 10, 283